Claims Operations: A Practical Guide

CLAIMS OPERATIONS: A PRACTICAL GUIDE

Michael T. Murdock

International Risk Management Institute, Inc.
Dallas, Texas

Third Printing October 2014
PRINTED IN THE UNITED STATES OF AMERICA

Edited by Bonnie Rogers, ARM

ISBN 978-1-933686-20-2

International Risk Management Institute, Inc.®
12222 Merit Drive
Suite 1600
Dallas, Texas 75251-2266
(972) 960-7693
Fax (972) 371-5120
www.IRMI.com

CONTENTS

Third-Party Administrators

Appendices

PREFACE

Claims Operations: A Practical Guide was written as a handbook for the property and casualty insurance industry to provide a basic understanding of claims operations and to help users gain a comprehensive overview of the claims process itself. While there are many insurance reference resources that can be utilized by insurance professionals to understand the claims process, few are contained within a single book. Fewer still provide specific examples relating to the claims process.

Whether you are a claims trainee, adjuster, manager, underwriter, program manager, customer service representative (CSR), broker or agent, program administrator, risk manager, third-party administrator (TPA), captive owner, captive manager, or work for a company that is self-insured, or if you just want to learn more about insurance claims, this book will help.

The Claims Function

The claims function is a necessary key component of every risk-bearing situation where the potential for damages exists. It differs from other insurance and risk management functions in that it is not exclusive to any particular aspect of the industry. For example, a self-insured entity may not be interested in the underwriting function, since there is no actual insurance policy to underwrite. But a self-insured would be very interested in the claims function as the claim frequency and claim severity directly impact the self-insured's ability to pay its own claims.

Likewise, a broker is very interested in claim activity as the historical claim activity directly relates to the broker's ability to place the risk with an insurer. A risk manager is concerned about claims as it is the essence of what a risk manager attempts to either control or mitigate. A program administrator's insurance program will not survive with poor claims service or adverse loss experience.

As mentioned above, the claims function crosses all risk-bearing situations. In insurance companies, the claims operation is a separate department, and necessary function, that directly affects profitability. At times, the cost of the claims function, in terms of both losses and expenses to process losses or claims, represents over 50 percent of the premium dollars paid to the insurer by its policyholders. As the cost of claims increases, the profitability of the insurance company decreases.

Many times there are disagreements between a claims professional and underwriting professional. The claims professional may establish a claim reserve or settle a claim which, in the underwriter's opinion, was excessive and unwarranted. At the same time, the claims professional will criticize the underwriter for improperly underwriting the risk that would have avoided the claim in the first place. This book addresses some of these issues, providing clear examples and illustrations.

Poor claims service results in a poor reputation. An insurer with a poor reputation is bound to lose existing policyholders as well as potential new business. This also will negatively affect the company's profitability. Other risk-bearing entities, such as captives and risk retention groups, will experience the same effect as indicated above; however, the overall impact could be even greater, as these entities may not have as much premium as a traditional insurance company to sustain losses and expenses.

Ideal claims personnel understand the technical aspects of claims handling and also have the people skills—empathy and ethics—to be effective and professional claims adjusters or managers. This book will discuss the type of person who fits this mold, along with the challenges faced by claims professionals on a daily basis. After reading this book, you will have a better understanding of their job functions and also the challenges they face, not only working with the public but also internally with other company departments.

The claims function may not be the most glamorous of the insurance or risk management roles, but in the author's opinion, it is the most interesting. Claims adjusters must rely on their own judgment, personality, and demeanor to be effective in their job. Claims service and results are also the most widely scrutinized, criticized, and monitored function in the industry, and for good reason, given the financial affect on insurers and insureds alike.

The Scope of the *Guide*

There are many other industry books, publications, and courses that provide information on the claims handling process. This book was written to provide an overview of not just claims handling but, more importantly, claims operations.

A theoretical approach to explain the claims process may not always be the best way for a new industry professional (or even an experienced one) to fully comprehend the process. This book provides the theoretical foundation but also provides examples and practical application. By providing "behind the scenes" information, it takes the mystery out of the claims function and correlates its impact on a risk-bearing entity's profitability and survivability. It also provides the reader with a clear understanding of the importance of the claims function and how an adjuster's (or even a company's) approach toward claims handling can seriously affect society's view of the insurance industry.

As an experienced claims professional, the author provides claims information and examples that will benefit any insurance or risk management professional. The book was written in a format that allows the reader to read the book in its entirety or simply refer to a section of interest. The book focuses on claims operations, the claims process, technical claims handling, and third-party claims administration. The appendices provide useful information, including legal theories and doctrines, ethics, the alternative market, and other reference material.

Of course, the views contained in this book are those of the author, and not necessarily those of the publisher, International Risk Management Institute, Inc., or its staff.

Michael T. Murdock, CPCU, ARe, ARM, ASLI, ACI
April 2010

About the Author

Michael T. Murdock, MSIM, CPCU, ARM, ARe, ASLI, ACI

Michael T. Murdock has worked in the insurance industry for over 30 years in various industry technical and management positions, including claims adjuster, supervisor, regional claims manager, vice president, chief operating officer, and president in insurance, reinsurance, risk management, and third-party administrator (TPA) firms, handling all lines of insurance.

With his diversified multiline insurance background, Mr. Murdock has not only personally adjusted and audited many insurance claims, but has also formed and managed two TPA firms. He is a licensed adjuster, and has been licensed as an insurance broker/agent, surplus lines broker, reinsurance broker, and certified insurance consultant. He has worked in the traditional, specialty, London, and the alternative insurance markets. These experiences have allowed him to write from both an insurance company and TPA executive perspective.

Mr. Murdock has a master's degree in Insurance Management from Boston University and holds the following insurance designations:

- Chartered Property Casualty Underwriter (CPCU)
- Associate in Reinsurance (ARe)
- Associate in Risk Management (ARM)
- Associate in Surplus Lines Insurance (ASLI)
- Associate in Captive Insurance (ACI) (from the International Center for Captive Insurance Education)

Mr. Murdock grew up in Massapequa, New York, and spent most of his career in the northeastern part of the United States. He is married with three daughters and currently resides in the Minneapolis, Minnesota area.

Currently, Mr. Murdock is the senior vice president of Claims and Program Services at Berkley Risk, a W.R. Berkley Company. Berkley Risk provides insurance management and claim administration services.

Mr. Murdock can be reached at:

Michael T. Murdock, SVP
Berkley Risk
222 South Ninth Street, Suite 1300
Minneapolis, MN 55402
Tel.: (612) 766–3800
Email: mmurdock@berkleyrisk.com

Chapter 1: Introduction

In many ways, the job of the claims professional has changed greatly over the years. In the 1970s, insurance claims professionals wore dark, three-piece suits with white shirts and conservative ties, worked in a large office, sitting at huge metal desks lined up in rows. Adjusters were constantly leaving for and returning from the field. The wide-open office was furious with activity: phones ringing, people smoking, rummaging through piles of claim files, typewriters clacking, with the bell on the return adding to the commotion. A very active environment indeed.

There were no personal computers, fax machines, cell phones, or copy machines. Hard copy claim files piled up on desks with handwritten and typewritten notes attached. Although signed statements were preferred, adjusters recorded statements in the field and by telephone (using a ring adapter over the telephone receiver). These adjusters were true "road warriors," conducting field investigations; recording statements from claimants, insureds, and witnesses; taking photographs; making diagrams; visiting accident scenes, police departments, and attorneys' offices; writing appraisals; testifying in court; performing activity checks; and dictating captioned reports.

An adjuster commonly carried the tools of the trade: a Dictaphone that used minicassette tapes, three-part statement paper, a measuring wheel and tape, clipboards, a Polaroid camera, claim forms, a checkbook (for first-call settlements), a bound planner, maps (lots of maps!), and a good supply of coins to make telephone calls from phone booths, to feed the meter to park the company car, to pay tolls, and to fill the ever-present coffee thermos.

It was a very exciting job, but it took a special type of person to be a claims adjuster. That hasn't changed. Being a claims professional—whether an adjuster or manager—involves working with people, helping them when they have a problem, offering solutions, and making good a bad situation. But it's not easy. At times, the adjuster's job can be confrontational, involve long or odd work hours, and can be frustrating. Adjusters must deal with all types of people from a variety of cultures and backgrounds. Having just experienced an accident or injury, they may be stressed, despondent, irrational, and angry. During any given workweek, an adjuster may be screamed at, cursed, and criticized by claimants, while also being pushed to meet production goals by the claims manager. All the while, the adjuster needs to be able to maintain an appropriate demeanor and disposition to objectively handle each claim assignment respectfully, effectively, and professionally.

Back in the day, new claims personnel underwent an intensive training period, often involving a company-sponsored claims school or other formal education. These training programs provided the fundamental training requirements necessary to be a multiline adjuster. Novice claims

LACK OF QUALIFIED CLAIMS PERSONNEL—WHY?

There is a lack of qualified and experienced claim resources in the industry. The lack of resources applies to insurance company Claims Departments, third-party administrators (TPAs), and any other claim facility requiring the skills of a professional claims person. The lack of experienced resources includes not only adjusters, but also claims supervisors and managers. This situation will only be exacerbated in the future. According to the U.S Department of Labor, Bureau of Labor Statistics, "[Adjuster] employment is expected to increase moderately, but many job openings will arise from the need to replace workers who retire or leave for other reasons."

As an industry, we are going to be faced with a serious problem as experienced claims professionals retire from the industry. The baby boomer generation includes many industry professionals who had established an insurance career back in the 1970s and 1980s that are now ready, or soon to be ready, for retirement.

Why does the industry have trouble recruiting and training new, qualified personnel?

- ✓ It takes a special type of person to be an effective adjuster. If employers who provide claims services do not offer a work environment that includes manageable caseloads, normal working conditions, opportunities for advancement, and generally a positive work environment, they will not be able to attract the necessary experience and talent.

- ✓ Over the years, many claim facilities have overloaded adjusters, which has prompted industry professionals to seek other industry opportunities or leave the industry completely. The perception of claims handling went from an exciting job opportunity to the bottom rung of the insurance industry ladder.

- ✓ The insurance industry's reputation has, in recent times, been tarnished by unethical and illegal behavior on the part of some insurance professionals, including senior managers and executives of insurance companies. This type of behavior even occurred during times when policyholders were relying on the industry to help them, such as during a catastrophe, like Hurricane Katrina. This adverse publicity may deter recent college graduates from considering a career in the insurance industry, particularly within a claims operation.

From where will qualified staff people be recruited? Will there be enough staff resources to actually provide the necessary claims services throughout the industry? If the industry continues to utilize a brick-and-mortar business model, competition for staff resources within a commuting distance of the office will be fierce, with it being almost impossible to recruit qualified staff resources. The lack of experienced claim resources will succumb to the law of supply and demand, and thereby drive up the cost of good claims personnel.

adjusters shadowed experienced adjusters to learn the ropes, and then started off slowly, on small and uncomplicated claims.

Today, things are not so formalized. There is a lack of adjuster trainee programs available in the industry. While certain companies currently provide some form of adjuster trainee program, they appear to be in the minority. More often than not, most companies provide new recruits with limited tools of the trade: telephone, digital cameras, recorders to take statements, a claim management system for the placement of notes and statistical information and/or hard copy claim files and claim forms.

Some of the more innovative companies provide new recruits with more technology driven tools, such as cell phones and BlackBerry smart phones,[1] voice-over Internet protocol (VOIP) telephone systems,[2] voice recognition software, remote telecommuting staff resources, paperless claim management systems, video conferencing, and the like. However, in both instances, the new recruits are expected to hit the ground running, and the basics of claims handling are often ignored or handled haphazardly. This book seeks to fill that informational gap.

[1]The BlackBerry, developed by Research In Motion (RIM), also known as a smart phone, is a wireless handheld device that functions as a mobile phone and can be used as well as for e-mail, text messaging, and Internet access.

[2]A general term for technology that delivers voice communication for faxes, messages, etc., over the Internet or other shared network. VOIP can reduce communication and infrastructure costs by routing phone calls over existing data networks and avoiding duplicate network systems.

Claims Operations: A Practical Guide is a resource for risk and insurance professionals who want to gain a better understanding of the claims function. It provides a complete overview of the fundamental aspects of the claims process. This makes it particularly useful to new adjusters entering the industry. It also will benefit those working in a professional, technical staff, or management capacity, such as claims adjusters and claims managers, underwriters, reinsurance personnel, third-party administrators, managing general agents, program administrators, insurance agents, and a host of others.

The focus of the book is on property and casualty insurance and professional lines claims handling, including both insurer claims operations and third-party claim administration. As the title conveys, this book is a *guide* and should be used in conjunction with other operational and claim resources to manage a successful claims operation. It provides examples and resources for the claims professional and also highlights areas that can improve or adversely impact a claims operation.

This *Guide* contains 30 chapters and 7 appendices so that you can quickly access information you need on a particular topic. Guides to more information are provided at the end of each chapter to help lead you to other chapters you may find of interest. By reading this book, you are embarking on a road to understanding the claims function and claims operations. Bon voyage!

Chapter 2: Claims Operations—Overview

Claims Operations: A Practical Guide is a tool designed to explain to the reader the intricacies of property and casualty insurance claims. We begin by describing claims operations, then move on to explain the claims process itself, the role of third-party administrators, and finally, how claims are actually handled. For the claims novice, it is probably best to start here, at the beginning. This section addresses:

- Different types of claims operations (Chapter 3, page 17)
- Core operational issues (Chapter 4, page 29)
- Claims management overview (Chapter 5, page 45)
- Management controls (Chapter 6, page 57)
- Recruitment and retention (Chapter 7, page 73)
- Financing and banking (Chapter 8, page 87)
- Technology (Chapter 9, page 93)

This chapter provides a general overview of claims operations, focumsing on the fundamentals and the key players.

The Claims Function

The insurance business has been around for centuries, and along with it, the insurance claims function. While the typical claims function probably looks very different today than it did in the 17th century, given the advancement in industry and technology, some of the same claim practices and protocols practiced hundreds of years ago still exist today. Claims operations have made many advances over the last 30 years and are certain to make many future advances—particularly in the use of technology—but the core function has not changed.

> Management of the underwriting results, through effective claim management, will ultimately control the profitability or unprofitability of an insurance company or underwriting program.

So, what is a claim? *Merriam-Webster's Online Dictionary* defines "claim" as a demand for something due or believed to be due, or a right to something. The word has its origin back to the 14th century. In the same vein, the word "adjust" means to bring to a more satisfactory state or to determine the amount to be paid under an insurance policy settlement of a loss. It, too, dates back to the 14th century. By definition, then, claims are basically demands against an insurance policy by the policyholder, and adjusting is the process whereby the settlement amount, if any, is determined.

The delivery of the claims function has changed because there are now many different insurance and noninsurance structures that require claims services. There are also many different types of claims operations and claim facilities. For example, most insurance companies maintain internal claims operations; reinsurance companies[1] have their own claims staff; third-party administrators (TPAs) provide outsourced claims services using their own staff; independent adjusters provide outsourced claims services to insurance companies and other risk-bearing facilities; agents or brokers may have internal claims operations; captives and risk retention groups have claim facilities; and self-insured companies have their own claims staff.

To fully understand the various types of claims operations, it is important to first understand how claims operations fit into various insurance market structures. The claims operation is just one of the insurance operational components; however, it is arguably the most important function. Therefore, the proper management of the claim function in any type of an insurance market structure is critical for the insurance market structure's profitability and success.

Management of the underwriting results, through effective claim management, will ultimately control the profitability or unprofitability of an insurance company or program. What do we mean by that? Well, there are two outcomes an underwriter will be faced with for each policy written—either losses in the form of claims or no losses will occur during the policy period. The policies with no losses obviously generate a profit. The policies with losses will adversely affect the profitability for that particular policy, contributing to the results of all the policies written. If the losses are managed properly, including the proper maintenance of claim reserves and appropriate

TRADITIONAL INSURANCE MARKET

The traditional insurance market is the most common market an insurance buyer is used to dealing with. This market differs from the alternative or specialty market in that it utilizes ordinary methods of underwriting and claims handling, and is structured as a typical insurance company. Traditional insurance markets include insurance companies where one would purchase property and casualty insurance coverage for vehicles, homes, and businesses, using standardized coverage forms and premiums. These markets are closely monitored by state insurance departments and may require various filings for premium rates and policy forms. This market includes both personal lines and commercial lines exposures.

[1]A reinsurance company provides additional insurance capacity to insurance companies. Reinsurance allows for companies to spread the risk so that one insurance company does not retain all the risk itself, and also increases its capacity to write more premiums. In essence, it is insurance for insurers.

settlement resolutions, the claims operation is managing the underwriting results.

In a traditional insurance arrangement, an insurance policy is purchased from an insurer, often with the assistance of an agent or broker. The insurer performs all the insurance functions, such as marketing, underwriting, binding, rating, and issuing the insurance policy; billing, investigating, and paying claims; and, in liability policies, defending the insured in the event of a lawsuit against the insured. If a retail agent is involved, the agent's role is confined to the sales and distribution function.

The claims function is typically an internal department within the insurance company operation. Many claims professionals in the industry work in the traditional market or have come from the traditional market, and are now working in other various insurance markets. The traditional insurance market, which most people are used to dealing with, differs from the alternative or specialty market in that it utilizes ordinary methods of underwriting and claims handling. The alternative market[2] does not. (See Appendix A for more information on the alterative market.)

Exhibits 2.1 and 2.2 illustrate a traditional insurance company's operations and Claims Department, respectively.

Claim Fundamentals and Key Players

A frequently stated rule of thumb in the insurance industry is that a quality claims opera-

[2]The alternative market represents over 50 percent of the insurance market and includes any insurance transaction which involves partial or total self-insurance, as well as pooling arrangements.

Exhibit 2.1: Traditional Insurance Company Operation

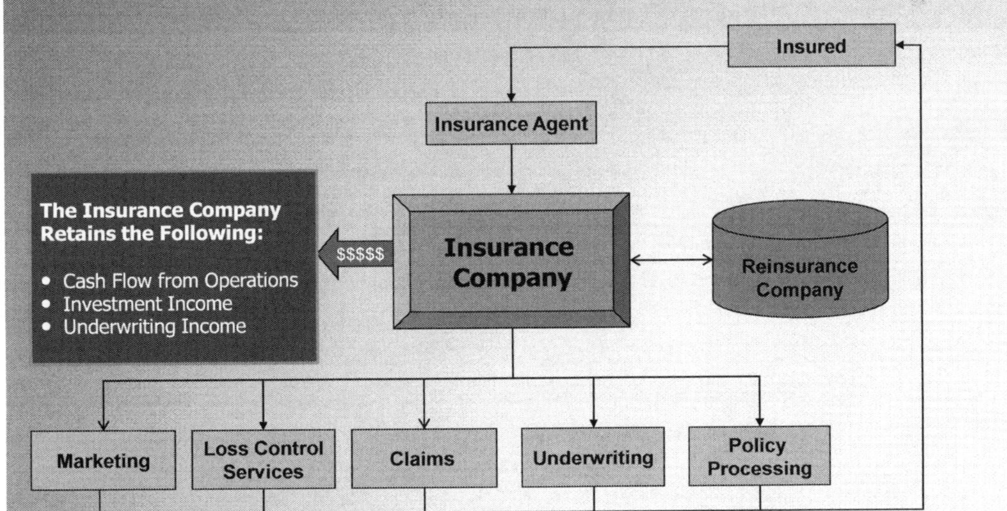

In the traditional insurance company model, the insurance company bears risk, and may cede (or transfer) a portion of the risk to a reinsurance company. The insurance company provides various services to the insured. The insurance company retains investment income and cash flow from the operations. Favorable results will yield underwriting income; unfavorable results will yield an underwriting loss.

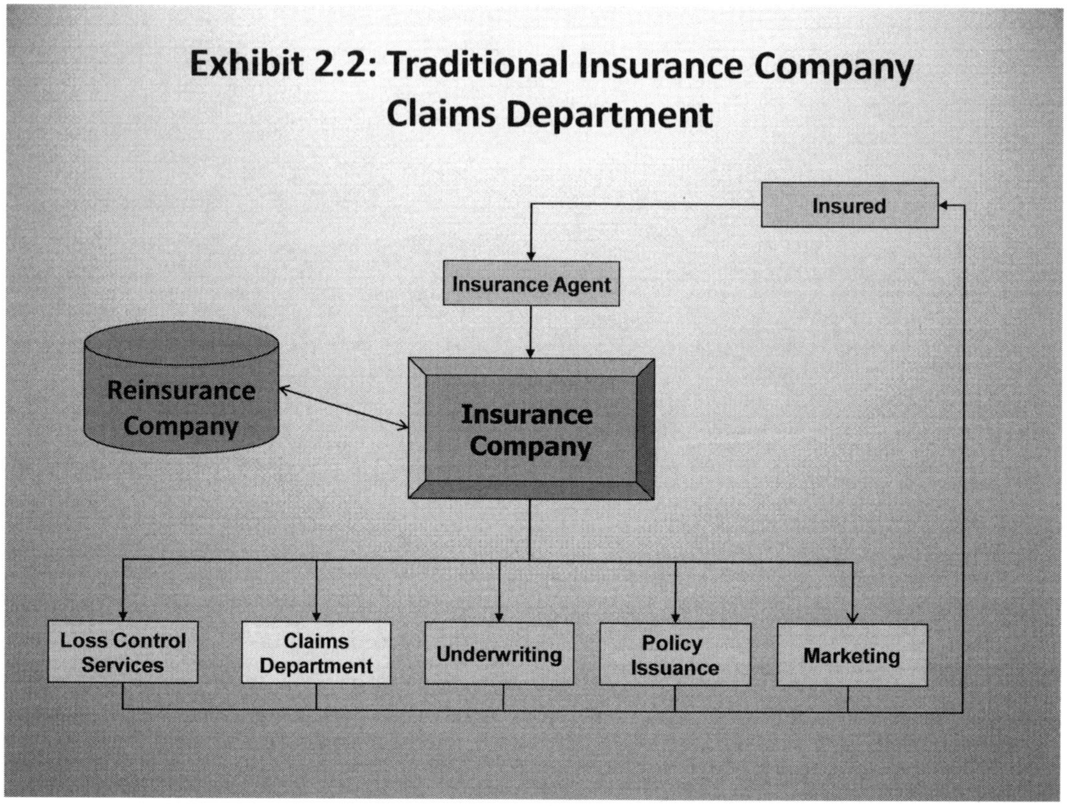

tion can save a company up to 4 points off the loss and loss adjustment expense (LAE) ratios through proper claims handling and controlled expenses. The key to a quality claim organization is its people—support staff, management, and the technical professional staff. It takes experienced and qualified personnel who are motivated to do a good job to produce a top-notch claims operation.

Within the Claims Department are various personnel—claim resources—responsible for handling, managing, or supporting various claims operations. These positions are divided into adjusters, claims staff, and miscellaneous others, often in peripheral positions.

Claims Adjusters

There are several types of adjusters, classified by the party they work for and their areas of expertise.

A ***staff claims adjuster*** (also referred to as a claims representative or associate) handles claims for an insurance company, third-party claim administrator, or self-insured entity.[3] Typically, they are employees; however, often they can be retained as consultants. Staff adjusters handle all lines of business (multiline) or just one line, auto for example, depending on their experience and qualifications.

Staff adjusters are usually supervised by claims supervisors or managers and can either work in the field, at a desk, from

[3]A self-insured entity absorbs part of the risk, either partially or fully, resulting in a premium reduction or no premium at all. The self-insured portion of the risk is called the self-insured retention (SIR). The self-insured entity pays for the losses and expenses within the self-insured retention from its operating funds, or funds set aside to specifically pay for claims. The self-insured entity may handle claims with its own claims staff or retain the services of a third-party administrator (TPA).

home, or a combination of these. Their duties include managing the claims process, including conducting claims investigations, evaluating damages and preparing estimates, communicating with insureds, claimants, and attorneys, and negotiating claim dispositions.

Staff adjusters may need to be licensed as adjusters in individual states, depending on the jurisdiction. Staff adjusters working for an insurance company may be exempt from licensing requirements in certain states. It is important to note that, as an employee of the insurer, third-party claim administrator, or self-insured entity, the staff adjuster's primary concern will be to protect the interests of the employer.

A ***multiline adjuster*** is an adjuster who is trained in handling multiple lines of business, such as automobile, general liability, property, inland marine, and workers compensation. There are also adjusters who are specifically trained in certain lines of business, such as property, workers compensation, and automobile exposures. These adjusters are typically referred to by the line of insurance on which they focus, such as a property adjuster.

Independent adjusters handle claims for a client insurance company, third-party claim administrator, self-insured entity, reinsurer, or any other entity requiring field claims services. Typically, they are not employees of an insurance company. Generally, independent adjusters are small business operations with just a few employees and consultants. However, there are large national adjusting firms as well. Independent adjusters may handle all lines of business, depending on their experience and qualifications, and usually provide field adjusting, appraising, and investigative services.

Often, staff claims adjusters will assign claim activities to independent adjusters, either on a task basis (only specific tasks to be assigned) or on a full adjustment basis (complete claims process including a captioned report). Independent adjusters are usually supervised by an internal claims supervisor, claims manager, or owner, but their work product is indirectly supervised by their client. Their duties may include managing the claims process (if the client has minimal claims staff resources), but often involves field adjusting activities, such as taking statements, appraising and evaluating damages, taking photographs, making diagrams, and canvassing witnesses.

It is important to note that independent adjusters have not only the duty to protect the interests of their clients, but also a duty as employees or consultants to the company for which they work. Independent adjusters bill the client for services rendered as an hourly time-and-expense rate or on a flat-rate basis. Most states require that independent adjusters be licensed.

Public adjusters (PAs) are adjusters retained by policyholders to represent their interests in a first-party claim against insurance companies. Public adjusters are paid by the insured, which is typically a percentage of the settlement amount. Public adjusters are trained and educated insurance adjusters who understand coverage, damage evaluations, and the insurance claims process. *They are the only type of adjuster that represents insureds, not insurance companies.* PAs represent policyholders in personal lines and commercial lines first-party property claims. Most states require that public adjusters be licensed.

A ***general adjuster*** can be a staff adjuster or independent adjuster who is trained in property and casualty claims handling and has achieved an advanced level of expertise. Typically, general adjusters are assigned to the more serious claims.

Other Claims Personnel

The size of Claims Departments can be large or small, corresponding to the size of the insurer in most cases. Following are descriptions of these positions.

Exhibit 2.3: Agent Types

Retail Agent: An insurance agent who acts as an intermediary between an insured and the marketplace. In some instances, retail agents deal directly with an insurer in arranging coverage, while in others, retail agents work with managing general agents or wholesale brokers to secure coverage for their client-insured. Often, retail agents have a dual responsibility to the insurance companies they represent or are appointed by and the insureds they are selling insurance to. If the agent only represents the insured in the insurance transaction, they are considered a broker. Agents and brokers are sometimes called producers. Most states require that agents and brokers be licensed.

Managing General Agent (MGA): Is authorized by an insurer to transact insurance business and may have authority to bind the insurer, issue policies, appoint producers, arrange for reinsurance, and provide other administrative support, depending on the specifics of the MGA agreement. MGAs usually require special licensing and have to meet other requirements specified by various state insurance departments. MGAs have to comply with the MGA Model Act developed by the National Association of Insurance Commissioners (NAIC). This is not to be confused with a managing general underwriter (MGU), who is essentially an MGA involved in the in life and health insurance business as opposed to property and casualty.

Wholesale Agent: Is an agent that functions as a distributor for retail agents. Wholesale agents are intermediaries, appointed by insurance companies, who distribute insurance products to retail agents and brokers, who in turn sell the insurance product to the insured. The wholesale agent is paid a commission by the insurance company, and the wholesale agent then pays the retail agent, or broker, a commission. Most states require that wholesale agents be licensed as agents or brokers.

General Agent: The term "general agent (GA)" has many meanings in the insurance industry. In program business, it usually refers to a program administrator who may perform some of the functions of a program administrator but is not considered a managing general agent. An important distinction is that general agencies are usually restricted as to the types and value of claims that can be handled, due to state licensing restrictions.

Claims examiners can be staff claims adjusters, home office personnel, or any other adjuster who primarily works in an office environment handling claims at a desk or overseeing or managing claims of others (even managing the technical claim work product of other claims adjusters). If the claim examiner is providing actual adjusting services, licensing will be required.

Claims supervisors or ***claims managers*** provide oversight or supervision to adjusters or claims representatives. However, at times, companies may give a "claims supervisor" or "claims manager" title to a person who only supervises or manages technical claims files. Claims supervisors or managers may manage people and claim files, and may have their own direct caseloads of claim files as well. This position may exist in any type of claims operation. When claims supervisors or managers are actively involved in the claims process, including communication with claimants and insureds, adjuster licensing is often necessary.

The ***claims support staff*** provides a very important function in a claims operation. The primary function of the staff involves data entry and claims processing, mail processing, check issuance, image scanning, and other support functions. It is important to note that this function continues to evolve and change with developments in technology and the move toward completely paperless claims operations. Typically, the claims support staff is not required to be licensed.

Claims attorneys have similar duties to the staff claims adjuster, but primarily are hired to handle professional liability, errors and omissions, and management liability (directors and officers liability, employment practices liability, etc.) claims. Claims attorneys are particularly well suited for these types of claims, given the complex legal and coverage issues involved. Their legal training in contract law and analysis can be very effective in the handling of claims. Some states exempt claims attorneys from adjuster licensing.

Independent appraisers or ***staff appraisers*** primarily estimate damages to vehicles and heavy equipment. Although they are not considered adjusters, they provide a component of adjusting services during the claim process by inspecting damages, taking photographs, and preparing damage estimates. Most states require appraisers to be licensed.

Agency claims representatives usually handle the claims function within retail or wholesale insurance agencies. Their function is typically limited to being claim liaisons between insurers and policyholders (their clients) to enhance customer service and control the loss ratio. Their services include managing the intake of new claims, requesting status reports from insurers, and reviewing insurance company claim files to be sure the claim reserves are appropriate. Some states require agency claims representatives to be licensed as adjusters; however, some states do not require licensing as long as the claims being handled are under a certain monetary threshold and only involve property damage.

Third-party administrators (TPAs) are outsourced claim facilities. They provide a claims service to organizations or companies that have limited or no claim resources. TPAs can provide claims services from the claim report date to file closure. They employ claims adjusters, managers, attorneys, and support staff to handle claims for various clients, such as insurance companies, reinsurers, self-insured companies, and program administrators. TPAs charge for their services as a percentage of the premium, fixed fees by line and class of business, flat administrative fees, or fees based on time and expenses. Adjusters employed by a TPA are required to be licensed, as well as the TPA firm itself, in some states. (See Chapters 18–20 for a detailed discussion of TPAs.)

Reinsurance claims staffs include employees or consultants of a reinsurance company. Their primary responsibility is the oversight of the primary insurers' (or TPAs') claims with the potential to impact the reinsurer financially. They may hold titles such as reinsurance examiner, officer, assistant vice president, or vice president. Usually, the reinsurance claims staff is not required to be licensed.

A ***program administrator,*** sometimes referred to as a managing general agent or general agent, typically manages a controlled homogenous or heterogeneous book of insurance business, which involves a block of insurance premium, sometimes referred to as program business.[4] Program premium volume often starts at $5 million,

[4]Program business is insurance business handled by a program administrator, managing general agent (MGA), or general agent (GA). Program business is a separate or niche part of the insurance industry devoted specifically to special insurance programs. Programs can provide a large block of premium for insurers; therefore, the need for program business will change with the insurance market cycle. In a soft market, when insurers are looking to increase premium volume to make up for the lower insurance rates, they tend to have a larger appetite for program business. However, in a hard market, when the insurance rates are higher, insurers seek to shrink the volume of policies, and may have less of an appetite for program business. Insurance companies and reinsurers devote resources exclusively to this type of business, which is conducted in both the soft and hard markets.

Exhibit 2.4: Program Manager Illustration

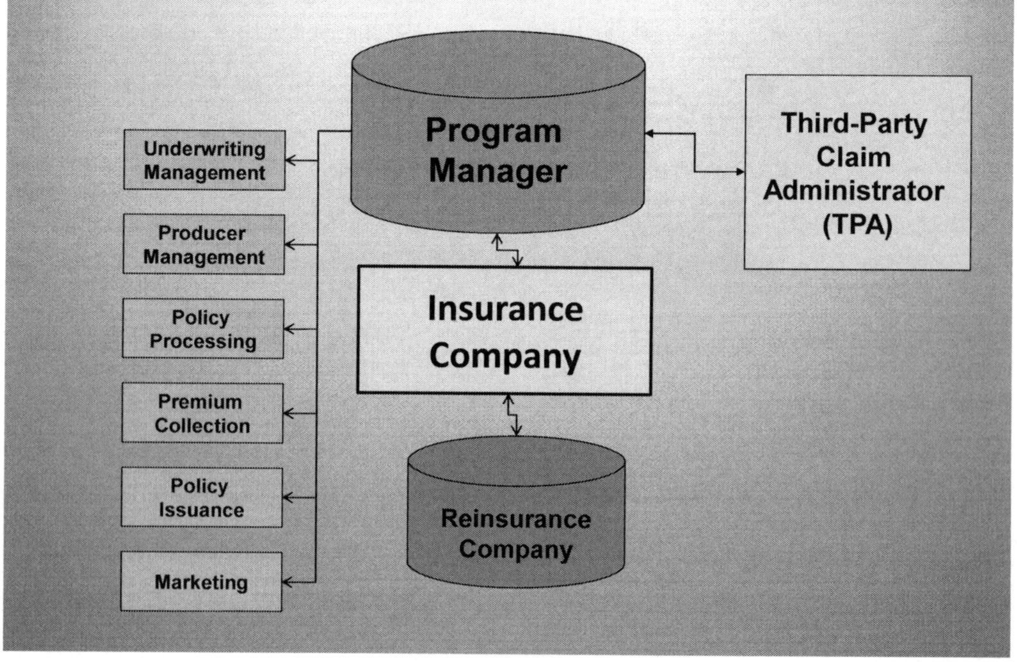

Claimant: An individual or entity who has presented a *third-party* claim.

Insured: An individual or entity who has presented a *first-party* claim.

Claim Feature: A single type of loss for one individual claimant involved in a claim occurrence, e.g., bodily injury or property damage.

Claim Suffix: Similar to claim feature, this term may also be used in *first-party* property claim handling to list separate components of the property claim, e.g., building, contents and business interruption.

Claim File or Claim Occurrence: One claim occurrence may include many claimants, the insured, and various claim features.

and can go up to hundreds of millions of dollars. The business may be written through a commercial insurer, reinsurer, or sometimes a captive insurer.[5] Retail agents or producers are utilized as a distribution mechanism. The program administrator may underwrite the business, issue policies, and collect premium—functions which would normally be handled by the insurance company.

A program administrator may have special expertise in a particular class of business, such as tow trucks, trash haulers, truckers, builders, or ambulance companies. This expertise may translate into a more profitable program, with an effective distribution mechanism, implementation of risk management programs, special claim expertise, special policy forms, association sponsorships, and other special programs to make the program unique and profitable.

It is important to note that the insurance functions handled by a program administrator can vary widely, from simply acting as a retail agent with the insurer handling all the insurance functions, to managing all aspects of the insurance operation including underwriting, claims (if not outsourced to a TPA), loss control, premium collection, and policy issuance. Adjusters employed by a program administrator are required to be licensed, as well as the firm itself, in some states.

Exhibit 2.4 provides an illustration of a program manager operation utilizing a TPA.

Claim Types

There are two general categories of claims: *first-party* and *third-party* claims.

- *First-party claims* involve only the policyholder and include claims such as property, business interruption, inland

[5]A captive insurer is an insurance company that is wholly owned and controlled by its insureds. Its primary purpose is to insure the risks of its owners, and the primary beneficiaries of its underwriting profits are its insureds. More information on captives can be found in Appendix A.

The Claims Department has systems that are integrated with the other functional departments within the insurance company (i.e., policy management and underwriting systems). The Claims Department produces claim data to meet various claim management reporting and data compliance reporting requirements.

The insurance company Claims Department overhead and expenses are paid from the premium dollars. A budget is established to pay the overhead and expenses of the claims operation. The primary expense in any claims operation is the cost of staff resources, such as payroll and benefits. Typically, a Claims Department budget is prepared after the premium projections are determined, with the applicable percentage of the premium allocated to the claims function. In other words, the claim budget will need to meet the overall allocation determined by senior management. This can be a problem if an inadequate amount is allocated, resulting in restrictions on proper claims staffing, potentially affecting the quality of claims handling. Exhibit 3.2 below provides an illustration of various insurance company Claims Department budget expense categories.

Agency Claims Operations

Some retail and wholesale insurance agencies or brokerages have claims operations to assist with the claims of individual policyholders insured with the agency or bro-

Exhibit 3.2: Budget Expense Categories for an Insurance Company Claims Department

- Payroll
- Payroll Processing & Taxes
- Automobile
- Corporate Filings
- Depreciation/Amortization
- Dues & Subscriptions
- Equipment Rental
- Employee Welfare
- Insurance—Employee
- Insurance—Operating
- Interest & Bank Charges
- Professional Licensing
- Miscellaneous Expenses
- Postage
- Printing
- Professional Fees
- Rent
- Utilities
- Real Estate Taxes
- Repairs & Maintenance
- Telephone
- Travel & Entertainment
- Office & Supplies
- Professional Development
- Recruitment
- Outsourced Services

kerage. Services include new loss reporting, follow-up status, monitoring, consultation on claim-related issues, and claim reserve reviews. Agency or brokerage claims operations can range from a one person claims unit with a customer service representative (CSR) position, to a large claims operation with many adjusters and claims managers.

The costs associated with agency or brokerage claims operations are generally absorbed by the agency from the commissions paid by the insurance company for the policies written. These claims services are considered ancillary services provided by the insurance agent or broker for its customers. However, when dealing with self-insured customers, large agencies or brokers may charge their customers a fee for claims services. It should also be noted that large agencies or brokers may have their own full-service TPA claims operations.

Self-Insured Claims Operations

Self-insured claims operations can range from a single risk manager directly handling claims to multiple adjusters and claims managers overseeing a large volume of claims. It is important to note that the risk manager is typically the primary contact at a self-insured claims operation, who usually reports to the chief financial officer or some other senior officer of the self-insured organization. Self-insured claims operations can resemble a TPA claims operation with a claim organizational infrastructure, systems, and a hierarchy of management. There are many self-insured claims operations that are very sophisticated, akin to an insurance company claims operation.

Self-insured claims operations are typically funded internally from operating expenses. Many self-insured organizations outsource the claims function to independent adjusters or third-party administrators due to a lack of claims resources or systems.

Independent Adjuster Claims Operations

Independent adjuster claims operations are businesses formed to provide field adjusting services to insurers, self-insureds, TPAs, reinsurers, captives, etc., as a separate, unaffiliated business. There are several different types of independent adjusting firms:

- ***National Adjusting Firms***—These adjusting companies have thousands of employees with offices nationwide, handling all types of property and casualty claims. Claims services are provided by desk adjusters, field adjusters, and investigators.

- ***National Franchised Adjusting Firms***—These adjusting companies are individually owned franchised adjusting businesses (franchisees). The franchisor provides the franchisee with name recognition and branding, marketing and billing support, as well as a claims system. (By claims system, we are referring to claims management information tracking and storage software. See Chapter 9, Claims Operations—Technology, beginning on page 93.) Typically, service fees and reporting are uniform among the franchisees. The franchisor receives payment from the franchisee to join the franchised organization and then receives a percentage of the billed service fees.

These firms can be a single adjuster or an adjusting firm with many employees and consultants.

- ***Privately Owned Adjusting Firms***—These firms are usually privately owned and may employ anywhere from 1–100+ claims employees. They can be run by one individual or structured similarly to the larger firms, with many employees and consultants handling claims for the adjusting firms. The claims services are provided by field adjusters and investigators. Sometimes a TPA may have an independent field adjusting division or subsidiary.

The independent adjuster or firm is usually paid on a time-and-expense basis, with fixed fees charged for certain task assignments. For example, a fixed fee may apply to a property appraisal assignment for property valued at under $7,500, or a fixed fee could be paid for photographs and diagrams of an accident scene.

Independent adjuster hourly rates vary by geographic location and are generally in the range of $55–$110 per hour, plus expenses (such as mileage, telephone, fax, and photos). Rates will also vary by the adjuster's experience, qualifications, location, and line of business.

Many years ago, most claims were handled by field adjusters. Most insurance companies either had their own field adjusting staff or outsourced this function to an independent adjuster. After telephone and desk adjusting became an effective means of adjusting property and casualty claims, many companies reduced or eliminated their field adjusting staff. Most large insurance companies currently maintain field adjusting staff; however, many companies (including self-insured organizations) outsource the field adjusting process to an independent adjuster.

Independent adjusters serve an important function within the industry. These adjusters can either handle task assignments or be assigned on a full adjustment basis. Even with the technological advances in the industry, adjusters are still needed to handle activities in the field, such as photographs and diagrams, statements, witness canvassing, and writing estimates or appraisals.

Managing General Agent (MGA) or Program Administrator Claims Operations

MGA claims operations are claims operations managed and integrated into a managing general agency. These operations may resemble a combination of an insurance company Claims Department and a TPA. Sometimes the MGA claims operation may actually be a TPA but organized as a separate entity or subsidiary of the MGA operation. Typically, the MGA operation and claims staff will be structured similar to the TPA claims operation.

The MGA claims operational costs may be incorporated into the MGA commission or fees, with a specific allocation for the Claims Department or TPA expenses. The MGA commission or fees are paid from the premium dollars that are generated by the MGA operation.

There are some specialty insurance companies writing program business (homogeneous groupings of insurance customers with common operations that often form associations or risk purchasing groups[1]) that will not allow the program administrator or MGA to handle or control the claims operation. Their reasoning is usually based on their need to exert full control over certain aspects of the claims operation, such as reserve management, investigations, settlement evaluations, litigation management, check issuance, and regulatory compliance. If the program administrator does not manage the process properly, this could potentially represent a financial risk to the insurance company.

Each program administrator or MGA should be individually evaluated to determine whether there are proper processes, systems, and controls in place to administer claims properly and effectively. When the program administrator or MGA does not handle the claims function, it will either be handled by an internal Claims Department for the insurance company or outsourced to a TPA.

Third-Party Administrator (TPA) Claims Operations

There are many types of TPAs in the insurance industry, including TPAs handling accident and health insurance, but this

[1]Risk purchasing groups are often formed by insurance professionals, including agents, brokers, and insurers, based on an identified need of commercial insurance buyers. For members, the purchasing group offers tailor-made coverage, broader coverage terms, lower rates, loss control and risk management programs, and often provides rewards for good loss experience, such as dividends in the form of credits against next year's premium. For insurers, purchasing groups offer the ability to achieve greater profitability. Purchasing groups can provide liability coverage only and are formed under the Liability Risk Retention Act (LRRA) of 1986.

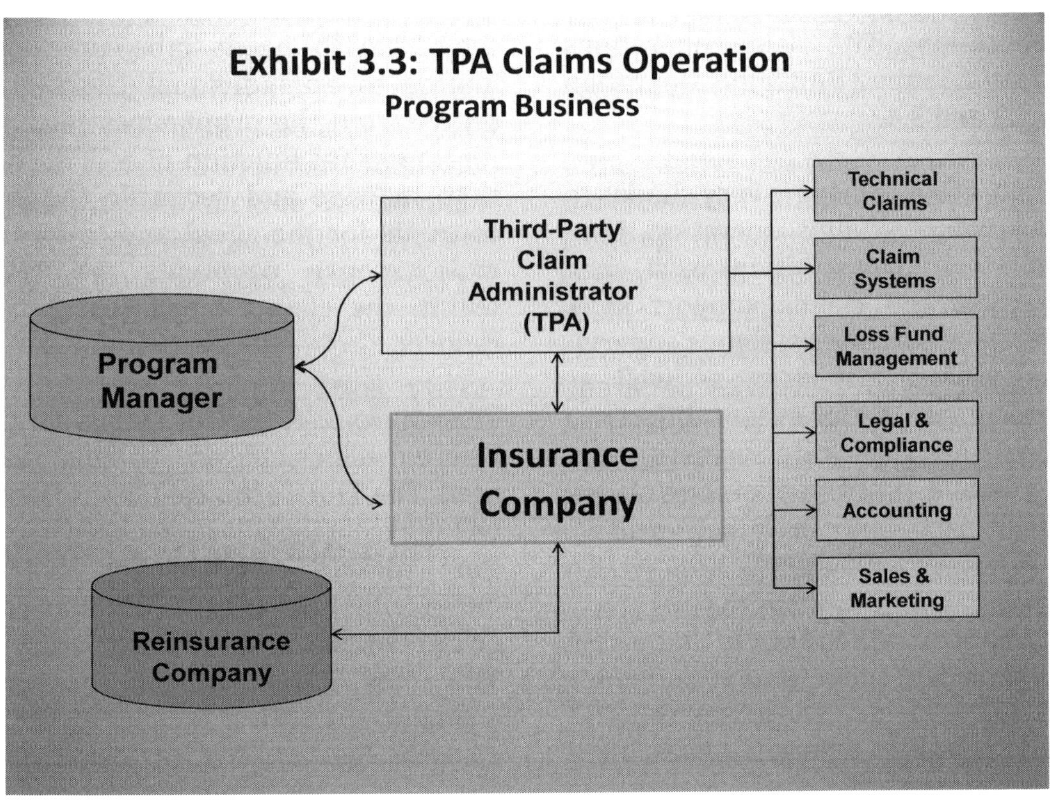

Chapter 4: Claims Operations—Core Operational Issues

This chapter focuses on core operational issues, such as human resources, management, reserve management, settlement, underwriting and loss control, loss ratios and profitability, finances and banking, insurance and bonding, business continuity and disaster recovery, and closed file retention. Let's start by looking at a sample organizational chart of an insurance company's Claims Department in Exhibit 4.1 below.

Human Resources (HR)

The HR Department is the backbone of any claims organization. Smart companies refer to their employees as their most important asset. Companies that recognize their employees as such are generally able to recruit better claims personnel and have lower employee turnover than those who have less respect for their personnel.

Exhibit 4.1: Sample Organizational Chart
Insurance Company—Claims Department

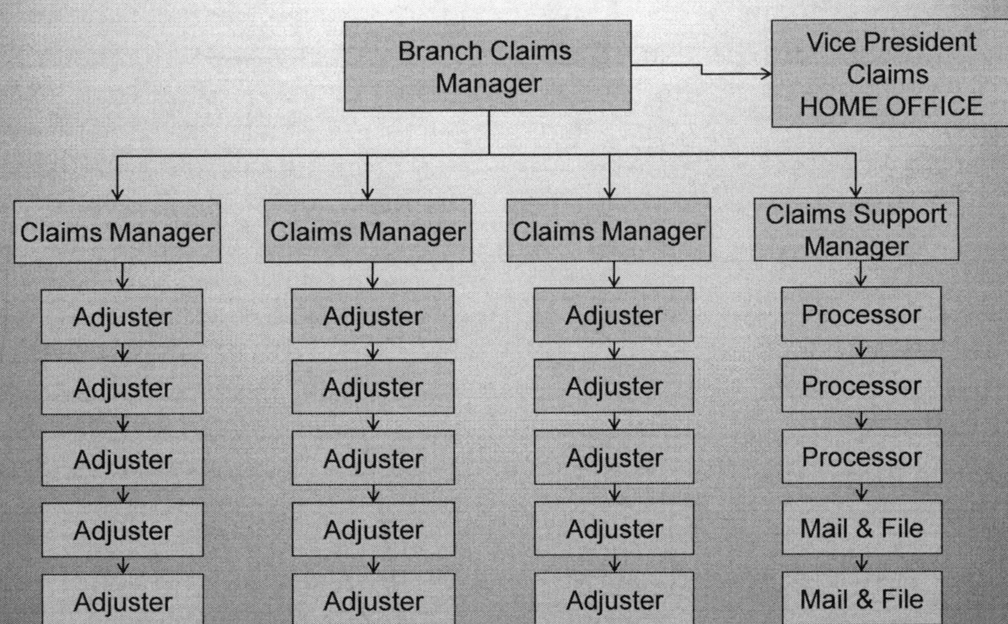

You cannot run a claims operation without experienced and knowledgeable claims people. Employees who enjoy working for a company will produce a higher quality work product, give above-average customer service, and operate as an effective team. The opposite occurs when employees do not enjoy their work environment and do not feel valued.

That said, probably the most important function of HR is the recruitment, hiring, and training of employees. It's so important, in fact, that we've devoted an entire chapter to it. See Chapter 7, beginning on page 73.

The Importance of Adequate Supervision

Most adjusters require some type of supervision. Proper supervision of a claim file typically involves instructions up-front when the claim is initially reported, periodic supervisory input as the claim file develops, and input as to the claim evaluation and ultimate resolution. This is usually done through the use of supervisory notes and instructions, and a calendar or diary—a formalized to-do list of what has happened regarding a claim, what needs to happen, and contingency plans in case of the unexpected.

Supervisors should monitor their adjusters through the use of a dual calendar or dual diary system to follow the progress of the claim, from initiation through closure. Naturally, the extent of the supervision will depend on the experience and knowledge of the adjuster being supervised. The supervisor must ensure the adjusters are maintaining timely diary management, particularly if the claim involves potentially time-sensitive dates, e.g., litigation handling. Another key responsibility of supervisors is to be sure claim files are timely and properly reserved. (Chapter 16, beginning on page 183, deals with reserve management.) Supervision in a claim organization is essential to maintain quality results.

As a service company or an internal Claims Department servicing claims for an insurer, human resources are the most costly expense within the operation. The quality of the staff resources has a direct and significant impact on the quality of claims handling and its results. With a class of insurance business that is complex and requires experienced and knowledgeable adjusters, poor results will occur if inexperienced adjusters are hired to hold down expenses.

The ratio of the technical staff to the management staff will vary by organization. For best results, however, it should generally be no more than 5:1, with the managers or supervisors having minimal responsibility for directly handling claims. The more people reporting to an individual claims supervisor or manager, the more likely that poor quality issues will develop. For example, if a claims manager has eight direct reports, there will probably be an adverse impact on the claim quality, given the amount of time necessary to actually provide substantive supervision to the technical staff. The manager will only be able to be peripherally involved. The basic supervisory comments may be in the claim file activity notes, but there is no substantive input from the supervisor or manager.

This is how problems with claim quality develop. Adjusters know their supervisors are monitoring the claim file with a dual diary on the claim. When the supervisor provides no comments or substantive direction and then advances their diary, they have every right to assume that they are handling the claim properly. However, when supervisors are busy trying to keep up with the workload, managing more than five adjusters, they will often overlook subtle errors and only become involved when problems arise. The end result is that a potential for a mistake exists, and mistakes can be costly.

For example, a time-sensitive date may pass due to an adjuster being unfamiliar with a particular claim jurisdiction or perhaps not having the appropriate experience to recognize a potential problem. As a result of the error or mistake, a bad faith claim[1] may develop and could result in an errors and omission[2] (E&O) claim against the company.

The same supervisory problem can occur if the supervisor only manages four adjusters but has a full workload of directly handled claims to manage at the same time. It is virtually impossible to function as an adjuster handling a full workload (or even a 50 percent workload) and manage four adjusters. Management does not only consist of file reviews and technical monitoring. It involves the management of people, including performance management, productivity analysis, administrative responsibilities, and training and development.

REMEMBER PROFITABILITY

Both insurance companies and TPAs are in business to make a profit. Both must develop operating budgets to control expenses.

If revenue declines (i.e., premium or TPA service fees), then the primary way to maintain profitability, or in some cases survival, is to reduce expenses. Reducing expenses usually means staff reductions.

The reduction of claims staff, with no corresponding reduction in claims volume, will develop into poor claim results. If there is not enough money to sustain the resources to properly handle claims, it won't take long for the inferior claims operation to produce a much larger increase in losses than was saved in expenses—a disaster!

Performance Management

Let's look at some of the positive and negative effects of managing human resources in claims operations. The primary and core issue regarding human resources in any organization is *financially* driven. Insurance companies (including the Claims Department) and TPAs are in business to make a profit, and they must develop operating budgets to control expenses. For example, if you are managing a claims operation for an insurer, the company, through its functional departments (Underwriting, Claims,

[1]Bad faith is a term used to describe blatantly unfair conduct that exceeds mere negligence by an insurance company or TPA. For example, a bad faith claim may arise if an auto liability insurer arbitrarily refuses to settle a claim within policy limits, where an insured's liability is incontrovertible. Bad faith damages, also known as extracontractual damages, are often substantial. They frequently exceed the limits of the insurance policy that is the subject of the claim.

[2]In the TPA environment, E&O claims develop as a result of mistakes or errors. Errors and omissions also refers to a particular type of insurance written under a claims-made policy.

Sales/Marketing, Accounting, Legal, etc.) have prepared an operating budget for each department. The budget includes all the expenses associated with the department, including the cost of human resources (salary, benefits, etc.). The revenue in an insurance company is derived from the premium it collects with the insurance policies it writes (sells).

If you have $1 of premium, you need to allocate the expenses associated with the premium as the cost of doing business. For example, we could allocate 32¢ for underwriting management, loss control, policy processing, boards, bureaus and taxes; 45¢ for losses, which translates into a loss ratio of 45 percent (which is good); and 12¢ for loss adjustment expenses (LAE). That brings us to a total of 89¢, leaving 11¢ for profit.

Let's now review the loss and LAE costs. LAE is the cost of investigating and adjusting losses. Loss adjustment expenses need not be allocated to a particular claim, but if they are, they are referred to as allocated loss adjustment expenses (ALAE). Examples include attorney, legal, adjuster, and appraiser fees.[3] If LAE costs are not allocated to a specific claim, but instead represent the expenses associated with the overall budget for the Claims Department, then they are unallocated loss adjustment expenses (ULAE). Examples include Claims Department payroll, benefits, supplies, equipment, or the cost of the contracted TPA.

In our example, 57¢ out of every premium dollar relates to claim costs. This is a prime reason why it is always wise to devote the proper resources to the claims function! If the Claims Department is able to improve the claims operation and save 4¢ off the loss ratio example above, the profit margin will increase by 4 points! Although this is a simplistic analysis, it is a reality, sometimes either overlooked or ignored by management. Being shortsighted or misunderstanding the impact of the claims operation on the overall company results will lead to problems.

UNDERPRICED TPA SERVICE FEES

If a TPA underprices service fees, the client will lose in the end. Those who outsource claim services often believe they are saving money. However, it's important to look closer at the transaction. All TPAs have to hire qualified people to handle claims and have similar operating expenses. And, they also need to make a profit. If the same price is charged for all TPA services—for example 4 percent of the gross written premium—this perpetuates the problem and reputation TPAs have in the industry. You always get what you pay for!

This situation not only occurs at insurance companies but may also happen when an insurer contracts the claims function to a TPA who inadequately prices its services or accepts a reduced fee proposed by the client. When a TPA's service fee is too low, it is virtually impossible for quality claims handling to be sustained, and the poor handling will severely impact the insurance program results. The consequence will ultimately be that the insurer loses money, and the TPA

[3] It should be noted that some insurance companies may code adjuster and appraisal expenses as an unallocated loss adjustment expense.

loses its client and faces the possibility of being sued by the insurance company. So, who was at fault, the insurer or the TPA? Actually, both—the insurer for getting what it paid for and the TPA for accepting the client's reduced fee structure in the first place, knowing it was underpriced.

The importance of understanding LAE, ALAE, and ULAE costs is that the claim budget is tied to the premium, and the premium is tied to the insurance rates being charged. If the insurer is not charging enough premiums with inadequate rates to cover its expenses and losses, then the only way to make a profit, other than the investments gained on its premium and loss reserves, is to reduce operating expenses. Remember the example of $1 or 100¢. If an insurance company spends more than 100¢ to operate, it is losing money.

The only way to correct this problem is to reduce the operating budgets for each department, which ultimately limits the ability to hire the staff resources necessary to handle and manage claims properly. The Claims Department reduces staff resources to get the budget to an acceptable level. The remaining claims staff becomes overloaded and backlogged, adversely affecting the quality of the claim file content and customer service. Claim mistakes are made, and shortly thereafter, turnover begins. Along the way, the company loses good employees because the job demands become increasingly difficult to meet, causing employees to be placed on performance warnings and ultimately terminated.

As turnover accelerates, the quality of claims handling deteriorates further. It becomes very difficult to replace people because past staff reductions indicate potential job instability, and continued turnover indicates a potentially poor work environment. The claims operation attempts to correct the problem by hiring temporary adjusters, which increases the expenses that could have been used to keep some of the people who were let go. All this can happen pretty quickly in a claims operation, but it can take years for the organization to recover, particularly the reputation for a poor work environment and high workloads that are unmanageable.

The same process occurs in a TPA claims operation. The TPA management staff prepares an operating budget for the company by department. The budget includes all the revenue and expenses associated with the company, including the cost of human resources (e.g., salary and benefits). TPA revenue is derived from the service fees it charges to its clients. If a TPA chooses to underprice its services to remain competitive, adversely affecting its profit margins, then the only way to improve results is to reduce expenses. In the end you have the same results as in the insurance company problem above, but probably with more significant consequences. Reducing the operating expense budget by reducing staff resources limits the TPA's ability to handle the claims properly. Mistakes are made, generating errors and omissions claims, and the client terminates the claims service agreement for poor service.

The solution to these problems is twofold. First, companies need to recognize these problems up-front and avoid the pitfall—conceivably saving money on the frontend while paying more on the backend to clean up or remedy the problem. Second, companies always need a contingency plan to allow for the handling of situations which change the operational or financial picture of the organization.

Settlement Philosophy

All claim facilities should have a settlement philosophy. Generally, a settlement philosophy serves as a guide to the Claims Department staff as to the proper approach to resolve a claim. It is very important that claims always be settled fairly and equitably. There is way too much bad publicity about insurers intentionally underpaying claims, much of it deserved. Claims should be paid promptly, fairly, and in accordance with the policy terms. An example excerpt of a settlement philosophy is shown opposite.

> **SETTLEMENT PHILOSOPHY**
>
> We investigate each claim to a point where we are able to properly evaluate our exposure in terms of liability, compensability, and damages. At that point, we utilize our judgment as to whether we require further investigation or whether the claim should be positioned for a proper defense, resolution, or settlement disposition.
>
> We should always continue to aggressively pursue a fair resolution through effective negotiations, utilizing our investigation and documentation contained within the claim file. We evaluate claims fairly and equitably, and comply with insurance department regulations.

Assume you are conducting an investigation, and you see that the insured could be held liable for injury to a third party. Should you initiate settlement discussions with the third-party claimant? This is a question that should be answered by your settlement philosophy. If you settle an injury claim with a claimant who is unrepresented by counsel for $2,500, when you would have paid $15,000 if the claimant was represented by an attorney, was the settlement fair and equitable? Of course not! Is it fair to deny a portion of the insured's personal property theft claim because the insured cannot locate every receipt? Of course not!

What about the property damage claim wherein the claimant agrees to settle a water damage claim at $5,000 after you advise him that there will be further delays if the settlement offer is not accepted. You also require a general release and intentionally neglect to tell the claimant about the mold potential caused by the water damage. Is this fair?

Oftentimes, these problems occur because there is no documented settlement philosophy to provide guidance and direction in the settlement of claims. An adjuster's job is not to look for ways to deny claims, but to investigate and adjust each claim fairly based on its own merits. All too often, adjusters deny coverage on first-party claims too quickly because they do not review the coverage forms properly.

Adjusters should strive to find coverage under the policy for an insured or policyholder, not look to deny coverage as quickly as possible. This is real problem in the insurance industry, which has contributed to its own tarnished reputation. Insurers write a policy for which the insured pays a premium. If the insured does not pay the premium on time, the insurer immediately cancels the policy. Insurance policy language is typically very complicated (even the so-called easy reading language policy). Even adjusters, claims managers, and coverage attorneys find it difficult to evaluate coverage. So, if the insurer had difficulty evaluating coverage under its own policies, how can policyholders be expected to do so?

The point here is that adjusters are the insureds' first point of contact after a loss. Policyholders are looking for guidance and direction, not adversity. It's the adjuster's job to read the policy and assist the insured in the handling of the claim with coverage advice and direction, with an eye toward finding coverage. Doing so will make the adjuster and insured partners rather than adversaries.

Underwriting

Underwriting involves all the activities necessary for the review and placement of the insurance business. It is imperative that underwriters and the claims staff work in harmony. Adjusters need not blame the underwriter for writing business that should never have been written. The underwriting function is not an easy job, and sometimes business gets written because the policyholder or agent may not have realized the hazards or exposures which ended up causing a loss. Or it's possible the underwriter may have missed something in the submission and review process.

"Underwriting as one of the major departments of the insurance company does its part to see that the insurer meets its survival goal. Specifically, the major goal of underwriting is the selection and maintenance of a profitable, growing book of business. A book of business, or simply a book, is the set of all the policies currently in force with an insurer of a particular kind of insurance (for example personal auto or workers compensation), a certain class of business or perhaps all the policies written by the insurer. There are a number of underwriting objectives or sub-goals related to this major goal:

(1) to provide proper coverage;

(2) to maintain selection standards;

(3) to maintain pricing standards; and

(4) to maintain high standards of professional competence."

J.J. Launie, J. Finley Lee, and Norman A. Baglini.
Principles of Property and Liability Underwriting. Malvern, PA: Insurance Institute of America, 1986.

premium. The expenses will include underwriting costs, acquisition costs (such as marketing, commissions, boards, bureaus and taxes). Insurance companies with low expense ratios are considered to be more efficient.

Often, underwriters refer to a combined ratio. It is the sum of two ratios, one calculated by dividing incurred losses plus loss adjustment expense (LAE) by earned premiums (the calendar year loss ratio), and the other calculated by dividing all other expenses by either written or earned premium (i.e., trade basis or statutory basis expense ratios). When applied to a company's overall results, the combined ratio is also referred to as the composite ratio or statutory ratio. Basically, the combined ratio measures the percentage of premium an insurance company uses to pay and process claims, as well as its expenses.

The combined ratio can be easily understood in terms of all expenses attributed to an insurance company's business to be profitable, not to exceed 100 percent. A combined ratio *below* 100 percent is indicative of an underwriting profit. If the combined ratio exceeds 100 percent, however, the insurance company is losing money for each percentage point in excess of 100 percent (investments may minimize the loss).

Combined Ratio

$$\frac{\text{Incurred Losses/LAE}}{\text{Earned Premium}} + \frac{\text{Expenses}}{\text{Written Premium}}$$

Sometimes the combined ratio term can be better understood in terms of expressing the 100 percent as $1. For example, an insurance company may pay out 55¢ in incurred losses (loss ratio) and 35¢ in underwriting expenses, which equals 90¢. The insurance company has earned 10¢ in this particular transaction, plus interest on the investment of the premium and loss reserves.

Profitability

Claims professionals need to understand the loss ratio, expense ratio, and combined ratio components. Claims managers are

Policy Year (the period between anniversary dates): All policies with an effective date in a particular year are included in the policy year data. Incurred losses are put back in the policy year, no matter when the claim occurred or when the claim payment and reserve transactions are statistically entered.

Calendar Year (the 12 calendar months beginning January 1): All policy and claim transactions are entered statistically and appear in the calendar year in which they were entered, e.g., 1/1/11 to 12/31/11.

Accident Year (any 12-month period for which losses from incidents taking place during that 12-month period are tracked): All claim transactions are put in the year that the claim occurred, without any regard as to the year the policy was written.

2009 Loss Ratio	*2010 Loss Ratio*	*2011 Loss Ratio*
50%	66%	68%
Incurred Losses: $2,500,000	Incurred Losses: $2,500,000	Incurred Losses: $6,800,000
Earned Premium: $5,000,000	Earned Premium: $3,800,000	Earned Premium: $10,000,000

responsible for making sure the Claims Department is not adversely affecting the loss ratio. While claims personnel cannot take responsibility for the actual losses sustained, they should take responsibility for the control of reserve redundancy and deficiency, improperly investigated claims, overpaid claim settlements, errors, and mismanaged claims with high jury verdicts. To properly analyze loss ratio fluctuations, claims managers should include a determination as to whether the loss ratio is being adversely affected by the insurance rates, premium volume, and the overall insurance market.

Consider the example above. Assume that in 2009 the total earned premium was $5 million. The incurred losses for the same time period were $2.5 million. This yields a loss ratio of 50 percent. This makes the underwriters happy.

In 2010, however, the total earned premium was $3.8 million, and the incurred loss for the same time period was $2.5 million, yielding a loss ratio of 66 percent. The underwriters are unhappy, and the Claims Department is criticized for contributing to a poor loss ratio with poor claims handling. While the incurred losses did not change from 2009 to 2010, the premium did. The premium may have changed due to lower rates with no increase in policy count caused by market and pricing. The end result was that the premium volume shrunk, causing the loss ratio to increase.

In 2011, the total earned premium is now at $10 million, the incurred losses for the same time period are $6.8 million, yielding a loss ratio of 68 percent. The policy count increased, and the rates also increased due to a more favorable market. But several large losses in 2011 adversely affected the incurred results. The underwriters are unhappy, and the Claims Department is blamed for contributing to a poor loss ratio by overreserving the recent large losses. Upon review of the large losses, it's determined that the reserves are proper. The loss ratio increased as a result of risk selection and underwriting, and not improper claims handling.

These examples are just an oversimplified explanation of how important it is to manage the claim data and information, and not just the actual claim files. The third example above, involving the 68 percent loss ratio, could have been due to poor claims handling. Perhaps there was a large reserve increase in the current calendar year, yet the loss occurred 3 years prior. The reserve adjustment may have been very late, which caused the loss ratio to increase substantially. Or the loss ratio could have been affected if there had been a large block of claims that were recently closed with payments exceeding the reserve amounts. Payments in excess of reserve amounts will increase the loss ratio, as the loss ratio is affected by the total incurred losses, which includes paid losses and outstanding reserves, less any recoveries. (Chapter 16, Claims Process—Reserve Management, page 183, deals with reserves in more detail.)

Claims managers must not only handle and manage claims, but also analyze claims and premium data to evaluate the impact of the losses and profitability on the company or client. To conduct an analysis, it is important to understand both claims and premium data to identify various claim issues. Loss ratios are affected by premium volume, which can in turn be affected by insurance rates. If insurance rates are reduced with the same policy count, the overall premium volume will reduce. The premium volume will also be reduced if the company's insurance rates are too high, and the insurance company becomes less competitive, losing premium volume to competitors. Identifying the cause of loss ratio fluctuations may not be an easy task, but it's important to resolve the problem.

Loss Triangles

Loss triangles are used by underwriters, claims professionals, and actuaries to evaluate the impact of losses (paid losses or total incurred losses) and premium over specified periods of time. Essentially, a loss triangle is a table of loss experience, with

Exhibit 4.2: General Liability Losses for XYZ Company

Months from the Beginning of the Policy Year

Policy Year	18	30	42	54	66
2007	$75,019	$108,638	$127,400	$143,897	$158,345
2008	$98,678	$109,837	$132,459	$147,323	
2009	$100,222	$127,415	$132,236		
2010	$108,234	$122,783			
2011	$111,382				
Total Incurred Losses					

total losses shown at regular periods, i.e., valuation dates, reflecting the change in amounts as claims mature. Older periods in the table will have one more entry than the next youngest period, leading to the triangle shape of the data in the table. Loss triangles are used to determine loss development for a given risk.

Exhibit 4.2 illustrates a loss triangle for general liability losses. In the first 18 months of the policy year 2007, incurred losses were at $75,019, and over the next 4 review periods over 66 months, those same losses increased to $158,345. So, when we look at the $111,382 in 2011, we are looking at incurred losses which are not fully developed; therefore, we should expect that the incurred losses will increase over time. Loss triangles are a very important tool to analyze profitability. Triangles can also be used to illustrate claim counts over specified periods of time.

Business Continuity and Disaster Recovery

Every insurance company and most TPAs have some sort of a business continuity and disaster recovery plan in place. They are critical for operational survival. Business continuity and disaster recovery plans can range from being very simple to very complex. Generally, a plan should include the following:

- Plan overview
- Business continuity team including managers and team leaders
- Explanation of current systems and disaster recovery process for each segment
- Systems backup and redundancy protocols
- Crisis management plan
- Emergency management plan
- General overview of each department and its function
- Identification of the critical areas that may be affected by a disaster
- Detailed plan to manage systems and data recovery in the event of a disaster
- Identification of a remote meeting location to continue operations
- Identification of necessary equipment, furniture, telephone, and other communication systems, computer systems, software applications, manuals, and supplies that will be needed by the disaster recovery team in the event of a disaster
- A telephone and e-mail contact list
- Staff training and testing

There are various risks to evaluate as part of the business continuity plan, such as:

- Information technology risks
- Risks of external or internal fraud
- Cyber risks
- Risk due to natural and unnatural disasters
- Terrorism
- Market risk

- Credit risk
- Interest rate risk
- Cash flow risk
- Errors and omissions (E&O) risks
- Reputation risk
- Other property and casualty risks

Business continuity and disaster recovery are even more critical with the use of paperless claim management systems and imaged documentation. In the event of a disaster, the claim facility needs to be able get back into operation as quickly as possible with minimal disruption and loss of information or data. This is particularly true if the disaster that caused the impact on the claim facility is the same disaster which will generate claims to be adjusted by the claim facility in a catastrophe claim environment.

As a TPA, the claim service agreement with the client will outline the TPA's responsibility to maintain the security of the claim data. It is absolutely imperative that the TPA have redundant backup systems to avoid the loss of claim data. It is also important that the TPA test these systems with the periodic exercise of data recovery. Loss of claim data by a TPA could result in a significant claim against the TPA by its client(s).

The business continuity and disaster recovery plans need to address the most important resource of any claim organization—its staff resources. Every plan should include a designated alternative work area or facility in the event of a disaster that is equipped with the systems, processes, and resources necessary to continue with the firm's operations.

Retention of Closed Files

Why is closed file retention so important? In addition to legal and regulatory requirements, noncompliance with the closed file retention procedures could have an adverse financial impact on a company that provides claim services (i.e., insurance company or TPA). For example, assume a Claims Department conducts a very thorough investigation of a fatality claim; however, the claim was never pursued. After 3 years, the Claims Department destroys the claim file and its contents. Six months after that, the estate of the claimant files a wrongful death action well within the jurisdiction's 4-year statute of limitations. All of the investigation and evidentiary documentation has been destroyed, leaving the claim facility with minimal documentation to properly defend the policyholder.

The premature destruction of the claim file could result in an excessive settlement or even an adverse or excessive jury verdict. Also, since the claim file was destroyed prematurely, the policyholder could bring an extracontractual claim[4] or action against the insurance company or TPA, exposing the policyholder to an excessive jury verdict due to the consequences of its failure to comply with the file retention procedures and laws.

The same situation could arise if the claim facility destroyed a claim file involving a minor, not realizing that the applicable stat-

[4]An extracontractual claim can occur when the insurance company mishandles a claim, commits a bad faith act, or does not adhere to unfair claim practice regulations. Coverage for extracontractual claims involving a TPA or adjuster is found in an errors and omissions (E&O) insurance policy.

ute of limitations does not even begin until the claimant reaches the age of 18 or majority. If the claim file was destroyed in 7 years, and the claimant would not reach majority until the tenth year, the claim file was destroyed prematurely.

There are various closed file retention requirements by state and federal law. Generally, claim file records are retained from 7 to 10 years from the closure date. If a minor child is involved, then the retention starts with the claimant's eighteenth birthday, and are retained 7–10 years from that date.

With technological advances, new claims are often completely paperless with all documents imaged into the claims system. Also, older claim files are now being converted to an imaged claim file to save file storage costs. Proper storage and maintenance of these files should help eliminate the retention problems discussed above. Record retention also applies to electronic records, including e-mail records. Business e-mail should not be deleted; it should be archived with a backup system in place.

Summary and Conclusion

The core claim operational issues discussed in this chapter illustrate their importance and impact on the overall claim operations. Experienced and knowledgeable human resources are critical in any claim organization. The supervision and management of human resources is critical to achieve quality results. If a supervisor or manager has too many adjusters directly reporting to them, there is less time to provide substantive supervision of adjusters and poor quality may result. There are various management controls which are utilized by a supervisor or manager to monitor adjusters, including a dual diary process, wherein the supervisor or manager has placed an additional diary on the claim as a method to monitor the activities of an adjuster. However, the claim supervisor or manager cannot place a dual diary on every claim, which will make the management control ineffective.

The chapter discussed performance management correlating it to operating budgets and the Claim Department's impact on profitability, including an illustration of loss triangles and a discussion of the two components of loss adjustment expenses: allocated loss adjustment expenses (ALAE) and unallocated loss adjustment expenses (ULAE). The Claims Department's operating budget is important as it dictates the amount of staff resources which can be hired in a given time and explains the financial restrictions sometimes faced by a claim facility. If the claim budget does not provide an adequate number of staff resources, claim workloads may increase, adversely impacting results and profitability.

The need for an effective settlement philosophy was also discussed, as well as underwriting and loss control issues. We further discussed loss ratios and profitability, detailing terms such as loss ratio, expense ratio, and combined ratio. A comparison of the underwriting cycle in terms of the hard and soft insurance markets was also provided.

Lastly, an ineffective business continuity or disaster recovery plan can be detrimental to any claim organization, as well as noncompliance with an established closed file retention process. Both could have a negative financial consequence on any claim operation.

Chapter 5: Claims Operations—Claims Management Overview

Effective management is critical to a claim organization and also the most difficult for many to understand. Oftentimes, adjusters are promoted to supervisors or managers because they were great technicians. They may be provided little to no supervisory or management training to expand on their solid technical skills. These adjusters understand how to handle their own claim files but may not understand how to manage subordinate employees to get them to also produce a quality work product.

As an industry, we place a lot of emphasis on technical skills because insurance is a technical job. Functional skills need to be learned, and this is usually accomplished through "on-the-job" training and coursework. As these skills are mastered, the natural progression is promotion to supervisor or manager. The problem is that not everyone is cut out to be a capable manager, and those so promoted may not want the job at all, which is why a professional technical path is needed as an alternative. This can be accomplished with technical positions that have more autonomy and responsibility, along with a higher salary structure.

Supervision and Management

Supervision and management are not always fun and rewarding. On the way up the career ladder, good adjusters work hard to produce a quality work product and thereby receive praise and positive feedback from management. Then, with a promotion to supervisor or manager, they become responsible for co-employees and the quality of their work. If members of their staffs are underperforming, it's up to the supervisor to take action, which could range from one-on-one performance meetings, formal verbal or written warnings, probation, or possibly termination. This can be a very unpleasant experience for both the adjuster and manager!

Success as a manager is driven by the ability to manage and lead the staff toward the organizational objectives, including the production of a quality work product. Inability to motivate staff to get the job done properly could result in the manager receiving a formal verbal or written warning, probation, or even termination.

The focus of this chapter is to highlight various management tools and management controls that can be used by supervisors and managers in a claims operation. There are many books written specifically on the topic of management, and, of course, this discussion is only intended to provide specific issues relating to claim management.

Staffing

Proper staffing is critical for claims operations to be successful. As a manager, you need to be able to evaluate staffing and workloads. This is accomplished through management reports available from the claims system (see Chapter 9 on technology beginning on page 93), as well as various staffing exercises that can be completed to provide further insight as to the necessary staffing for the organization.

If you are preparing budgets or are asked how many people you need to get the job done, you need to understand how to complete and effectively use a staffing analysis. A staffing analysis is a detailed analysis comparing adjuster workloads and productivity. In a Claims Department, there are various levels of support, technical, supervisory, and management staff. The staffing analysis will reveal the staff needed based on the pending and new claim volume.

New Claim: A newly reported loss that has been assigned to an adjuster for handling. Once the claim is set up as a new claim, it then becomes a pending claim.

Pending Claim: A claim that is open at the time of review and currently assigned to an adjuster.

Closed Claim: A pending claim that is statistically closed by payment or nonpayment.

Reopened Claim: A claim that was previously closed and is now reopened for investigation, handling, or processing.

Incident or Report Only Claim: A claim wherein no payment is expected.

Before beginning to prepare a staffing analysis, first evaluate the staff workloads. Realistic workloads will yield the best results and also minimize turnover. Asking adjusters to handle a pending caseload of 250 to 300 claims is simply a recipe for disaster. But, of course, this fact must be weighed against the reality of the budget. A well-prepared staffing analysis will not be a "wish list," but a working document to manage the technical claims handling and, at the same time, meet the organizational objectives.

Another aspect of the staffing analysis is to be sure to make "apples-to-apples" comparisons. For example, one claim organization counts each claim feature as one claim, while another may count each claim occurrence as one claim. The difference may not be significant with some lines, like general liability, but it will be with other lines, such as automobile, that have the potential for multiple claim features (e.g., bodily injury, no-fault, property damage, collision, uninsured motorist) in a single claim file occurrence.

As mentioned previously, there is a direct correlation of workloads to quality results. As an illustration, assume Adjuster Ann is handling a commercial general liability (CGL) insurance bodily injury claim. The facts involve Claimant Claire falling on the insured's walkway, sustaining a fractured elbow. Claire is represented by an attorney who provides a photograph of the defective walkway. Adjuster Ann has 250 pending claims and is under pressure to reduce her pending claims, while at the same time she is receiving 3 new claims per day. She conducts an investigation of the alleged defective walkway, which the insured (owner of XYZ Corporation) indicates has been there for many years. Constructive notice—the knowledge of facts that would lead a reasonably prudent person to take action—is established. Adjuster Ann determines the insured is primarily liable and settles the bodily injury claim for $18,000.

Adjuster Betty is assigned an identical CGL bodily injury claim but currently has a lower workload of 150 claims. She digs a little bit deeper in her investigation to learn that the building and adjacent walkway are actually owned by another entity (YYY, LLC), which has the same principals as the named insured entity but is actually a separate entity, insured under its own liability policy with a different insurance company. Adjuster Betty denies the claim based on no liability (as the named insured does not own maintain or control the location of the fall) and closes her file.

This may not be a common occurrence, but it illustrates the ways that a more thorough investigation will result in higher quality claims results. For example, it isn't uncommon for very busy adjusters to settle smaller claims on the higher end of the ranges than they are valued because they simply do not have time or resources to effectively negotiate them. Another frequent problem is when the adjuster won't take the time to get an appraisal of the vehicle damage, even though the appraisal may reduce the total claim to a level within the deductible. Other adjusters, in their rush to close claims, improperly evaluate coverage issues and pay losses that are not covered under the terms of the insurance policy.

Workloads vary by claim facility. The operating budget will dictate the workload standards in a claim organization.

There are hundreds of examples, but the point is that management may think reducing staff saves money, but in reality, considering the concomitant increase in adjuster workloads, this could result in hundreds of thousands of additional loss dollars.

Just do the numbers. If a Claims Department had 30 bodily injury adjusters, and they each handled 180 bodily claims in 1 year (15 per month), there would be 5,400 bodily claims. If all those claims settled, and the adjusters paid an additional $1,000 on each claim (paying more toward the higher settlement range), the total overpayment would be $5.4 million! This problem would be so subtle that the harried and overworked claims manager may not notice until it is too late.

The more overworked a person is, the poorer the work product. The poorer the work product, the higher the financial impact. The higher the financial impact, the higher the loss ratio. (See Chapter 4, Core Operational Issues, beginning on page 29, for more info on loss ratios.)

It should also be noted that higher pending claim volumes may indicate a performance problem and may not be a staffing issue at all. If an adjuster does not close claims in the normal course of business and continues to have newly reported claims assigned, it is inevitable that the pending claims will be very high, which also has an impact on the ability to handle new claims. Managers must remain cognizant of this problem, particularly when requesting additional staff. Thus, it is important to also consider closing ratios of the claims staff to effectively evaluate the reasons for the current workload.

Claims Attorney: Handles professional liability and management liability claims as well as other claims which involve complex coverage issues.

Claims Specialist: Handles complex and large exposure claims (all types), including litigation claims and high value first-party property claims.

Senior Claims Adjuster: Handles high exposure bodily injury, property damage and workers compensation indemnity claims, including some litigation claims and first-party property claims.

Claims Adjuster II: Handles low-to-medium exposure bodily injury, property damage, workers compensation (indemnity and medical), and first-party property claims.

Claims Adjuster I: Handles all low exposure damage claims, including property damage, collision and comprehensive, and first-party property, as well as workers compensation medical-only claims.

Claims Adjuster Trainee: Involved in a formal training program, handling low exposure damage claims under close supervision.

A closing ratio is the comparison of new claims to closed claims during a given time period. For example, if an adjuster were assigned 30 claims in a month, and closed 25 in the same month, the closing ratio would be 83 percent. If an employee consistently has a closing ratio under 75 percent, the claims manager should be very concerned as, over time, the pending claim volume will go through the roof! Every month, pending claim volume will be increasing, adversely affecting the quality of the claims handling because the adjuster cannot manage the workload. It also needs to be determined whether claim files have been recently transferred to the adjuster from another adjuster. The reassigned adjuster needs time to review the newly assigned pending claims, which could take weeks or months, given the need to handle other pending claims and new assignments.

When evaluating new claims, claims managers need to look at their complexity and severity. Comparing the workload of an adjuster handling property damage claims to an adjuster handling bodily injury claims is inappropriate. The bodily injury claims are more time-consuming and require more work than property damage claims. There are also distinctions in the amount of time and effort necessary to handle a claim pending in litigation compared to nonlitigated claims.

Staffing Analysis

So, with the stage set, let's perform a staffing analysis.[1] To keep the illustration simple, the analysis shown below uses *claim files* (one claim occurrence that may include many claimants, the insured, and various claim features) as the basis for staffing, as opposed

[1]Please keep in mind that this approach illustrates just one staffing analysis methodology. There are many different types of staffing methodologies.

to *claim features* (a single loss for one claimant). When evaluating staffing of a claims unit that is handling claims with many features, such as auto claims, perform the analysis on a claim features basis.

Exhibit 5.1 depicts what this organization or manager feels are reasonable workload objectives for each type of claim position in the unit. The technical or professional positions used are standard in the industry. They may have different labels in some organizations, but the same job requirements will exist with different position names.

Exhibit 5.2 illustrates the actual workloads of the unit claims staff by position. *Pending claims* is the actual number of claims open for each staff member at the time of the analysis. The new claim monthly average represents an average of the new claims for the time period of the staffing analysis. When using a 6-month period, for example, the total new claim count by staff member will be divided by 6 to arrive at the average.

Exhibit 5.3 then compares the actual to the original objectives to allow evaluation of the unit's staffing level. New and pending claims are reviewed separately. The first column lists the staff positions. The second column simply restates the maximum number the manager feels is reasonable for each position as depicted in Exhibit 5.1, and the third column shows the number of people in each position. The fourth column shows the sum of the number of claims for each person (from Exhibit 5.2) to depict the actual number of pending claims or new claims by position instead of by individual.

The fifth column in Exhibit 5.3 shows the average number of pending or new claims, which is calculated by dividing the actual number of claims for each position (column 4) by the number of staff for that position (column 3). For example, the 142 average for claims attorney pending claims is calculated by dividing 283 by 2 and rounding the 141.5 result up to 142.

Exhibit 5.1: Workload Objectives

Position	Pending Claims	New Monthly Claims
Claims Officer	0	0
Claims Manager	0	0
Claims Supervisor	0	0
Claims Attorney	100–125	15–20
Claims Specialist	100–125	15–20
Sr. Claims Adjuster	125–150	20–25
Claims Adjuster II	125–150	25–35
Claims Adjuster I	100–125	35–60

Column six, then, provides a comparison of the maximum number of pending or new claims per position objectives (from Exhibit 5.1) to the average workloads calculated in column 5. This is calculated by subtracting column 2 from column 5, yielding a plus or minus difference in column 6. Thus, on average, the claims attorney position is assigned 17 more pending claims and 7 more new claims than the maximum range objectives for the position of 125 pending and 20 new claims.

Now that acceptable workloads have been projected and sorted (pending claims and new claims) by position with averages, staffing can be evaluated in terms of the total full-time and part-time adjusters and attorneys required.

The pending claims section in Exhibit 5.3 shows that, spread over 12 adjuster positions, there are 43 more claims than the objective for maximum pending workloads. This difference is quite manageable. By realigning claim file assignments for the claims attorneys and senior claims adjusters, the pending claim volume can be leveled with no staff additions or reductions.

Exhibit 5.2: Actual Workloads

#	Name	Position	Pending Claims	New Claim Monthly Average
1	John Patterson	Claims Attorney	165	36
2	Christine Carson	Claims Attorney	118	17
3	Jackie Rogers	Claims Specialist	129	19
4	Samuel Jackson	Claims Specialist	137	26
5	Rita Woolworth	Claims Specialist	126	14
6	Peter Gonzalez	Sr. Claims Adjuster	186	32
7	Austin Limits	Sr. Claims Adjuster	147	39
8	Kathy Augustine	Claims Adjuster II	150	47
9	Mary Smith	Claims Adjuster II	167	38
10	Herbert Oakes	Claims Adjuster II	139	27
11	Michael Jorgensen	Claims Adjuster I	118	46
12	Theresa Cohen	Claims Adjuster I	133	58
	Totals:		**1715**	**399**
	Averages:		**143**	**33.25**

Similarly, the new claims section shows that, spread over these 12 adjuster positions, there are 12 claims more than the objective for maximum new assignment workloads. Again, by realigning new claim assignments for the claims attorneys and senior claims adjusters, the new claim volume can be leveled with no staff additions or reductions.

So, is the unit staffed properly using the above illustrations? Well, that depends! It depends on the financial budget as well as the technical requirements and the experience of the adjusters. If claims operation position allocation has been adjusted down by the organization to 10 adjusters, equivalent to perhaps $500,000 in salary, then staff must be reduced and workloads

Exhibit 5.3: Staffing Analysis

#1	#2	#3	#4	#5	#6
		PENDING CLAIMS			
Position	**Max Pending Claims**	**Total Staff**	**Actual Pending**	**Average Pending**	**+/– Difference**
Claims Attorney	125	2	283	142	+17
Claims Specialist	125	3	392	131	+6
Sr. Claims Adjuster	150	2	333	167	+17
Claims Adjuster II	150	3	456	152	+2
Claims Adjuster I	125	2	251	126	+1
Totals:		**12**	**1715**	**143**	**+43**
		NEW CLAIMS			
Position	**Max New Claims**	**Total Staff**	**Actual New**	**Average New**	**+/– Difference**
Claims Attorney	20	2	53	27	+7
Claims Specialist	20	3	59	20	0
Sr. Claims Adjuster	25	2	71	36	+11
Claims Adjuster II	35	3	112	37	+2
Claims Adjuster I	60	2	104	52	–8
Totals:		**12**	**399**	**34**	**+12**

increased. Another possibility might be to change the claims handling methodology and outsource some of the claim activities; however, this will result in increased allocated loss adjustment expenses.

Another alternative is to reduce the cost of staff resources in a manner to allow for the operation to maintain 12 adjusters but with the same salary budget. This would result in staff realignment by replacing adjusters who have higher salary levels with lower salaried employees (possibly even claims trainees). Obviously, this is not a pleasant task or outcome for the personnel and possibly not for the company. This could negatively affect the quality of the claims operation if less experienced adjusters are hired. Sometimes, staff levels may be reduced with attrition or voluntary turnover, making the transition easier.

Workload Variations

Workloads can vary for a variety of reasons, all of which need to be taken into consideration when determining optimal staffing levels. Some of these reasons are discussed below.

Type of Claim

Some claims require a lot of very detailed work, such as a fatality claim in litigation. Others may require minimal handling, such as a collision or windshield claim.

Line of Business

Workloads for different lines of business may vary considerably. For example, an automobile liability claim involving two vehicles with injury and property damage may not be as time-consuming as a complex professional liability or directors and officers liability claim. A property claim involving $50,000 in damage may settle in 90 days, yet a $50,000 workers compensation indemnity claim could be pending for 2 years.

Class of Business

Underwriters distinguish classes of business to make a distinction between certain types of exposures within a line of business. For example, tow trucks and waste haulers may be separate classes of business within the automobile line of business. Some classes of business may have nuances that require more detailed and/or specialized claims handling, such as environmental or taxicab liability claims handling.

Complexity and Severity

The more complex and severe the claims, the less volume an adjuster can handle. This is important, as claims managers must know the number of complex claims an adjuster is working on to adjust the overall workload accordingly. There are different ways to identify complex claims, such as home office or client reporting claim lists, litigation lists, loss runs, and claim reserve reports, which can identify reserve amounts by claim feature.

Litigation

Litigation claims, if handled properly with a comprehensive litigation management program, are time-consuming. There are legal pleadings and depositions to review, a litigation process to manage, analysis of caselaw and statutes, and comprehensive ongoing investigations and discovery. (See Appendix F—Litigation Management.)

Subrogation Only Claims

If an adjuster is only handling the subrogation aspect of the claim, wherein the underlying investigation or adjustment process has already been completed, then the subrogation adjuster can be expected to handle a larger volume of claims. It's not unusual to see subrogation pending claim levels at 250–300 claim files. However, even if the adjuster is superhuman, a pending of 500 subrogation claims is unmanageable. Remember, the subrogation recoverables reduce the incurred losses and should be a priority, as the recovery dollars go right to the bottom line.

The proper workload for the subrogation adjuster also needs to take into consideration whether the claims are first-party property or automobile collision. First-party property subrogation claims handling can be more time-consuming than automobile subrogation claims handling. This is primarily due to the potential extent of damages involved, as well as the depth of the subrogation investigation.

Claim Methodology

Workloads are dependent on the methodology of claims handling. For example, take Adjuster Andy who takes statements, makes telephone calls, types all of the correspondence, and enters claim data transactions. Now compare the handling with Adjuster Bert who relies on an independent adjuster to tackle most of the claims investigations (with written summary reports), with a support unit that types all correspondence and

enters all data. Adjuster Andy's workload should be less than Adjuster Bert's, as the tasks assigned Adjuster Andy will eat up much of his workday.

Claim Requirements

Sometimes, claims operations have different claims handling requirements that impact workloads and staffing. For example, instead of taking statements and making telephone contacts, some organizations may require the claims adjusters to simply send form statements and other claim form documents to all the parties to the loss, reducing the work necessary to investigate a claim. Claims operations may require adjusters to prepare formal reports at certain intervals during the claims handling process. Full reporting takes time and should be considered when evaluating workloads.

If the claims operation has a detailed litigation management program, which will control expenses, the time necessary to properly manage a litigated claim will impact the number of litigation claim files an adjuster can handle at any given point in time. If the same litigation claim file is simply abandoned to defense counsel for handling, with no substantive input by the adjuster, a litigation adjuster will be able to handle more claims.

Claim Position

Various claim positions may dictate the workloads. A claims specialist handling only fire losses in excess of $100,000 should have a lower workload than an adjuster handling property claims at $5,000 and lower.

Active versus Run-Off Claims

Active claims are claims that are open and pending in a claims operation. *Run-off* claims are those open claims in a special program that has been shut down (or where the insurer no longer writes that line or class of business) and for which all policy periods have expired. In a run-off situation, only a minimal number of new claims are expected to be reported. The insurer's goals are to run off or close the pending claims and finalize the overall incurred losses. (See Chapters 18–20, pages 221–270, on TPAs for more details on run-off claims.)

Adjuster Experience

An experienced bodily injury adjuster can handle a higher workload of bodily injury claims than, for example, an inexperienced bodily injury adjuster who was recently transferred from a property damage adjuster unit and has just started handling bodily injury claims. Unfortunately, some claims managers underestimate the time necessary for adjusters to understand, adapt, and learn how to handle other lines of business. These types of situations require adjustments to workloads.

Summary and Conclusion

In this chapter, we focused on claims management. Effective supervision and management are critical to a successful claims operation, and a career path toward management may not always be the right path for every claims person.

Workloads and staffing are the core of any claim facility and drive the quality and results of a claim organization. Unrealistic workloads with an understaffed claims operation will be detrimental to the organization and the underwriting facility or self-insured involved. Although there will always be budgetary constraints in any organization, it is important to evaluate the ultimate direct and indirect costs to a claim organization and the insurance company or client it represents. For example, the overpayment of claims or paying noncovered claims has a direct impact on profitability. Often, mistakes can be avoided if the claims staff has enough time to manage the claim workload properly.

The chapter includes a sample staffing analysis to illustrate the various components that should be addressed when staffing a claim organization. Workloads can vary considerably by the types of claims, lines of business, class of business, complexity and severity, litigation involvement, number of subrogation claims, claim methodology, claim requirements, claim position, active versus run-off claims, and adjuster experience. It is important to determine whether the increased workloads are due to increased claim volume or due to adjuster performance in not meeting claim closing ratios on a monthly basis.

FOR MORE INFORMATION ON:	GO TO:	PAGE(S):
Core Operational Issues	Chapter 4	29
Management Controls	Chapter 6	57
Recruitment and Retention	Chapter 7	73
Claims Process—Reserve Management	Chapter 16	183
Third-Party Administrators	Chapters 18–20	221–270
Claims Handling Guidelines	Chapters 21–30	271–354

Chapter 6: Claims Operations—Management Controls

Any claims operation must have supervisory or management controls in place to manage and monitor the quality of the claims operation and administratively manage employees. These types of controls will vary by claim operation and, by necessity, this discussion covers only those universal controls that apply to most claims operations

Claim Authority

Claim authority is the maximum monetary amount that a claims unit employee may use in the establishment of a claim reserve, negotiation of a settlement, payment of a claim, or processing of a claim payment without seeking the approval of a higher-ranking claim person. Each claims technical and management person should have some type of claim authority. Without some level of claim authority, a claims person is not really making technical claim decisions, which is part of an adjuster's professional developmental process.

How much claim authority does an adjuster need? It depends! Claim authority should be based on the adjuster's knowledge and experience level, and should be earned. When adjusters improperly make decisions that exceed their claim authority, it is important that the manager address the issue, which can be serious depending on the circumstances, particularly if the employee exceeded the authority established by the client (i.e., in a third-party administrator environment). Depending on the incident, it could involve adjustment of the employee's authority and/or disciplinary action.

All claims specialists and adjusters should be assigned an individual claim authority. This will outline the limitations on their ability to set reserves, settle the claim, and approve expenses and payment. Only claim management and officers should have print check authority and check signing authority. Adjusters should be required to strictly

MANAGEMENT CONTROLS

- Claim Authority Levels
- Management Dual Diary
- Payment/Check Approval
- Large Loss Review
- System Controls
- Business Rules
- Quality Controls
- Quality Review Program
- Claim Metrics
- Productivity Reporting
- Management Reports
- Performance Management
- Security

adhere to their claim authority and request additional authority as necessary from the appropriate manager. Claim authority extended by a manager to an adjuster should be documented in the electronic claim file notes outlining the authority extended. Although adjusters may be required to work within their respective claim authorities, it is a good practice to encourage handling adjusters to maintain an open dialogue with their respective managers to discuss individual claim values for both reserve and settlement purposes when necessary, even if the claim is within the adjuster's established claim authority.

Typically, the claims adjuster and management staff receive a formal memo or e-mail confirming claim authority levels. The claim management system is programmed to control the claim authority process with regard to reserve entry, reserve approval, payable approval, and check issuance or printing. Whenever settlement, payable approval, or reserve authority is increased by a claims manager, it should be clearly documented in a formal memo or e-mail.

Management Dual Diary

A claims diary is a calendar diary established to review or handle a claim file at a certain point in time, or follow up on a particular task or adjustment activity. The claim diary process is also used to meet deadlines, including time-sensitive dates. For example, diaries are established for periodic reviews of a claim (including reserve reviews), follow-up contacts, outstanding investigation or adjusting items to be completed, and responses to arbitration notices or litigation activities. A diary can be established for any claim file activity.

The claim file includes all notes, e-mails, correspondence, investigative and adjustment documentation and financial transactions. The diary review process may involve a review of the file documentation to determine the claim value or prepare a file report or memorandum.

A management dual diary is the placement of a claims manager's diary on a claim file right along with the adjuster's diary. It is designed to provide supervision, guidance, and direction to the claims adjuster. This ensures that the manager will also periodically look at the claim file. For this reason, a management dual diary is critical during the claims handling process. There are various reasons to place a dual diary on a claim file, and a specific process, which is outlined in the Claims Handling section of this book.

A claims manager cannot possibly dual diary every claim on the adjuster's diary. This is ineffective in managing the claims process and also handicaps the adjuster's ability to develop skills and confidence. If all claims were subject to dual diary, the claims manager would be spread so thin as to be unable to provide any type of substantive input. This results in mistakes. Therefore, a claims supervisor or manager will dual diary claims that exceed the adjuster's monetary claim authority, require home office approval, are classified as client reporting files, are likely to be subject to litigation, or involve coverage issues. The process will vary by claim organization and adjuster.

An important responsibility of a claims manager is to understand the areas that require actual management involvement. If a claims manager has 5 adjusters, each with 125 claims, then there are 625 claims pending in the unit at any given time. Claims managers need to prioritize their involvement in claim files and only become involved in the technical claims handling of an individual claim when necessary and appropriate. If a claims manager feels strongly that he or she needs to be involved in every single claim file for an individual adjuster, the adjuster is either not capable or willing to do the job, or the claims manager needs management training.

It is a good practice for claims managers to consider removing a dual diary when a claim has reached a certain development stage (if the claim is being handled properly) and extend additional claim authority to the adjuster. The final note by the claims manager could outline what needs to be accomplished, along with some closing comments. For example, the note could indicate:

> Jack, you've done a nice job handling this claim file to date. Please follow up and contact the claimant's attorney to initiate settlement discussions. You should be able to settle this claim in the range of $15,000–$20,000. I'm extending $20,000 in settlement authority. We will need a general release, releasing both the named insured and the insured operator. If you have any questions, see me. Thanks.

This type of management direction gives the adjuster an opportunity to make decisions beyond the standard authority that is in place.

Take as another example an adjuster with $15,000 in settlement authority. The adjuster is working a claim that *may* have a value up to $50,000, and this is the current reserve amount. Once the investigation is complete, and the claim only requires some additional documentation of special damages, the claims manager might extend claim authority up to $40,000, and remove the diary with a note indicating:

> Nice job to date. The claim looks like it is moving in the right direction. Please follow up to complete the outstanding items indicated in my last memo. I am extending settlement authority up to $40,000 to settle this claim. If you need more authority, please let me know. Good luck!

By referring the claim file back to the handling adjuster to direct the claim toward a resolution without the need for close monitoring (referred to as "charging back" the claim), the claims supervisor or manager reduces the number of claims to oversee, providing more time to review the claims that require management attention. It also provides an opportunity for the adjuster to work autonomously on a claim, which is another opportunity to develop skills and confidence.

Payment or Check Approval Process

The payment or check approval process will vary by claim organization. Usually, in an electronic claim environment, either the claims support, technical, or management staff will enter amounts to be paid—the claim payables—within the claims system, which is the entry stage of the check issuance process. All payables above the payment approval authority of the individual claim employee should require approval by the supervisor, claims manager, or an officer of the company, in accordance with their individual claim authority level. If the payment exceeds the adjuster's authority, prior to the payable approval stage, there should be a note in the claim file extending authority to settle the claim at or below the requested payment amount.

Large Loss Review

Large loss referrals are notices sent to the home office or client advising of claims that exceed the office's or third-party administrator's claim authority level. The large loss reports are comprehensive and often have attachments. Since these types of claims generally exceed the manager's authority, the claims manager should review and approve all large loss referrals.

System Controls

Claims systems have various controls that are used to monitor and prevent employees from exceeding their claim authority for both reserves and payment approval. Controls can also be used to block the ability to make any data changes without manager approval, backdate transactions, or change any file notes or documents.

Depending on the sophistication of the technology being utilized, some claim organizations can develop system business rules, which provide further controls during the claims handling process. In an electronic claim environment, system controls are critical.

Business Rules

Business rules are usually system generated and assist the management staff in managing the claims process. Here are a few examples of business rules that a claims operation might have in place:

- When any legal process or arbitration decision is received and entered by the claims support unit, an automatic e-mail is generated and sent to the adjuster and manager.
- A reserve worksheet with mandatory fields must be completed on any workers compensation claim before a claim reserve can be entered.
- A notification is automatically generated if the incurred losses within an aggregate self-insured retention (SIR) exceed a certain percentage of the SIR, e.g., 50 percent, since this would trigger a reporting requirement to the excess insurer.

Quality Controls and Quality Review Process

There are many quality controls claims managers can utilize during the normal course of business. (Some of these controls are detailed in the Management Reports section beginning on page 64.) Managers should evaluate whether management controls are being utilized effectively. If there are management controls in place that the staff never abides by or pays attention to, then they should either be enforced or eliminated. Management controls should be managerial tools and not simply a requirement that has no value or purpose.

The most important management control is the quality review process. Every claim facility should have a documented quality

Exhibit 6.1: Quality File Review Process

- Claims Supervision and Management
- Coverage and Contacts
- Investigation and Documentation
- Reserve Management
- Expense Control
- Diary Management and Claim Control
- Claim Evaluation and Analysis
- Disposition, Negotiation, and Claim Resolution
- Litigation Management
- Recovery/Contribution
- Large Loss and Client Referral
- Client Specific Categories

review process. This process allows managers to select a representative sample of claim files monthly for each technical claims employee (adjuster) and then conduct individual claim file reviews. The file review will typically focus on the categories indicated in Exhibit 6.1.

There should be a review sheet (electronic), or entry, for each claim file reviewed as well as a master sheet that categorizes and trends the results. The results should be one component of each technical claims employee's performance review, with a target percentage achieved. The quality review process, including file review forms, can easily be automated either using a spreadsheet or a database program. The automated process will allow for custom trending of results.

Most claim facilities are subject to quality reviews by either a home office or client (i.e., client insurers, reinsurers, self-insurers, or third-party consultants retained by clients). These reviews are typically called claim audits or claim reviews, and will involve similar categories as those used in the quality review process. The review may also involve an administrative or operational review, as discussed below.

The results of these reviews should be utilized as a management tool to identify areas for improvement as well as for training and development purposes. Although claims managers may not always be provided with

Exhibit 6.2: Audit Worksheet Categories

- Coverage
- Contacts
- Investigation
- Documentation
- Evaluation and Analysis
- Litigation Management
- Diary Management
- Reserve Management
- Recovery and Contribution
- Claim Resolution
- Supervision
- Client Reporting
- Reinsurance Reporting

an audit report from client or home office auditors, they should insist on a wrap-up of the auditor's findings at the conclusion of the audit. A wrap-up, in the claims context, is simply a discussion between claim management (and possibly other staff) and the audit team. The wrap-up should review the technical claim category results, any findings related to the overall claims operation, and include a discussion about the claim facility's strengths and weaknesses—possible areas for improvement.

Frequently, the senior claim management staff may only be involved in the claims operational review outlined in the administrative and operational review shown in Exhibit 6.3. Administrative or operational reviews provide a complete analysis of a claims operation. The focus is on many operational issues, including contracts, human resources, regulatory compliance, accounting, best practices (i.e., industry recognized and proven practices), management controls, and claims systems.

Claims managers and auditors should not criticize file handlers personally but provide constructive feedback concerning the work product itself. Sometimes claims manager monthly file reviews and claim audits can be emotional, as there may be a lot at stake if the results are not acceptable, such as the loss of a client or employee or management probation. The goal should always be to provide positive feedback along with any areas for improvement. Though a perfect claim file is rarely found,

Exhibit 6.3: Administrative and Operational Review

- Organizational Overview and Contracts
- Claim Management and Adjuster Interviews
- Regulatory Review:
    - Professional Licensing
    - Fair Claim Act Compliance
- Loss Fund Account Management:
    - Check Issuance Process
    - Reconciliation
    - Security
    - Office of Foreign Assets Control (OFAC) Compliance
- Claims Handling Guidelines (Best Practices)
- Litigation Management
- Reserve Management Processes and Procedures
- Review of Quality Controls and Claim Standards
- Large Loss/Client Reporting
- Reinsurance Reporting
- Claim Authority Levels by Employee
- Staffing and Employee Productivity
- Claims Systems Review
- Training and Development
- Insurance and Bonds
- Client-Specific Categories

claims managers often have very high standards and an expectation that all their employees should embrace the same standards. Some claim files do not need absolute perfection, and this should be kept in mind while conducting reviews.

Lastly, it is important for claims managers and auditors to be open and honest. In an attempt to avoid conflict, it is not unusual for managers or auditors to soft pedal issues during the wrap-up only to include brutally honest results about issues in the written report. Misleading people into thinking that they performed well and then criticizing them in a written report is unfair and demoralizing.

Claim Metrics

Claim metrics involves the tracking of quantitative information to evaluate performance of the unit and claim trends that may impact the claims operation and insurer or self-insured. Metrics are commonly maintained on average contact times from the date reported to initial contact, new losses, closed claims, reopened claims, closing ratios, claim duration, percentage of litigation claims, average reserves, average claim costs, average expense costs, workloads, productivity, and turnover.

Properly used, claim metrics serve as an early warning system for developing problems. If, for example, average paids (the total volume of paid losses for a particular category, divided by the number of claims) are being monitored, and the average loss payments increase substantially in a single month, the claims managers are alerted to a potential problem area. The specific claims might then be identified and reviewed to determine whether this is a trend or just an anomaly. Claim metrics reports should be generated and reviewed each month.

Productivity Reporting

Productivity reports are used to monitor and manage claims employee workloads and overall production. Generally, productivity reports should include the information listed in Exhibit 6.4. Productivity reports are a tool, and like any other tool, should not be relied on exclusively to manage, or staff, a claims operation. Most claim facilities have mechanisms in place to allow managers to obtain productivity reports on a regular basis, either manually or electronically. These reports should be reviewed routinely—at least monthly.

Productivity results should be discussed with each claims employee on a monthly basis to review overall production, identify claims that should be directed toward closing, and monitor the employee's progress for performance management purposes. Performance management objectives should always include productivity goals.

Exhibit 6.4: Summary Productivity Report

- Employee Name
- Open Pending Claims by Month
- New Claims by Month
- Reopened Claims by Month
- Closed Claims by Month
- Closing Ratios by Month

A simple monthly productivity report is illustrated in Exhibit 6.5. When evaluating productivity, it often makes sense to track reassigned claims as a separate category because a reassigned claim reduces one adjuster's pending and increases another's without actually increasing the claim volume in the new, open, or closed claim categories. If there were a significant number of new claims reassigned to an adjuster, it would involve a review process of each new reassigned claim affecting the adjuster's ability to handle new incoming claim volume and current pending claims.

The closing ratio, the ratio of closed claims to the total of new and reopened claims, is a good indicator of claim productivity. When an adjuster has a high pending claim volume, it is beneficial to review the closing ratio for the current and prior months. Low closing ratios will increase the pending claim volume each month, and, on the surface, it may look like an adjuster has been overloaded. High workloads will always make it difficult to close claims and will lead to quality problems. With a steady volume of new claims coming in, and the need to manage open pending claims, minimal time is left to close claims and handle claims properly.

Productivity reports can provide useful information, but it is important to trend the productivity and evaluate any identified problems so they can be corrected. The corrective action may include realignment of workloads and/or possibly a performance action plan for a particular adjuster. If the new claim volume is increasing, the corrective plan may include adding staff resources.

Management Reports

Many types of claim management reports are used by claim managers, and some examples of commonly used reports are listed in Exhibit 6.6. Often, the generation of these reports, or logs, is automated and available for retrieval electronically from the reporting module of most claim management systems.

Exhibit 6.5: Simple Monthly Productivity Report

Adjuster	Status					
	Prior Pending	New	Reopen	Closed	Current Pending	Closing Ratio
Smith	135	25	3	27	136	96%
Abrams	165	42	2	42	167	95%
Jones	156	18	1	5	170	26%
Peters	129	19	4	20	132	87%
Kaminski	185	16	1	3	199	18%
TOTALS	**770**	**120**	**11**	**97**	**804**	74%

Exhibit 6.6: Management Reports and Logs

- Loss Runs
- File Lists
- Check and Financial Registers
- Reserve Change Report
- Recovery Reports:
  - Subrogation
  - Salvage
  - Deductibles
  - Loss refund
- Diary Reports
- Open and Closed Payable Reports
- Litigation Claim Lists
- Suit Log
- Complaint Log
- Coverage Disclaimer Log
- Large Loss Report

Loss Runs

Loss runs are generated on a summary and detailed level, and with many claims systems, can be sorted or filtered hundreds of different ways. Loss runs typically include claim details such as claimant and insured names, date of loss, date reported, reserves, loss and expense payments, recoveries, and the claims handler's name. Loss runs are traditionally used by underwriters to evaluate the desirability of an account based on its loss history. The underwriter may review various losses to evaluate the account, to set factors used in a rating plan, and to determine a premium to charge.

Loss runs may also be used to identify the need to implement safety and risk control techniques, such as a slip-and-fall prevention program, to reduce the probability of common losses from occurring, or reducing the severity of those that do. Claims managers also use loss runs to identify specific claims for review (client reporting or high-value claims, claims with zero or low reserves, etc.) or to complete special claim review projects.

Claim File Lists

These are simply lists of claim files falling within certain categories, including a list of clam files by employee name. Claim file lists are often used in combination with productivity reports to review performance. Claim file lists with detailed information can also be used by management to identify claims that require a dual diary or a report to the home office or the client based on the incurred losses to date. They can also be used to determine the need to reassign claims from one adjuster to another.

Check Registers and Financial Registers

These include lists of issued checks, payments, reimbursements, and other financial transactions by check number, date, and payee.

Reserve Change Reports

These reports provide a detailed or summary list of reserve changes in a given time period. Reserve change reports are used to provide information regarding stepladder or stair step reserving (the improper practice of frequently raising claim reserves to cover payments that come due instead of establishing a proper reserve up-front), late or untimely reserve adjustments, and errors. This reporting mechanism should include the ability to show reserve changes by individual adjusters to assist in evaluating performance. Finally, a claim system should always have the ability to generate reports of historical reserve transactions and not just current or the most recent reserve transactions. Reserve management is the topic of a separate chapter, Chapter 16, beginning on page 183.

Recovery Reports

Detailed or summary lists of recovery transactions in a given time period, these reports provide information on several types of recovery, including subrogation, salvage, deductibles, and loss refunds. These reports are used to identify recovery potential and monitor collection in the various recovery categories. If a high-deductible or self-insured program is involved, it will be important to have management reports available to track aggregate deductibles and self-insured retentions (SIRs) with a mechanism to notify the insurer (primary or excess) as the aggregate deductible or SIR reaches a certain level within a policy period.

Diary Reports

As discussed above under dual diaries, diary management is a critical function within a claims operation. When adjusters or claims managers are not current with their daily diaries review of claims, claim quality problems will develop. Late diary management may generate customer service complaints, delayed investigations, late claim payments, potential lawsuit defaults,[1] late reserve entries, and cause many other potential problems and issues.

Diary reports are used to monitor this critical function. They provide a detailed list of claims employee diaries for a specified time period. These reports reveal which adjusters are current with their diary entries. They also provide an indication as to whether adjusters are using the diary function properly.

Claims managers should monitor diary management on a daily basis. An adjuster with a propensity to be disorganized will be even more disorganized with late diaries. Late diaries translate into a backlog of work, which could take a long period of time to correct. When evaluating diary management, it is important to determine whether substantive activity is occurring during the diary review process, or is the diary simply being advanced forward so that it no longer appears on a late diary report. The latter contributes further to the problem and may require a performance action plan.

Open and Closed Payable Reports

These reports provide a list of claim payments that require approval to allow check

[1]A default occurs when a summons and complaint goes unanswered within the statutory time frame. In some states, a default could mean that the insurance company would be responsible for the judgment, which could be equivalent to the amount sued for. This could be devastating to a claim facility, particularly if the policy limits were below the judgment amount. Most claim facilities supplement the diary function with a suit log to monitor this process.

processing and issuance as well as a list of payments already approved for payment processing.

Litigation Claim Lists

A list of litigation claims by adjuster and claims operation may be a simple list of all claim files pending in litigation or a more comprehensive report detailing important litigation information, such as the parties to the litigation, date filed, state, venue (where filed), liability percentages, reserves, costs to date, offers and demands, plaintiff attorney and defense attorney contacts, trial dates, and other important information about the case.

Suit Log

Used to monitor the intake of new lawsuits and the referral of lawsuits to defense counsel, the suit log typically includes the case caption, the insured's name, the claim number, the date suit was served, the answer due date and extension (if any), the date answered, and the defense firm assigned. The suit log, maintained by claim management, should be monitored daily to avoid a default judgment by not responding to time-sensitive pleadings, such as a summons and complaint, writ, or petition.

Complaint Log

This is a log of all claim complaints, including complaints made by state insurance departments to the claim facility. Typically, most state insurance departments require the maintenance of a complaint log to monitor and respond to insurance department complaints. Claim complaints should be taken very seriously with the understanding that the complaint may, or may not, be legitimate. All complaints should be dealt with quickly and according to formal written procedures.

Generally, all written complaints are brought to the attention of claims managers. They are responsible for logging the complaint into the complaint log, reporting the applicable complaints to the client or home office, and ensuring that the complaint is answered in a timely fashion. The complaint log should include the complaint disposition as well. Although the handling adjuster or the claims manager may prepare the actual response, a senior level claims person, such as the vice president of the Claims Department, should be advised of complaint activity on a monthly basis. Some claim facilities require the involvement of general counsel in the preparation and response to state insurance department complaints.

Many state insurance departments publicly list the number of annual insurance department complaints for each insurer admitted in their states for use by insurance consumers. A high volume of claim complaints could be detrimental to the insurer's reputation and ability to sell insurance. If, for example, retail agents are consistently hearing complaints by their policyholders about a particular insurer's claims handling, they may decide to place the business with another insurer. Thus, it is important to expeditiously deal with performance problems that lead to claim complaints.

Coverage Disclaimer Log

This is a log of all claims wherein coverage was disclaimed or denied. These logs are very helpful in identifying claims that require management involvement and also assist the insurer's Underwriting Department in tracking the types of coverage disclaimers.

Large Loss Report Log

This log is a list of claims that have been, or need to be, reported to the home office or client based on the exposure or claim category.

Performance Management

Performance management is the ongoing monitoring of employee accomplishments to be sure they are on track to achieve individual and companywide goals and objectives. Performance management includes all methods and tools used by management to monitor, manage, control, and evaluate the performance of all employees.

Most companies rely heavily on a performance evaluation or appraisal process to conduct this function. This method of evaluating the performance of employees involves setting objectives at the beginning of a review period and then monitoring performance against those objectives with a periodic reporting function, such as quarterly and annually. The key to successful performance management and a proper performance evaluation is to have goals that are achievable and measurable with complete buy-in by the employee. These goals should be documented in writing at the beginning of the review period. The goals should never be ambiguous and should always be clear and concise.

It is critical for the goals and objectives to be defined and measurable. If goals and objectives are not measurable, it is virtually impossible to objectively evaluate an employee's performance. Ambiguous goals that are not measurable frustrate employees and are typically subjective in nature. The individual goals and objectives of an employee should contribute to the overall goals and objectives of the organization. Therefore, when establishing goals and objectives, a good starting point is to outline organizational objectives, then specify individual objectives that will contribute to the overall company goal.

The goals and subsequent performance evaluations should contemplate employee development in addition to handling assigned claims. Claims managers should encourage employees to pursue insurance coursework and insurance designations. There are many insurance designations offered by various industry educational organizations. The American Institute for Chartered Property Casualty Underwriters and the Insurance Institute of America (http://www.aicpcu.org) offer various associate programs with the Associate in Claims (AIC) and Associate in Risk Management (ARM) probably being the most

> ***Management Note***
>
> Always, prepare and complete employee performance appraisals timely! Expect the same with your own performance appraisal!

appropriate for most claims personnel. The Chartered Property Casualty Underwriter (CPCU) designation is the most prestigious in the industry. Claim Law Associate designations covering legal principles, casualty, property, workers compensation, automobile, and fraud are available through the American Educational Institute (http://www.aeiclaimslaw.com). Another option is the Registered Professional Adjuster (RPA) (http://www.rpa-adjuster.com). There also numerous online continuing education courses that may be taken to further knowledge and earn credit for adjuster licensing, such as those offered by IRMI (http://irmi.webce.com).

While the performance review process can be a very beneficial management tool if conducted in a timely and open manner, delays in performing the process can be very demotivating. When managers are late preparing reviews, they send a message that other activities are more important than their staff. Performance evaluations are important to employees and also affect their salary reviews. Thus, they have every right to expect them to be done as promised. Performance meetings with employees will achieve a lot more for managers than performing a few more file reviews. Employees are the most important assets of any claim facility, and they should be treated that way!

Often, managers get so caught up in the daily claim activities that they forget to say "good job" or "well done" or even "thanks for doing a nice job, it is appreciated"! Those words are so important to all employees, no matter how old they are or how much experience they have. Such compliments make a person feel good and spread a positive environment throughout the company. They help sustain a positive culture.

This all leads to recognition and reward—the recognition of a job well done with appropriate rewards for employees. The recognition and reward should always be commensurate with the task or situation being rewarded. There are many different types of rewards, such as store gift cards, plaques or certificates, days off, the president's prime parking spot, employee of the month status, etc. The recognition and reward process needs to be sincere and involve all employees. Group participation is critical for the recognition and reward process to be effective, and these types of activities should be done in an open meeting environment.

Handling errors and mistakes can sometimes be a very awkward experience for both the person who made the mistake and the manager who is addressing it. The key is to learn from mistakes. Mistakes can be embarrassing to an employee and could potentially involve some type of performance action. As opposed to rewards, it is important to address mistakes and any corrective action with the employee in a private environment. Addressing employee mistakes in an open environment can be very detrimental to the operation. It is never wise to make an example of an employee with criticism in the presence of coworkers or peers.

Security

Security is a critical function that should not be overlooked in a claim facility. A claim facility is managing a process that involves significant financial transactions. Typically, claim payments are processed as checks issued from a loss fund account, which is a separate fiduciary bank account from which claim payments are issued and to which claim reimbursements (e.g., loss and expense refunds, subrogation, salvage, deductible collection) are deposited.

The financial transactions make claim facilities targets for both internal and external theft and fraud. Internal thefts are instigated by employees or consultants within the claim facility itself. They can involve fraudulent schemes in which claim payments are issued to either the perpetrators, under fictitious names, or to some third-party accomplice. Another common fraud is for an unscrupulous adjuster to intentionally inflate an appraisal, bodily injury claim evaluation, salvage value, or other element of the claim process and receive a monetary kickback from the recipient of the inflated settlement.

Another scheme involves "fraud rings," where a group of perpetrators stage accidents to bilk money from insurers. These fraud rings may involve policyholders, claimants, attorneys, medical professionals, body shops, and adjusters. Unfortunately, some fraudulent schemes are difficult to detect, and it is important to employ various controls to uncover them.

Exhibit 6.7: Fraud Avoidance Techniques

- Require dual signatures on checks and wire transfers.
- Institute a tiered claim payment approval process.
- Make claims system edits to only allow payment approvals and checks issued up to established claim authority levels.
- Develop reserve worksheets to outline claim settlement values and the thought process involved.
- Do not allow check signers to take part in reconciliation of bank accounts.
- Insist on timely correction of claim errors, particularly any errors related to issued checks or reimbursements.
- Log all recovery checks for immediate deposit with a bank deposit stamp.
- Use uniform check stock with bank security paper.
- Conduct management oversight during the claims process to review claim documentation relating to financial transactions to detect any irregularities.
- Control salvage and vehicle title processing.

If the claims system and management controls are not in place, this type of activity can occur virtually undetected. Often, insurance companies have Internal Audit Departments that conduct random and scheduled audits of Claim Departments. The internal audits focus on the financial transactional history of the claims process to determine if there are any irregularities. Auditors may also send questionnaires to claim payment recipients to verify receipt of the payments, payment amounts, and confirm proper payees and addresses.

Internal theft can be very costly to an organization, but it can be minimized with proper management oversight and claims system controls. Careful management of the payment approval process and check issuance functions, along with reconciliation of the loss fund account, are two of the controls that can assist in minimizing internal theft. It's important to remember that internal theft can be committed by anyone, including claims processors, adjusters, managers, house counsel attorneys, or officers. Some controls and loss avoidance techniques are shown in Exhibit 6.7.

The handling of potentially fraudulent claims is discussed further in other chapters. When fraudulent claim activity involves internal employees, internal auditors will typically be involved in the process. If potentially fraudulent claim activity involves external parties, such as the claimant, policyholder, vendors, or professionals, a special investigative unit (SIU) will be involved. An SIU is a division or department within an insurance company involved in detecting and pursuing action against fraudulent activities on the part of insureds or claimants.

SIU investigators are trained in law enforcement and insurance. Because they are assigned to investigate external insurance fraud, they typically work with law enforcement agencies in the investigative process. SIU investigators usually report to claim management or the home office.

Summary and Conclusion

Experienced and knowledgeable human resources are critical in any claim organization. The supervision and management of human resources is crucial to achieve quality results. If supervisors or managers have too many adjusters directly reporting to them, there is less time to provide substantive supervision of adjusters and poor quality may result. There are various management controls which are utilized by a supervisor or manager to monitor adjusters, including a dual diary process, wherein the supervisor or manager has placed an additional diary on the claim, as one method to monitor the activities of an adjuster. However, the claim supervisor or manager cannot place a dual diary on every claim, which will make the management control ineffective.

There are a variety of other management controls available, including established claim authority levels, payment and check approval process, large loss reviews, other periodic claim reviews, and claim system controls. The ability to control quality in any claim organization will lead to positive financial results and enhanced customer service. By conducting claim file reviews, management can monitor the quality of the claim organization and take any necessary action toward improvement. In addition to individual claim file reviews, claim management as well as claim auditors may conduct an administrative and operational review of the claim facility. These reviews focus on operational issues, such as contracts, employee interviews, licensing and regulatory compliance, claims handling guidelines, reserve management, authority levels, staffing and productivity, home office or client reporting, claim systems, and training and development.

Claim metrics, productivity analysis, and claim management reports are necessary to effectively manage employees and the overall claims process. They provide the necessary information to identify potential trends or problems, and to evaluate adjuster performance.

Security in a claim organization, although sometimes overlooked, is critical given the financial transactions handled by adjusters and their fiduciary capacity (i.e., claim authority). Fraud is quite common, but there are ways to deter fraud with claim systems and management controls and fraud avoidance techniques. Internal auditors and SIU investigators are important in any insurance or claim organization to assist in this process.

FOR MORE INFORMATION ON:	GO TO:	PAGE(S):
Claims Operations	Chapters 2–9	5–104
Core Operational Issues	Chapter 4	29
Management Controls	Chapter 6	57
Recruitment and Retention	Chapter 7	73
Claims Process	Chapters 10–17	105–220
Reserve Management	Chapter 16	183
Recovery	Chapter 17	205
Third-Party Administrators	Chapters 18–20	221–270
Claims Handling Guidelines—Overview	Chapter 21	271
Ethics in Claims Handling	Appendix E	409
Litigation Management	Appendix F	421
Legal Theory and Doctrines	Appendix G	427

Chapter 7: Claims Operations—Recruitment and Retention

The hiring of personnel, and its impact on the claim organization, is probably the most important function of the claims operation. An experienced and knowledgeable claims staff will ultimately produce a quality claim organization. This chapter discusses how to attain that goal through recruitment and hiring, setting performance objectives, training, and employee development and retention. Turnover and layoffs are also addressed.

Recruitment and Hiring

The hiring practices of an organization will impact its overall claim results. What type of recruitment program is in place? Where are the candidates coming from? What are the job requirements and qualifications? Are there budgetary constraints limiting the ability to hire additional staff or necessary *experienced* staff due to salary level and benefit limitations? Answers to these questions will vary by organization.

What type of person becomes a claims adjuster? In the mid 1970s, according to some industry professionals, insurance claims jobs were for those who wanted to work in a business environment but did not have clear direction as to the type of job they wanted. The claims adjuster jobs did not pay very well, and the hours were long. Insurance companies and recruiters were searching for candidates with a particular type of disposition or background, which would make the candidate more successful as an adjuster and a long-term employee. There were various insurance company in-house claim training programs that would provide the fundamental adjuster textbook education and the development of field adjuster skills. Adjusters would complete the comprehensive training programs, locate another job paying a better salary, and leave. Eventually, the companies that offered the in-house claim training programs were responsible for training many adjusters and managers working in the industry.

Today, the claims adjuster position may have a better reputation, but as an industry, it is becoming increasingly difficult to recruit and retain qualified candidates. The job is not for everyone, but it does take a certain type of person to become a successful adjuster. Keep in mind that there are many reasons for adjuster turnover, and it is possible to hire the right person for the job only to have him or her leave because the job environment does not suit the adjuster's disposition.

The adjuster job is unique in many ways and hiring the claims applicant who possesses the personal characteristics shown in Exhibit 7.1 will help ensure success.

Exhibit 7.1: Characteristics of a Successful Adjuster

- **Organizational Skills:** Adjusters need to be organized to stay current. They also need to be able to prioritize activities and diary on a daily basis.
- **Flexibility:** In a claim environment, things change. Successful adjusters are flexible to changing conditions.
- **Analytical Skills:** Adjusters analyze and evaluate claim documentation. These skills are necessary to manage claim files and direct them toward closing.
- **Good Retention of Facts and Figures:** Each claim file represents a "story" replete with financial transactions. Successful adjusters have the ability to remember all their stories and be able to communicate them along with their recommendations to others.
- **Solid Writing Skills:** Being able to communicate well in written form, through e-mail and reports, is absolutely essential in a claims operation. Adjusters do these tasks routinely, typically on a daily basis. If you can't write, don't become a claims adjuster.
- **Empathy:** Claimants and insureds are not criminals! Successful adjusters are empathic toward their claimants' situations and the impact on their lives. Empathy will open communication channels.
- **Ability To Visualize and Record:** Successful claims adjusters must be creative enough to visualize the claim as it occurred and reduce it to writing. If they cannot do this, they probably will be handicapped in a claim environment.
- **Negotiations:** Having good negotiation skills allows adjusters to manage their workload effectively. As new claims are assigned, the adjuster needs to direct pending claims toward closing. These negotiation skills are very similar to sales skills, as they do require "selling" your position on liability issues, damage issues, and claim values.
- **Willingness To Continuously Learn:** Adjusters who think they know everything do not last long and are probably dangerous! Claims professionals continue to learn and expand their knowledge of the law, regulations, and claims handling procedures throughout their careers.
- **Technology and Computer Skills:** As with writing and communicating, computer skills are crucial to the insurance adjuster. Knowing how to use certain applications, such as e-mail, word processing, spreadsheet development, and making slide/visual presentations, is essential in today's business environment, including the claims environment. Also, solid typing skills are a must. Those that don't possess these skills need to either learn them quickly or else consider another industry. Time is of the essence when closing claims. Computer skills are absolutely essential to all claims personnel.

Technology

It is important to have good hiring practices that are both documented and consistently applied. Most Human Resource Departments in larger companies utilize software programs to manage the recruitment and hiring process. They may also have specific staff devoted to staff recruitment. However, in a smaller claims operation, the human resource function may be a part-time position for one person. Therefore, it is important that technology be used to supplement the recruitment and hiring process.

Technology-driven solutions, such as recruitment portals from company websites, can be very effective. Job candidates complete online applications and upload their confidential resumes to the company portal. The online applications and resumes are retained in a database with the ability to sort, filter, and retrieve candidate information, as necessary.

Honesty

When recruiting claims professionals, it is important to be honest and open about the job and the work environment. We have all been there at some point in our career (particularly early on when you are a novice at being interviewed). As a candidate, you have an interview and meet with several managers or supervisors who paint a very attractive picture of the claims operation in terms of the workload, job satisfaction, and future advancement. Once hired, however, you see that some of the interviewers significantly embellished about the organization to get you to accept the job! Or, you don't get to interview with the direct supervisor or manager who you will be reporting to because they are "unavailable," only to learn later that their personality is comparable to "Attila the Hun," and they are the cause of perpetual turnover!

Be professional and honest in the recruitment process. Provide a full picture of the claim organizational environment and culture. It is unethical and unprofessional to be less than honest and fully open during the interview process. You will recruit a better candidate and reduce future turnover if you are. As a job candidate, ask a lot of questions and always request an interview with the direct supervisor or manager for that position.

Preemployment Screening

Hiring an adjuster is more than just adding an employee. An adjuster is a professional member of the staff who makes financial decisions on a daily basis. Look for the best candidate for the job, with a focus on education and experience, as well as certain traits, such as being ethical, noncriminal, and trustworthy. For these reasons, it is recommended that all job candidates undergo a comprehensive background check including a credit check, criminal check, and a drug screen. There are many vendor companies available that perform these types of services.

Positive Work Environment

Another aspect of the job environment worth mentioning is the physical environment, including furniture, equipment, and resources. Employees want to be appreciated, and a quality work environment may be as important as salary and other compensation. Old beat-up furniture, outdated equipment, and decades' old technology only adds to a poor work environment.

Job Descriptions

All employees, in all industries, need a description of their job responsibilities, activities, and the company's expectations of the employee. Job descriptions should be prepared for each position outlining the position, title, salary ranges, job requirements and prerequisites, educational requirements, and responsibilities.

Performance Objectives

These objectives should be implemented for every employee, and should be achievable and measurable, not vague or ambiguous. Too often, performance planning becomes a "form-over-substance" exercise, resulting in performance objectives that are meaningless, not even understood by the line management employees who are charged with implementing them.

Performance objectives should be implemented as a part of an overall organizational performance management plan, which rolls up all departments to the top of the organization. In other words, the development of performance management plans should be a foundation for the organization to meet its goals and objectives. Each individual within an organization contributes toward the overall organizational objectives. In this environment, each department needs to manage the performance planning process to be sure that it benefits the organization, the department, and the employee.

Some examples of core individual claims employee performance objectives may include:

- ***Quality Results***—Achieving quality claim results as demonstrated through monthly claim file audits by the supervisor or manager. This could involve a review of 7–10 claim files per month, with a focus on specific categories. The results of these individual claim audits affect many areas of claims handling that impact the organization overall. For example, some of the review categories include reserve management (affecting the company's financial results), customer service (influencing policy and customer retention), investigation and evaluation (affecting adequacy of claim reserves and loss payments), recovery (recovering loss payments, which makes a positive impact on the organization's financial results), diary management (making sure quality customer service is maintained and time-sensitive dates are not missed), and expense control.
- ***Claim Productivity***—Each month, adjusters receive new claim assignments while at the same time they are closing claims. Meeting claim closing ratios is critical to the claims operation. The reality is that claims need to close at some point in the claims handling process. There will be claims that will not close in the short term, either due to no liability involved or damage disputes resulting in litigation. However, for the claims operation to effectively manage productivity, claims need to close at a ratio of one to one, or additional staffing may be required. If an adjuster's closing ratio becomes gradually worse, the supervisor or manager should not only look at workloads, but also at whether the adjuster has a performance or training issue affecting his or her ability to close claims or the overall management of the adjuster's

claim assignments. Closing claims requires both evaluation and negotiation skills.

- ***Customer Service***—Adjusters need to provide quality service, which not only affects customer retention but also the overall reputation of the insurer, self-insured, or third-party administrator (TPA). The number of claims service complaints is one indicator of the quality of service being rendered. There will always be claims service complaints in the insurance industry. The key is to determine whether the complaints are legitimate. Claim facilities should maintain a complaint log that includes details concerning each claim complaint, including the handling adjuster's name. If an adjuster has an excessive number of legitimate complaints, an action plan developed for an employee (a performance plan) may be necessary.

- ***Employee Attitude***—With its adverse affect on other employees, a poor attitude can be as destructive to a claims organization as poor quality claims handling. A poor attitude can be subtle or obvious. Poor attitudes affect not only other employees, but also customers, including claimants, insureds, and vendors. Basically, employee attitudes have a serious effect on the overall organization and a negative connotation with regard to professionalism. Employees with poor attitudes should be positioned for performance warnings or even termination.

- ***Professional Development***—Ongoing education and completion of continuing education requirements is critical in the insurance industry. In the best organizations, adjusters are continuously seeking to expand their knowledge and improve their skill sets. All claims employees should be encouraged to enroll in insurance coursework, including programs leading to insurance and professional designations. Continuing education provides an organization with employees with greater knowledge, skill sets, and, usually, morale. (See IRMI education programs at http://irmi.webce.com.)

Lack of an effective performance management program can increase turnover. Those employees who contribute greatly to the organization should be rewarded. The performance management process should be clear, concise, and understood by all employees. If everyone is rated the same, those employees who are the heavy contributors may get frustrated and leave as the marginal performers are receiving the same rating (and possibly the same salary adjustment).

In many claim organizations, adjusters get promoted to supervisor or manager because of their claims technical skill level and experience, and not because of supervisory or management experience. Many adjusters strive to get promoted to supervisor or manager because it is the traditional career progression for both increased compensation and possibly satisfying their egos. Unfortunately, not everyone can be successful at being a supervisor or manager, or may not want the position in the first place. The best claim organizations make a technical path available for employees so that the supervisor or manager promotion is not the only available course for future opportunity and advancement. Ideally, there will be technical positions available that have a comparable compensation structure to a supervisor or manager.

Training and Employee Development

Employee development is important to a claims organization and should be an ongoing process. At a minimum, training should be completed monthly. The topics should be relevant and include outside guest speakers. Employee development should be a category in every performance management program, both technical and management, and is essential to maintain the quality of a claim organization. Development can be self-study coursework, working toward the achievement of various insurance designations, or formal education in a college degree program.

Policy and Procedural Manuals

Lack of formal operational policies and procedures can also have a detrimental effect on a claim organization. A claim organization needs policies and procedures in place to properly manage the claims operation. Policies and procedures guide the staff in addressing operational requirements, technical claims handling issues, development of a consistent approach to claims handling, and establishment of a foundation to create ongoing goals and objectives. The policies and procedures need to be consistent and updated periodically. Outdated policies and procedures confuse the staff and create mistakes.

Exhibit 7.2: Training Manuals

Claims Technical Manual: Details the processes and procedures in handling claims. Generally, these manuals are for the claims technical and management staff.

Claims Processing Manual: Provides specific detailed instructions on claims processing issues, including new claim, reserve, and payment entry. A claims processing manual may be used by the claims support staff as well as the claims technical and management staff.

Claims Systems Manual: Provides specific instructions and support concerning utilization of the claims system, including claim report management.

Claim Form Letters and Forms Manual: A claim manual or catalog containing various form letters and claim forms utilized in the normal course of business, including state-specific form letters and claim forms.

Employee Manual: A comprehensive manual detailing the personnel policies and procedures of the organization.

Claim organizations can have a variety of policy and procedural manuals, and some examples are described in Exhibit 7.2. Policy and procedural manuals may include a claims technical, processing, and systems manual, a manual of form letters and claim forms, and an employee or human resource manual.

Employee Retention and Turnover

Employee turnover is the absolute worst problem any claim organization can have, yet it is very common in the industry. Turnover is very difficult to correct and can be

Exhibit 7.3: Causes of Employee Turnover

- Excessive Claim Workloads
- Unrealistic Management Expectations (or New Management)
- Negative Working Environment
- No or Little Future Advancement or Promotional Opportunities
- Unacceptable Work Hour Expectations
- Compensation Dissatisfaction Regarding Salary Level and Lack of Future Compensation in the Form of Cost of Living and/or Merit Adjustments as Well as Benefit Packages
- No Organizational Leadership
- Lack of Management Support
- No Consistent Operational Policies and Procedures
- No Performance Management Process
- No Training and Development Programs
- No Claim Authority or Limited Authority To Make Decisions
- Interviewers Were Untruthful about the Organization during the Hiring Process
- Lack of the Necessary Resources To Do the Job Properly
- TURNOVER! (Continued Turnover Causes More Turnover)

very costly. A management-related problem, turnover is caused by management actions and decisions, and is very difficult to resolve without the full support and cooperation of all levels of management.

Exhibit 7.3 shows some of the many reasons for employee turnover, some of which are discussed in more detail below. The most important aspect of managing voluntary turnover is to recognize its cause in the first place. You can't correct a problem if you don't understand its cause. Some of these causes appear on the surface to be simple to resolve, but it's usually not that easy.

Excessive Claim Workloads

Claims managers are often under an enormous amount of pressure to produce a quality work product, meet production goals, control expenses, avoid errors, and provide good service. Without adequate financial resources in the operating budget to hire the staff necessary to achieve these results, problems arise. People with less experience are hired with the notion that they will be trained and developed. But if, after they are hired, no one has the time to train them, they will be unable to handle the same workload as fully trained adjusters, regardless of management goals and expectations to the contrary. This is obviously not a good situation for the new employees, many of whom will become disappointed and resign.

It is a good practice for supervisors, claims managers, and even vice presidents of the Claims Department to sit at an adjuster's desk for the day. The daily challenges an adjuster encounters may be quite shocking. Many times, turnover is caused by management's unrealistic expectations and demand for quality results.

There are Claims Departments in some organizations that have been understaffed for years (primarily due to continued turnover without replacement staff), yet the organization is profitable. So when the vice president of the Claims Department approaches the senior management and requests approval for additional staff, the request is denied simply based on dollars and cents. The vice president could accept this type of decision as long as management understands that being understaffed leads to many other issues that cause organizational problems such as poor quality, errors and omission claims, and continued turnover.

Unacceptable Work Hour Expectations

We all understand the concept of running a *lean* claims operation, but don't expect people who are consistently overloaded and pressured to achieve results that cannot be accomplished unless they work 65–70 hours per week. Employees become frustrated and leave, perpetuating the turnover problem. Managers who constantly communicate to their staff that they need to work harder and smarter in this type of work environment lose credibility and respect. It's better to just communicate the truth.

Working long hours does not necessarily translate into doing a good job or producing quality work. It usually ends up in dissatisfaction and resentment due to its impact on employees and their personal lives. Some claims professionals and managers feel that working late every night will get them ahead in the organization. This actually may work but will probably be regretted later. When senior managers work late all the time, they tend to expect others to do so as well. This type of work environment or culture ultimately distorts staffing and contributes to other human resource problems, such as job resentment and burnout, not to mention errors.

When employees work late consistently, it adds work hours to the week, allowing more time to handle additional claim volume and hopefully yield an improved quality work product, without having to add to staff. The result is that those claims adjusters who have good skills, but do not put in the extra hours, become overloaded and end up on a performance action plan or leave because they can't handle the workload or provide the same quality as adjusters who put in more hours.

Those adjusters putting in all the extra time may be meeting or exceeding the quality standards by putting in an extra 10–15 hours per week, which is comparable to one-half of an adjuster position, and at the same time raising the bar with regard to standards. At the other end of the spectrum is the adjuster who consistently works late and still cannot keep up with the workload. Either the workload is too high, or possibly the adjuster may not be a right fit for the job.

Adjuster workloads should be manageable. There will always be time periods when extra effort is required; however, if extra effort is always required, the workloads are not manageable. If the workloads are manageable, the manager can then insist on a solid day's work from employees, which should be a sufficient amount of time to complete daily work activities. Those adjusters who give extra effort should be rewarded for their contributions through merit increases, promotions, and bonuses.

Unreasonable Management Expectations

Oftentimes, claims managers in insurance companies are transferred to poorly performing claims offices to help these underperformers improve their quality. Unfortunately, the very act of putting a new manager in place will, in itself, cause morale problems and possibly turnover that is very difficult for the new manager to combat. People generally do not like, and are resistive to, change. The new manager arrives at the office, implements new programs, policies, and procedures, and enforces quality expectations. The resignation letters come one by one, and the new manager can't understand why. The reason the new manager doesn't understand why is because he or she does not have the management skills to be equipped to handle the situation.

A new manager should not expect change overnight. It is essential to communicate, communicate, and communicate some more! If the claims staff is resistive to change, then the best approach is to properly and effectively communicate the reasons for the changes while remaining open and flexible for suggestions, or else mass turnover will occur, which is very costly for an organization.

Unresolved Departmental Complaints

Some managers want to avoid conflict at all costs and will not address employee complaints. Whether these complaints are warranted or unwarranted, minor or major, if unresolved or not addressed, the complaints fester and disgruntlement may spread throughout the department and company. The potential exists for the complaints to negatively impact department or company morale, and can spill over to clients and prospective employees (i.e., during the employee interview process, word of mouth in the industry). Complaints may not be able to be resolved, but if not addressed, can create more conflict and have a detrimental effect on the organization. Claim managers need to handle all complaints, even if the end result is that nothing can be done.

Negative Working Environment

A negative work environment is probably one of the most common root causes of turnover and spreads very quickly throughout the organization. Do poor attitudes and lack of communication cause negativity? No, actually these are the residual effects of negativity. Negativity usually results from the work environment, either caused by a fellow employee or the job itself. Coworkers, or even managers, who are negative toward the job and organization, for any number of reasons, can have an undesirable influence on the organization. It quickly spreads to all levels of the organization and breeds rapid turnover.

Negativity issues must be resolved to avoid such consequences, and this is an area where managers can easily lose credibility. One solution is to terminate the employee who is the cause of the negativity, but this may not be an easy decision, particularly if the adjuster has good technical skills that are needed. There are other alternatives in lieu of termination, and it is important to provide employees with an opportunity to correct the situation. The manager needs to effectively communicate with the employee to determine the reasons for the negativity and then look for a resolution. Perhaps there are personal issues in the employee's life causing the negativity, or a work event that the manager is unaware of involving the employee and a coworker or another manager. A manager should exhaust all options prior to termination and never ignore the problem, hoping it will go away, because it will not. Also, the failure to take the necessary steps will often cause many excellent members of the staff to become discontented with the bad attitudes and leave as a result.

No Organizational Leadership

Lack of organizational leadership and support can ruin any firm. It all starts at the top. If management is not leading the organization effectively, it will fail. Keep in mind that leadership is not management, and management is not leadership.

There are many different leadership styles, which are probably beyond this text; however, it is important to know and recognize the type of leadership style to use. Some management styles are absolutely useless in a claim environment, and the manager who uses these styles probably has high turnover and manages a claim organization which is in turmoil. The successful manager uses a variety of different leadership styles, blending an appropriate style to effectively manage the organization.

Whatever style is used, the manager must seek some participation by employees. If the manager makes all the decisions and never considers input from subordinates, employees are not participating. If a manager always criticizes and never praises, the firm will not have a very motivating work environment. There needs to be a balance so that goals are achieved and, at the same time, employees are motivated to get the job done.

What makes a successful claim manager? A successful claim manager will have the traits listed in Exhibit 7.4. Can a manager be successful without leadership skills? The

Exhibit 7.4: Characteristics of a Successful Claim Manager

- **Basic Management Skills:** New managers need to have management training to develop management skills such as planning, organizing, controlling, delegation, problem solving, coaching, and conflict resolution.
- **Motivational Skills:** Managers need to understand how to motivate their staffs to accomplish the departmental and organizational objectives.
- **Communication and Presentation Skills:** Managers need to be able to convey their intent to employees and management with effective verbal and written communication.
- **Time Management and Organizational Skills:** Managers need to be organized individually and be able to prioritize activities so that there is a sufficient amount of time to interact and coach subordinate employees.
- **People or Human Resource Skills:** Simply stated, managers with poor human relations or "people skills" will have a difficult time managing others, particularly in small groups. Employees want to be able to approach their direct manager and interact. Managers deal with all sorts of employee problems, even some personal problems that may adversely affect the job. Being empathetic, and occasionally practicing humility, can go a long way in successfully managing people. A manager needs to be looked upon as a mentor.
- **Organizational Sensitivity:** Managers need to know the organization not only from a procedural and process viewpoint, but also the political environment. Unfortunately, every organization has this underlying environment that can be extremely detrimental to a manager's ability to manage effectively if he or she does not understand who the key players are in the organization and recognize their influence on management and employees.
- **Technical Skills:** A claims manager needs to possess claim technical skills, but does not necessarily need to be an expert technician. Remember, great claim technicians do not necessarily become great claims managers!

answer will depend on the work environment and the number of subordinates involved. Leaders come in all sizes, types, and ages. The key is that effective leadership skills are necessary to motivate the staff at all levels. Companies with effective leaders are successful because they are able to achieve company objectives through their employees and management. Successful managers get the job done with the right people; managers who do everything themselves, or do not think anyone else can do the job better than they can, are not leading.

Leaders manage people effectively by coaching, training, motivating, and mentoring subordinate employees. Claim management is not an easy job, and there are many challenges a manager is faced with on a daily basis. Even if there is poor leadership above the claim managerial level, claim managers can still be effective leaders with their own staffs.

Staff Downsizing/ Employee Layoffs

Claims operations experience staff downsizing, layoffs, or as some companies called it, staff reengineering. The primary reason for staff downsizing is financial. The economy plays a role in these actions, but not always. Business downturns are not always affected by a poor economy. Downsizing sometimes develops with loss of business due to poor claims handling, exiting a business segment, company mergers, and sale of the business.

Staff resources represent over 50 percent of most budgets in a service organization. There are several reasons that lead an organization to downsize or lay off employees, several of which are outlined below.

Company Financial Objectives Not Being Met

Operational budgets are prepared that record the projected revenue and expenses in a given time period. If the revenue projection is not being met to support the expense budget, the company may need to reduce expenses to achieve profitability or break even. Typically, the quickest way to reduce expenses is to cut staff, given its immediate impact on the expense budget. This action has the potential to impact the quality of the claim organization if the claim volume has not decreased with the loss of business, as there will be less staff to handle the remaining claims.

Reduction in Business or Revenue

A company may have lost a key client that supported a large portion of the projected annual revenue. This would generally result in employee reduction to continue to maintain profitability.

Business Shutdown or Structure Change

A company may shut down the business entirely due to the loss of clients or change its business structure by merging with another company or being sold.

Summary and Conclusion

The adjuster job is unique in many ways, and there are certain characteristics that may be indicative of the long-term success of an adjuster. These characteristics include organizational skills, flexibility, analytical skills, good retention, solid writing skills, empathy, ability to visualize, good negotiation skills, a willingness to continuously learn as well as technological and computer skills. In the author's opinion, lack of these characteristics will cause the adjuster to be unsuccessful in the job.

Employee turnover is the "curse" of any claim organization. Hiring the right person for the job may be challenging; however, managing the employee is even more difficult. Establishing performance objectives and addressing employee issues are critical for a successful claim operation.

The claims manager's job is not an easy one. It involves motivating the adjusting staff to produce quality claims results with the workloads authorized based on the approved financial budgets. The claims manager must be resilient and balance task and people skills to get the job done.

This chapter outlines some characteristics of a successful claims manager. Although not an all-inclusive list, it does highlight some of the important skills a claims manager needs to be successful on the job. While many of these skills are learned, they may also be part of a person's personality. Finding and keeping claim employees with these traits is a large part of a manager's job.

FOR MORE INFORMATION ON:	GO TO:	PAGE(S):
Claims Operations	Chapters 2–9	5–104
Core Operational Issues	Chapter 4	29
Claims Management Overview	Chapter 5	45
Management Controls	Chapter 6	57
Technology	Chapter 9	93
Claims Process	Chapters 10–17	105–220
Claims Handling Guidelines	Chapters 21–30	271–354
Ethics in Claims Handling	Appendix E	409

CHAPTER 8: CLAIMS OPERATIONS—FINANCING AND BANKING

As is true of all businesses, financing and banking are integral to claims operations. Budgets have to be developed and followed, bank accounts need to be established and funded, checks need to be written, regulations need to be adhered to, and so on. This chapter delves into this area of claims operations.

Budgets

It is impossible and very irresponsible to run a Claims Department or any claim facility without an operating budget, which includes revenue and expense projections as well as an indication of profit and loss. Budget types and categories can vary by claim facility. An insurance company budget for a Claims Department will look different than a budget for a third-party administrator (TPA), as a TPA is a separate claims business, generating revenue from its claim services. But both will include all the functional departments, such as Accounting, Human Resources, Legal and Compliance, and Sales and Marketing.

A Claims Department budget, then, is a departmental budget that only includes expenses related to the Claims Department function along with overhead allocations from other departments, such as Legal, Home Office, Technology, and Human Resources. Budgets are used to forecast revenue and expenses by monitoring financial progress with a comparison of the budget versus actual results.

Loss Fund Account

Loss fund accounts are used by claim facilities to manage the claim payment process. They are funded to pay claims and process any reimbursements or recoveries. Basically, loss fund accounts are bank checking accounts that may earn interest, depending on the type of account and banking institution. Various types of bank accounts are outlined below.

- ***Zero Balance Account (ZBA)***—This is a checking account in which a zero balance is maintained with the automatic transfer of funds from a master account to process checks presented at given point in time.

- ***Demand Deposit Account (DDA)***—This is a checking account or deposit account held at a bank or other financial institution for the purpose of quick access to the funds. These are called "demand accounts" as the funds are available on demand.

- ***Sweep Accounts***—These are offered by the cash management division of a bank. Excess funds from a company bank account are automatically moved into a money market mutual fund overnight and then moved back the next morning. This allows interest to be earned overnight.

Loss fund accounts may receive or disburse funds in a variety of ways, including the following:

- ***Positive Pay***—This service is provided by banks. A company issuing checks shares its check register with the bank, listing all written checks. The bank will only release funds for the checks listed on the register, which reduces the potential for check fraud.
- ***Automated Clearing House (ACH)***—An electronic system used to transfer funds between banks, this service is usually offered by the cash management division of a bank.
- ***Lockbox Accounts***—An insurance company may receive a large number of check payments, and the bank establishes a post office box to hold them. The mail is opened by the bank, and checks received are deposited.
- ***Wire Transfer***—A wire transfer is an electronic transfer of funds. A bank wire transfer is a message to the receiving bank requesting it to process payment in accordance with the settlement instructions provided.
- ***Escheatment***—This is the process of turning over unclaimed or abandoned property to the state after a specified time period established by that state has elapsed. Unclaimed property can involve claim checks never cashed. A claim facility cannot simply void a claim check (if it has not been cashed)

BUDGET CATEGORIES

Revenue (TPAs):

- ✔ Service Fees
- ✔ Consulting Fees
- ✔ Recovery fees

Expenses:

- ✔ Payroll
- ✔ Payroll Processing and Taxes
- ✔ Automobile
- ✔ Corporate Filings
- ✔ Depreciation/Amortization
- ✔ Dues and Subscriptions
- ✔ Equipment Rental
- ✔ Employee Welfare
- ✔ Insurance—Employee
- ✔ Insurance—Operating
- ✔ Interest and Bank Charges
- ✔ Professional Licensing
- ✔ Miscellaneous Expenses
- ✔ Postage
- ✔ Printing
- ✔ Professional Fees
- ✔ Rent
- ✔ Utilities
- ✔ Real Estate Taxes
- ✔ Repairs & Maintenance
- ✔ Telephone
- ✔ Travel and Entertainment
- ✔ Office and Supplies
- ✔ Professional Development
- ✔ Recruitment
- ✔ Outsourced Services

and deposit it back into the loss fund account. Each state has its own escheatment regulations, which require the taking of unclaimed funds and turning them over to the state, which will keep the funds until claimed by the owner. All claim facilities need to understand the escheatment process since there will always be issued checks that are not cashed. This escheatment process can be handled by the Accounting Department or be outsourced to a third party.

Check Issuance Process

Claim checks are issued from a loss fund account or some other designated bank account set up to handle loss and expense checks. Typically, there are only designated authorized signers on the loss fund account, and certain monetary levels usually require dual signatures. Checks may be issued daily or weekly.

Many claim facilities utilize a check writing software program, which may be a component of the claim management system or a stand-alone program. The check-writing component of the claim management system usually interfaces with the claim management system, updating the claim file record along with compiling statistical and historical data.

Although some claim facilities still issue checks manually, most claim facilities typically issue laser check stock directly from the claim management system on specialized, secure check stock or security paper. Computerized checks may be prenumbered, with the check numbers printed on the check stock in sequential order. When computerized checks are issued, the same check number should appear on the claim check, which is generated by the claims system. A person should not be able to change the check sequence numbers within the claim management system. Should a claim check have errors after printing, the check should be either voided or spoiled.[1] The check register should reflect all check numbers in sequence, with a zero monetary value for all checks voided or spoiled.

All blank check stock should be retained in a secure location, such as a locked steel file cabinet or safe. Only certain officers and Accounting Department employees of the claim facility have access to the check stock supply. When check stock is retrieved for use, there is often a log to be completed and signed by the person requesting check stock. It is a good idea for security purposes to have a manager initial and review the log, verifying the check sequence numbers being utilized. The check stock log should also be retained in a separate locked cabinet or be stored electronically. Any unused checks need to be returned to management at the end of the day, along with any checks voided or spoiled.

Ordinarily, the claims support, technical, or management staff will enter claim payables within a claim management system, which is basically completing the processing entry stage of check issuance. All claim payables above the payable approval authority of the claim employee may require approval by the manager or an officer of the company, in accordance with their individual claim authority level.

[1] A spoiled check is a check that may have misprinted or became mutilated during the check issuance process. The check is deemed nonnegotiable, not to be used or reissued.

Only certain individuals within the company's Accounting Department should have authority to print claim checks after open payables are approved. It's a good practice to have payable approval reports reviewed prior to the check issuance. After claim checks are printed, an officer or senior authorized claims manager should be required to sign each claim check over a certain dollar threshold. Checks under the dollar threshold may be stamped with a magnetic ink character recognition signature of an officer of the company. An officer of the company usually cosigns all claim checks in excess of a certain dollar threshold.

A TPA will typically establish an individual bank account for each claim administration client or program. At the end of each month, each TPA loss fund account is reconciled by the TPA Accounting Department. The monthly bank statement is then reconciled against the debits and credits listed in the banking component of the claim management or accounting system.

Office of Foreign Assets Control (OFAC) Compliance

All claim facilities need to be familiar with the OFAC and verify all claim payments against the master list published by the OFAC. According to the ISO ClaimSearch® website:

> All U.S. insurance companies and their employees—as well as U.S. citizens and permanent resident aliens employed by non-U.S. insurers—are responsible for screening claims against the master list published by the Office of Foreign Assets Control (OFAC) of the U.S. Department of the Treasury. The purpose of the screening is to ensure that you do not pay out money to a person or organization involved in terrorism, international narcotics trafficking, or activities related to the proliferation of weapons of mass destruction. Failure to comply with your legal requirement can result in corporate or personal fines of up to $1 million and up to 12 years in prison.[2]

The ISO ClaimSearch® system provides a service to facilitate the OFAC verification process. (See Appendix B, beginning on page 363, for more information on the ISO ClaimSearch® system.) Many insurance computer systems and TPA claim systems have been upgraded to provide the verification service as well. Basically, all claim payments, losses, and expenses should be processed through OFAC verification prior to issuance. In the event a verification result indicates a reportable item, your Legal Department or general counsel should be notified.

Internal Revenue Service (IRS) Compliance

IRS filings are part of the claims process for both insurance companies and TPAs. An IRS Form W–9: Request for Taxpayer Identification Number (TIN) and Certification is used to provide the correct tax identification number to the person requesting it. Failure to provide the form can result in a fine of $50, and providing false information can yield a penalty of $500.

---

[2] "OFAC Compliance Service." Jersey City, NJ: ISO ClaimSearch.® http://www.iso.com/products/ISO-ClaimSearch/ISO-ClaimSearch-OFAC-Compliance-Service.html.

Claim facilities request the W–9 form to certify that the TIN number is correct and that the vendor is not subject to any back withholding of taxes. These forms are usually sent to vendors who are paid as an allocated loss adjustment expense. Often, their assigned vendor identification number is actually their TIN number.

An IRS 1099 Miscellaneous Income form is used by taxpayers and tax exempt organizations to report financial information to the IRS. The vendor record will usually reflect the proper code to qualify for 1099 year-end reporting. The vendors that qualify will receive the 1099 report indicating the total amount paid to the vendor. An IRS 1096 form is used to provide a summary of the 1099 forms being filed, which can be filled out and filed electronically. It should be noted that failure to file the 1099 forms can result in IRS penalty fines.

Summary and Conclusion

Budgets and loss fund accounting are integral parts of the claims operation. Operational budgets are essential for both an insurance company Claims Department and for a TPA. The TPA budget will be more comprehensive as the budget will not only include the Technical Claim Department but also the other functional departments as well.

Insurance companies maintain loss fund accounts from the premium received on the sale of their policies. TPAs receive loss funding from their clients, such as an insurance company or self-insured. However, in both instances, the loss fund account is used to pay claims, both losses and allocated loss adjustment expenses.

Check security is essential at any claim facility. By segregating duties and being vigilant in the check entry, approval, and issuance process along with secure storage of the check stock, the chance of having a fraudulent act committed against the company is reduced.

FOR MORE INFORMATION ON:	GO TO:	PAGE(S):
Claims Operations	Chapters 2–9	5–104
Core Operational Issues	Chapter 4	29
Management Controls	Chapter 6	57
Technology	Chapter 9	93
Claims Process	Chapters 10–17	105–220
Reserve Management	Chapter 16	183
Recovery	Chapter 17	205
Third-Party Administrators	Chapters 18–20	221–270
Claims Handling Guidelines	Chapters 21–30	271–354
ISO ClaimsSearch®	Appendix B	363

Chapter 9: Claims Operations—Technology

Although technology in the insurance industry continues to change rapidly, as an industry, we are way behind other industries. When referring to *technology,* we are primarily referring to systems that manage the claims handling process for any type of claim facility. Generally, an insurance company claims system is a component of the overall insurance management system, which may include underwriting, policy processing, policy issuance, accounting, billing, imaging, agency interface, claim management, and other third-party interfaces. A third-party administrator (TPA) claims system is typically geared toward claim management only, which includes claim records and file management (i.e., claim data, financial transactions, notes, correspondence, attachments), claim management reporting, loss fund account management, policy maintenance, and integration of general accounting functions.

Information Technology Challenges

There are many challenges in an increasingly complicated and fast paced information technology environment. Some of these challenges include:

- ***Building or buying a system, or a combination of both approaches***—Should the system be maintained on the company's own servers (client server) and accessed via personal computers and terminals, or should the system be deployed via the Internet using the latest technology? Should the company maintain the data on its own computer servers or outsource this function using a managed hosting service?

- ***Multiple data sources and data accuracy***—Many companies, and their clients or vendors, have multiple formats and types of data, combined with multiple sources of data including data from TPAs. Unfortunately, electronic data is rarely stored in the same system or formats, potentially causing informational errors. Integration can sometimes be complicated, time-consuming, and costly.

- ***Complex and diverse reporting needs***—The primary output of any claim management systems is its ability to provide comprehensive reporting. The reporting tools need to be user-friendly and flexible enough to provide a detailed analysis, without having to modify the system with each new report request. Systems also need to have output in a variety of formats, including database, PDF, word processing, and spreadsheet formats.

- ***Business intelligence tools***—Systems must have the ability to quickly and efficiently provide data and information in an organized and productive manner, without sacrificing time and money.

- ***IT support***—Can the company get the proper level of IT support, either internally or through outsourced resources, with potential budgetary constraints or the unavailability of qualified IT talent? When a claims system is purchased, it may have the basic components and modules. However, with the levels of modifications required by many organizations (TPAs and insurers), the additional modifications can be very costly. With limited resources, some vendors may require a long time to provide the level of support needed.

- ***Technology obsolescence***—This can have a serious effect on an organization, particularly larger companies. A huge investment over time in current technology makes it cost-prohibitive to make technological changes quickly to keep the organization current with the latest technology.

- ***Technology costs***—Licensing fees, service and support, custom modifications, and dealing with other technology costs can drain an organization's financial resources.

Although these challenges exist for many companies, information technology is the core of most service-related businesses and is particularly important in the insurance industry. Technology changes at a very rapid pace, and it will continue to do so in the future. Companies that do not embrace current technology, and keep pace with its evolution, will not survive in the long term.

Leaving the Brick and Mortar Behind

Changes in technology occur daily, and it is sometimes impossible for large insurance companies with outdated "legacy" systems to implement current cutting-edge technology, despite the new advancements and improvements they offer. Legacy systems severely impair the insurance industry's efficiency and overall productivity. In fact, the insurance industry still operates in a vast sea of paper in the 21st century! Eventually, however, the insurance claims process is sure to become virtual, with all claim activities, including investigations and adjusting services, being processed online. The maintenance of hard copy claim files by claim facilities is becoming obsolete, being replaced by paperless claim management systems with integrated imaging of all claim documents. More and more often, other technology, such as video conferencing and Internet informational Web portals, are utilized to deliver claim services that exceed expectations.

The claims function does not need a physical office environment to operate efficiently and productively. The old "brick-and-mortar work environment" business model is outmoded and unnecessary. Technology needs to become the foundation of the claims operation, and not just a method to capture and retrieve data.

Some of the challenges faced by claim facilities in recruitment and employee retention can be improved by adapting to a virtual business model, which emphasizes advanced technology, utilization of physically remote employees, and the elimination of large office locations. The claims function can be effective and efficiently implemented anywhere with Internet access. It's just a matter of time, money, and commitment.

Claim and Risk Management Information Systems

The primary system maintained by a claim facility or TPA is its claim management system, sometimes referred to as a risk management information system (RMIS). There are many different types of insurance company and TPA claim management systems, a discussion of which is beyond the scope of this book. However, Exhibit 9.1 on page 96 shows some of the key components of a claim management system.

What Is a Claim Management System?

The key word in defining a "claim management system" is the word *system,* which is generally defined as a group of interacting, interrelated, or interdependent elements forming a complex whole. A claim management system combines all of the manual and automated claim tasks and operations into one interacting, interrelated, and interdependent group, to make the claim process more efficient, productive, and, it is hoped, cost effective.

What constitutes a claim management system may differ from organization to organization. Some claim management systems may be a simple spreadsheet or a Microsoft Access database, while others may be very comprehensive, including accounting, loss fund management, and other interrelated functions. The type of system used by various claim facilities will depend on the size of the organization and the functionality required. Although the larger organization may require a more comprehensive system, some smaller organizations may also need the comprehensive functionality of a more robust claims system, based on the services they provide.

Exhibit 9.1 provides an illustration of the types of functionality in claim management systems. Systems will differ in the functionality provided. In general, the more functionality, the higher the cost.

There are certain features and benefits to look for in a claims system, which are outlined below.

- ***Flexibility***—The system needs to be flexible in a changing industry, with the ability to implement system modifications at a minimal cost. The user administrator should be able to make changes at the desktop to fields, screens, drop-down menus, security levels, and other areas without the need to involve a programmer.
- ***Imaging***—The ability to scan or image all documents and attach them to the claim file with descriptive categories is crucial.
- ***Recorded statements***—The system needs to be able to upload recorded statements into the electronic claim file or have the recorded statement taken from within the claims system through an interface telephonic function.
- ***Interfaces***—The claims system must be able to interface with other system components, such as policy and accounting modules, as well as industry databases.

Exhibit 9.1: General Claim Management System Functions

- Policy Maintenance
- File Notes
- Diary Management
- Integrated E-mail (Preferably with a Hot Spot[a] To Drag E-mail into the Claim Record)
- Integrated Correspondence and Claim Forms
- Integrated Imaging System
- A Web-Based Loss Reporting System
- Client Inquiry Access Anywhere in the World through a Web Browser
- Reporting and Business Automation Tools
- Laser Check Issuance
- Loss Fund Bank Account Management and Reconciliation
- User-Defined Claim Fields
- Customized Statistical Reporting
- Integrated Risk Management Reporting Engine Tool
- Ability To Develop Data Interfaces with Insureds, Clients, Insurers, and Reinsurers
- Interfaced ISO ClaimSearch® (See Appendix B beginning on page 363.)
- Recorded Statements in a Usable, Transferable File Format
- Ability To Integrate with Office of Foreign Assets Control[b] (OFAC) Database
- A Medical Bill Review Interface Providing a Standard Medical Bill Review Process
- Workers Compensation Data Electronic Data Interchange (EDI)[c] with Various State Insurance Facilities

continued

[a]For example, the claim management system allows you to take an e-mail from Outlook by dragging it (with a left click) from the Outlook inbox to a section in the claims system specifically designated for receiving the e-mail (an icon location on the screen). A pop-up box appears, and you then have the ability to file the e-mail (with all of its attachments) within the appropriate claim record. It avoids the necessity of copying and pasting the e-mail into the claim notes or as a PDF attachment.

[b]See Chapter 8, page 90, for more information on the Office of Foreign Assets Control (OFAC), which requires that insurers screen claims for terrorism or narcotics involvement.

[c]Many states have adopted Electronic Data Interface (EDI) standards, which contribute to the reduction of workers compensation claim administrative paperwork, foster improved accuracy, faster turnaround for payment of benefits, and uniform reporting. The primary objective of EDI for workers compensation data is improved transmission of information from its source, such as the healthcare providers to insurers, and from the insurers to state and federal workers compensation regulatory agencies. The more advanced claim management systems have an integrated EDI reporting system.

Exhibit 9.1: General Claim Management System Functions (cont.)

- Positive Pay or Similar Banking Interface as a Fraud Detection Tool (See Chapter 8: Claims Operations—Financing and Banking, beginning on page 87.)
- IRS 1099 Reporting Capability
- Health Insurance Portability and Accountability Act (HIPAA)[d] Administration Integration and Compliance
- Comprehensive Claim Management Reporting with Report Scheduling Function for:
    - Loss Runs
    - Financial Registers
    - Check Registers
    - Large Loss Reports
    - Safety Analysis and Risk Analysis Reports
    - Claim List Reports
    - Reserve Management Reports (Including Reserve Changes)
    - Productivity Reports
    - Closing Ratio Reports
    - Diary Management Reports
    - Claim Expense Reports (Summary and Details)
    - Client Reporting File Reports
    - Vendor Reports
    - Litigation Reports and Suit Log
    - Recovery Reports (Subrogation, Deductibles, and Salvage)

[d]The Health Insurance Portability and Accountability Act (HIPAA) was enacted by the U.S. Congress in 1996. Title II of HIPAA, known as the Administrative Simplification (AS) provisions, requires the establishment of national standards for electronic healthcare transactions and national identifiers for providers, health insurance plans, and employers. This is intended to help people keep their information private. The Privacy Rule standards address the use and disclosure of individuals' health information—called "protected health information"—by organizations subject to the Privacy Rule—called "covered entities"—as well as standards for individuals' privacy rights to understand and control how their health information is used. The Rule strikes a balance that permits important uses of information, while protecting the privacy of people who seek care and healing. Given that the healthcare marketplace is diverse, the Rule is designed to be flexible and comprehensive to cover the variety of uses and disclosures that need to be addressed.

- ***Data exports***—The ability to import and export data into the system without significant programming time and money is critical.

- ***Screens***—The claim screens need to be easy to use and have drop down fields wherever possible to avoid free-form entry.

- ***Ad hoc report writer***—The system needs the ability to allow users to create specific, customized claim management and risk management reports at the desktop, without the need for special programming.

- ***Periodic updates and releases***—The system should include the release of periodic updates—at no cost—to include any changes to the product resulting from industry or regulatory changes, or overall product enhancements.

- ***User groups***—The software vendor should have an established user group to exchange ideas and issues regarding the software product and also establish the foundation for product updates and enhancements.

What Is a Risk Management Information System (RMIS)?

Some industry professionals may describe a claim management system as an RMIS. However, there are differences in both systems. For example, an RMIS may include the following functionality not found in claim management systems:

- An RMIS may be a composition of software applications and databases providing the risk manager with the ability to gather and analyze data from various sources, and make informed decisions regarding risk financing and loss control issues.

- The RMIS system may store more comprehensive policy information, as well as exposure lists, vehicle schedules, insurance certificates, and contracts.

- The system may include comprehensive enterprise risk management (ERM)[1] functionality, expanding the risk management process to business risk, speculative risk, market risk, and compliance risk (i.e., compliance with state and federal regulations).

- The system may include a claim administration component or module.

Use of Other Technology

Technology also encompasses other areas, such video conferencing, Voice over IP (VOIP) telephone systems, voice recognition software for notes and reports, digital cameras and video cameras, and recorded statement Web portals, such as N2uitive™ (http://www.n2uitive.com).

A claim facility may also maintain other systems in order to operate effectively. For example, the claim facility may maintain the following systems:

- Accounting (general ledger)

- Imaging system (interfaced with the claim management system)

[1]Enterprise risk management (ERM) is the process of planning, organizing, and controlling the risk management activities of an organization to minimize or reduce the effects of risk on an organization's financial stability.

- Human resources
- Sales and marketing
- E-mail (exchange server)
- Smart phone (enterprise server)
- Data servers (LAN and WAN)
- Backup systems
- Telephone and fax, including VOIP
- Video technology
- Website
- Webinars
- Group collaborative Web location or portal
- Access to various databases and online resources (i.e., ChoicePoint, ISO ClaimSearch®)

Some claim facilities, such as a TPA, must maintain an accounting system to manage the general ledger and its billing processes. Often, the accounting system interfaces with the claim management system. Claim management systems not only manage the technical process but also provide the necessary data and reporting for clients and may also manage the loss fund accounting process.

Claim facilities may maintain human resource systems to track employee information, including recruitment, benefits, and other personnel information. The Sales and Marketing Department will maintain customer relations management software to track and monitor sales prospects and customers. The software usually includes the ability to diary information for the future and produce detailed reports. This type of software enhances the productivity of the sales force and helps manage the sales cycle and control the process.

Maintaining e-mail systems, either outsourced to an application service provider or maintained internally with an e-mail server, is essential in a claim environment. Some claim management systems have a fully interfaced internal e-mail component, eliminating the need to copy over e-mail documents to the claim management system. Since the BlackBerry and other smart phones and devices have become an essential tool in the business environment, many TPAs issue such equipment to staff, maintaining either an internal BlackBerry enterprise server or outsourcing the entire process.

Most businesses, including a claim facility, maintain data servers. Depending on the claim management system, the data servers may include the clients' claim data. The data servers are required to be backed up routinely as outlined in the claim facility's disaster recovery process. Typically, data can be accessed within a local area network (LAN) and a wide area network (WAN). The LAN includes the network within the physical office location, whereas the WAN includes other office locations and remote employees.

As technology improves, there are various methods to communicate with physically remote employees and other office locations, such as a Citrix[2] connection and virtual private networks (VPN).[3] To maintain an appropriate speed for data connections, a claim facility will maintain T-1 data and telephone lines or faster fiber optic technology. The increased speeds of broadband data connections have contributed to the use of the Internet as a method to deploy and maintain Web-based claim management systems, as well as the use of VOIP telephone technology. See Exhibit 9.2 below.

Since most of the investigative and adjustment process at a claim facility is done by telephone, telephone technology is very important to the claim environment. Either the claim facility maintains a telephone private branch exchange (PBX) at each of its physical office locations, or it may utilize newer technology consisting of VOIP and a virtual PBX. A virtual PBX is much more flexible and can incorporate many employees and offices with minimal hardware investment. A virtual PBX can be maintained internally or provided by an outsourced service provider. Often, the entire system functionality and administrative

[2]Citrix Systems, Inc., is currently the leader in access infrastructure solutions, which includes network access, single sign-on, VPN capabilities, presentation services, remote control and remote support applications. Citrix uses two technologies: WinFrame and Independent Computing Architecture (ICA).

[3]Virtual private networks (VPN) are utilized by organizations to provide remote access to a secure network. The VPN is a private network that typically uses the Internet to connect remote sites or users together.

Exhibit 9.2: Broadband Connections

Cable Modem: A cable modem is a type of Network Bridge and modem that provides bi-directional data communication via radio frequency channels on a cable television (CATV) infrastructure, primarily used to deliver broadband Internet access in the form of cable Internet. Most providers offer data speeds of 1 to 10 Mbps (megabits per second). Higher speeds are often available for businesses.

DSL Digital Subscriber Line: This is a telephone circuit that transmits data over the wires of a local telephone network using high frequency bands. Most providers offer data speeds of 1 to 7 Mbps.

T-1 Data Line: This is a data transfer system that transfers digital signals at 1.544 Mbps. Typically, the data transfer is guaranteed at a certain speed, eliminating any loss of speed using the public Internet. Many businesses have multiple T-1 lines for both data and telephone.

Fiber-Optic Cable: This is a data transfer system that can transfer digital signals starting at 1.5 Mbps to 150 Mbps. Fiber optic technology is more efficient, given the ability to increase bandwidth without the installation of additional cable or wiring.

changes are done through an Internet Web portal at the desktop.

Video conferencing has become very advanced and much more affordable, with the availability of increased levels of Internet bandwidth through cable and telephone lines. No longer reserved for the corporate boardrooms, it is now being deployed to remote staff as a means to communicate on a daily basis. High definition video conferencing can be used on a one-on-one basis via a high speed Internet connection, or include multiple parties on one large screen, called multi-point conferencing. Video conferencing will most likely be the single advanced technology that will change the way claim facilities operate. New business models will emerge, using video not only between employees, but also by field staff streaming video back to the desktop of an adjuster or manager, giving the ability to adjust property claims anywhere in the world.

Most claim facilities maintain a website describing their services and company. Websites are important from a sales and marketing perspective. However, websites also serve other functions. For example, clients' access to the claim management system may be achieved through the website as a convenient way for clients to access their records with a secure user ID and password. The website may also have what is called a File Transfer Protocol (FTP) site, which can be used to transfer and exchange data files between the claim facility and the client, avoiding the use of e-mail for data file exchange.

Webinar's are utilized for many purposes, such as to demonstrate various software and systems, provide a resource for client presentations (thus eliminating or minimizing travel), for staff continuing education, etc. There are several vendors who provide webinar resources, including WebEx and GoToMeeting.

Many companies, including claim facilities, maintain Web portals which allow for collaboration among all employees, including documents, employee meetings, calendars, announcements, access to databases, links to various websites, expense reporting, and company documents. The Web portal may also include the ability to access human resource documents. An example of this type of portal is Microsoft Sharepoint.

To properly investigate and adjust claims, a claim facility will need to maintain access to various databases and online resources. For example, claim facility employees may need to access the ISO ClaimSearch® system, Choicepoint® databases, official records or police report databases, motor vehicle record databases, and others. There are various online claim resource websites, some of which are listed below:

- http://www.claimsites.com
- http://www.claimsdesk.com
- http://www.claimspages.com
- http://www.claims-portal.com
- http://www.ambest.com/legal/statelawdigest.html

Importance of Data Security and Backup

Most claims systems have an administrator module that controls the security within the claims system. For example, check issuance, reserve and settlement authority levels, and certain system modules such as system coding, loss fund account management, and billing. These functions require specific security levels. Access to management reports, various claim screens and claim fields, as well as the day of the week and time of day a system can be accessed will also require specific security levels. The effective management of the systems security component is critical to any claim facility and is reserved for only a designated few within the organization.

Since an organization's data is vital to its survival, it is critical that all systems are backed up properly and regularly. Claim systems have databases that include important claim data necessary for an insurance company or TPA to operate. The loss or theft of this data could have a serious negative impact resulting in a potential business shutdown. If the TPA lost the entire client database, it could result in serious litigation between the client and the TPA, as the TPA contract typically requires the TPA to provide redundant data backup systems.

The process of data backup can be as simple as a tape backup run nightly and then retained off premises, or a comprehensive data backup process of consisting of redundant servers and systems across the organization, at different intervals, using a combination of computer hardware devices and software programs. Data may also be backed up using Internet connections, storing huge amounts of data remotely. Data backup is also necessary to comply with business record retention. E-mail archiving and retention of other important business records are critical components of a disaster recovery plan.

Backup is critical, but so is the ability to recover in the event of a loss of data. Most companies require a periodic backup restoration to be sure the process is working properly.

Technology Case Study—A Virtual Adjuster!

To help illustrate the importance of technology in claims management, it might be a good idea to follow a day in the life of a typical claims adjuster. We'll call him James.

James wakes up in the morning, has breakfast, and takes a short commute down the hall of his home to his office. He is a virtual worker! The office is equipped with a high speed personal computer with dual 19 inch monitors, a high-definition Web video camera, as well as business grade high-speed Internet connection, and a VOIP telephone. The software on his computer includes the Microsoft Office suite of products, including Outlook, Word, Excel, Power Point, Access, and Info-Path. Additionally, the computer is equipped with high definition video conference software.

James boots up the computer and accesses the claim management system and the Microsoft Sharepoint employee collaborative website, using the Web browser. He views the Sharepoint website for important company announcements, to research medical terminology on a claim he is handling, and to place a medical claim for his son on the Human Resources Department site. His day has begun with the handling of claim files using an automated diary process within the claims system, while fielding telephone calls using a wireless headset and documenting the electronic claim file notes with activities.

James takes five recorded statements in a digital format using a recorded statement Web portal interfaced with the claim management system and the VOIP system, with the statements parked as attachments in the claim file record. He receives e-mail throughout the day, which is fully integrated into the claim file record, and requests claim checks to be electronically issued on claims he has settled. The company has implemented debit cards for workers compensation indemnity benefits in lieu of issuing benefit checks. At the outset of a lost-time claim, the claimant or employee receives a debit card which is replenished by James as benefits are paid, eliminating the need to issue biweekly checks.

Workers compensation medical benefits are received electronically from providers and are automatically repriced by the claim management system, with each bill ready for payment and an electronic explanation of benefits (EOB) printed along with the check. Workers compensation claim forms are requested by James within the claims system and then are printed electronically and mailed directly to the claimant from a centralized location.

While working through his diary, James receives two new claims requiring initial contacts, one being a first-party property claim (James is very experienced with these types of claims). His claims manager assigns his coworker, Peter, who is a field inspector, to inspect the loss using video conferencing technology. Peter is dispatched to the loss location using global position satellite (GPS) technology with the address sent to him via text by James. Equipped with wireless video conference head gear (with microphone), Peter scopes out the property, loss streaming back video, takes still digital photos, and sends measurements to James so that he can prepare a damage estimate. James uses a Web-based property estimating software to complete the damage estimate while on the phone with Peter. James completes the damage estimate and sends the completed estimate to the policyholder via e-mail, with photographs attached.

James receives medical documentation via an e-mail attachment directly into the claim file record from an attorney who is interested in settlement discussions. James has annotated the medical records in a TIF file format with his notes outlining questions for the attorney. In the meantime, he wants to be sure he has an updated ISO ClaimSearch® confirming that the claimant has not had an intervening accident which could have contributed to the injuries being claimed. He pushes one key and instantly receives back results indicating a subsequent accident with similar injuries. James begins the negotiation process.

James receives a video conference call for a mediation he is attending electronically. Using multipoint conferencing, he can view the claimant and his attorney, as well as defense counsel and the mediator. After an hour of mediation, the claim is settled, and closing documentation is distributed to all parties as e-mail attachments. James requests the settlement check electronically after reviewing the closing documentation.

At the end of the day, James and the three other adjusters in his unit have a multipoint video conference meeting with the claims manager. The manager wants to discuss the automated quality file reviews being conducted remotely by the home office claims staff. Since the claims operation is virtual, the home office claims staff can view the entire claim file record, including all attachments and recorded statements remotely.

So ends anther busy day for James, the virtual adjuster.

Summary and Conclusion

Technology is the backbone of any claim facility, whether the facility is an insurance company claim operation or a TPA. The claim management system is the primary resource used by the claims staff to handle and manage claim activity. There are information technology challenges, ranging from a decision to build or buy a system, the different multiple data sources, complex reporting needs, technology obsolescence, and the technology resources that are required versus what is available.

For claims operations to survive, the brick and mortar claim facility will need to be left behind! As a service organization, the virtual model is a perfect fit and will be the only cost-effective method to deliver high quality and efficient claims services in the future. By integrating a virtual business model, including remote staff with manageable caseloads, Web-based claims systems, and video conferencing, service and the quality of the claim work product will improve dramatically.

Claim and risk management information systems are standard in today's business climate. Other technologies, from smart phones to virtual offices, are often utilized by claim facilities. Data security and backup are critical elements of any claim facility and need to be monitored closely, including documented restoration tests.

We ended the chapter with James, the virtual adjuster, and went through his day looking how technology has made claim services more efficient, productive, and cost-effective.

FOR MORE INFORMATION ON:	GO TO:	PAGE(S):
Claims Operations—Overview	Chapter 2	5
Claims Process—Overview	Chapter 10	105
Third-Party Administrators	Chapters 18–20	221–270
Claims Handling Guidelines	Chapters 21–30	271–354
ISO ClaimSearch®	Appendix B	363

CHAPTER 10: CLAIMS PROCESS—OVERVIEW

The claims process is everything that happens from the date the claim is reported to the date the claim is closed. It includes all activities performed by the claims adjuster (or claims attorney), supervisor, manager, and claims support staff. It's important to note that various stages of the claims process are more significant than others. This section discusses these critical stages in detail because of their impact on the progressive development of an individual claim file and the overall claims process. These stages are:

- Investigation and adjustment (Chapter 11, page 115)
- Statements and interviews (Chapter 12, page 127)
- Coverage issues (Chapter 13, page 143)
- Evaluation and resolution (Chapter 14, page 155)
- Going to court (Chapter 15, page 173)
- Reserve management (Chapter 16, page 183)
- Recovery (Chapter 17, page 205)

This chapter provides a general overview of the claims process, focusing on its duration—from first report to closing and archiving.

Claim Duration

How long is the claims process? Well, it depends on a number of factors, such as the type of claim (i.e., physical damage, bodily injury, workers compensation, professional liability); the number of parties; the claim features in the claim; whether the claim is pending litigation; if injuries are involved, the type of injury and disability; if damages are involved, the extent of the damages; and, of course, the level of staffing in the organization. If the staffing is inadequate, the workloads will be higher, with less time to handle each individual claim and extending the time period in the claims process. By extending the time period, the claim value or exposure may increase.

For example, if the adjuster does not control the medical management process effectively (including arrangements for an independent medical exam[1]), the claimant may overtreat or be on disability for a longer duration than necessary. If the claims adjuster handling a property damage claim does not control the loss of use (i.e., rental claim) due to excessive work-

[1]An independent medical exam (IME) is a physical examination (PE) conducted by a physician on behalf of the insurance company or defendant in a lawsuit. Exams are typically conducted at the physician's office with the physicians having the benefit of the medical and hospital records provided by the claimants or their attorneys in advance of the exam. The purpose of physical examinations is to determine and evaluate the injuries sustained in the accident, any disability, the causal relationship of the injuries to the treatment and disability, future treatment options, diagnosis, and prognosis. The exams may be arranged by the adjuster or defense attorneys and may involve several exams if there are multiple specialties involved, such as orthopedic, chiropractic, neurologist, etc. In litigation proceedings, defendants are typically entitled to IMEs for each specialty.

loads, the property damage exposure will increase. If an adjuster is delayed in inspecting a property loss, and repairs are completed before the adjuster has an opportunity to inspect, the repairs may be more than the appraisal that adjuster would have written.

These examples are common in a claims operation, and are often referred to as "leakage." Although the amounts may seem to be minimal for an individual claim file, multiplied by hundreds or thousands of claim files, leakage can have a profound effect on the financial stability of the claims operation. Leakage can be avoided with manageable workloads and proper supervision.

Claim First Report

Where and when does the claim begin? Every claim begins with some type of first report. The first report normally includes all the necessary information to verify coverage and establish a claim record. The report may include the insured's name and address, policy number and effective dates, policy limits, the date of loss, the loss location, the parties involved, contact information, vehicle or property damage information, and a description of the accident or incident.

The first report can be an industry standard first report, such as the Association for Cooperative Operations Research and Development (ACORD)[2] Loss Notice form. There are four primary ACORD Loss Notice forms: property, automobile, general liability and workers compensation. [See Appendix D,

[2]ACORD (Association for Cooperative Operations Research and Development) is a global, nonprofit standards development organization serving the insurance industry and related financial services industries. ACORD's mission is to facilitate the development of open consensus data standards and standard forms. ACORD members include hundreds of insurance and reinsurance companies, agents, and brokers, software providers, and industry associations worldwide. ACORD works with these organizations toward a goal of improved data communication across diverse platforms through implementation of standards. About ACORD. New York: ACORD, 2010. http://www.acord.org/about/.

Exhibit 10.1: New York Fraud Statement

"Any person who knowingly and with intent to defraud any insurance company or other person files an application for commercial insurance or a statement of claim for any commercial or personal insurance benefits containing any materially false information, or conceals for the purpose of misleading, information concerning any fact material thereto, and any person who in connection with such application or claim knowingly makes or knowingly assists, abets, solicits or conspires with another to make a false report of the theft, destruction, damage or conversion of any motor vehicle to a law enforcement agency, the Department of Motor vehicles or an insurance company, commits a fraudulent insurance act, which is a crime, and shall also be subject to a civil penalty not to exceed $5,000 and the value of the subject motor vehicle or stated claim for each violation."

beginning on page 389, for copies of the ACORD Loss Notice forms.[3]]

The ACORD Loss Notice form is a comprehensive form, which includes the state fraud language, warning of the penalties for submitting a fraudulent claim report. For example, the New York fraud statement is shown in Exhibit 10.1 on page 106.

These forms may be submitted by an agent or broker, or a policyholder. Sometimes, when taking a telephone first report, the claims support staff will utilize the ACORD form to record the accident or incident information, either online or in a handwritten format. A first report may be submitted in the form of a letter, e-mail, or even a first notice lawsuit, and may be submitted by the policyholder, agent, broker, or directly by a claimant or their representative.

It should be noted that in workers compensation, the first report is commonly referred to a as "First Notice of Injury." Many states mandate the use of their own state required first notice report, which must be completed by the employer within a statutory time period. For example the First Notice of Injury in Connecticut is called an "Employers First Report of Occupational Injury or Illness." The reporting instructions indicate:

> The Form "EMPLOYER'S FIRST REPORT OF OCCUPATIONAL INJURY OR ILLNESS" is to be completed by an employer or its workers compensation insurance carrier to notify the Workers' Compensation Commission of occupational injuries or illnesses that result in incapacity for one day or more. Unlike many Commission forms, **the Employer's First Report Form must be sent directly to the** Commission Chairman's Office in Hartford."[4]

[3]**Important use limitation:** ACORD forms are provided solely for educational and reference purposes. Insurance companies must be licensed directly by ACORD to use any of these forms.

The first report provides the necessary information to set up the claim file in the claim system and assign a claims handler, or adjuster. For this reason, it is important that the first report be completed accurately and in its entirety.

Proper claim acknowledgements eliminate mail matching, image identification, and telephone call volume.

Coverage Verification

Coverage verification is the process of verifying that the loss being presented is covered under the insurance policy purchased by the insured or policyholder. Initially, the claims support unit will confirm or verify coverage in terms of the named insured, policy number, effective dates, locations, covered vehicles, covered property, coverage limits, deductibles, and endorsements.

It is then the adjuster's responsibility to confirm that, based on the details of the loss and possibly the initial investigation, the claim is covered and not excluded under the policy. The adjuster may need to review the coverage forms, endorsements, and

[4]*Workers Compensation On-Line Forms.* Hartford, CT: State of Connecticut Workers Compensation Commission, 2009.

Claims Process

schedules for additional insureds, exclusions, limitations, policy limits, and potential sublimits for ancillary coverages.

Claim Acknowledgement

A claim acknowledgement is a statement made to the parties to the claim or loss (insured, claimant, agent) acknowledging receipt of the claim and referencing the claim number, policy number, claim caption, date of loss, adjuster assignment, and insurance company name. Claim acknowledgements can be sent by mail, fax, or electronically.

Claim Setup

Typically, new claims are received by the claims operation by mail, e-mail, fax, or electronically. Thereafter, the claims are "set up" in the claim facility's claim system by transferring the information from the loss notice or first report and entering the information in the claim file record. The transfer of loss notice information can also be done electronically through a data import function.

The claims support staff will usually enter all of the claim information provided with the initial loss notice into the claim file record, either as a hard copy or electronically. The claim setup also includes entry of the necessary claim coding and statistical information required to track the claim data for the insurance company or client (as a third-party administrator). These coding or statistical entries provide the foundation to be able to produce the necessary statistical and financial information, either electronically or in reports, for the company or client and regulators, if applicable. The claims support staff will also either organize the documents received with the initial claim report and place them in a hard copy claim jacket or file, or if the claim file is electronic, facilitate the imaging or scanning of all the documents, labeling each image for ease of future retrieval and review. Initial loss and expense reserves may be established by the handling adjuster or claims manager with the entry of new claims.

Error free claim setups can eliminate typographical errors on correspondence, reserve entry errors, and possibly an errors or omissions (E&O) claim if mail attachments are not properly posted to the correct claim file.

After the initial processing entry, the claims support unit will place initial adjuster and manager diaries on the claim file and refer the claim file to the adjuster or claims manager, depending on the claims operation protocol. Upon receipt of the new claim assignment, the handling adjuster initiates the claims handing process.

Claim Assignment

The claim assignment process involves assigning the newly reported claim to an adjuster for handling. This process may be done by the claims support staff with predefined assignment protocols based on claim types or lines of business, or by the claims supervisor or manager. If the assignment is made by the claims supervisor or manager, there may be supervisor comments or instructions concerning the handling.

The claim assignment process is critical. Each claim needs to be assigned to the proper adjuster with the right experience and qualifications. If a claim is assigned improperly, the claim could be mishandled, costing the claim facility valuable time and expense. It is also important to monitor the assignment process to be sure that any individual adjuster is not being assigned too many claims in a given day, precluding the adjuster from being able to handle the claims properly and effectively. This may be particularly true in the high volume of claim assignments during weather-related property losses.

This stage is important to the initial direction of the claim. If the supervisor or manager wants certain investigative or adjustment items addressed during the investigation or adjustment of the claim file, this is usually included at the time of the claim assignment.

Claim Initial Contacts

The initial contacts establish the foundation for the claim investigation and adjustment process. These contacts allow the adjuster to evaluate the necessary future investigation by using the information developed during the initial contacts. The scope of the initial contact may include securing comprehensive details of the accident or incident and the taking of a statement.

Most claims operations require same day contact (or within 24 hours) with the parties to the loss, particularly the insured and claimant. Leaving messages may be acceptable, as long as the follow-up activity is the next day. Claim file notes should not consistently indicate, "left message," which usually indicates a problem. After a second contact attempt, a contact letter, postcard, e-mail, or fax should be sent to the party involved, requesting contact.

When handling an errors and omissions, professional liability, management liability, or public entity claim, the adjuster's goal should be to make contact with the named insured or their designated representative (i.e., risk manager or insured attorney) upon receipt of a new loss notice. Care should be used in making sure contact is first established with the appropriate member of the insured organization (i.e., risk manager, clerk, selectman, police chief). Insured employees should not be interviewed without the permission of the appropriate contact person.

Discretion and judgment should be used in making contact with the claimant or claimant's attorney, depending on the type of claim and issues involved. If the claim is reported indicating no liability on the insured, or a notice only claim[5], it may not be prudent to make contact with the claimants. Doing so could, rightly or wrongly, give the claimants the impression that they can expect payment of the claim, even when the insured is not responsible.

As a claims service organization, it is essential that telephone messages be returned promptly. All telephone and voice mail

[5]A notice only claim is a claim where no payment is expected. It is comparable to an incident report.

messages should be returned the same day as received. Claims professionals should be proactive and make themselves available to claimants and insureds. This means adjusters should make actual contact with the person leaving the message, and not simply leave a return message and re-diary the claim file for follow up. It can be very frustrating to consistently get a voice mail message and then get a return call and have to call again. It perpetuates the "telephone tag" problem!

Technical Claims Handling

The technical claims handling process involves the claims process activities handled by the claims adjuster, supervisor, or manager, and basically includes the entire claims process, except for the claims support tasks. The claim file record is updated as the claim progresses.

This process includes the claim investigation and adjustment activities (discussed in Chapter 11, beginning on page 115), as well as reserve management (discussed in Chapter 17, beginning on page 205). Activities include ongoing contacts, letters, e-mails and correspondence, statements, ISO ClaimSearch,® entering payables for loss and expense payments, issuing claim forms, securing or preparing estimates and appraisals, taking photographs and making diagrams, litigation management, broker/agent interaction, supervisory or management input or direction, and file reporting.

The technical claims process drives the progression and development of the claim file. As the investigation and adjustment activities are completed, the claim is evaluated and analyzed to determine liability, compensability, and damages. Claim reserves are adjusted, and the claim is either directed toward a defense, settlement, or compromised resolution. During this process, the adjuster may be communicating with the supervisor, manager, and assigned attorney if the claim is in litigation. There may be formal reports prepared for the file that provide the status of the claim and its future direction.

Diary Management

To properly manage claim diaries, as well as maintain quality service, it is very important that claim diaries be managed effectively and remain current. Diary management is the responsibility of the handling adjuster, overseen by the supervisor or manager. All claim files should have an active diary date until the claim file is closed. Realistic diary dates should be utilized to avoid having too many claim files for review and handling on a given date.

Thereafter, the claims manager should continue to maintain a manager diary date on the claim categories listed on page 111. A claims manager should exercise individual discretion in maintaining a dual diary on claims with gross damage exposure—the full value of claim without any offsets for liability, contribution, or second injury fund—that is over the handling adjuster's authority. A dual diary should also be kept on litigation claims and on certain coverage-issue claims by charging back (allowing the handling adjuster to work the claim without supervision based on the adjuster's experience and qualifications) the claim after the first 90 days. However, the claims manager should always remain responsible for the claim after the charge back and take care in this management delegation process.

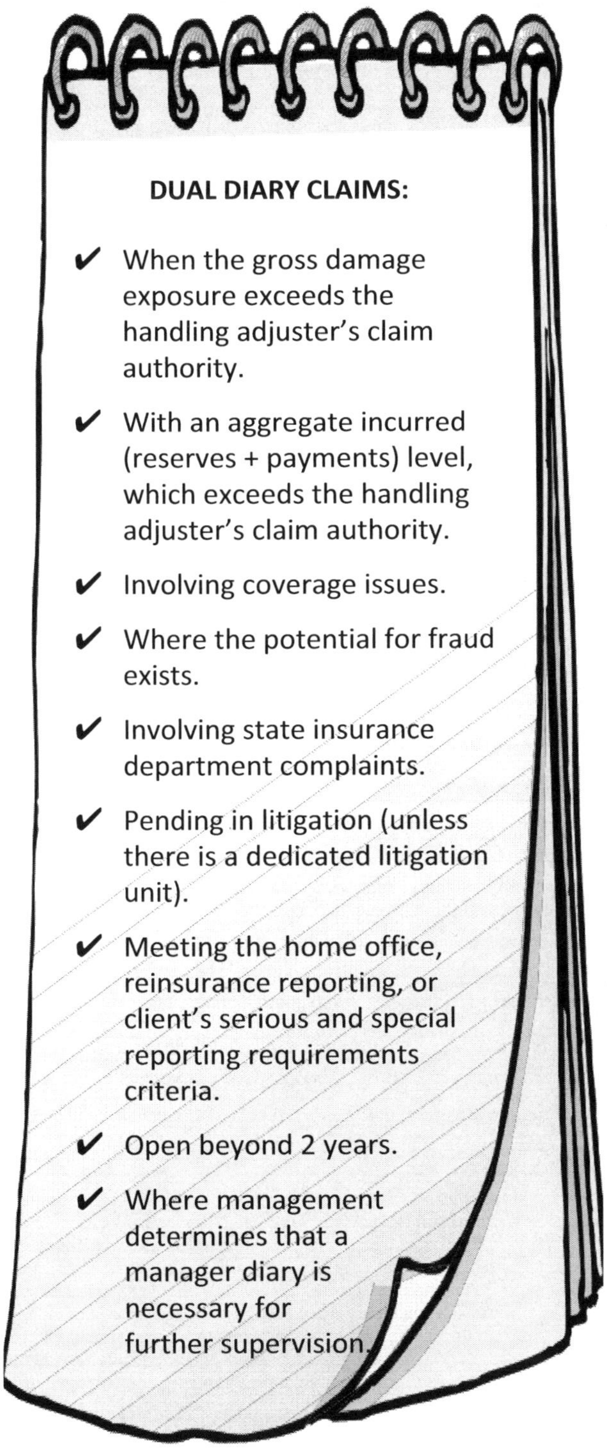

When a claim file is initially set up, each individual claim should have both a handling adjuster and a claims manager diary date entered. A terminal reserve[6] diary date needs to be established for the adjuster and claims manager at 9 months from the claim report date as well as a 30-day diary for the initial claim status report to be completed by the handling adjuster. Thereafter, a proper handling adjuster diary date must be established to effectively manage the claims process, including completion of the outstanding claim investigation.

The handling adjuster's initial diary date should be no longer than 7 days from claim opening, depending on the type of claim involved (i.e., first-party loss), the follow-up investigation needed, or if there are other claims handling or statutory requirements. The claim investigation should be well underway, with enough information to properly evaluate the current claim reserves, within a 15-day time period after claim opening.

Generally, the handling adjuster diary dates should be no longer than 30-day intervals. If the claim file is a home office reporting file or client reporting file, a specific diary date for the handling adjuster should be established referencing the diary type. The home office reporting file or client reporting file diary date must be prior to the next reporting [due] date (NRD) to allow timely reporting.

All handling adjusters and claims managers should either utilize a manual diary or an

[6] A terminal reserve is an exposure based reserve which represents what the claim facility would expect to pay on a claim at that point in time, based on what is known to date.

electronic diary management system to effectively handle claims. Computerized online diary reports are typically available for use by the adjuster and claims manager.

Overdue diaries can cause a host of problems for a claims operation. Diaries control various activities necessary on a claim file. If diaries are not current, service complaints, reserve management issues, and missed important deadlines could occur. It is important to note that the pushing ahead of overdue diaries to a future date—to avoid the appearance of being overdue—does not resolve the potential problems that may develop; it will just compound the potential adverse results.

Claims Processing

Claims processing encompasses a variety of tasks performed by the claims support unit. The extent of the tasks performed will depend on the organizational structure of the claim facility. Some of the tasks performed may include reserve entry (new and adjustments), payment of loss and expenses, requests for IRS W-9 forms, issuance of IRS 1099 forms, error corrections, typing of letters and claim forms, etc. In some organizations, these tasks are performed by the handling adjuster.

Mail and File Process

Prior to electronic claim files being used, the mail and file unit was critical to the claims operation. Mail came into the organization and needed to be matched to the hard copy claim file jackets. The hard copy claim files were somewhere in the claims office, but often, it took time to locate the files to attach the claim mail and refer the claim file with mail attached to the appropriate adjuster or manager. If the claim was initially located on the file shelf, a charge out card may have indicated it was delivered to an adjuster on a specific date. However, in the interim the adjuster may have requested a manual check to be prepared so the claim file would then be routed to another location. The adjuster's instructions may have also indicated to enter an ISO ClaimSearch® after the check was prepared, routing the claim file to another location. A supervisor or manager might have had a dual-diary date due, referring the file to the manager for review.

This whole process was inefficient, and it was very difficult to determine where a claim file was located at any given point in time. It created the need to have "rush searches" that took valuable time from the claims support unit to handle other priorities. Eventually, some claims operation used "bar coding" to track claim files throughout the operation, which improved efficiency. However, the use of electronic claim files and the scanning of mail eliminated these problems and changed the mail and file job responsibilities.

In an electronic claim environment, the claims support unit opens the postal mail and retrieves e-mailed and faxed documents, and then date stamps[7] all correspondence. Thereafter, the mail is indexed to determine the name of the handling adjuster and claim number, and then imaged or scanned to the electronic claim file. The handling adjuster and manager

[7]It should be noted that some states require that all claim mail placed in the hard copy or electronic claim file must be date stamped. Some imaging systems provide the date stamp function as part of the imaging process.

then address the mail delivery in the electronic claim file.

All lawsuits, legal pleadings, state insurance department complaints, arbitration notices, and arbitration decisions should be immediately delivered to the claims manager by the claims support unit, as these documents may be time sensitive and require immediate handling.

E-mail documents may not make it to the claim file if the claims are not completely electronic. Some adjusters copy and paste or print the e-mails. This may be cumbersome and subject to human error, and is not a recommended process for any claims operation. Interfacing e-mail with the electronic claim file is an essential component of any claim management system.

Recovery checks and voided checks, when received by mail, should be delivered to the administrative cashier for processing. Even when the operation is paperless or electronic, certain legal or regulatory documents may not be suitable for shredding after being scanned to the claim file, and need to be maintained in a hard-copy format. For example, all *original* vehicle titles should be delivered to the appropriate claims office and maintained in a hard-copy format according to the claims operation's established vehicle title processing procedures.

Claim Closing Process

The claim closing process involves several steps, depending on the claim facility. First, the adjuster will secure the appropriate closing documentation. If the claim involves bodily injury or property damage liability, a signed release may be required. If the claim involves a first-party loss (i.e., automobile physical damage claim or first-party property claim), a proof of loss may be required. Second, a memo or note will document that the claim is going to be closed. It will contain brief details concerning the claim outcome. Third, the claim party will need to be statistically closed either with a final claim payment or closed without payment (CWP). This is also called "closed no payment (CNP)."

After the closing process is completed, the claim no longer remains on active diary unless unusual circumstances require follow up at a later date.

Claim File Storage or Archive Process

Physical claim files are typically stored on-site for 6–9 months and then shipped off-site either to a company-owned location or a storage facility. Physical file storage can be very costly and cumbersome when files need to be retrieved for reopening or further handling.

Electronic claim files may be stored indefinitely, and as the databases get too large, older claim files can be archived and then transferred to another database location. Generally, claim file records are stored 7–10 years; however, bodily injury claims involving a minor will be required to be stored 7–10 years from the date the claimant reaches the age of majority.

Summary and Conclusion

In this chapter, we examined the entire claims process, focusing on various stages and how they interrelate with other claim stages. As the claim progresses—with the initial first report, with coverage confirmation, the claim acknowledgement, claim set-up, assignment, and contacts—it then enters the technical claims handling process, where most of the claim activities are conducted and monitored.

During the technical claims handling process, diary management is essential to control and manage the claims process for both the adjuster and manager. The claims support unit is involved along the way to support the technical claims handling process with claims processing activities, as well as mail and file support. When the claim is ready to be closed, the closing process finalizes the claim with the necessary closing documents and statistical closing of the claim file. Lastly, the claim file is either stored physically or electronically, depending on the particular claims operation.

Other chapters discuss some of these claims processing stages in more depth.

FOR MORE INFORMATION ON:	GO TO:	PAGE(S):
Claims Operations	Chapters 2–9	5–104
Claims Process	Chapters 10–17	105–220
Investigation and Adjustment	Chapter 11	115
Claim Statements and Interviews	Chapter 12	127
Coverage Issues	Chapter 13	143
Evaluation and Resolution	Chapter 14	155
Going to Court	Chapter 15	173
Reserve Management	Chapter 16	183
Recovery	Chapter 17	205
Third-Party Administrators	Chapters 18–20	221–270
Claims Handling Guidelines	Chapters 21–30	271–354
ISO ClaimSearch®	Appendix B	363
Ethics in Claims Handling	Appendix E	409

Chapter 11: Claims Process—Investigation and Adjustment

The claim investigation and adjustment process includes various claim activities and file documentation. These activities continue to be updated as the claim progresses. Claims investigations are critical and represent the foundation for the evaluation and assessment of a claim. The key to a proper claim evaluation is to review all the investigation and documentation material and then summarize the key elements of the claim in terms of liability and damages. The claim investigation serves as the basis for the coverage analysis and evaluation of the claim. If the investigation is inadequate or incomplete, then the evaluation may be flawed or incorrect.

For example, in an automobile liability claim, if the adjuster fails to get the police report (which cited the claimant for failure to yield the right of way), the evaluation of the claim could result in the insurer paying a claim that was not warranted. Or, in a property loss, if the adjuster neglects to retain an expert to inspect the portable heater that caused the fire, a viable subrogation claim may not be able to be pursued. The examples go on and on! The point is that the claim investigation must be properly conducted and completed so the claim can be evaluated and adjusted.

There are many different aspects of a claims investigation as well as the adjustment activities which bring a claim to resolution. This chapter provides an overview of some of these activities.

VARIOUS CLAIM INVESTIGATION ELEMENTS

- ✔ Coverage Verification
- ✔ Adjuster Assignment and Action Plan
- ✔ Attorney Allegations
- ✔ Interviews and Statements
- ✔ Use of Experts
- ✔ Documents
  - Claim Forms
  - Contracts
  - Official Reports
  - Authorizations
  - Medical, Diagnostic, and Hospital Records
  - Photographs
  - Diagrams
  - Estimates and Appraisals

Coverage Verification

Coverage verification is one of the most important aspects of the claims handling process. While the process can vary by claims operation, at many claim facilities, the claims support unit initially verifies coverage to establish the claim file record. Analyzing and evaluating coverage rests with the handling adjuster and the claims manager. The claim file notes should clearly outline the coverage analysis, including reference to the applicable policy forms and endorsements. Particular attention should be paid to the actual date of loss and the policy effective dates.

Chapter 13, Claims Process—Coverage Issues, beginning on page 143, will review the coverage verification and coverage analysis processes in greater detail.

Adjuster Assignment and Action Plan

Once coverage for a claim is verified, an adjuster is assigned to investigate and adjust the claim. During the course of a claim investigation, there are many desk adjuster and field adjuster activities. Both adjusters work together in completing an investigation. However, it is not uncommon for the field adjuster to be an independent adjuster retained to handle specific task assignments.

The desk adjuster works in the claims office, handling all claim activities by telephone, e-mail, and correspondence. In contrast, the field adjuster primarily works outside the office, "in the field" so to speak, conducting investigation tasks such as taking photographs, preparing diagrams, conducting activity checks[1] and witness canvasses,[2] viewing and recording traffic light sequences, taking statements (both recorded and signed statements), inspecting damages, and writing appraisals.

Upon receipt of a new claim (or reassignment of a claim), the claims manager should provide instructions to the handling adjuster via a file note or e-mail. The handling adjuster needs to review the claims manager's instructions and complete a file note acknowledging receipt of the new claim, or reassignment, and outline an adjuster action plan for further handling. An adjuster action plan typically consists of the components shown in Exhibit 11.1. For workers compensation (WC) claims, it would also include compensability; accident, notice, and causal relationship; and a medical management plan.

Use of Independent Adjusters

The assignment of independent adjusters is sometimes necessary for fieldwork where there's a lack of staff field adjusters, for whatever reason. When utilizing independent adjusters during the adjustment process, the handling adjuster or claims manager should approve the assignment, documenting the approval within the claim file notes.

---

[1] An activity check is when a field adjuster or investigator checks on an injured claimant to confirm that the injuries are real and disability is continuing. The activity check may involve speaking with neighbors.

[2] A witness canvass is when an adjuster visits all businesses and residences near an accident scene to locate any potential witnesses to the accident or loss.

Independent adjuster assignments can be very narrow, sometimes called a "limited assignment," or quite broad. In a "full adjustment," the independent adjuster handles all aspects of the claim and report back in a captioned report, i.e., a complete description of the loss broken down into categories, such as coverage, liability, damages, investigation, etc. Full adjustments are typically used in first-party property losses. Whether for limited or full adjustments, independent adjusters should be assigned in writing, using a detailed assignment letter or form, which provides specific instructions. The independent adjuster then reports back to the handling adjuster or claims manager with the results.

Where more specialized vendor investigative work is needed, such as a surveillance or private investigation, the appropriate vendor should be selected by consultation with defense counsel and/or the client. (*Note:* some clients require prior approval to use these types of vendors.)

Independent adjuster invoices should be scrutinized to be sure the billing hours and service fees are appropriate and in accordance with the agreed billing schedule. All independent adjuster vendors must be reviewed and approved prior to making any assignments. The review process includes a company brochure, a list of services provided by line of business, an insurance certificate (with errors and omissions coverage), references, a signed IRS W-9 form, and a current fee schedule.

Attorney Allegations

When the claimant is represented by an attorney, the adjuster needs to secure basic information in lieu of speaking with the claimant directly. This information is nec-

Exhibit 11.1: Adjuster Action Plan Components

- Coverage Verification
- Compensability (WC)
- Facts of Loss
- Liability and Damages
- Accident, Notice, and Causal Relationship (WC)
- Medical Management Plan (WC and PIP)
- First-Party Claim Details and Plan
- Reserves
- Investigation Completed and Outstanding
- Recovery
- Future Action Plan
- Litigation Management (If Applicable)

essary to complete the investigation and also for evaluation purposes.

Contact with the claimant or plaintiff[3] attorney involves securing basic information, such as:

- Attorney and law firm name, business address, telephone, fax number, and e-mail address
- Claimant name, address, age, date of birth, and marital status
- Date of accident, time of accident, description of accident, and weather conditions
- Attorney's theory of liability[4]
- Claimant occupation, employer name and address, wage rate, and disability period
- Physician names, addresses, specialty, injuries and diagnosis, treatment and prognosis
- Hospital name and address with inpatient dates or service dates
- Itemized special damages[5] including medical, hospital, diagnostic, wages, property damage, etc.
- Third-party involvement/other parties on notice (with insurer and attorney names)
- Witness names, addresses, and telephone numbers
- Responding police agency and/or ambulance company
- Claimant vehicle make, model, and year; claimant vehicle damage and any available estimates
- Photographs of accident scene or vehicles
- Workers compensation and/and no-fault insurer and claim reference numbers
- Litigation: yes/no (If yes, consider securing an extension of time to answer without waiving any defenses[6])
- Names and contact information for any experts retained

Interviews and Statements

Statements are a necessary component of the investigative process and serve as a

[3]The claimant is called a *plaintiff* once a lawsuit is filed by the claimant. Both terms are used to describe the third party presenting a claim.

[4]A theory of liability is the claimant attorney's basis for presenting the claim against the insured. It will involve some type of legal theory to be able to sustain the claim in the event of litigation. For example, a theory of liability could be that the insured failed to maintain the walkway where the claimant fell down and also had actual notice of the defective condition in the form of prior written complaints to the building tenants.

[5]Special damages are expenses incurred by the claimant or plaintiff as a result of the accident, such as medical and hospital expenses, wage loss, property damage, and other out-of-pocket expenses.

[6]Often, the lawsuit requires either 20 or 30 days to provide a formal answer to the complaint, which may not be an adequate amount of time to respond. The adjuster may request an extension of time to answer the complaint. The adjuster should not agree to waive any defenses in exchange for being granted an extension. These defenses can include statutes of limitations, proper and timely service of the complaint, jurisdictional issues, and the like.

tool to evaluate both liability and damage issues. As we discussed in Chapter 10, initial contacts establish the foundation for the claim investigation and adjustment process. These contacts allow the adjuster to evaluate the necessary future investigation by using the information developed during the initial contacts. The scope of the initial contact may include securing comprehensive details of the accident or incident and taking a statement.

Some companies no longer take actual statements. Instead, they either document the interviews in the claim file notes or use statement forms that are sent to the parties involved in the loss for completion and signature. When statements are taken, they can be written or recorded. Written statements are called signed statements. Recorded interviews or statements are taken in person or by telephone. These days, recorded interviews are more common than "signed statements." They are easy to obtain and can be transcribed if necessary. Signed statements can be more restrictive as they are typically written in the first person and generally take much longer. A recorded interview can be secured in about 15 minutes with the ability to ask many initial and follow-up questions based on the answers provided.

Statements can also be taken utilizing computerized recording software. The statement is saved in a wav. or mp3 file format and then maintained in the electronic claim file as an attachment.

When a coverage issue exists, or any other concern requiring the insured's testimony (because the insurer needs information from the insured to further investigate the claim), an examination under oath (EUO) may be requested. This is a formal deposition held in the insurer's attorney's office with a court stenographer present to document the proceeding. The insured may or may not be represented by an attorney. EUOs are prevalent in first-party claims where fraud or misrepresentations are alleged on the part of the insured.

Chapter 12, Claims Process—Claim Statements and Interviews, beginning on page 127, provides a more detailed overview of the statement and interview process.

Use of Experts

Experts should always be considered during the adjustment process. The expert's findings and report will either assist in the defense of the claim or support the claimant's theory of liability. It is important to assign the expert early on in the investigation to be sure the evidence is available in the same condition as it was immediately after the accident. Secure evidence in a safe place after the accident, so that an inspection can be arranged later on if necessary. Generally, experts are not used in small claims; however, if there is a chance of recovery against a responsible party, use of an expert should be considered, weighing the expense against the possible contribution toward a successful recovery.

In automobile and property claims handling, an expert inspection may be called a "cause and origin inspection" in that the expert has been retained to determine how the loss was caused and its origin, such as with a fire loss. When an expert has been retained to reconstruct a serious accident scene, the expert is called an accident reconstructionist. Experts may have advanced credentials and experience, giving them the ability to testify to their findings and opinions. When assigning an expert, it is important to confirm the expert's experience and qualifications by requesting a curriculum vitae (CV), which is a summary of the expert's relevant skills, professional experience, and education.

The following are some of the more common expert types:

- Medical (specialized physicians)
- Engineer (electrical, mechanical, building, civil, chemical, biotechnical)
- Heating, ventilating, and air-conditioning (HVAC)
- Accident reconstructionist
- Accounting expert
- Legal expert
- Economist
- Fraud expert

Investigative and Adjustment Documentation

The claim investigation includes securing various documents relevant to the claim. Examples include leases, contracts, letters, business records, damage estimates, inspection reports, photographs, product information, complaint records, and any other documentation that would add value to the claim result, either negatively or positively. Many of these are discussed in more detail below.

Claim Forms

Claim forms include industry standard forms and state-mandated forms. Each claim form serves a purpose and may be used by an adjuster during the claims process. The claim form will either be sent out by the claims support staff at the request of the adjuster or sent directly by the adjuster.

Claim forms are used during the investigation process to secure investigative information and documentation (such as medical, hospital, and wage records) to further develop the claim, validate or confirm claim information, and direct a claim toward closing. State-mandated forms may include state workers compensation and no-fault or personal injury protection (PIP) forms, or an industry standard form with state-mandated language that has been incorporated into the form based on statutory requirements. For example, the claim form may have a required fraud statement, indicate the statute of limitations, or have other language to protect a claimant's rights. Some examples of claim forms are indicated below:

General claim forms include:

- Releases (for bodily injury and property damage claims)
- Proof of loss and subrogation receipts[7]
- Medical, hospital, and wage authorizations

[7] A subrogation receipt, sometimes referred to as a loan receipt, is a document attached or incorporated into a proof of loss, providing the insurance company with the right of subrogation.

- Driver statement forms
- Witness statement forms
- Vehicle odometer reading forms
- Nonwaiver agreements (See Chapter 12 beginning on page 127.)
- Medical and attending physician report forms
- Building estimate forms
- Contents or personal property list forms
- Affidavit of vehicle theft form
- Affidavit of salvage retention form

State-mandated forms may include:

- PIP application for benefits
- PIP attending physician report
- PIP hospital verification form
- PIP employer wage form
- Workers compensation first notice of injury
- Workers compensation medical report
- Workers compensation employer wage verification form

Letters, E-mail, and Correspondence

Throughout the claims process, there are letters, e-mail, and other correspondence sent and received by the adjuster. This documentation should always be retained in sequential order within the claim file. It is important that letters received, requiring a response, be responded to timely and address any requests. Not only is this good customer service, but it also avoids service or regulatory complaints or noncompliance with state statutes. For example, in some states, if the claimant attorney sends a letter requesting insurance policy information relative to a claim, the adjuster has only 30 days to respond.

Form letters can include claim acknowledgement letters, contact letters, cover letters requesting completion of an attached form (i.e., statement form, release, proof of loss, or PIP form), letters to the claimant attorney requesting special damage documentation, and denial letters. Most form letters are sent electronically from the claim management system.

Just as there are state-mandated forms, there are also stated-mandated letters used during the claims process. Some states, such as New York and California, require that certain language be included within claim letters. The letters are sent to the claimant or insured at the time when the claim is initially acknowledged and throughout the claims process, including status reports and claim denials. For example, in New York, when handling an automobile property damage liability claim, the adjuster must send a letter to the claimant within a specified time period advising that the insured's liability coverage provides coverage for property damage, loss of use, and any other out-of-pocket expense reasonably attributed to the accident, an explanation of comparative negligence and how reimbursement is affected by it, and a request for an estimate and other relevant documentation.

Authorizations

Throughout the claims process, the adjuster needs to secure information or documentation that can only be obtained with authorizations signed or executed by the party releasing the records. The claim authorizations are typically sent out by the claims support unit or directly by the adjuster, and may be sent to the claimants or insureds or to their legal representatives. Claim authorizations will be sent early in the claims process. For example, when medical or wage claims are presented, the adjuster should request all medical and wage records as soon as possible.

Estimates and Appraisals

Estimates are written projections of damages. They are used in most automobile and property damage liability claims as well as first-party property claims. Generally, the adjuster requests a damage estimate before assigning a field adjuster to inspect the damages. The estimate is requested to determine the extent of the damages and whether an appraisal is necessary. Estimates are written by a third party who has an interest in repairing the damages, such as a body shop, contractor, or other repair facility.

An appraisal is different from an estimate. The appraisal is written by the field adjuster based on his or her actual inspection of the damages, often using computer estimating software. The appraisal should be written on an agreed or binding appraisal basis, or it ends up simply being another estimate. An agreed appraisal means that the adjuster's appraisal has been agreed to by the body shop or contractor that has agreed to repair the damages for the agreed upon amount. The agreed appraisal should always be with the claimant's or insured's body shop or contractor of choice.

All vehicle total losses require a total loss evaluation report (including salvage comments and other required calculations) prepared by the appraiser as part of the adjustment process. The total loss evaluation report is prepared by an automobile appraiser and involves vehicles considered to be a total loss. the total loss evaluation report is prepared in conjunction with an automobile appraisal and includes a detailed valuation of the vehicle (actual cash value). The report may also include an indication of salvage value and other costs, such as towing and storage, photographs, and the damage appraisal report indicating that the damages have exceeded the actual cash value of the vehicle. Typically, if the written appraisal is 75–80 percent of the vehicle's actual cash value, the vehicle will be declared a total loss, as the chance for hidden or supplemental damages exists.

When appropriate, vendors may be used to review damage estimates in lieu of an actual physical inspection and appraisal. Automated Computer Estimating (ACE) (http://www.ace-it.com) is one vendor used for this purpose. ACE can also be utilized to review third-party property damage subrogation supporting documentation.

All automobile physical damage, property damage, and general liability claims with damages exceeding a certain dollar threshold, such as $500, should have an appraisal assigned, unless the insurance company's procedures or client's special claims handling instructions differ. The handling adjuster's judgment is utilized when assigning appraisals under the dollar threshold level.

Use of Independent Appraisers

Staff appraisers often assess the value of damage or losses to automobile and property claims. If there are no appraisers on staff, the claims adjuster may use independent appraisers to perform these tasks. The handling adjuster should not need approval to assign an independent appraiser during the claims handling process.

As with independent adjusters, independent appraiser vendors are reviewed and approved prior to making any assignments. Their brochures, services by line of business, insurance certificates, references, tax forms, and fees should be assessed.

Claim File Documentation

Proper claim file documentation is essential to effectively manage the claims process and also to comply with various state claims handling statutes and regulations. All claim file notes are placed in either the hard-copy claim file or within the electronic claim file, avoiding the use of telephone messages or handwritten "sticky" notes. All claim file mail and other correspondence should be date stamped, i.e., stamped with the date received, and then scanned to the claim file if an electronic file system is used. All correspondence pertaining to lawsuits or litigation, claims service complaints (including insurance department complaints), appraisals, and damage estimates is a priority and must be handled promptly.

The subsequent notes by the handling adjuster pertain to individual items completed during the investigation and adjustment process. At every diary review date, or when interim substantive file activity develops, all file notes should comment on the adequacy of the current claim reserves and outline the follow-up items required on diary.

All claim activities documented in the claim file notes need to be clear so that any person reviewing the claim file will know the status of the investigation and adjustment of the claim. The file notes should be concise, but understandable, and not be entered in an abbreviated or cryptic manner. When entering a file contact note, the date, time, full name of the party spoken with, the company name, their position, if applicable, and telephone number should appear in the file note.

All communication, discussions, and interaction between the handling adjuster and claims manager is clearly outlined within the claim file notes, including settlement, payable, and reserve authority. All claim settlement negotiations should be clearly documented in the claim file notes indicating demands and offers discussed during the negotiation process.

Typically, within 15 days from the assignment date, the handling adjuster should have completed most of the initial investigation. Thereafter, the handling adjuster completes claim status reports at various intervals during the claims handling process or at the request of management. Generally, claim status reports include the same information as the adjuster action plan; however, they may be revised or tailored depending on what stage the claim is in. The claim status report provides an explanation of where the claim currently stands, what has been done to date, and what needs to be done in the future.

During the initial 6 months of a claim, claim status reports are required at the 30-, 90-, and 180-day increments and include the same adjuster action plan items referenced above. The claims manager reviews all claims status reports, providing written comments and instructions as necessary in a note format, and further diaries the claim file in accordance with diary management requirements. Any necessary reserve adjustments should be either processed by the claims manager with an explanatory note to the handling adjuster within the claim file, or referred to the handling adjuster with specific instructions.

If the claim file is subject to client large loss reporting, the large loss report should replace the claim status report if the completion dates are within the same time period. A large loss report is a report to management or a client triggered by the reserves (or payments) exceeding a certain predefined level, or a certain type of claim requiring special reporting. The monetary trigger level will vary by company and can be start as low as $25,000. The report may be on a large loss reporting form, in electronic format, or in a word processing document. Large loss reports may be in a captioned report format, as well.

At every review date, the handling adjuster and claims manager need to comment on the adequacy of the current claim reserves. A claim reserve review is generally mandatory on all claim reserves open for 9 months from the initial report date. A case reserve is an estimate of the value of a claim or group of claims not yet paid; an estimate of the amount a particular claim will ultimately be settled for or adjudicated. Insurers will also set reserves for their entire books of business to estimate their future liabilities. See Chapter 17, beginning on page 205, for more information on reserving practices.

Justification for any reserve adjustments should be clearly documented within the claim file notes. If a factor reserve[8] is being converted to a terminal reserve,[9] the notes should reflect any special handling instructions regarding the reserve conversion.

Summary and Conclusion

This chapter focused on claims investigations and the adjustment process, the foundation for the evaluation and assessment of a claim. Although this chapter did not include every aspect of the claim investigation or adjustment process, it did illustrate how important the investigation is and how it interrelates with claim reporting. Timely completion of the investigation is essential so that claim can be evaluated early on and not stretched out over a long period of time. Late investigations cause other problems such as witnesses not being available or having poor recollection.

Chapters 21 through 30 (pages 271–354) provide specific claims handling guidelines for various types of claims.

[8]Factor reserves are temporary values that are set before further investigation is conducted. They are explained in more detail in Chapter 16. Similar to average value reserves, the factor reserve is entered initially and then converted at a later date to an individual case reserve.

[9]A terminal reserve is an exposure based reserve which represents what the claim facility would expect to pay on a claim at that point in time, based on what is known to date.

CHAPTER 12: CLAIMS PROCESS— STATEMENTS AND INTERVIEWS

For many years, the insurance claims industry has used statements and interviews during the claims handling process to document witness accounts of an accident or incident. This chapter examines these two methods in detail.

Statement Basics

There are various methods of taking statements, including a signed statement, a recorded statement, or a statement with a court reporter or stenographer present. Signed statements are written and may have a better chance of being admissible into evidence at the time of trial. Recorded statements, or recorded interviews, are easier to take and can capture more information in a shorter period of time. Sworn statements made in front of a court reporter who administers an oath to the person being interviewed are the most effective method of taking a statement, and usually involve attorneys being present. Lastly, an affidavit may be taken, which is a sworn statement witnessed by a notary public.

The most important aspect of the statement is to be sure the statement is accurate and truthful. The statement must also meet its intended purpose of documenting the facts about an accident or incident. There are many reasons why a statement may not be accurate or truthful. For example:

- The witness has poor recollection of the events or accident.
- A head injury impacts the ability to remember the details.
- A witness is too young to accurately describe the events.
- A witness intentionally holds back information that could be detrimental to the claimant's position or defense.
- A witness is protecting another person.
- Too much time has passed since the accident for any reasonable person to accurately remember specific details.
- A fraudulent and/or criminal act has been committed.

Statements are typically taken during the initial claims handling stages; however, if witnesses are located or come forth later on, the statement could be taken years later. Adjusters take statements as part of the investigative process to develop factual information to properly evaluate liability and damages. The purpose of the statement is also for the insurance company or third-party administrator (TPA) claims staff to evaluate the claim to determine the insurance company's obligations under the insurance policy.

The job of the claims adjuster is not to try to trick the person being interviewed into saying something that can be used against them at a later date. The adjuster's job is to gather the factual information to evaluate the claim. The adjuster should not ask leading questions that could cause the witness to change the facts. Open-ended questions are acceptable, as the responses may lead to other issues requiring further questioning.

Most claimant attorneys will advise their clients to refuse the request to take a statement, whether over the telephone or in person, without an attorney being present. It is rare that claimants' attorneys will allow their clients to provide statements in liability claims. The reason is that the claimant attorney may be concerned that the statement could contain information detrimental to their client's claim. They might also prefer their client be deposed during litigation rather than making a statement. The defense will have an option to depose the claimant, but only after litigation has been filed and the discovery process has begun.

By not having the claimant's statement from the outset, the claims adjuster is forced to evaluate the claim based solely on all other available information obtained from the investigation, such as statements from the insured and witnesses, police reports, photos, and diagrams. If the claimant's statement is favorable to the claimant's claim, it could be beneficial for the claimant to voluntarily provide a statement.

The policyholder or insured[1] must provide a recorded or signed statement to comply with the insurance contract. If the insured refuses to provide a statement, the adjuster should determine the name of the insured's attorney and then make arrangements to take the statement at the attorney's office. There are reasons for insureds not providing a statement. The insureds may have criminal proceedings or companion litigation pending from the accident that could jeopardize their defense.

If a coverage issue is pending, a statement should not be taken from the insured until a nonwaiver agreement[2] is secured or a reservation of rights letter[3] is issued. If the claims adjuster initiates the claim investigation prior to securing a nonwaiver agreement or issuing a reservation of rights

[1]This includes the driver who was operating the insured vehicle in an automobile accident.

[2]A nonwaiver agreement is a form of reservation of rights used in property and casualty claims (most often in property and inland marine claims). The primary difference between the reservation of rights letter and the nonwaiver agreement is that the nonwaiver agreement is signed by both the insurance company representative and the insured and is, therefore, considered a bilateral agreement. Nonwaiver agreements are usually brief and do not go into any detail with respect to the coverage issue and policy language. They may be used by the field claims staff and sometimes by the desk adjuster. Nonwaiver agreements are used as a method to continue with the investigation and the adjustment of a claim, with each party understanding that a potential coverage issue exists. It preserves the rights of both the insurance company and the insured.

[3]A reservation of rights letter (sometimes referred to as an "R of R letter") reserves the insurer's right to deny coverage and/or withdraw from the defense of the claim at a future date. The letters should be comprehensive and cite all the applicable policy language, including the insuring agreement, definitions, exclusions, exceptions, and conditions. The letters should always be sent certified mail, return receipt requested, along with a separate letter to the named insured, with a copy to the agent and any additional insureds requesting coverage under the policy. The reservation of rights letter should be sent as soon as the adjuster is in a position to formulate a coverage opinion, within 30 days from the initial claim report date or the date of receipt of the summons and complaint. Be careful in the issuance of reservation of rights letters and know the jurisdiction and state laws. Some states may require the insured to acknowledge and sign the reservation of rights letter for it to be valid.

letter, the insurer could be estopped and the company's rights to disclaim coverage waived.[4]

Never force a witness to provide a statement or make comments that could be interpreted as the statement was made under duress. If a claimant or insured indicates that they wish to consult with an attorney before providing a statement, that is their right. Their request should be honored. Some states have laws holding that the adjuster may not take a statement from a hospitalized claimant within a certain number of days after the accident.

An adjuster's job is to gather factual information. Unfortunately, the factual information gathered may be used to deny the claimant's claim or cause it to be severely compromised. Obviously, this is the primary reason for the claimant attorney to advise their client to refuse to provide the statement without the attorney being consulted or present.

An adjuster should never use trickery or deceit when securing a statement from a claimant or insured. Claims adjusters do not have a very good reputation in the industry. The reasons for this involve unscrupulous, unethical, or poorly trained adjusters who are looking for ways to deny a claim, as opposed to simply conducting the investigation to accurately evaluate liability and damages. Some adjusters think every claim they handle is fraudulent in terms of the accident facts or the injuries and damages. This is not the right attitude to take and only contributes to adjusters' poor reputation. It's also why most states have enacted unfair claim practice regulations that are designed to protect both the insured and third-party claimants.

Mentioning these issues in this particular chapter is important as the statement is typically taken at the initial stages of the claims investigation, which usually establishes the foundation for initial evaluation of the claim. The topic of adjuster behavior and ethics is further discussed in Appendix E beginning on page 409.

Statement Process and Guidelines

The remainder of this chapter discusses the statement process. Various guidelines utilized to take statements are provided in Appendix C beginning on page 369.

Signed Statements

Signed statements are often taken on lined paper in the presence of the claimant, insured, or witness. Carbon paper or noncarbon paper (NCR paper)[5] can be used to provide a copy of the statement to the person providing the statement. In the alternative, a copy of the statement should be sent to the person by mail or e-mail. Some technologically proficient adjusters may use a laptop to take the signed statement and send the statement back for signature. (*Note:* This may not be as effective as a handwritten signed statement, signed at the time it was taken.) Others use a per-

[4] A waiver is generally the voluntary surrender of a right or privilege. Waivers can be written or oral. Estoppel occurs as a result of the waiver, precluding the person who voluntarily surrendered their right or privilege from asserting that right later on.

[5] NCR paper is an alternative to carbon paper and is used to make a copy of an original, handwritten document without the use of electronics.

Page 1 of 2

May 31, 2008 at 9:00AM
139 Main Street
Windsor, CT 06095

Today's date is 5/31/08 at 9:00am. My name is Nancy P. Johnson and I reside at 139 Main Street, Windsor, CT 06095. I have lived at this address for five years. My home telephone number is 860-668-1956. My work number is 860-456-1390. My cell number is 860-490-6790. I am single, age 35 and my date of birth is 4/6/73. My social security number is 044-36-1247. I am employed by Century Realty located at 45 Carson Avenue, Windsor, CT 06095, as a realtor, and have been for the last five years. My manager's name is Michael Peterson. On 5/27/08, at 9:15am, I was involved in an accident at McDonald's Restaurant located at 1482 Route 22, Bloomfield, CT 06002. I was on my way to work and stopped at the restaurant to get breakfast and coffee. I was not under the influence of alcohol, drugs or any other medication at the time of the accident. My work day begins at 10:00am and I was not in a rush to get to work. I was alone at the time of the accident. The accident took place on the walkway to the left of the restaurant, leading to the entrance of the restaurant. The concrete walkway is approximately five feet wide and thirty feet long with grass on both sides of the walkway. At approximately ten feet from the entrance, the walkway had a crack in the concrete about seven inches wide and three inches deep, in the center of the walkway. The walkway had no obstructions, or other defects, foreign objects or foreign substances, and was otherwise well maintained. There were no mats or carpets on the walkway. I was walking at a normal pace, looking straight ahead when I tripped and fell in the hole. I was carrying my pocketbook but nothing else. I do not wear glasses, was not wearing sun glasses at the time of the accident, and I was not using a cell phone at the time of the accident. The weather was clear and dry with a temperature of 80 degrees. I was wearing a blue pants suit, no hat, no coat or jacket, with low rubber heels no higher than an half inch. The area where the crack in the concrete was located had no warning signs, construction tape, fences or barriers. I have never observed the crack in the past as this was my first visit to the restaurant. As I walked over the

X Nancy P. Johnson X Beth Lawson

Page 2 of 2

May 31, 2008 at 9:00AM
139 Main Street
Windsor, CT 06095

crack in the concrete, I tripped and fell to the ground. The toe of my right foot became caught in the hole causing me to trip and fall. When I fell, I used my hands to break my fall to the ground. As a result of the accident, I fractured my left wrist and tore my clothing. The Bloomfield Volunteer Ambulance Company arrived and transported me to the hospital for emergency room treatment at Hartford Hospital located in Hartford, CT. The Bloomfield Police Department also arrived and took a report. At the hospital, I recieved X-rays and an evaluation from the emergency room attending physician. The wrist fracture was casted with no surgery. Thereafter, I recieved treatment with an orthopedic Surgeon who is Dr. Peter Quinn, located at 34 Asylum Street, Hartford, CT. The treatment consisted of additional x-rays, orthopedic evaluation and prescribed medication. I continue to be under Dr. Peter Quinn's care. I am currently disabled from work at Century Realty. Dr. Peter Quinn has indicated that I will be disabled for four weeks. I earn $50,000 per year and not being paid by my employer while I am out of work. I have never been involved in any prior accidents nor have I ever sustained any prior injuries. I have no physical impairments or disabilities. The accident was witnessed by David Greco who reside at 578 Echo Avenue, Windsor Locks, CT 06096. Mr. Greco was leaving the restaurant when I fell. After the accident occurred, the restaurant manager, whose name I do not recall, came out to help me. The manager is about six feet tall, 180 pounds, brown hair and wearing a blue McDonald's shirt and hat. He had also called 911 for an ambulance. The restaurant manager said that the hole in the concrete had been there for three days, due to excavation and repairs by a contractor as a result of a water main leak. The contractor was apparently returning the following week to complete the repairs to the walkway. The restaurant manager indicated that there were orange warning cones in front of, and in back of, the hole, but apparently stolen by unknown teenagers the night before. I have nothing else to add to this statement. I HAVE READ THE ABOVE TWO PAGES OF THIS STATEMENT AND IT IS THE TRUTH TO THE BEST OF MY KNOWLEDGE.

X Nancy P. Johnson
Nancy P. Johnson
139 Main Street
Windsor, CT 06095

Witness X Beth Lawson
444 Route 168
Suffield, CT. 06078

sonal computer tablet, which can accommodate a handwritten or typed statement and signed electronically.

The adjuster will actually write the statement in their own handwriting, as interview questions are asked and responses are given. The process is much more time consuming than other statement methods, as the adjuster must ask questions and then write the answers. The signed statement is written in the first person and reads like story. It can take time to formulate questions between sentences and may involve discussion or clarification between the adjuster and the person providing the statement. The statements can be lengthy or short, depending on the status as a claimant, insured, or witness.

Negative Statements

Sometimes, adjusters take negative statements to rule out any factual knowledge of the accident or incident and to prevent the witness from coming forward later to provide inaccurate or untruthful testimony. An example would be when an adjuster asks a potential witness whether he actually saw the accident. He says he did not. The adjuster records this negative statement to ensure the witness will not come forward at a later date stating otherwise.

Forum and Format

The environment should be conductive to taking a signed statement. Choose a quiet location with the ability to write on a hard surface. As the statement is being taken, the adjuster writes down the responses to the questions as stated by the person providing the statement. There are no spaces skipped in the statement body, and the sentences run from the left to the right sides of the pages, leaving no room to insert additional text after the statement has been completed and signed.

Typically, the adjuster will utilize a statement guide, which provides a series of questions to be sure all the necessary questions are addressed in the statement. See Appendix C for examples of statement guides for auto, general liability, and workers compensation claims. More experienced adjusters have memorized the statement guides and can take a statement without referring the actual guide during the statement taking process.

The statement will begin with the date, time, and address of where the statement is being taken indicated in the upper right. The current page of the total number of pages (e.g., page 1 of 3) is indicated to the left; this is entered after the statement is completed. The last line of each page (except the last page) should be left blank for signatures of the person being interviewed and a witness or the adjuster taking the statement. The person providing the statement should read the statement to be sure it is accurate and truthful. Any corrections made should be initialed by the interviewee.

On the last page of the statement, the following should be written after the last sentence: "I have read the above __ pages of this statement, and it is the truth to the best of my knowledge." The next line of the statement, to the left, should have the signature, printed name, and residential address of the person being interviewed. On the same lines, to the right, the witness or the adjuster taking the statement should print their name, business address, and signature. A slanted line should then be drawn from the rest of the page, starting from underneath the last line on the right of the page to the lowest left corner of the page, blocking out the ability to add any information after the statement has been signed.

Advantages and Disadvantages

The advantages of a signed statement are that it preserves evidence, is actually signed by the person providing the statement, is easier to read as it flows like a story, requires no transcription, and is more apt to be admissible into evidence at the time of a hearing or trial. The disadvantages of a signed statement are that the process is very time-consuming with most people not wanting to take up to an hour or so to provide a statement, it is a paper product that will require scanning into an electronic claim system, and it is difficult to use a statement guide when taking a statement, as it is cumbersome to look at a statement guide, ask questions, and write down the answers.

Also, the signed statement typically is not as descriptive as a recorded statement, as there may be additional information or conversation about the accident or incident in a recorded interview that would otherwise not be included in the signed statement.

An example of a signed statement from a claimant who tripped and fell at a fast food restaurant can be found on pages 130–131.

Recorded Statements

Recorded statements or interviews are typically taken using a recording device, which can be a portable handheld device, a desktop tool, or a feature built into the telephone system (with recording software), including Voice Over Internet Protocol (VOIP) virtual telephone systems.

Many years ago, recorded statements were taken using a recording device with a belt which had grooves, similar to a music record. Eventually, standard cassette tapes were used, graduating to the usage of mini-cassette tapes. The cassette tapes were labeled and placed in an envelope along with a handwritten summary of the statement details. The recorded statement envelope was then placed in the hard copy claim file. The claim file jacket could become quite thick if there were many statements included. There was no way to determine the number of statements taken by an individual adjuster as the statements were contained in each individual claim file, with no master record.

Nowadays, most adjusters use mini-cassette tapes with a recorder or use a digital recorder which produces a computer file such as a wav or mp3 file. Many insurers and claim facilities integrate their statement-taking process into their telephone systems, storing the record in a computer format. There are various vendors that provide Internet Web portals for statement taking, such as N2uitive (http://www.n2uitive.com). With these advances in technology, claims managers can now review the statements easily online and also track the volume and quality of statements by adjuster, claims office, and company.

Forum and Format

Recorded statements can be taken in most environments, as long as the interviewee's voice can be heard. For example, if the adjuster is at the scene of an accident or on a construction site, a recorded statement can be taken very easily with a portable recording device. Also, the adjuster can ask more questions, allowing the person being interviewed to expand more freely on their answers. An adjuster can secure much more information in a recorded statement as opposed to a signed statement. Also, the time necessary to secure a recorded statement is much less than what it takes to secure a signed statement.

Recorded statements are taken using a question-and-answer format. The adjuster asks questions concerning the accident or incident, waits for appropriate responses, and then moves onto the next question. Throughout the interview process, the adjuster may change the line of questioning, depending on the answers being provided. Recorded statements tend to be more authentic as the responses are in the interviewee's own voice. One major difference between a recorded statement and signed statement is that there is not much time between questions and answers to consider a response. The whole process is less time-consuming than taking a signed statement and typically provides much more detail concerning the information necessary to evaluate liability and damages.

The adjuster should prepare the person being interviewed by explaining the recorded statement process and the questions involved, the time necessary to complete the statement, and that the interviewee must be amenable to the process. An adjuster should never take a recorded statement without the permission of the person being interviewed. If the person being interviewed requests that the recording device be turned off, this request should always be honored. If the person requests a transcription of the recorded statement, this request should be complied with as soon as practicable.

Recorded statements are not routinely transcribed. The statement will be transcribed if the person providing the statement, or their legal representative, requests a copy. Transcription will also be necessary if the claim moves into the litigation stages or arbitration is filed. Occasionally, a defense attorney will request that the witness sign the recorded statement transcription on the last page to authenticate and attest to its content.

Five Phases

There are five phases of the recorded statement process. The first phase involves the introduction or opening format. Here, the person being interviewed is identified as well as the date and time stated. Permission to secure the interview needs to be asked and obtained. In the second phase, the adjuster secures all personal information of the person being interviewed, such as name, address, telephone, date of birth, Social Security Number, and marital status. In the third phase, the adjuster asks questions regarding the details of the accident or incident, and in the fourth, questions regarding injuries and/or damages are asked. In the fifth phase, the adjuster closes the interview by asking whether the person being interviewed understood all the questions being asked, whether any additional information would like to be provided, making sure that the answers were true and correct, and confirming that permission was granted to record the interview.

Exhibit 12.1 provides an example of the five phases of the recorded statement process.

Exhibit 12.1: Five Phases Recorded Statement

#1—Opening

This is John Smith at telephone number (800) 458–3232, extension 1123. It is now 3:00 pm on January 3, 2010. I speaking with Janet Burke regarding an accident which occurred on December 13, 2009. Ms. Burke, do you understand that I am recording this interview? Do I have your permission to record this interview?

#2—Personal Information and Identification

Personal information of the person being interviewed:

- Name, address, and home telephone number
- Mobile telephone number
- E-mail address
- Any aliases
- Date of birth
- Social Security Number
- Marital status (spouse's name)
- Dependents—name and ages
- Parents' names (if minor)
- Occupation
- Employer's name, address, and telephone number
- Other employment
- Physical impairments

#3—Accident or Incident Details

Refer to the individual statement guides for questions to ask.

#4—Injuries and/or Damages

- Describe the nature and extent of injuries (in detail).
- How were injuries caused?
- What treatment was received at the scene of the accident?
- Were you rendered unconscious?

continued

Exhibit 12.1: Five Phases Recorded Statement (cont.)

- What treatment was received after the accident?
- Was an ambulance called, or were police involved?
- What was the name of the hospital or medical facility?
- Was emergency room treatment provided?
- Where you hospitalized (location, duration, and dates)?
- Provide the names and addresses of all treating physicians (with specialty).
- Were x-rays taken? Provide the name of and contact information for the radiologist.
- Describe any previous accidents, injuries, and illnesses (details).
- List the disability dates.
- Were wages paid by your employer? If so, at what rate?
- Lost wages to date?
- What is the expected return to work date?
- What is the expected future disability?
- List all medical and hospital bill expenses to date.
- If this is a fatality claim, please list:
    - Funeral expenses
    - Cost of burial plot
    - Cost of tombstone
    - Length of time between accident and death. Was there conscious pain and suffering?
- List the general property damage details (if applicable).
    - Details of item(s) damaged
    - Age of item
    - Purchase price
    - Repair or replacement cost

#5—Interview Closing

Ms. Burke, do you have any questions? Is there anything else you would like to add about the accident? Were all your answers true and correct to the best of your knowledge? Do you understand that this interview has been recorded? Was the interview recorded with your permission? This is John Smith at telephone number (800) 458–3232, extension 1123. I am ending this interview at this time with your permission.

Advantages and Disadvantages

The advantages of a recorded statement are that the statements tend to be more detailed and are provided directly by the person being interviewed, in their own words. Recorded statements are easier and faster to secure, either by telephone or in person. Typically, a recorded statement can be secured within 10 to 20 minutes. Also, the recorded statement record can be attached directly to the electronic claim file record.

Insurance companies and claim facilities utilize recorded statements because they are less expensive than taking a signed statement. A signed statement can take from 1 to 2 hours, depending on the complexity of the accident involved. Since many claim facilities do not have staff field adjusters, a signed statement will require an assignment to an independent field adjuster to secure the statement. The field adjuster assignment will add to the cost of the claim process.

The disadvantages of recorded statements are few. However, there are issues with regard to making sure that you are actually interviewing the correct person by telephone. Also, if the recorded interview is going to be used as evidence for a hearing or trial, any gaps or noises indicating the recorder was turned off during the interview could cause the entire interview to be inadmissible. Typically, for a recorded interview to be admitted into evidence, the recorded interview must be played for the jury with the person who was interviewed present. In situations where the recording device malfunctions, causing the recorded interview to be either inaudible or incomplete, a second interview will need to be conducted.

It is also important *not* to mention *insurance* or *coverage* during a recorded statement involving a liability claim. In the event the claim reaches the litigation stages, this could preclude the statement from being admissible into evidence, as the jury could prejudicially render a higher verdict if they know insurance is involved.

Sworn Statements

Sworn statements are more formal than a signed statement or recorded statement. A sworn statement is made in front of a court reporter who administers an oath to the person being interviewed. Usually attorneys are present. This type of statement is the most effective method because it is taken under oath and can be used at the time of trial. After the transcript is reviewed, the person providing the sworn statement must sign the transcript. An affidavit, witnessed by a notary public, may be attached to the sworn statement, attesting to the content of the statement under penalty of perjury.

There are several terms used to describe sworn statements, such as an affidavit, deposition, examination before trial, or examination under oath.

Affidavits

An affidavit is a legal document, consisting of a sworn statement, typically prepared by an attorney, which provides details of a claim. The affidavit is limited in that there is no way to ask questions or rebut the content of the statement. It is basically a notarized sworn statement. Sometimes an attorney will provide an affidavit in lieu of the adjuster taking a statement from the claimant or insured. The person providing the affidavit is called the affiant. Typically, the affiant provides the statement under oath in front of a notary public.

Depositions

A deposition is basically a sworn statement in front of a court reporter who administers an oath to the person being interviewed. Depositions are usually taken before trial by separate attorneys representing the plaintiff and defendant in the litigation process. The defense attorney and the plaintiff attorney have the option to depose each other's clients. Depositions can also be secured from nonparty wit-

Exhibit 12.2: Sample Affidavit

STATE OF ______________

COUNTY OF _____________

APPEARED BEFORE ME, the undersigned Notary on this ___ day of _______, 20___, ________________________, who resides at__________________________, known to me to be a credible person and of lawful age, who upon his or her statement under oath and affirmation states:

____

____

____

(A statement of facts)

____

[Signature of Affiant]

Subscribed and sworn to before me, this ___ day of _________, 20___.

NOTARY PUBLIC

My commission expires: _____________, 20___. *(Notary Seal)*

____

(signature of Notary)

____

(Notary Name)

nesses, meaning those who saw the accident but are not directly involved in the litigation.

Examination before Trial

In some jurisdictions, such as New York, a deposition taken before trial has begun is called an examination before trial has begun.

Examination under Oath (EUO)

A deposition taken prior to any litigation being filed is commonly referred to as an examination under oath. An EUO is ordinarily taken during a first-party claim from a policyholder or a claimant who has a claim for benefits under the policy as an insured. Insurance companies may use the EUO process in an automobile first-party or personal injury protection (PIP) claim, first-party property claims, and claims where fraud or misrepresentation is suspected. The conditions section of the insurance policy provides the insurance company with the right to an examination or statement under oath.

During an EUO, the person being deposed has the right to be represented by legal counsel. A court reporter administers an oath to the person being interviewed. The EUO can be used as an important investigative tool in both automobile and property claims, and is admissible into evidence at the time of trial.

Statement Guides

Statements provide the foundation and framework for the basis of the claim investigation, and ultimately are an important component of the liability and damage analysis. Statements should be taken as soon as possible during the initial stages of the claim process to avoid any memory or recall issues. Naturally, most claims involve statements from parties to the loss. However, some claims with only minor damages may not require a formal statement, while more complex claims will necessitate statements from witnesses and extraneous parties as well. There are also certain types of claims where the statement is taken directly by defense counsel. This ensures the statement is considered to be protected under attorney-client privilege, preventing it from being discoverable in the litigation process.

Statements can be taken from various parties involved in a claim. For example, an automobile claim investigation may require statements from the insured operator, adverse operator, vehicle passengers, the claimant, pedestrians, and any witnesses. Statements may also be taken from the responding police officers. A general liability claim investigation may require statements from the claimant, property owner, insured, ambulance attendant or responding police officer, and any available witnesses. A property claim investigation will typically involve statements from the insured and any witnesses. A workers compensation claim investigation will involve statements of the claimant, employer representative (insured), and any witnesses. Basically, statements should be taken from any party to the loss who might provide important information affecting liability, compensability (workers compensation), and damages.

Many experienced adjusters do not use a formal recorded statement guideline format. However, a recorded statement guideline is recommended and should be utilized. By starting with the statement guide, then listening closely to the person being interviewed, the adjuster can hone in, asking additional questions that probe deeper into the facts of the situation. The recorded statement information also provides a basis for a formal claim report, including the adjuster's evaluation of liability, compensability, and damages. If a recorded statement is taken in person, a diagram by the person being interviewed may assist in conveying the accident details.

It's important for adjusters to be able to visualize how the accident or incident occurred. If the adjuster is unable to visualize the accident, he or she will be unable to form the proper questions. The line of questioning should be orderly and consistent with the recorded statement guide. After the statement is transcribed, it should read as a question-and-answer document, providing the reader with a complete story of the accident. If the adjuster haphazardly asked questions in no particular order, and jumps around during the interview process, the statement will end up being very confusing and potentially not useful.

Various formal statement guides that can be utilized by adjusters handling different lines of business are provided in Appendix C beginning on page 369. The first phase (opening) and fifth phase (closing) of the recorded statement guide have not been included in the guides below, as these phases have been illustrated above and are basically the same for all recorded statements.

The guides cover the basics for typical claims. However, situations tend to differ, and an individual claim may require additional information. Adjusters should supplement the guide with whatever questions are necessary to properly evaluate the claim. If there are complicated factual issues, coverage questions, or legal issues involved, the claims adjuster may need to consult the claims supervisor or manager for specific instructions. There is a direct correlation between the preparation necessary to take the statement and the resulting quality of the statement. Again, it is important that claims adjusters not rush when taking statements and listen very closely to the responses given by the person being interviewed.

Summary and Conclusion

In this chapter, the various types of statements used by adjusters were reviewed, including signed statements, recorded statements, and sworn statements. The most important aspect of the statement is to be sure the statement is accurate and truthful. The statement must also meet its intended purpose of documenting the facts about an accident or incident. The adjuster's job is to gather the factual information to evaluate the claim.

An adjuster should never use trickery or deceit when securing a statement from a claimant or insured. As an industry, adjusters may not have a very good reputation. The reasons for the poor reputation involve unscrupulous, unethical, or poorly trained adjusters who are looking for ways to deny a claim, as opposed to simply conducting the investigation to accurately evaluate liability and damages. Since the statement process may be the only contact with the claimant, insured, or witness, it is important to be forthright and professional.

There are five phases of the recorded statement process: the opening, securing all personal information of the person being interviewed, the details of the accident or incident, the injuries and/or damages, and closing where adjuster asks whether the person being interviewed understood all the questions, whether any additional information would like to be provided, affirming the answers were true and correct, and confirming that permission was granted to record the interview.

The statement is an important tool to record and document the claim investigation, and provides a foundation to evaluate liability, compensability and damages in a claim.

Chapter 13: Claims Process—Coverage Issues

There are two components of coverage in a claim environment: *coverage verification* and *coverage analysis*. Although both are the responsibility of the adjuster and claims manager, the claims support staff may assist in coverage verification when the claim is first set up.

Coverage analysis or evaluation is an important function for an adjuster and claims manager, and requires education, training, and experience to become proficient. As young adjusters become more experienced and advance their professional careers with industry coursework and on-the-job training, they become more proficient at coverage analysis. Understanding and applying coverage to a loss is critical in the claims process, particularly when working with common forms and endorsements utilized during the normal course of business (e.g., commercial auto, general liability, homeowner policies). Since some policy forms and endorsements may have policy language deemed ambiguous by the courts, it is important that the claims staff also understand the local jurisdiction to determine if any caselaw will modify the coverage analysis.

There is no mystery to coverage analysis. Basically, it involves understanding the various sections of the policy as well as other information that can affect the coverage evaluation. This chapter discusses the insurance policy sections, such as the insuring agreement, definitions, conditions, and exclusions, how they affect coverage provided, and then how to convey coverage or noncoverage to the insured/claimant.

Coverage Verification

Coverage verification is one of the most important aspects of the claims handling process and is typically the responsibility of both the handling adjuster and the claims manager, sometimes with the assistance of the claims support staff. The actual process can vary by claims operation. For example, in a traditional insurance company claim environment, the adjuster and manager have access to the policy administration system along with all the forms and endorsements.

To properly set up the claim, then, coverage must first be established in the policy administration system. The claims support staff may set up the initial claim with available information indicated on the first report of claim, such as the named insured, policy number, policy dates, and vehicle information. Other claims operations may have access to a policy administration system through a program administrator or general agent. Lacking that, coverage may need to be verified the old-fashioned way by requesting and reviewing a hard copy of the policy, including declarations, schedules, forms, and endorsements.

Coverage verification needs to come first, before a claims investigation is initiated or the claim is processed. The claim file should be documented with an imaged or scanned copy of the policy declarations page, applicable coverage forms, vehicle schedules, driver and location schedules, and other endorsements as needed. A review of these documents can be referenced in the claims system notes or policy screens. Copies of policy forms and endorsements can usually be requested from the applicable underwriting facility.

Most insurer claims systems, and some third-party administrators (TPAs) are fully interfaced with the policy administration system. This allows full integration of coverage verification with the claims process, eliminating the need to post any policy documents to the claim file record .

As mentioned above, verifying and evaluating coverage rests with the handling claims adjuster and manager. As part of the investigative process, a claims professional will need to look at basic coverage issues before doing an in-depth review of the forms and endorsements. For example, the following coverage issues apply to most losses:

- ***Verify named insured status***—Is the party requesting coverage a named insured under the policy? A named insured is any person, firm, or organization, or any of its members specifically designated by name as an insured in an insurance policy. Named insureds are distinguished from others who may fall within the policy definition of an "insured" but are not specifically named on the policy itself. The first named insured is listed in the policy declarations page; however, there may also be a separate endorsement listing all the other named insureds under the policy
- ***Verify additional insured status***—Is the claimant an additional insured under the policy? An additional insured is a person or organization not automatically included as an insured under an insurance policy, but for whom insured status is arranged, usually by endorsement. A named insured's impetus for providing additional insured status to others may be a desire to protect the other party because of a close relationship with that party (e.g., employees or members of an insured club) or to comply with a contractual agreement requiring the named insured to do so (e.g., customers or owners of property leased by the named insured). While considered an *insured* under the policy, additional insureds do not have the same rights and privileges as the named insureds. It is not uncommon that commercial policies have multiple named insureds and additional insureds. When additional insureds are listed on a policy, they will typically be listed in an endorsement as well.
- ***Determine the coverage period***—Does the loss fall within the policy's effective dates? Was the policy in force the entire coverage period, i.e., not canceled prior to the expiration date? Some claim systems have a built-in edit feature that will not allow a loss to be entered in the claim system if it does not fall within the policy period.
- ***Beware of claims-made policies***—Pay particular attention to the actual claim notice date and any policy provi-

sions that affect coverage written on a claims-made basis (e.g., directors and officers, employment practices liability). Generally, coverage is only provided if the claim is reported during the policy period. However, an extended reporting period endorsement can expand the time during which a claim can be made and covered under the policy, while a prior and pending exclusion precludes coverage for claims that were pending prior to the inception of the policy. A retroactive date provision eliminates coverage for injuries or damage that occurred prior to a specified date, even if the claim is first made during the policy period. Thus, the claim file notes should comment on the actual claim notice date on claims-made policies and also address any of the above issues that might provide or preclude coverage.

- ***Ascertain whether any deductibles apply to the loss***—Does the loss fall within the deductible? Are there any exceptions to the applicability of the deductible? For example, the insured may have purchased full glass coverage under the "other than collision" or "comprehensive" coverage. This would eliminate the comprehensive deductible for all glass losses.

- ***Ensure that the alleged acts are covered under the policy***—Does the applicable liability coverage form provide coverage, and are there any applicable exclusions? For example, if there is claim presented by a manufacturer for damage to its products, the claim would be excluded as there is no coverage for property damage to the insured's own products.

- ***Verify that the location and property are covered***—Is the policy properly endorsed with the location where the loss occurred, and is the property covered (e.g., building or personal property or contents)? This is particularly important when handling property losses, as the adjuster needs to confirm that the location is covered as well as determine the limits on the property covered.

- ***Determine the applicable policy limits***—Are there per occurrence, aggregate per loss, or aggregate per policy period limits? For example, a coverage limit of $1 million/$2 million for product liability means that there is a per occurrence limit of $1 million and an aggregate limit of $2 million. Are there any sublimits that apply to the loss? For example, the policy may provide coverage for property of others with a small limit. Does the damage claim exceed the policy limits?

- ***Verify whether there is other insurance***—Is there other available insurance applying to the loss that could respond on a concurrent or excess basis?

Coverage Analysis

It is very important that the adjuster and claims manager evaluate coverage with the objective to provide coverage and not to deny coverage. The policyholders paid premium dollars for the coverage, and the only time they will receive any benefit is when a claim occurs. The claims professional should explore all available opportunities for coverage, carefully reviewing all coverage forms and endorsements. If the claims professional's coverage evaluation is geared toward a determination as to how a claim can be denied, then the adjuster may not be treating the policyholder fairly and may also be engaging in unethical behavior.

Reading a policy form or endorsement may not be exciting, but must be done to fully understand and evaluate coverage. Adjusters who "skim" the coverage forms for sections that they "think" apply to the loss may miss an important section that affects coverage. Consider the coverage forms or endorsements to be an adjuster's tools of the trade. Without understanding their content or not taking the time to familiarize yourself with their application, you have not fully developed your claims professional skills. Claims adjusters must understand and apply coverage, and then fully explain to the insured how coverage applies to that particular loss. Being less than proficient in this area means a claim may be paid by mistake or denied when the claim was actually covered. This could result in an errors and omissions or bad-faith lawsuit against the adjuster.

Coverage analysis basically consists of evaluating whether a particular claim is covered under the insurance policy. If coverage applies, then there needs to be a determination as to the extent of the defense and indemnity provided under the policy and if there are any coverage limitations. Coverage cannot be properly evaluated unless the adjuster has a complete copy of the policy with all forms, schedules, and endorsements. There is nothing more embarrassing to an adjuster who denies coverage only to learn that the coverage exclusion cited did not apply as the insured had an endorsement buying back the coverage. When evaluating coverage, the coverage forms need to be read, understood, and explained to the insured or claimant. If the adjuster or claims manager cannot understand the policy language, then how can the insured be expected to comprehend it? If in doubt, seek clarification from the underwriter or claims manager.

Remember that "ambiguity" in a policy or coverage form may result in the insured being granted coverage because the insurance policy is a contract of adhesion. This means that the insured must accept or adhere to the entire contract, with all of its terms and conditions. The insurer develops and prints the contract or policy, and the insured typically has to accept it in its entirety or reject it. Note, however, that some amendments are allowed, such as endorsements that restrict or expand coverage. The insurer, though, also writes these endorsements. As a result, courts normally rule that any ambiguities within the policy should be ruled in favor of the party with lesser knowledge (i.e., the named insured). This encourages insurers to draft policies that are clearly written, and it also promotes the use of definitions to help clarify important terms.

To analyze coverage properly, then, there needs to be an understanding of how the insurance policy is structured and where to look to find the necessary information to include in the coverage analysis. Listed below are various provisions and sections of an insurance policy and how they may relate to coverage analysis.[1] In addition, part of the coverage analysis process is to determine whether there is any applicable caselaw or

[1]Portions of this discussion are taken from the online continuing education course *Commercial Lines 101*. Dallas, TX: International Risk Management Institute, Inc., 2006. http://irmi.webce.com/.

state-required amendatory endorsements that could modify the coverage under the policy. Once the coverage analysis is complete, the claim file notes need to be written clearly, outlining the coverage analysis, including reference to the applicable policy forms and endorsements.

Policy Declarations

The policy declarations page(s) provides information about the insured, the policy, and the insurer. It includes items such as the name and address of the insured business, the type of organization (partnership, corporation, LLC), the policy period, policy limits, deductible(s), additional interests (mortgagee or loss payee), and premium. Any endorsements attached to the policy are also normally listed in the declarations pages as well. It is important to make sure that the endorsements being reviewed are actually attached to the policy; they are indicated on the declarations page. The endorsement edition dates are also very important as policy forms and endorsements may change from time to time, expanding or limiting coverage.

Insuring Agreement

The insuring agreement grants the coverage provided by the policy and outlines what the insurer agrees to do, and its obligations and promises, under the [policy] contract. For example, the standard commercial general liability (CGL) insurance policy insuring agreement promises that the insurer will pay for all liability arising from bodily injury or property damage occurring during the policy period within the policy territory. A commercial property policy might promise to pay for all direct damage to insured property arising from any cause, subject to applicable policy exclusions. The insuring agreement places only a few restrictions on the coverage provided by the policy. The real scope of coverage, therefore, is determined by the policy's exclusions and definitions.

Where multiple coverages are provided in a single policy, each coverage section is likely to have its own insuring agreement. This allows the policy drafters to tailor the insurer's promise for each coverage area. For example, the insuring agreement under a liability coverage form might obligate the insurer to:

> pay on behalf of the insured all sums which the insured shall become legally obligated to pay as damages because of bodily injury or property damage arising out of the ownership, maintenance, or use of the insured premises and all operations incidental thereto.

Policy Conditions

Insurance contracts are conditional contracts. This means that the insurance company's obligations to pay for damages are conditional based on an occurrence being covered under the policy. The policy conditions place contractual obligations on both the insurer and the insured or policyholder. For example, if the insured does not pay the premium, the insurance company does not owe coverage. If a claim is not reported timely, the insurance company could disclaim coverage for late notice. The insurance company could also disclaim coverage for failure to cooperate—a policy condition as well.

The conditions section enumerates both the insured's and the insurer's rights and responsibilities under the policy. For example, the terms under which the policy may be canceled are set forth here. Other items typically addressed in the conditions section of an insurance policy include subrogation rights, the insured's duties in the event of a loss, and how losses will be apportioned between insurers when more than one policy applies to a loss.

Policy Definitions

Key words and phrases in insurance policies are often assigned precise definitions as they are used in the policy. Undefined terms are assigned their ordinary meanings, such as those found in a regular dictionary. The definitions of key terms should be carefully studied as they can play just as important a role as exclusions in determining coverage under a policy. Defined terms are usually marked in some way when they appear in the policy; some policies use bold print, while others use italics or quotation marks to denote defined terms. Most policies define terms in a separate "Definitions" section, but sometimes the same term will be assigned different meanings in different sections of the policy. In that instance, the term may be defined separately in each section of the policy.

For example, "occurrence" could be defined as a continuous or repeated exposure which results in "bodily injury" or "property damage" neither expected nor intended by the insured. "Bodily injury" is often defined as bodily injury, sickness, disease sustained by a person, including death. "Property damage" is defined as physical injury to tangible property, including all resulting loss of use of that property. There are over 20 definitions in the standard general liability policy form. It is important that adjusters know them all and understand the implications of each.

Policy Exclusions

Exclusions limit the coverage granted in the insuring agreement. Exclusions can apply to specified perils (earthquake or flood), certain types of property (trees or money), or specified types of losses (testing losses or intentional losses). For example, the standard workers compensation and employers liability policy excludes bodily injury occurring outside the United States, its territories or possessions, or Canada; however, the exclusion does not apply if the injury is to a citizen of the United States or Canada who is temporarily outside these countries. Most exclusions serve one of the following purposes:

- Eliminating or reducing overlapping coverage
- Removing coverage not needed by typical insureds
- Reducing the incentive to create losses and providing the insured with an incentive to try to prevent losses
- Removing coverage for uninsurable risks

An example of a policy exclusion is the "expected or intended injury exclusion," which is defined as "bodily injury" or "property damage" expected or intended from the standpoint of the insured.

Policy Endorsements

Because most insurance policies are drafted to meet the common needs of a variety of insured businesses, some insureds' needs will not be adequately addressed by the policies. Rather than drafting a specially designed policy for each insured with special needs, called a "manuscript policy," insurers use endorsements to tailor the terms of the standard and nonstandard policies to the needs of the individual insured businesses. (Sometimes endorsements are called "riders," most commonly in commercial crime insurance.)

Some of the purposes for which endorsements are used include the following:

- Granting additional coverage
- Restricting or eliminating coverage provided in the basic policy
- Modifying coverage by changing or adding definitions
- Modifying the rights of the insurer or insured by changing or adding conditions
- Scheduling covered persons, projects, or property

Standard endorsements exist for many common modifications, such as adding another party as an additional insured on the policy. For example, manufacturers are commonly required to add vendors as additional insureds on their general liability policies, and standard endorsements are available for achieving this.

If no standard endorsement is available for making the desired modifications, a manuscript endorsement may be drafted and added to the policy. Legal counsel is generally consulted in drafting manuscript endorsements to ensure they accomplish the intended purpose and to avoid making unintended alterations to the policy. As these are, by definition, nonstandard endorsements, it's important for adjusters to read them very carefiully and seek clarification from the claims manager or underwriter if needed.

Some endorsements are straightforward and brief; others resemble a separate insurance policy, having their own grant of coverage, exclusions, and conditions. Although they may seem to stand on their own, endorsements are attached to the policy, and are thus subject to the same terms and conditions of the policy, except where they specifically declare the terms of the basic policy to be changed or replaced by those in the endorsement.

Endorsements are often added to policies during the policy term. Adjusters need to look for any such endorsements that are added midterm and carefully review them to understand their impact. Insurers have very limited rights to alter the coverage provided by an insurance policy after its proposal is accepted and bound, so any midterm coverage restrictions may be negotiable. All endorsements should be physically attached to the policy.

Policy Exceptions

These are typically included in the exclusion section of the applicable insurance policy, carving out coverage as an exception to the exclusion. An example of a policy exception would be the policy exclusion for "expected or intended injury," which is defined as "bodily injury" of "property damage" expected or intended from the standpoint of the insured. The second half of the exclusion indicates that this exclusion does not apply to "bodily injury" resulting from reasonable force to protect persons or property. This reverses the exclusion by providing an exception and grants coverage for an intentional act only under the circumstances indicated.

State Amendatory Endorsements

These endorsements are mandated by various states, based on individual policy form filings. It is very important to review state amendatory endorsements as they may change the language in the base policy forms and/or other applicable policy endorsements. These endorsements will be available from the underwriters; however, they may also be found on various state insurance department websites.

An example of an amendatory endorsement may be in a personal auto policy which specifically addresses when the personal auto policy provides coverage for a rental vehicle, modifying the personal auto policy form by expanding coverage.

Policy Schedules

Policy schedules, typically located after the policy declarations pages, provide important information relative to covered vehicles on commercial automobile policies. A policy schedule in a commercial auto policy will include a list of all the scheduled vehicles, providing specific rating and coverage information. On property policies, property locations and pertinent coverage information is shown on the policy schedule, such as exposure, locations, rating, and other important coverage information. The schedule of locations will list the location address, the buildings, and business personal property at each location, including specific rating and coverage information.

Caselaw Interpretation or Statutes

It is important for adjusters to note that certain caselaw or statutes may change the interpretation or applicability of the policy forms and endorsements. This information is typically available from local defense counsel retained to defend claims for the claim facility. If the claim facility is an insurance company Claims Department, then the insurer may have a house counsel[2] legal operation, where this information is available. A good source for caselaw interpretation and statutes is the litigation unit of the claim facility. Given their communication exchange with defense counsel on many claims, they will be able to provide much of the necessary information on any given jurisdiction.

Coverage Position

It is very important to review all the allegations either in the claim notice or lawsuit pleadings. These allegations will establish the framework for the claims adjuster's coverage analysis. A good approach is to list all the allegations in numerical sequence and address the coverage for each allegation or cause of action separately.

[2]House counsel is a law firm owned by an insurance company. The law firm generally has a separate location, and the signage and stationery will indicate the name of the law firm and not the insurance company name (i.e., Smith & Johnson, Attorneys at Law). Insurance companies may establish house counsel operations to reduce legal costs in lieu of using an outside law firm. The house counsel attorney must make sure to avoid any conflict of interest, as the policyholder of the insurance company is their client.

When a claim facility is faced with a potential or real coverage issue, there are certain steps that need to be taken quickly. If coverage is not accepted (if coverage is accepted, there will be no coverage issues raised in the claim), then the next step typically involves the preparation of a coverage position letter or a nonwaiver agreement. A coverage position letter can be either a reservation of rights letter or a coverage disclaimer letter.

Coverage Position Letter

After finishing the analysis of each allegation, a coverage position letter is developed. A coverage position letter should include the following:

- Introduction and policy information (i.e., named insured, policy number, effective dates, and policy limits)
- Acknowledgement of the claim or lawsuit (i.e., venue, style of case, amount claimed)
- Details of documents submitted acknowledging the coverage review and analysis
- A review of each allegation or cause of action, citing specific corresponding policy language such as the insuring agreement, exclusions, definitions, etc., outlining the insurer's position on coverage (*Note:* this is only done when a claim is not covered.)
- Closing remarks indicating whether the policy will respond, if the insurer intends to reserve its rights, or if coverage will be denied (The closing remarks section is a summary of the insurance company's position at that time, what the next steps are necessary either for the insurance company or policyholder, and any relevant information being requested from the policyholder.)
- Thanking the insured for the submission and offering future assistance to answer questions

Reservation of Rights Letter

A reservation of rights letter (sometimes referred to as an "R of R letter") reserves the insurer's right to deny coverage and/or withdraw from the defense of the claim at a future date. The letters should be comprehensive and cite all the applicable policy language, including the insuring agreement, definitions, exclusions, exceptions, and conditions.

The letters should always be sent certified mail, return receipt requested, with a separate letter to the named insured, along with a copy to the insurance agent or broker as well as the applicable additional insureds requesting coverage under the policy, if that's the case. The reservation of rights letter should be sent as soon as the adjuster is in a position to formulate a coverage opinion. This should be no longer than 30 days from the initial claim report date or receipt of the summons and complaint. Be careful in the issuance of reservation of rights letters and know the jurisdiction and state laws.

Here are some important points relative to reservation of rights letters:

- Failure to cite the applicable policy language, or issuance of an ineffective letter, may result in a flawed defensible coverage position, resulting in the waiver of coverage defenses and being estopped from raising any other future coverage defenses. For example, a claim is submitted 6 months after the loss, but the driver is not listed on the policy, or is specifically excluded as a driver. If the initial coverage position letter indicated that the insurer was reserving its rights under the policy because the vehicle operator was not listed as a driver or was an excluded driver, but failed to raise the "late notice" issue, the insurance company may be precluded, or "estopped" from raising the late notice issue at a later date.

- Some states require specific language on all reservation of rights letters, such as mandatory fraud language warning the policyholder of the consequences of submitting a fraudulent claim or their rights to submit a complaint to the state insurance department if they disagree with a coverage denial.

- Some states require the reservation of rights letters to be signed and acknowledged by the insured, and will not uphold *unilateral* reservation of rights letters. A unilateral reservation of rights letter means that the letter is written by the insurance company or claim facility to protect its rights under the policy and is then sent to the policyholder. The policyholder's rights may not be protected in the letter as it was written by one party, and then signed by the insurer or claim facility. A nonwaiver agreement would be considered *bilateral,* as it protects both the insurance company and the policyholder, and is signed by both parties.

- A late reservation of rights letter could result in a waiver of any policy defenses.

- In some states, a reservation of rights letter triggers the insured's right to retain its own counsel to defend the insured for the noncovered causes of action, i.e., detailed allegations within a writ, petition, or complaint.

A reservation of rights letter is not forever! Claims adjusters must eventually take a coverage position to accept coverage, partially deny coverage for certain aspects of the claim only, or deny coverage for the total claim.

Nonwaiver Agreements

A form of reservation of rights used in property and casualty claims, nonwaiver agreements are used as a method to continue with the investigation and the adjustment of a claim, with each party understanding that a potential coverage issue exists. It preserves the rights of both the insurance company and the insured. They are used more often in the handling of property and inland marine claims, but can be used in liability claims as well. The primary difference between the reservation of rights letter and the nonwaiver agreement is that the nonwaiver agreement is signed by both the insurance company representative and the insured and is, therefore, considered a bilateral agreement because both parties agree.

Typically, nonwaiver agreements are brief and do not go into any detail with respect to the coverage issue and policy language. They may be used by the field claims staff and sometimes by the desk adjuster.

Coverage Disclaimer Letter

A coverage disclaimer letter is a letter directed to the insured denying coverage for the claim in its entirety or for only certain aspects of the claim. The primary difference is that a coverage disclaimer formally denies coverage. It should be noted that a reservation of rights letter can incorporate a partial coverage disclaimer.

The coverage disclaimer letter should be comprehensive and cite all the applicable policy language, including the insuring agreement, definitions, exclusions, and conditions. As with reservation of rights letters, the letter should always be sent certified mail, return receipt requested, with a separate letter to the named insured, and if the claim is made by an additional insured, to the applicable additional insureds requesting coverage under the policy.

Summary and Conclusion

Conducting the coverage analysis and conveying the insurer's position is one of the most important aspects of the claims process. It sets the stage, so to speak, for what is to come. Therefore, it is crucial to review and evaluate coverage very carefully.

This chapter referred to many legal terms that novice adjusters may not be familiar with. Refer to Appendix G, Legal Theory and Doctrine, for further information and explanations.

Another source for coverage verification and analysis advice is coverage counsel, i.e., attorneys retained to assist with the coverage analysis depending on the complexity and severity of the coverage issues. When appropriate, seek their help to prepare coverage position letters if necessary and warranted. Although coverage evaluation is generally the responsibility of the claims professional, consideration should be given to assistance from coverage counsel, particularly if coverage litigation is expected.

When preparing a coverage letter directed to the insured, be sure to take into consideration the insureds' emotional involvement and be empathetic toward their position. A coverage letter can be written denying coverage or reserving the insurer's rights without sounding "cold" or unfriendly. Remember, the insured purchased a policy and paid premium to the company. They are still a policyholder and a customer. Be courteous and helpful.

FOR MORE INFORMATION ON:	GO TO:	PAGE(S):
Claims Operations	Chapters 2–9	5–104
Claims Process	Chapters 10–17	105–220
Claims Process—Overview	Chapter 10	105
Investigation and Adjustment	Chapter 11	115
Evaluation and Resolution	Chapter 14	155
Going to Court	Chapter 15	173
Reserve Management	Chapter 16	183
Recovery	Chapter 17	205
Claims Handling Guidelines	Chapters 21–30	271–354
Litigation Management	Appendix F	421
Legal Theory and Doctrines	Appendix G	427

Chapter 14: Claims Process—Evaluation and Resolution

The claims process begins with a claim being made and an investigation conducted. The investigation seeks to determine the facts of the loss as well as to determine the injuries and damages sustained. These were the topics discussed in Chapter 11 (page 115). Insurance coverage then needs to be verified and analyzed. Coverage analysis is used to ascertain whether the claim is covered under the insured's policy. This was addressed in Chapter 13 (page 143). Now we turn to the task of determining how much, if anything, the claim is worth.

Claim Evaluation

The analysis and evaluation of claims will differ by line of business, jurisdiction or venue[1] (location of claim), and type of claim. The key to a proper claim evaluation is to review all the investigation and documentation developed during the claims process and then summarize the key elements of the claim in terms of liability and damages. The claim investigation serves as the basis for the analysis and evaluation of the claim. If the investigation is inadequate or incomplete, the evaluation may be flawed or incorrect. Remember, the evaluation of the claim also affects the claim reserves established for that claim. If the claim has been undervalued or overvalued, it will impact the company's financials.

In an injury claim, after the claim investigation has been completed, and the claimant is no longer being treated medically, liability and damages are evaluated. Thereafter, claim settlement negotiations will ensue. Depending on the extent of the liability determined, and the damages being claimed, negotiations may be simple or can be protracted over a long period of time. They may involve the use of mediation—a dispute resolution process wherein a third party assists in the resolution of the claim. Mediation can be court ordered, and may be binding on the parties to the mediation. To settle claims effectively, claims adjusters need to be skillful at settlement negotiations. It is important to note that a properly documented claim evaluation will assist in the claim negotiation process and ultimate resolution of the claim.

Evaluation Outline

The format used to document the claim evaluation process may differ by organization, manager, and adjuster. However, no matter what format used, the same process is needed to evaluate the claim properly. Some use a claim evaluation form or electronic claim screen that guides the user through the process, providing all the necessary sections to be completed so there are no miss-

[1] Venue is where a lawsuit is filed and also means the court the lawsuit is filed in, such as state superior or supreme court or federal court.

ing items. Other adjusters may use a structured format but include the evaluation in the file notes in narrative form.

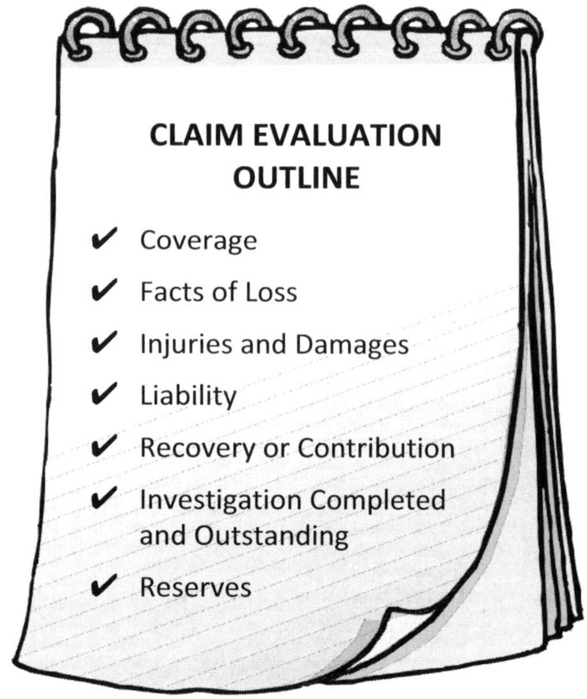

The claim evaluation process has several components, and the key to a proper evaluation is to be sure to cover all of them in the evaluation. A sample outline of a claim evaluation is shown opposite. The outlined items are developed through the claim investigation process. Let's take a look at these items and how they impact the claim evaluation.

Coverage

As indicated in Chapter 13, coverage includes both coverage verification when the claim is initially reported and coverage analysis to review any pertinent policy language which may impact the scope of coverage. Coverage verification is limited to a review of the named insured's, policy effective dates, vehicle schedule, limits and deductibles, loss payees, etc. Coverage analysis requires a skillful review of the coverage forms and endorsements to determine if the loss is actually covered under the policy and if any limitations apply.

Facts of the Loss

The facts of the loss are basically the facts developed during the claim investigation used to evaluate liability. For example, assume an adjuster's investigation reveals that the insured operator ran the red traffic light because she dropped her cell phone while driving, reached down to retrieve it, and didn't see the light had turned. This was supported by a statement from a passenger in the insured's vehicle. This factual information is relevant to the liability evaluation and confirms that the insured is liable in the claim.

Injuries and Damages

These refer to the damage component of the evaluation. "Injury" encompasses more than a note in the claim file indicating there was a fractured arm. The adjuster must elaborate, specifying the type of fracture, the specific bone fractured, how the fracture was repaired (i.e., cast applied with closed reduction[2] or with surgery using an open reduction[3]), the number days hospi-

[2]Closed reduction refers to the treatment of a fracture without the need for surgical intervention, typically treated with a hard or soft cast.

[3]Open reduction refers to the treatment of a fracture requiring surgical intervention, which may include the use of pins, staples, bone grafts, and other means to repair the fracture. An open reduction is more serious than a closed reduction and will generate more medical and hospital bills, as well as an extended disability period.

talized, the amount of physical therapy, hospital and medical costs, disability period and lost wages, and the claimant's occupation. A fractured arm without surgery to a construction worker will have a higher value than for an office worker, as the construction worker may use his arm during the manual labor process. A fractured arm requiring surgery will involve a more extensive disability and recovery period, increased medical and hospital bills, and lost wages, and may also involve scarring.

"Damages" also pertain to property damage, including loss of use, if applicable. Depending on the extent of the damages, it is always wise to inspect closely to verify the extent of the damages and take photographs.

Liability

Liability refers to the legal liability on the insured and is based on statutory and caselaw. Please see the section below regarding how liability is determined.

Recovery or Contribution

These are two separate terms. "Recovery" refers to the reclamation of payments made to the insured or claimant from the responsible party. "Contribution" refers to one party seeking payment assistance from another responsible party in a claim.

For example, a claimant is a passenger in an automobile intersection accident and is injured. There is a question as to which vehicle had the green traffic light. She files a lawsuit against the vehicle she is a passenger in as well as against the adverse vehicle. Both vehicle operators and owners are named as defendants in the lawsuit, and each file a cross-claim against the other based on contribution. In other words, each defendant may contribute toward the settlement, or share in any verdict, depending on whether both parties are deemed to be negligent.

Investigation Completed and Outstanding

This is a list of what investigation has been completed up to that point in time and also lists the investigation necessary in the future. This provides the reader of the evaluation with the information needed to formulate the liability and damage decisions. It also indicates what further investigation remains and how it may impact the current evaluation.

Reserves

Lastly, the adequacy of the claim reserves should assessed as part of the evaluation process. The reserves could prove to be inadequate or deficient, or end up being more than adequate or redundant. Remember that the reserve represents the amount that may be paid on a claim. Therefore, the reserve amount should always be consistent with the adjuster's claim evaluation.

Determining Liability

The insuring agreement of a liability insurance policy indicates that the insurance company will provide insurance coverage for all liability losses where the insured is legally responsible, as long as the loss is covered under the policy. The standard commercial general liability (CGL) insurance policy insuring agreement promises that the insurer will pay for all liability arising from bodily injury or property damage occurring during the policy period within the policy territory. A typical insuring agreement says:

> We will *pay all damages* [indemnify] for bodily injury and property damage for which any insured may become legally responsible ... we will *settle or defend* [indemnify and defend], as appropriate, any claim or suit asking for these damages. Our duty to *settle or defend* [indemnify and defend] ends when our limit of liability for coverage has been exhausted.

Even if the insured is not responsible or legally liable for the loss, the insurance policy will provide liability coverage as long as the loss is not excluded, and subject to the policy limitations. There are situations where a policyholder demands coverage for a loss that on the surface may not be covered. However, the duty to defend is broader than the duty to indemnify. In this situation, even though coverage for the loss is questionable, the insurance company provides a defense, reserving its rights to withdraw its defense at a later date if the legal discovery indicates coverage does not apply, and also reserving on indemnification of any potential jury verdict. Reserving rights on indemnification is important as the verdict may result in only certain causes of action or counts that are not covered under the policy.

A key part of the claims handling process is establishing who is to blame—who is liable or responsible for the accident—and whether there are other responsible parties who will share in the loss (these are often referred to as a third parties or codefendants). Establishing liability is a critical component of the evaluation process. If the injuries (damages) are very serious, but the investigation indicates no liability, the adjuster may end up denying the claim. If there is no liability, it will also affect the claim reserve in two ways. The bodily injury claim reserve may be lower based on the liability evaluation, and the expense reserve may be higher given the potential legal expenses necessary to defend the claim.

Many companies utilize narrative terms to describe the degree of liability involved in an investigation. For example, the following terms may be used. These terms provide an indication as to the extent of the insured's and claimant's liability and are very common in the industry. For illustrative purposes, these definitions include percentage ranges, which vary by company.

- ***Clear liability***—Refers to a liability evaluation where liability has been evaluated at 100 percent, meaning there is no negligence on the part of the claimant. These claims are typically settled quickly, without the need for extended investigation or trial.

- ***Probable liability***—Involves a situation where the claimant may bear a small percentage of liability with the insured being the primary negligent party. The claim will typically be settled prior to trial. The percentage range of liability may range from 80–90 percent.

- ***Questionable liability***—Refers to a loss where the claimant and insured may both be liable. The percentage range of liability may range from 25–75 percent. The claim may result in a compromised settlement or possibly trial if the claim cannot be resolved. The questionable liability evaluation category is the broadest category in terms of the liability ranges, and many adjuster evaluations routinely fall within this category. When adjusters utilize this category during a claim evaluation, it is important to specify the percentage of liability attributed to both the claimant and the insured. At times, adjusters may overuse this category, not wanting to commit to either the doubtful or probable liability category. The adjuster should carefully analyze the investigation and make a decision on liability, as it directly impacts the claim evaluation, including the reserve.

- ***Doubtful liability***—Is used to describe a liability evaluation where both the claimant and insured are liable; however, the claimant is the primary negligent party. The percentage range of liability may range from 5–25 percent. This may result in a sharp compromise, a denial, or possibly trial.

- ***No liability or zero liability***—These categories are used when the liability evaluation reveals that the insured is not at all liable for the loss. The claim will be denied and may go to trial.

Damage Evaluation

The evaluation of damages during the claim process is important to develop the gross damage exposure of a claim. The gross damage exposure is the full exposure of a claim without any offsets for the negligence of the claimant or contribution from a third party.

Gross damage exposures in property damage claims are relatively easy. Typically, there will be a damage estimate or an appraisal by a field adjuster that will provide an indication of the total itemized damages in the claim. There may also be a loss of use element in the damages being claimed. However, injury claims are much more difficult to evaluate. Although there may be available computer programs to assist in the evaluation of claims, there is no one source that provides the evaluation of an injury claim by injury category. The same injury can be valued very differently for several reasons, some of which are outlined below.

The value of an injury may be what the injured person or claimant wants the claim resolved at based on their own evaluation, which sometimes may be unrealistic. This is the emotional component and often causes a delay in getting a claim resolved. The claimant attorney indicates his client is angry at the insured (particularly in fatality or serious injury claims) and wants an amount of money that far exceeds the adjuster's evaluation, which may have been based on industry practice (i.e., claims settled in the past with similar injuries). The danger with the emotional component is that if the claim is ultimately tried to a conclusion, the claimant may receive the amount they sought in the first place.

As indicated later in this chapter, a jury is composed of laypeople and not claims adjusters or attorneys. If the jury sympathizes with the claimant, it may award the claimant a large sum of money that was never contemplated by the adjuster. This is why it is important to understand the difference between settlement value and jury verdict value. Settlement value is what an adjuster expects to pay on a claim; jury verdict value is the projected verdict if the litigated claim is tried to conclusion. Although there are jury verdict statistics and verdict reporters, no one can predict what the actual verdict will be in a given claim.

So, how does an adjuster evaluate an injury claim? Custom and practice usually dictate the value of injury claims, which can vary by state, jurisdiction, and venue. What is "custom and practice," and where's the book to determine injury values for liability claims? The book does not exist, and if it did, it would probably be flawed as there are so many individual factors involved when evaluating an injury claim.

The evaluation of injury claims usually comes from experience in handling similar claims in the past, input from a claims supervisor or manager, and input from the defense attorney. Sometimes injury claims are discussed in a claim committee format wherein several members of the claims staff (and possibly other staff) discuss the facts and value of claims to arrive at reserves and settlement values. For example, a New York claim involving a lower back sprain with $500 in medical bills and 1 week of lost wages at $750 may yield a gross settlement value in the area of $5,000–$7,500. A claim involving a fractured hip with surgery may yield a gross settlement value of $150,000 to $250,000.

The gross value of the claim is established without any offset for negligence or contribution from another party. Adjusters then apply the percentage of negligence on the insured. For example, if the adjuster feels the gross claim value is $10,000, and the insured is 40 percent negligent, then the net claim value is $6,000. The adjuster then establishes a range for the net claim value. No adjuster is perfect on the liability or damage assessment, which is why a range is set. In this case, the range might be $5,000–$7,500.

Damages can be classified into several categories.

- ***Compensatory damages***—Consist of general damages and special damages.
- ***General damages***—Damages based on physical and emotional pain and suffering, loss of companionship, loss of consortium,[4] disfigurement, loss of enjoyment of life, permanency, and mental or physical impairment.
- ***Special damages***—Include expenses incurred by the plaintiff (or claimant) as a result of the accident, such as medical and hospital-related expenses, wage loss, property damage, and other out-of-pocket expenses.
- ***Punitive damages***—Sometimes called exemplary damages, refer to damages which serve to punish a defendant for its conduct. Typically, punitive damages are awarded when the defendant committed acts which are grossly negligent, intentional, or egregious. Punitive damage awards can far exceed general damage awards. In some juris-

[4]Loss of consortium refers to the lack of the benefit of a family relationship due to injuries sustained in the accident. Family in this context typically involves a husband and wife. This is why a general release should be taken from both the husband and wife when settling a bodily injury liability claim.

SPECIAL DAMAGES:	$2,150
Injury:	Fractured humerus (closed reduction and no surgery)—minimal permanency.
Medical:	Hospital emergency room treatment; x-rays, 3 orthopedic visits; 6 physical therapy visits; prescriptions—**$1,200**
Wages:	Employed as telemarketing representative earning $950/week. Total disability period 7 days—**$950**
GENERAL DAMAGES:	**$12,000**
Pain and suffering:	**$ 8,000**
Loss of consortium:	**$ 1,500**
Permanency:	**$ 2,500**
Disfigurement:	**$ 0**
GROSS VALUE	**$14,150**

Claims Process

dictions, a plaintiff may receive treble or triple the general damages.

Although there is no exact science in arriving at a gross damage bodily injury evaluation, there are steps that can assist in the process. Generally, the adjuster should be concerned with general damages and special damages. General damages are much more difficult to project given the subjectivity of the damages. How much money do you attribute to pain and suffering? Should a child receive more money than an adult? How much money is a facial scar worth to a woman whose occupation is a fashion model versus one who is a truck driver? Special damages are easily calculated if you have been provided with the medical and wage documentation. The calculation above may assist an adjuster to arrive at an appropriate gross damage evaluation.

In the example above, we arrived at a gross damage calculation at $14,150, keeping in mind that the general damage calculation is subjective. This is where custom and practice applies, which can vary by state, jurisdiction, and venue. By itemizing the damages, a monetary amount can be assigned to each component of the damage evaluation, arriving at a more accurate reserve.

Determining Negligence

Negligence is a tort or civil wrong, and generally means a person's conduct does not meet the standard of a reasonable or prudent person. In other words, negligence involves the failure to use a degree of care considered reasonable under a given set of circumstances. Acts of either omission or commission, or both, may constitute negligence. The four elements of negligence are: a duty owed to a plaintiff, a breach of that duty by the defendant, proximate cause, and an injury or damage suffered by the plaintiff. Liability policies are designed to cover claims of negligence.

A duty owed means a duty of care has been established to prevent injury or damage, such as the duty to prevent someone invited to your home from being injured. Breach of duty is basically one party's failure to protect another party from injury or damages. Causation means it has been established that the breach of duty is causally related to the injuries or damages sustained, i.e., the proximate cause. And damages relate to the injuries or property damage resulting from the breach of duty.

The concept of negligence will always be present in liability claims handling, so it is very important to understand this rather complicated concept during the claims handling process. As a claim adjuster, the most important concept of negligence is to understand the various defenses of either contributory negligence or comparative negligence, and how they apply during the claims handling process. These defenses vary by jurisdiction, and it is important to be familiar with these defenses and doctrines in each state in which the adjuster operates.

Contributory negligence is a much harsher negligence standard. In a contributory negligence jurisdiction, if the claimant's own actions constituted a partial cause or otherwise aggravated his or her injury in any way, the claimant receives nothing. This means that if the claimant is 1 percent at fault, he would be barred from recovery. Contributory negligence has been superseded in many states by other methods of apportioning liability.

In a comparative negligence jurisdiction, each party bears a certain percentage of fault or responsibility, and the claimant's recovery is reduced by their degree of fault or liability. If the claimant's negligence is found to be greater than the insured's, the claimant will receive nothing. There are two types of comparative negligence: modified and pure.

Modified comparative negligence means that the claimant or damaged party may be barred from recovery if their negligence exceeds a certain percentage. There are two types of modified comparative negligence. One type is the "50 percent rule," where a claimant cannot recover if found to be 50 percent or more at fault. However, if the claimant is 49 percent or less at fault, he may recover, but the recovery will be reduced by their percentage of fault. The other type is called the "51 percent rule," which puts the line at 51 percent instead of 50.

In a pure comparative negligence jurisdiction, the claimant can recover damages even if the claimant was 99 percent at fault or negligent, but the recovery will be reduced by their percentage of fault.

At the time when this book was written, most states followed the comparative negligence doctrine (either pure or modified). There are five jurisdictions that follow the contributory negligence doctrine: Alabama; Washington, DC; Maryland; North Carolina; and Virginia.

Understanding the concept of negligence is important for all adjusters. At one time, there was an emphasis on various levels of a claimant's status described as to whether the insured or defendant would be liable. For example, the business invitee describes a person on the premises who was invited, e.g., a customer or patron for whom the highest degree of care is owed. Licensee refers to a person who is on the premises with permission for a specific reason; the property owner has an obligation to warn licensees of a dangerous situation. A trespasser, on the other hand, is not owed such an obligation, although the owner should not willfully harm or injure the person.

Most jurisdictions follow the doctrine of reasonable care, which is based on a legal duty to act as an ordinary, prudent, reasonable person would and to not do something that would cause injury or damage to another person. If an adjuster is evaluating a claim and relying on a reasonable care standard, how does the adjuster know whether the insured acted reasonably? As explained above, there are distinctions between negligence in terms of comparative negligence and contributory negligence, as well as different categories of comparative negligence in terms of pure and modified. Each state will follow a particular contributory or comparative negligence rule. There are also other legal defenses and doctrines involved in the claim process which are discussed in Appendix G beginning on page 427.

For example, assume an automobile accident occurs in Alabama, which follows the pure contributory negligence rule. The insured operator had a stop sign, and the claimant operator had no traffic signal. The insured operator ran the stop sign and was struck by the claimant vehicle. Based on the investigation, the claimant is found to be 10 percent negligent for speeding. The claimant operator may be completely barred from recovery, even though the accident was primarily caused by the insured operator. If this same accident occurred in a pure comparative negligence jurisdiction, such as New York, The claimant would recover 90 percent of her damages, with the award being reduced by 10 percent for her own negligence.

Assume again that an automobile accident occurs in Colorado, which follows the modified comparative negligence 50 percent rule. The claimant operator made a left-hand turn in front of the insured operator. Based on the investigation, there was a no left turn signal for the claimant, and both the claimant operator and the insured operator maintain that they each had a solid green traffic light. The claimant operator contends that the insured operator was speeding at the time of the accident. The claims adjuster's investigation indicates the claimant is 60 percent negligent for the accident and damages. Since the claimant was over 50 percent negligent, he is completely barred from recovery.

As can be seen from the above examples, there are two important points to keep in mind when assessing negligence. First, it is important to know the laws of the jurisdiction or state where the accident occurred and, second, what negligence doctrine or defense does it follow: pure contributory, pure comparative, or modified comparative negligence. These points are all utilized to evaluate liability and determine an appropriate settlement evaluation and claim reserve.

Unfortunately, the percentage applied or apportioned in a claim can only be specific if a claim is tried to a conclusion, and a jury makes the liability decision. Therefore, since most claims are not tried to a conclusion (probably less than 5–8 percent are), the percentages of liability for most types of accidents are projected based on custom and practice. What does this mean? Adjusters take into consideration their own experience and the litigation of similar claims in the past when evaluating liability issues.

For example, some insurance company claim adjusters may state that auto accidents occurring in an uncontrolled intersection (i.e., no traffic signal) should be evaluated on a 50/50 liability apportionment. Claims involving a left turn accident without a turn signal may involve a liability apportionment of 75 percent against the party making the turn. An automobile accident involving a rear-end collision will probably result in 100 percent liability against the party causing the rear-end collision. However, if the rear-end collision resulted from the vehicle ahead stopping short, liability may be less than 100 percent.

That said, each claim should be evaluated based on its own merits. Although the claim details may be similar to other claims handled in the past, there may be other issues that could change the liability percentage.

When a claim reaches the trial stages, and testimony has been completed, the jury decides the issues of liability and damages. In some states, the jury may be composed of six jurors who are members of the community. Although the jurors are not supposed to consider that the defendant may or may not have insurance coverage, most

Exhibit 14.1 Sticky Liability Situations

If a claimant stopped properly at a stop sign, proceeded into the intersection, and was struck by your insured's vehicle, how much liability would you place on the claimant operator? 75 percent? 50 percent? 25 percent?

If an accident took place on a 4-lane divided highway with two lanes each way, with each lane divided by separated white lines, and the insured strikes another vehicle while attempting to pass the vehicle traveling in the right lane, how much liability should be placed on the insured? Did the vehicle the insured was attempting to pass speed up just prior to impact? Did the insured move over into the other lane too quickly, not looking back before passing? What were the points of impact?

A claimant slips and falls on an accumulation of water located on the floor of the insured supermarket. Since the claimant was wearing footwear which may have contributed to the accident, you feel the claimant is partially negligent. Therefore, when evaluating the claim for reserve and settlement purposes, you place 50 percent negligence on the claimant. If the injury claim has a gross settlement value of $25,000, then the net settlement value of the claim is $12,500. If the claimant is only 25 percent negligent, the claim has a net settlement value of $18,750. What is the actual value of this claim? Is the claimant 25 or 50 percent negligent? To compound the problem even further, how did you evaluate the gross value of the claim at $25,000? If the claim went to litigation, and a jury decided the damages, the damages could be $100,000 and liability could be assessed at 100 percent on your insured.

jurors are sophisticated enough to understand that insurance coverage exists. Some jurors may sympathize with a severely injured plaintiff and ignore the liability issues in order to render a substantial verdict. (See Appendix G, page 427, for more discussion of the legal theories and doctrines that apply to claims handling.)

Negotiations

The negotiation process is part of the adjuster's daily responsibility. Whether handling a first-party or third-party claim, the negotiation process is always front and center. Many issues will come into play: damage values, injury values, salvage values, and loss of income.

Negotiating an insurance claim is a give-and-take process. It is important to be absolutely prepared before entering into negotiations. If a claimant attorney calls on a claim file the adjuster is not totally familiar with, the wise course of action is to return the call after having an opportunity to review the claim file thoroughly. Being unprepared can result in an underpayment or overpayment.

The initial step is to closely examine what is being negotiated in the first place; the gross claim value needs to be determined. This is the full value of the claim without any offset for comparative negligence or contribution from other parties. Then the net claim value range is developed. This is the value of a claim after discounts or offsets, including liability and contribution, have been applied. It's a good idea to come up with a range rather than a precise amount because it's easy to be off on the liability or damage assessment. After this has been developed, a list of negotiation points should be made. An example will help illustrate this process.

Assume there is a liability claim involving a fall due to liquid on the floor, and the claimant sustained a fractured arm with a closed reduction, and received limited disability and treatment. The investigation indicates that the claimant is comparatively negligent (in a modified comparative negligence jurisdiction). The liability issue is estimated to be at 60 percent on the insured and 40 percent on the claimant. The injury required a closed reduction, and the claimant's own physician indicates there will be no permanency. The adjuster feels the gross claim value is $10,000, and the claimant is 40 percent negligent. This makes the net claim value $6,000. The adjuster establishes a range for the net claim value of $5,000–$7,500.

Armed with this information, it's time to develop negotiation points. The following are examples of negotiation points for our loss scenario above.

- The gross value ranges of fractured arm claims with similar facts and circumstances in the venue where the claim is pending.

- No permanency expected, per the claimant's physician. Limited disability and medical treatment.

- Minimum special damages and little pain and suffering.

- The claimant is at least 40 percent negligent, *if* the jury believes that the claimant's high heeled shoes and cell phone activity were the primary cause of the accident. If so, then the claimant could be barred from recovery at trial (if a jury finds her over 51 percent negligent).

- Notice is a factor.[5] For example, the investigation may indicate that there was no prior verbal or written notice (actual notice) of the dangerous floor condition which may have allegedly caused the accident. And, if the condition only existed for a short period of time just prior to the incident, the insured could not have been aware of the condition (and not have constructive notice). Without any prior notice, the claimant could end up being barred from recovery as she would fail to prove her claim.

- It's common knowledge that the claimant attorney does not like to try cases, and 99 percent of all his cases get settled.

Get on the telephone, and solicit a settlement demand. If the demand is outrageous, then consider a very low initial offer to stimulate some further discussion. Ask the claimant attorney how he arrived at the demand. Continue with the negotiation process. Don't negotiate against yourself—the claimant attorney needs to come down in his demand, and you may need to come up in your offer. If the attorney is not being reasonable, then discontinue until a later date, and try again.

Be sure to document claim file notes with the negotiation process. Confirm the settlement demand and the last offer to the claimant attorney in writing. This may require that the claimant attorney confer with the client. Also, stay in the low range of your settlement range, and only move into the high range if the claim is likely to settle.

Reporting Requirements

Should the claim investigation and negotiation indicate the potential for damages is in excess of the insured's policy limit, or litigation has been filed with an amount sued for in excess of the policy limit, it is crucial that this fact be conveyed to those who need to know, such as excess insurers and/or reinsurers. Claims handlers need to inquire with the retail agent, general agent, program administrator, and insured as to whether umbrella or excess coverage is available and promptly report the claim to those insurers.

Excess Insurer Reporting

If it appears the primary layer may be exhausted, excess insurers and reinsurers should be notified. The umbrella or excess insurer should be placed on written notice. This is very important to avoid a late-notice issue being raised by the umbrella or excess insurer for late reporting. Excess letters[6] should be sent to all insureds involving litigation and serious exposure claims. Such letters should be sent via certified mail, return receipt requested.

---

[5] Notice can be *actual,* meaning the insured had written or verbal notice of the defect or dangerous condition, or *constructive,* meaning that the condition existed for such a period of time that the insured should have had knowledge of it.

[6] Excess letters advise the insured or other defendants that an amount sued for does, or may, exceed the insurance policy limits. They are also called excess and damnum letters.

Excess letters may need to be tailored to comply with individual state requirements and may also require a written acknowledgement from the insured. If there is a pending coverage issue, the excess letter language may be incorporated into the reservation of rights letter. In claims involving liability policies, a letter should be sent to each defendant in a lawsuit who is covered under the liability policy, advising that the amount sued for exceeds or may exceed the policy limits.

In certain jurisdictions, the amount sued for may be open or provisional. This means that the complaint pleads the minimum jurisdictional limit the court will allow; the amount sued for can be amended or increased at a later date. Since the amount sued for can be amended or increased, the adjuster should advise the insured(s) that although not indicated in the complaint, the amount sued for could exceed the policy limits at a later date. A letter will need to be sent to each defendant on all claims pending in litigation.

Reinsurance, Client Company, and Home Office Reporting

Generally, the following claims should be reported immediately to the reinsurer, the third-party administrator (TPA) client-company, or the home office Claims Department of an insurance company, depending on the established protocols and requirements:

- Claims with an incurred level in excess of the claim facility or office's loss or expense authority
- State department of insurance claim or regulatory complaints
- Coverage issues (reservation of rights and coverage disclaimers)
- Fatality
- Traumatic brain injuries (including seizure, coma, and physical/mental impairment)
- Spinal cord injuries (including quadriplegia and paraplegia)
- Heart attacks (including stroke and myocardial infarction)
- Hearing loss
- Blindness (total or partial blindness in one or both eyes)
- Amputation of any body parts
- Major organ injury (including heart, liver, lungs, and spleen)
- Serious burn injuries resulting in disfigurement or scarring
- Lacerations involving serious disfigurement and/or scarring
- Non-union bone fractures
- Vertebrae injuries involving surgical intervention
- Occupational disease claims
- Claims involving rape, sexual assault, molestation, or sexual harassment
- Police professional liability claims involving use of deadly force or weapon discharge
- Jail or correctional facility riots
- Claims involving employment discrimination

- Claims involving wrongful termination
- Class action lawsuits
- Allegations of criminal conduct by an insured

REINSURER OR TPA CLIENT OR HOME OFFICE REFERRAL OUTLINE

- ✔ Coverage:
  - o Forms and Endorsements
  - o Proposed Coverage Letter
- ✔ Compensability (WC)
- ✔ Accident, Notice, and Causal Relationship (WC)
- ✔ Facts of Loss
- ✔ Liability
- ✔ Injuries and Damages
- ✔ Medical Management Plan (WC)
- ✔ Investigation
- ✔ Reserves
- ✔ Contribution, Indemnity, and Subrogation
- ✔ Any Applicable Governmental Immunities
- ✔ Recommendations and Action Plan
- ✔ Litigation Management Plan

- Any environmental, pollution, asbestosis, or toxic tort claim
- Any claim or suit alleging bad faith
- Any claim or suit alleging punitive damages
- Claims involving extracontractual damages
- Claims involving demands in excess of policy limits
- Claims alleging violation of the law by the claim facility or insurer
- Litigation naming the insurer as a defendant
- Litigation claims seeking declaratory relief on behalf of the claim facility or insurer
- Any other specific reporting category outlined in an individual client special claim reporting instructions

Reporting requirements will vary by reinsurer, client, and insurance company. When reporting a loss or referring a claim to the home office, reinsurer, or TPA client company, the information shown opposite should be included or addressed in the referral.

Settlement Disposition and Claim Resolution

After a claim is resolved, the appropriate closing documentation needs to be drawn up to finalize the settlement. The closing documents could include:

- ***A signed and notarized proof of loss***—Should be secured on all first-party losses, including automobile, property, cargo, and inland marine. A proof of loss is a formal statement made by the insured to the insurer regarding a claim, especially in property insurance, so that the insurer may determine its liability under the policy. A proof of loss should also be secured when handling first-party automobile claims, e.g., collision and comprehensive, including total vehicle theft claims. A proof of loss is the insured's formal claim under the policy. It contains the policy and claim information and must be signed by the named insureds in front of a notary public. The insurance policy sets forth when the proof of loss must be filed. Some claim facilities only use a proof of loss if the settlement exceeds a dollar threshold amount or when, in the judgment of the handling adjuster, a proof of loss is required to protect the interest of the company.

- ***A loan receipt or subrogation receipt***—An additional form signed by the insured giving the insurance company the right of subrogation against the responsible party for the loss. Sometimes, the proof of loss has language included that provides the insurer the right of subrogation, in lieu of a loan receipt.

- ***A general release***—In a liability claim this is a legal document, prepared after a settlement has been finalized, that sets forth the date and place of the loss, the settlement amount, the defendants being released, and the date signed. The general release is signed by the claimant or plaintiff, releasing the defendant or insured from any and all claims resulting from the accident or incident. The general release is typically signed by both husband and wife, and should be notarized. A signed and notarized general release should be taken on all bodily injury and property damage liability claims. Some claim facilities only use a general release if the settlement exceeds a dollar threshold amount or when, in the judgment of the handling adjuster, a general release is required to protect the interest of the insured and/or the client company.

  Releases can pertain only to property damage (property damage release), allowing settlement of a property damage claim only without releasing any claims for bodily injury. When taking a release from a corporation (corporation release) or other similar entity, it is important to confirm that the person signing the release has the authority to do so and their title is indicated on the release. If a fatality claim is involved, the claimant's estate will need to provide proof of being the personal representative of the claimant's estate either as an administrator (no will) or executor (with will), indicating they have the authority to execute the release.

- ***Workers compensation claims closing documentation***—Includes stipulations, which are used to reflect the settlement agreement, and documents from a hearing at an administrative board or commission.

- ***A withdrawal or stipulation of discontinuance***—This is a formal pleading that discontinues legal action against the defendant(s). In a civil lawsuit, a discontinuance will be necessary if a claim is settled prior to or during trial. The discontinuance is provided by the plain-

Claims Process

tiff to the defendant, and filed with the court where the lawsuit was pending. When settling a litigation claim, both a general release and a withdrawal or stipulation of discontinuance is needed. The original is filed at the court with a copy to the adjuster for the claim file.

- ***An infant compromise order or infant petition***—If the claim involves a claimant under the age of 18, this formal pleading should be submitted to the court requesting the court to approve the infant claimant's settlement. The judge will generally request an updated medical report from the claimant's attending physician to evaluate the injuries, diagnosis, and prognosis. The infant claimant is a ward of the court until age 18, and the claimant's parents cannot sign a release on behalf of the infant claimant. After the judge approves the settlement, a formal order will be prepared, which is a legal pleading filed with the court, outlining how the settlement payments are to be made. An attorney is necessary to assist in filing an infant compromise order or petition, and if the claimant is unrepresented, the claim facility may retain an attorney to represent the infant claimant.

Disposition Payments

Payments made to settle claims can come in many forms. There are direct payments, advance payments, payments to other parties of interest, and structured settlements. These are discussed below.

Direct Payments

Direct payments are settlement or court-ordered payments made directly to the claimant, plaintiff, or policyholder in the case of a first-party claim and their legal representatives. If a claim is tried to a conclusion and results in a verdict against the insured, judgment is entered by the court, and payment must be made promptly in accordance with the statutory requirements.

It is important that payment be made promptly, and the payee names are correctly indicated on the claim check. For example, if a claimant, who is married, is represented by an attorney, the claim check should indicate as follows:

> John Smith and Mary Smith, individually and as husband and wife, and Johnson & Jones, as attorneys.

Advance Payments

Sometimes, in liability claims handling, an adjuster may want to issue advance payments to an unrepresented (or even a represented claimant) as a good-faith gesture if the investigation has indicated the insured is liable and if the claim warrants it. Advance payments are advances toward the bodily injury liability settlement to be paid out at a later date. These payments are not considered as payments under a medical payments coverage form, even if they are being advanced to pay medical bills. Each payment reduces the total limit of liability coverage.

Some liability policies provide a separate medical payments coverage section or form, which provides reimbursement of medical and hospital bills, subject to a policy limit, without regard to liability. Payments under this coverage do not reduce the liability coverage limits and are paid in addition to payments made under the liability policy.

The advance payment is issued from the liability claim feature[7] of the claim file. When making advance payments, all intentions should be clearly documented in writing and confirmation received that the claimant/insured understands such payments will reduce the policy limit available.

Lienholder, Loss Payee, and Mortgagee Payments

All lienholders, loss payees, and mortgagees should be listed on all claim payment checks unless the adjuster's claims handling guidelines or internal requirements differ or the adjuster has been provided with written authority for the removal of the name from the claim check by the designated lienholder, loss payee, or mortgagee. Some states require the loss payee to be included on the claim check even if the payment is to a third party. Therefore, a copy of the vehicle title and/or registration would be necessary during the adjustment process for an auto claim.

If an adjuster neglects to add a lienholder, loss payee, or mortgagee to a claim check, and the policy has been endorsed listing these parties, the adjuster may end up paying the claim twice to the extent of the outstanding amounts owed to the third parties. The adjuster will then have to go back to the insured to get reimbursed.

[7]Claim feature is a single type of loss for one individual claimant involved in a claim occurrence, e.g., bodily injury or property damage.

Structured Settlements

Structured settlements are typically used to fund long-term casualty claim payment obligations as a result of settling serious injury or catastrophic claims. The use of structured settlements is also very common in the settlement of infant claims, as the payments can be spread out for many years. The future payments are referred to as periodic payments, which can be paid as lump sums or weekly or monthly benefits in the future. The longer the duration of the structured settlement, the more potential exists for a higher payout. The insurance company utilizes the claim funds it would have normally paid to the claimant directly and purchases an annuity to fund the payment obligation. The insurance company may assign the payment obligation to a third party, which will in turn purchase the annuity.

Structured settlements can also be used to "bridge the gap" in settlement negotiations. The cost of the structured settlement to the insurance company may be the same amount of money if the insurance company paid a cash settlement today. However, the benefits paid under the structured settlement in the future would be higher, potentially "bridging the gap" between the settlement demand and the offer. Structured settlements can be effective in most liability claims; however, some companies may only utilize structured settlements for claims with values in excess of $100,000, unless the claimant is an infant.

Summary and Conclusion

After investigation and coverage determination, the next step is claims evaluation.

Evaluating claims is not an easy task, particularly injury liability claims. It takes experience and training. The more input into the evaluation process, the better. Remember, the general damages component of the gross damage exposure calculation is a subjective evaluation; therefore, the projection will vary by each individual who provides an opinion.

Negligence evaluations are not a clear-cut percentage to be applied to the gross damage exposure. Can the evaluation be so refined that an adjuster can determine that a party is 40 percent versus 50 percent liable? Of course not, but for purposes of evaluation, a consistent method needs to be used so that the claims staff understands the claim facility's custom and practice.

Negotiation is a skill required by all adjusters. Some are better than others. The objective is to bring the claim to an equitable conclusion. Not every claim is going to settle in the range calculated. Since the general damage component of compensatory damages is subjective, it would be impossible for an adjuster to be exact with every bodily injury claim evaluation. Some claims may settle for more and others for less.

As part of the evaluation process, certain types of claims may need to be reported to a reinsurer, client company, or home office Claims Department. Prompt reporting is essential, and it is the adjuster's responsibility.

Lastly, when concluding claims, it is important that the appropriate closing documentation is secured to protect the interests of the parties involved.

FOR MORE INFORMATION ON:	GO TO:	PAGE(S):
Claims Operations	Chapters 2–9	5–194
Claims Process	Chapters 10–17	105–220
Claims Process—Overview	Chapter 10	105
Investigation and Adjustment	Chapter 11	115
Claim Statements and Interviews	Chapter 12	127
Coverage Issues	Chapter 13	143
Going to Court	Chapter 15	173
Reserve Management	Chapter 16	183
Recovery	Chapter 17	205
Claims Handling Guidelines	Chapters 21–30	271–354
Litigation Management	Appendix F	421
Legal Theory and Doctrines	Appendix G	427

Chapter 15: Claims Process—Going to Court

Claims Process

Sometimes, going to court to resolve a claim is inevitable for a number of reasons. For example, the investigation indicates no liability, the claimant or their attorney may have an unrealistic settlement demand, or the claimant simply wants his or her "day in court." Going to court is costly to both the plaintiff and the defendant (or the insured) in terms of both time and expense.

As a claim reaches the litigation stages, claim expenses or allocated loss adjustment expenses (ALAE) may increase substantially with attorney, court, and other legal costs, and the claim could be pending for a much longer period of time, sometimes for several years. While going to court is not the most desirable approach toward the resolution of a claim, it may be the only way to resolve it.

This chapter reviews the legal process, as well as other methods to resolve claims without the need for litigation, such as alternative dispute resolution. Litigation management, another salient feature of claims management, is discussed in detail in Appendix F, and more information on legal theory and doctrines can be found in Appendix G.

Litigation Basics

For those new to the industry, even the thought of going to court can send chills down the spine. However, litigation is sometimes the outcome in a claims situation, and it is important for claims personnel to understand the basics of the system and the process.

U.S. Court Structure

Injury and property damage claims are heard in various court systems throughout the United States. When handling litigation claims, an adjuster should be familiar with the various courts and their jurisdictional limitations. Exhibit 15.1 shows the various court structures in the United States.

Service of Process/ Summons and Complaint

When a plaintiff files legal action against a defendant, the pleading may be called a writ, a petition, a summons and complaint, or just a complaint. This legal document, or pleading, details the plaintiff's claim with individual causes of actions or counts outlined within. Each cause of action or count will contain allegations detailing the reasons for the cause of action against one, all, or some of the defendants. The complaint is typically delivered or "served" on each defendant personally or on the defendant's legal representative.

Most legal complaints require a formal answer within 20 to 30 days from the date the complaint was served. Sometimes, a defendant, its legal representative, or even an adjuster may secure an extension of time to answer the summons and complaint. When granted by the plaintiff attorney, this type of extension should always be confirmed in writing. Extensions may be

Exhibit 15.1: U.S. Court System

Municipal Court—This is a lower level local, city, village, or town court that may have a jurisdictional limit with a certain dollar threshold amount.

State Court—Most claim litigation fall in the state court system, which may include the following types of courts:

- **Small Claims Court**—A court environment developed for the unrepresented claimant which wishes to pursue legal action against a defendant. The amount claimed in a small claim court will be limited, such as a maximum amount of $5,000 in damages.
- **District Court**—Some states have their own district or county court with monetary limitations on the amount the court will hear.
- **Superior Court or Supreme Court**—The highest state court where most injury claims will be heard. Typically, there will be no monetary limitation for the amount sued for in this court.
- **Appellate Court or Court of Appeals**—Most states have an appeals court to hear matters referred from a lower court. Some states have an appellate division of the superior or supreme court as well as a court of appeals being the highest court in the state.
- **Court of Claims**—Exclusive venue to seek damages against a state or its related entities (i.e., New York Court of Claims).

Federal Court

- **District Court**—There are 94 federal district courts in the United States. Most federal courts only hear cases that involve a violation of federal law, such as civil rights violations and cases which involve citizens of different states.
- **U.S. Court of Appeals**—A federal appeals court to hear matters referred from a lower district court.
- **Federal Court of Claims**—A jurisdiction over most claims for money damages against the United States.
- **U.S. Supreme Court**—The highest judicial body in the United States.

requested to provide more time to respond to the complaint, engage in settlement discussions, and avoid the potential for a default judgment. A default judgment is the result of an answer or appearance not being filed timely in accordance with the jurisdiction's requirements.

Default judgments can occur for a number of reasons, such as an insured not referring the pleadings to the claim facility in a timely manner or as a result of an error on the part of the claim facility. Proper management control of incoming and outgoing lawsuit activity is critical for a claims operation, including date stamping pleadings as received. If a default judgment is received, some states are not lenient in vacating the judgment, or setting aside the default judgment, which could result in a substantial judgment with no ability to challenge it.

If an extension of time to answer is required, the adjuster should make sure that the extension will not waive any affirmative defenses in the action. An affirmative defense is a fact or issue that is a valid defense to a claim, even assuming the alleged facts asserting liability are true. For example, despite a defendant's negligence in causing an automobile accident, the plaintiff's contributory negligence may establish an affirmative defense to a bodily injury claim if it is proven that the plaintiff would have suffered no injuries had he or she been wearing a seatbelt. Other affirmative defenses include assumption of risk and statutes of limitations.

Appearance and Answer

After the defendant is served with the petition, writ, summons and complaint, or complaint, an answer is required, along with an appearance. The answer will provide detailed responses, in writing, to the complaint in the form of admissions or denials. The appearance will indicate the defense firm representing the defendant. Typically, the answer and appearance are filed with initial discovery demands, as indicated below.

Cross-Claims and Counterclaims

If multiple defendants are involved, one defendant may file a cross-claim against another defendant in an effort to shift liability to the other defendant. The cross-claim is a separate complaint served on the offending defendant. In most litigation proceedings, cross-claims are filed among all defendants. Cross-claims can be based on contractual liability issues (when one defendant may have agreed in a contract to defend and indemnify another defendant) or based on common law, which is unwritten law derived from court case decisions, based on custom and precedent. This is in contrast to statutory law, which is enacted by legislative bodies.

If a plaintiff is also negligent, the defendants may file a counterclaim against the plaintiff for damages or based on liability. For example, if the plaintiff, as the driver in an automobile accident, is comparatively negligent, a counterclaim may be filed against the plaintiff for property damage to the defendant's vehicle. The counterclaim is a separate pleading served on the plaintiff.

Discovery

After the answer and appearance are filed, the litigation progresses through the discovery stage. "Discovery" is a broad term that includes many activities from the point when the legal pleading is first served up to trial. Basically, it's investigation of the facts of a claim or the alleged proximate cause of an injury. Discovery may include such activities as interrogatories, depositions, expert examination of a product, and review of a plaintiff's medical history.

During this time, information and documentation are exchanged through various demands. In some jurisdictions, these demands and responses may be called interrogatories, and in other jurisdictions, such as New York, it may be called a bill of particulars. Interrogatories are essentially a list of questions for the plaintiff or defendant regarding the claim, liability, and damages. They require an admission, denial, or explanation. A bill of particulars is similar, except it may be formatted differently and can be supplemented as damages change.

Depositions

The discovery process will also include depositions of the plaintiffs, defendants, and witnesses, whether party to the lawsuit or not. A deposition is pretrial testimony given under oath, without the presence of a judge or jury, for the purpose of discovering evidence relevant to a lawsuit's issue. Depositions are usually taken at the attorney's office with a court reporter present. After the deposition is completed, the transcript is sent to the deposed parties for review, changes, and signatures.

Testimony may need to be taken from nonparty witnesses, i.e., witnesses who are not a party to the litigation. If unwilling to cooperate, it may be necessary to force a nonparty witness's testimony through the use of a subpoena, which is a legal document served on a person commanding him or her to appear at court under a penalty for failure to do so. Subpoenas may be signed by the judge requiring or ordering the witness to appear. Subpoenas may also be utilized to request records as part of the discovery process or at the time of trial. These subpoenas are called record subpoenas or a subpoenas duces tecum.

Summary Judgments and Declaratory Judgments

After discovery has been completed, if a defendant is not liable based on the results of discovery, a defendant may file a summary judgment motion with the court. A summary judgment is a detailed legal pleading summarizing the litigation, with exhibits, requesting that the court rule in favor of the defendant based on the evidence indicating that defendant is not liable. Factual questions or factual issues are reserved for a jury decision. Upon review of the summary judgment motion, if a judge feels there are factual issues outstanding, the judge will rule against the motion, meaning that the litigation will continue to trial.

A summary judgment motion should not be confused with a declaratory judgment (DJ) action. Either the insured or the insurance company can file a declaratory judgment action to litigate the coverage issues surrounding a claim. It is a legal action to decide the duties, rights, and obligations of the parties, but does not necessarily result in an award for damages. This methodology of resolving coverage issues is an excellent tool and eliminates any potential bad-faith claims resulting from delay in arriving at a final decision concerning coverage.

Declaratory actions, sometimes called "DEC actions," can sometimes involve multiple insurance companies. Depositions and legal discovery are utilized to establish the foundation to resolve the coverage issues through litigation. If the coverage claim does not settle after discovery is completed, the litigation will go to trial. There are two disadvantages to DJ actions: first, they are expensive with legal costs; second, the plaintiff or defendant may receive an adverse court decision, which could be used as precedent in future coverage issues in litigated claims.

Motions

Throughout the discovery process, a defendant or plaintiff may file a motion with the court, such as a summary judgment motion. Other motions may include a motion to change the venue, or location, of the lawsuit, a motion to produce a witness, a motion to preclude the submission of certain evidence, or some other request for the court or judge to intervene.

Settlement or Pretrial Conferences

Settlement conferences can be voluntary among all parties to the litigation or be court ordered. The purpose of a settlement conference is to discuss the liability and damage issues among all parties, with particular emphasis on the possibility of a settlement resolution. A pretrial conference is a meeting with the assigned judge and all parties to the litigation prior to trial. It is used to discuss the discovery completed to date and the outstanding discovery to be scheduled. The judge may order that certain discovery be completed within specific time frames so that the litigation moves along without delay. In court ordered pretrial conferences, the presiding judge may participate and assist in the negotiations of a claim in an effort to resolve it before trial. This is a good time to discuss settlement resolution as the judge may be able to convince both parties to compromise.

Some insurance companies have special adjusters called court adjusters or suit adjusters who participate with the defense attorneys at the settlement conference to assist in the resolution of the claim. The adjuster will typically have some type of settlement authority in advance of the pretrial conference to allow for further negotiations. Court adjusters or suit adjusters also participate in settlement discussions at the time of trial and may monitor the trial proceedings.

Trial

Once discovery is complete, the litigation will move into the trial stage with the filing of a notice of trial. Typically, a jury is selected from a jury pool. The jury pool is composed of laypeople that are required to participate in jury duty as part of their civic responsibility. The prospective jurors are questioned by both the judge and the participating attorneys. Depending on the jurisdiction, a participating attorney may challenge a prospective juror who may be biased toward their particular case. This is commonly referred to as a peremptory challenge, which refers to a right to reject a certain number of potential jurors who seem to have an unfavorable bias, without having to give any reason for the rejection. Voir dire refers to the jury examination process wherein the defense, plaintiff, or judge may question jurors and potentially object to a particular juror.

After jury selection, the trial begins with opening statements by both the plaintiff and defense attorneys. If there are multiple defendants, each defense attorney may provide its own opening statement. Thereafter, the plaintiffs will have an opportunity to submit their case, commonly referred to as the plaintiff's case, which will include testimony from various witnesses as well as the admission of documentary evidence. The defendants will then have the opportunity to submit their case, commonly referred to as the defendant's case, also including testimony from witnesses and admission of evidence.

Once the plaintiff's case and defendant's case are concluded, each party will have an opportunity for a closing argument, which is basically a summary of the testimony and events of the trial.

Verdict or Judgment

After closing arguments, the case is presented to the jury for deliberation, which is basically a secret meeting of the jurors behind closed doors. Prior to the deliberation, the judge will provide specific instructions to the jury, including an explanation of the law as it pertains to the case. A vote is taken at the conclusion of the jury deliberation, and once all jurors agree, their decision is presented to the judge on a signed verdict form. If the jury cannot reach a verdict by the required margin, it is said to be hung or deadlocked, and a new trial may be held.

The jury verdict or decision may be read by the court clerk, judge, or some other court official. The verdict will include issues of liability and damages. In some jurisdictions, the trial may be bifurcated, meaning that the liability issue is tried separately from the damage issue. If the defendant(s) are not found to be liable, the damage trial will not take place.

Once the verdict is rendered, the judgment is entered by the court. A copy of the judgment is provided to each party to the litigation. If the verdict involves monetary damages, the defendant has a certain amount of time to pay the damages to the plaintiff, the payment of which is referred to as a satisfaction of judgment. If an insurance company is involved, it will pay the judgment up to its policy limit.

Prejudgment interest may apply to the verdict, which is interest accruing on the amount of a legal award from the time of the injury or damage to the time the judgment is entered by the court. When awarded as part of a judgment against the defendant or insured, prejudgment interest is usually covered by the supplementary payments provision of standard general liability policies. It is not uncommon for prejudgment interest to apply to property damage claims in various states. When evaluating a damage claim pending in litigation, adjusters need to be aware of the prejudgment interest on any potential award as it can increase the value of a claim—a good reason to settle out of court! The amount of prejudgment interest is determined by state statute. For example, in some states, the interest rate is tied to the U.S. Treasury Bill rate, plus 2 to 4 percent, or a flat 12 percent per year.

If damages are not paid timely, postjudgment interest may apply. This is interest accruing on the judgment amount after a verdict has been rendered. If an insurance company does not pay a judgment timely, postjudgment interest will accrue from the date judgment was entered by the court until paid.

Sometimes, the defense may make a motion to appeal the judgment to a higher court, such as a court of appeals or the appellate division of a superior court, and the process begins again.

Litigation Claims Handling

The handling of litigation claims requires experience and knowledge of claims handling and the various jurisdictions where litigation claims are pending. There are several important factors relating to the handling of litigation claims that are discussed further below. (Appendix G provides a sample litigation management program, with a view toward keeping costs down.)

Complexity

Litigation claims may be complex, involving serious or catastrophic injuries. It is important that the adjuster understand all relevant issues involving the litigated claim, including damages, liability, and legal issues. Understanding the litigation process and all of its stages is important; various stages are critical to setting reserves and settlement and jury verdict evaluations.

For example, when the interrogatories or bills of particulars are completed, and the injury and special damage information, outlining the extent of the injuries sustained and special damages being claimed are confirmed, it's a good time to reevaluate claims reserves. Or, once depositions are completed, and a nonparty witness has testified supporting the plaintiff's case, it's a good time to revisit the liability evaluation.

Defense counsel should be used as a resource for information but not relied on exclusively for everything. The claims adjuster and claims manager need to stay involved through claim closure. As indicated in other chapters regarding claim evaluations, defense counsel is only one element of the evaluation process.

Time Sensitive Handling of Legal Process

Legal process, such as the summons and complaints, need to be handled within the time restrictions. Otherwise, it could cost the adjusting company millions of dollars if the documents are mishandled and not responded to in a timely manner. In some jurisdictions, it is difficult to reverse a default judgment because the adjuster failed to refer the pleadings to defense counsel on time. As a result of a default judgment, the insured as the defendant will be placed in an unfavorable position with the possibility of an award in excess of policy limits. This will trigger an extracontractual claim against the insurance company and an errors and omissions claim against the third-party administrator (TPA), if a TPA is involved.

Venues and Jurisdictions

Know your jurisdiction and venue, and don't assume that a venue in a rural area of the country will have low jury verdict potential. To the contrary, the verdict potential could be higher, particularly if the economic climate is poor.

Venues and jurisdictions not only impact jury verdict potential but also the court system and assigned judges. The value of the claim can be affected by the court where the lawsuit has been filed, such as federal court versus state court. Also, plaintiff attorneys have been known to "shop" venues and file where judges are "plaintiff oriented." Claims adjusters need to be aware of this. Although judges are supposed to be impartial, they may be predisposed to siding with the plaintiff. A change in venue request may be in order.

Attorney Qualifications and Trial Experience

When handling a litigation claim, the adjuster should always research the ability and experience of the plaintiff attorney handling the claim. If the plaintiff attorney is an experienced trial attorney with successful verdicts, this should be factored into the claim evaluation. Likewise, when assigning defense counsel to handle a litigation claim, be sure to use an experienced attorney with the legal credentials to effectively handle the litigated claim, including going to trial.

Ethical Protocols

Remember, defense counsel is retained to protect the legal interests of the insured defendant. Although the legal bill is paid by the insurance company, the insured defendant is defense counsel's client. This may prove to be a quandary for defense counsel at times. For example, defense counsel must protect his or her client from an adverse verdict, which could generate a legal malpractice claim if not handled properly. As another example, the insurer may pressure the defense attorney to settle, regardless of the effect on the defendant's reputation. These situations are not uncommon, particularly when the insurance adjuster is trying to control expenses.

Verdict Evaluations and Settlement Value

Once a claim gets to the litigation stage, there should be no surprises, but unfortunately, this is not always the case. At various intervals in the legal process, the adjuster should request legal opinions from the assigned defense attorney. For example, when the lawsuit is referred to defense counsel with a copy of the claim file documents, including the claim investigation, an evaluation of the claim in terms of liability and damages should be requested. The evaluation should include settlement value and jury verdict potential.

This is important for several reasons. First, it will assist with the reserve evaluation. Second, it will provide an indication to the adjuster as to whether the adjuster should engage in settlement discussions now or at a later date. And third, it will provide the adjuster with an idea of the assigned attorney's understanding of and experience in handing similar claims.

After the initial referral to defense counsel, an evaluation should be made after the interrogatories are completed or the bill of particulars is received. An evaluation should be made after depositions are completed. Prior to trial, defense should provide a comprehensive pretrial evaluation of the claim. Facts change with additional discovery and depositions, which can change the value of a claim. However, a claim should never go to trial without understanding the potential impact of a jury verdict. Defense counsel should always be consistent with their evaluation unless the facts have changed due to new testimony or other evidence.

An adjuster needs to follow the litigation process closely and know when to initiate settlement discussions, if at all. Settlement value is the claim value decided by the adjuster, claims manager, or other claim professionals, with input from defense counsel or even possibly a claim committee. However, this value can mean little if the claim is going to be decided by a jury. The jurors are laypeople with no claims background, and although a jury verdict may be predicted, there's no guarantee the prediction is right! No one can actually predict the final verdict. Rather, it's only a best guess based on prior verdicts involving similar claims in a particular venue or jurisdiction.

The potential financial impact of adverse jury verdicts can be very costly to an organization. Be careful before letting a jury decide the claim value, and make sure all are involved in the decision to go to trial by jury, including claims management, the insurance company home office, the client, and the insured defendant.

Alternative Dispute Resolution (ADR)

The utilization of alternative dispute resolution (ADR) methods to resolve disputes with the insured, third-party claimants, and insurance companies is preferable to costly litigation. The goal of ADR is to resolve legal disputes without resorting to full litigation through formal trial.

Arbitration

Arbitration is one form of ADR and the most commonly used ADR technique. Arbitration is the referral of a dispute to an impartial third party chosen by the parties in the dispute who agree in advance to abide by the arbitrator's award, which is issued after a hearing at which both parties have a chance to be heard.

The American Arbitration Association (AAA) (www.adr.org) administers ADR claims programs. It works with the parties, counsel, and the judiciary to come to an appropriate settlement. A variety of nonbinding and binding ADR techniques can be used, including neutral evaluation, mediation, and arbitration. Arbitration through the AAA may encompass a number of options, including telephonic hearings, "desk" arbitration that relies on documents only, or oral hearings.

Most insurance companies are members of Arbitration Forms, Inc. There are various forums, or methods to arbitrate, available for arbitration. This information is listed on the Arbitration Forms, Inc., website: www.arbfile.org.

Mediation

Mediation—the act of a third person in assisting two adverse parties adjust or settle their dispute—is another commonly used ADR method. Mediations can take place anywhere and are often used as a pretrial mechanism to resolve insurance claims. Mediation is typically nonbinding and used to bring both parties together in an attempt to resolve the claim. A third party selected and agreed to by the plaintiff and defendant serves as a mediator, and meets with both parties individually and then together in an effort to arrive at a settlement disposition. The mediator may be a retired judge or attorney or even a claims professional.

Summary and Conclusion

The handling of claims that may end up in litigation is difficult, at best, and requires knowledge of the litigation process, venues, jurisdictions, and settlement options. Litigation adjusters need to be very organized as well as experienced in legal and claim litigation matters. At this point, time matters, and missing a due date to answer and appear in a legal action could result in an adverse financial impact on a company.

Once a claim reaches the litigation stages, it has the potential for increased loss and expense costs, which can affect reserves. If a claim is decided by a jury, the outcome is uncertain. It is the responsibility of the adjuster to properly evaluate the litigated claim to be sure it is a claim that should be litigated in the first place. Sometimes, claims are litigated so that the discovery can be completed to get the necessary information to properly evaluate the claim. Adjusters need to know when to settle claims and not miss the opportunity to resolve the claim prior to a jury verdict.

Given the overall costs of litigation, using other alternative methods to resolve a conflict, such as arbitration or mediation, is an effective way to resolve claims. These should always be considered by an adjuster.

FOR MORE INFORMATION ON:	GO TO:	PAGE(S):
Claims Operations	Chapters 2–9	5–104
Claims Process	Chapters 10–17	105–220
Claims Process—Overview	Chapter 10	105
Investigation and Adjustment	Chapter 11	115
Claim Statements and Interviews	Chapter 12	127
Coverage Issues	Chapter 13	143
Evaluation and Resolution	Chapter 14	155
Recovery	Chapter 17	205
Reserve Management	Chapter 16	183
Claims Handling Guidelines	Chapters 21–30	271–354
Ethics in Claims Handling	Appendix E	409
Litigation Management	Appendix F	421
Legal Theory and Doctrines	Appendix G	427

Chapter 16: Claims Process—Reserve Management

Claims Process

The claims reserve management function is probably one of the most important aspects of the adjuster's and claims manager's responsibility. Establishing adequate claim reserves as part of the claims process is critical to the financial stability of an insurance organization. Insurance companies rely on claim reserves (case reserves) to set aside funds to pay future claims. If the funds are inadequate, then the company may need to use part of its surplus to pay future losses. By doing so, the insurance company may reduce its ability to write more business in the future.

For example, if the insurance regulators require a ratio of 3:1 for premium to surplus, and the insurance company writes $30 million in premium with $10 million in surplus, additional reserve strengthening of $1 million (e.g., reserve deficiency) could adversely impact the company's surplus position by a negative 10 percent. Establishing inadequate claims reserves have resulted in many insurers going bankrupt. Reserving is so critical, yet it is probably the one area in which claims people receive the least amount of training and development. That is why it is the subject of this chapter

Claim Reserve Basics

What is a claims reserve? Basically, when a claim is made, the claims adjuster assesses the claim value in terms of liability and damages, and sets aside monies to pay for its resolution. It is a budget, of sorts. Remember, as we learned in other chapters, incurred losses include paid and reserved losses, less any recovery. Incurred losses are used to calculate the loss ratio; therefore, claim reserves financially impact the company.

Over-reserving (called redundancy) and under-reserving (called deficiency) can both have a negative effect on a company. Redundancy can adversely affect insurance rates as the actuaries look at historical loss trends to develop insurance rates or pricing. If the reserves are redundant, inflating the incurred losses, then the future developed insurance rates may be too high or not competitive. On the other hand, if the reserves are deficient, the company may have to use its surplus to supplement case reserves to make claim payments. It is never possible to be absolutely precise, but if you can get in the 5 percent accuracy range, you'll be a hero!

When is a claim reserved? It is recommend that initial claim reserves be established when entering a new loss in the claims system, at the time the claim file is set up. The initial case reserves are established based on the information and documentation reported with the initial loss notice. Thereafter, as the investigation and adjustment process develops, and new information and documentation is received, including verbal information, the adjuster will adjust the claim reserves accordingly.

It's common for the handling adjuster to evaluate the initial reserve adequacy within 15 days from the date the claim is reported to the claim facility. This will provide enough time to conduct an initial investigation and secure documentation to properly evaluate liability or compensability, damages, and develop a medical management plan if the claim involves workers compensation or personal injury protection (PIP) or no-fault benefits. Claim reserves are then adjusted as needed. Don't fall in the trap of waiting for written documentation to adjust claim reserves—it could take years to get the needed documentation. Verbal indications of serious injuries should not be taken lightly.

Which claims are reserved? All claims should be reserved unless the claim is filed as a report-only or incident report where no claim payment is expected. Typically, these reports get entered in the claims system for tracking purposes, with minimal information entered.

How much reserve training does an adjuster receive? Some claims operations do little to no reserve training because it is perceived to be such a routine exercise, and the adjuster staff is seen as being experienced. So, how do adjusters and managers learn how to reserve bodily injury claims? Basically, through on-the-job training and continued experience. It is recommended that all claims operations hold regular training activities involving case reserving, utilizing real examples that will assist adjusters in understanding the reserve process and various evaluation techniques.

Reserve Methodologies

There are various reserve methodologies used in property and casualty claims handling:

- Individual case method
- Average value method
- Fast-track method
- Loss value or formula method
- Computerized method
- Tabular value method

These are discussed in detail below.

Individual Case Estimate Reserve Method

Arguably the most common claims reserve method, the individual case estimate, is reserving on a case-by-case basis. The adjuster assesses each component of the claim in terms of its viability, worth, and cost to the insurer. This is a subjective damage assessment and is based on many factors, including the extent of the injuries, the anticipated medical costs, the duration of disability and wage loss, the property damage assessment (if applicable), the liability evaluation, and any anticipated litigation costs.

Often, although not intentionally, the adjuster sets the reserves on a particular claim based on what was reserved for similar claims the adjuster has resolved in the past. This is referred to as pattern reserving. Although this may seem an appropriate and quick way to set reserves, it can result in under- or over-reserving if the unique facts of particular case and investigation are not taken into account. This is not to say that past experience plays no part.

Evaluation of property damage claims is much easier and more objective, as the evaluation is based on a known damage estimate or appraisal. However, when reserving for property damage claims, the adjuster needs to take into consideration any potential loss of use claim. Certain types of vehicles, such as taxis or limousines, can have a loss of use claim (sometimes referred to as an indirect loss) with a value in excess of the direct property damage claim.

For liability claims, however, one fractured elbow claim may be worth $18,000, while another may be valued at $35,000. This is why it is important to establish ranges for both reserve and settlement purposes. If an adjuster uses pattern reserving or a subjective evaluation without taking into consideration the claim investigation results or medical documentation, it may result in over- or under-reserving.

For example, how much additional value should be placed on a fractured leg claim involving a 9-year-old boy, when there is potential damage to the growth plate of the bone, which could cause a permanent limp as the child gets older and one leg to grow longer than the other? Should the value be more than a similar fractured leg claim? Of course it has a higher value, but how much?

A plumber driving a van rounds a curve in the roadway, and a tractor-trailer coming from the opposite direction dumps a load of lumber on top of the van, crushing the van and pinning the driver in the vehicle. The driver sustains two fractured legs, but while pinned in the vehicle, acid used by the plumber during plumbing operations drips onto his back over a period of 20 minutes, as the firemen attempted to extract him from the vehicle, resulting in extensive burns. How much money should be given to the driver for extensive burn injuries to his back?

When establishing reserves on an individual case basis, the adjuster may seek input from other claims personnel and defense counsel as well as research jury verdicts for similar claims in the same jurisdiction. It's important to remember that, if a claim does not settle prior to or during trial, it goes to the jury for value determination. The jury is typically composed of six laypeople with no experience in claim evaluations. Many factors could contribute to an adverse jury verdict, such as witness demeanors, jury sympathy, venue, the presiding judge, the economy,[1] and the type of defendant (insured). For example, a jury may not be favorably inclined to side with a gun manufacturer in a shooting or an oil drilling company in a pollution claim.

Since the bodily injury reserve methodology is so subjective, it is important to remain flexible in the valuation process. Not all claims have the exact same details; therefore, they may not fit into past injury valuation ranges. For example, two claims may have identical details, but one claimant is diabetic and is not expected to heal as quickly or completely, complicating the medial prognosis and prolonging disability.

[1]In a poor economy, jury verdicts may be higher as jurors may be more inclined to give more money to the plaintiff.

When using the individual case methodology of reserving, it is critical to document the reserve process in terms of liability and damages—both in terms of *general damages* (a subjective monetary award that is designed to compensate an injured person for pain and suffering) and *special damages* (objectively assessed monies awarded to an injured party for tangible losses, such as wage loss, loss of use, hospital and medical expenses, etc.). When evaluating liability, it is also essential to address legal issues or doctrines affecting liability. For example, liability may be established based on contributory negligence (negligence of a plaintiff could bar any recovery) or comparative negligence (the plaintiff's damages are reduced by a percentage representing the degree of his or her contributing fault). Legal theory and doctrines are discussed in Appendix G beginning on page 427.

Average Value Reserve Method

This type of reserve methodology, also referred to as a factor reserve or actuarial reserve, typically constitutes a temporary value until further investigation is conducted. These reserve values are not established by the adjuster, but by actuarial analysis of historical paid losses. An example would be reserving automobile property damage claims at $1,500 and bodily injury liability claims at $3,500 for the first 90 days of the claim. After 90 days, these claims would be assessed on an individual case estimate basis. The average value of the various types of claims can go up or down from the initial estimate, depending on the loss payment history, inflation factors, etc.

This reserve methodology is often used to streamline the reserve process. The adjuster or claims manager does not have to establish an initial individual case estimate reserve at the time a claim is set up when little is known to evaluate an accurate reserve. After 90 days, or some other predetermined time period, more investigation has been conducted, and additional information will be known to assist in establishing an accurate reserve.

Although this methodology may ultimately yield accurate individual case estimate reserves, there are two potential problems. First, management oversight and adjuster follow up are needed to identify and timely convert the average reserves to individual case reserves. Second, a claims operation may decide to develop its own average reserve basis, without any statistical analysis or actuarial input. There are some claims operations that may use a $3,500 bodily injury liability average reserve and leave the reserves at the same level permanently. However, the $3,500 reserve has no statistical analysis or actuarial input, and is simply management's estimate of the value of each bodily injury liability claim settlement. In the end, the aggregate case reserves may be totally inadequate. Additional reserves, called incurred but not reported (IBNR) reserves, discussed later, may have to be added to account for such deficiencies.

Fast-Track Reserve Method

"Fast-track" or "one-shot" reserves are used for simple, small claims that are expected to be settled quickly within a specified dollar amount. In the industry, these claims are commonly called "small claims," which have a value under a certain level, e.g., $5,000, or do not involve any injuries. The basis is similar to the average value method in that the reserve values are

Exhibit 16.1: Mortality Tables

In actuarial science, a mortality table (also called a life, expectancy, mortuary, or actuarial table) is a table indicating life expectancies for people in various categories, e.g., age, family history, occupation, smoking status, and socioeconomic class. It shows, for a person at each age, what the probability is that they will die before their next birthday. Other statistics that may be included in the table are:

- The probability of surviving any particular year of age.
- The remaining life expectancy for people at different ages.
- The proportion of other similarly aged persons who are still alive.

Mortality tables differ for men and for women because of their substantially different mortality rates.

established by an actuarial analysis of historical paid losses. Years ago, these claims were placed in a thin paper envelope or jacket instead of a thick hard copy file jacket. Since many companies now use electronic paperless claims systems, this process may be either eliminated or modified for an electronic claim environment.

Loss Ratio or Formula Reserve Method

This method establishes aggregate loss reserves for a specific coverage line, where the expected loss ratio is used to estimate the claim reserve. Sometimes prescribed by state statute, these percentages represent the portion of the annual insurance premium that would presumably be paid out in claims. An example would be a statutory reserve of 60 percent of the expected loss and loss adjustment expense to premium earned for workers compensation claims. The reserve values are not established by the adjuster.

Computerized Reserving

Some companies utilize computer software to assist in the evaluation of bodily injury claims, e.g., Colossus.® The software utilizes a series of interactive questions that assist the adjuster through the bodily injury claim evaluation process. With technological advances in the future, it seems certain that we will see other computerized programs to assist in the reserve evaluation process.

Tabular Value Reserve Method

This method uses a table of values for permanent disability and death claims. When handling workers compensation claims, the use of the tabular value method reserve process is very common, particularly on death cases of individuals with a spouse and dependants as well as long-term claims involving permanent disability. It is important to utilize the proper mortality tables for reserve calculation. Exhibit 16.1 explains mortality tables.

Incurred but Not Reported (IBNR) Reserves

This method is an estimate of the amount of an insurer's (or self-insurer's) liability for claim-generating events that have taken place but have not yet been reported to the insurer or self-insurer. The sum of IBNR losses plus incurred losses provides an estimate of the insurer's eventual liabilities for losses during a given period. IBNR reserves are typically established through an actuarial analysis. Often, claims management is consulted concerning potential deficiencies and the need for residual reserve supplements.

These reserves are actuarially based and are not set by the adjuster or claims manager. However, the claims operation's reserve methodology contributes to the IBNR calculation. If the claims operation changes the reserve methodology, yielding increased case reserves, the IBNR could adversely affect the overall loss ratio. The actuaries may become concerned that the claim costs are increasing, precipitating increased IBNR reserves.

Reserve Philosophy

A reserve philosophy is a specific process or approach to claim reserves that should be consistently followed by all members of the claim facility. The key word here is *consistently.* Changing a reserve philosophy, or

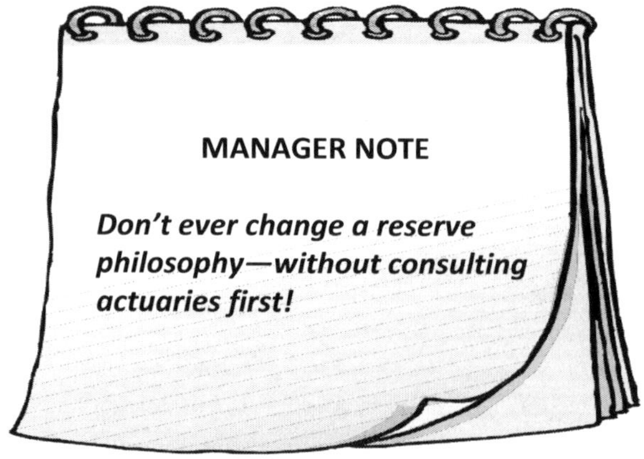

not following the established reserve philosophy, can be detrimental to any claim facility and the insurer that established the premium rates and wrote the policies. A reserve philosophy excerpt is shown in Exhibit 16.2.

Disregarding Reserve Philosophy

Let's look at the impact if the reserve philosophy is not followed properly. Assume the claims manager knows the reserve philosophy but decides to mandate that all soft tissue injuries be reserved at $5,000. The claims manager is not specific as to what constitutes a soft tissue injury and assumes that the claims staff understands. The claims manager communicates this philosophy change with staff at a weekly staff meeting.

Eighteen months later, a home office audit is conducted and determines that there are 1,000 "soft tissue" injury claims reserved at an aggregate of $500,000. However, after reviewing each individual claim file, the home office examiners determine that there needs to be an aggregate reserve increase of $4 million because many of the claims are grossly under-reserved.

The negative impact is that the actuaries who developed the insurance rates for the insurance policies were using the incurred loss results of $500,000, not $4 million, increasing the overall projected loss ratio. With inadequate rates, and a higher loss ratio, profit was overprojected, and the insurance company will lose money. Also, the agents who wrote the policies may have received bonuses based on results which were not legitimate, resulting in overpayment of commissions. In this example, the claims manager unknowingly implemented an average value reserve method

Exhibit 16.2: Formal Reserve Philosophy Excerpt

Individual case reserves are based on the most probable outcome, which is the amount that we expect to ultimately pay on a claim as a result of settlement, administrative hearing, or litigation. (A settlement value is different than a jury verdict value, which is when the jury decides the value of a claim.) The reserve should reflect a realistic but cautious view of the ultimate resolution value of the claim. We do not establish claim reserves based on a worst-case scenario or on a jury verdict exposure. Individual case reserves are established for each party (claim feature) and exposure unit involved in the claim process.

Individual case reserves are based on the judgment of the claims manager and handling adjuster, given the investigation and file developments to date. The initial case reserve can be established based on verbal information. Claim reserves are adjusted as new information, documentation, or investigation is developed or received. We do not establish claim reserves based on a pattern, factor, or average reserve method.

Generally, we look to have an accurate terminal reserve within 9 months from the claim report date, based on the current verbal and written investigation and documentation developed during the claims process. The terminal reserve should reflect the most probable outcome based on our knowledge and experience with respect to the liability and damages as alleged, rather than solely on the liability and damages as verified and documented. It should also be noted that the terminal reserve may be adjusted upward or downward if there is a material change in facts or circumstances.

We establish allocated loss adjustment expense (ALAE) reserves. Expense reserves are established when an ALAE exposure is recognized (i.e., when the loss is reported, placed in litigation, etc.) based on expected payments and are adjusted as the claim file develops.

Claims involving coverage disclaimer issues are reserved at $100 and are considered for closing within 60 days from the date the coverage disclaimer is issued to the insured, or you decide to afford coverage after the investigation is completed, unless other instructions are provided by the client.

that was inappropriate. The average value reserves were used for all claims with so-called soft tissue injuries which were never adjusted based on the actual injuries and damages, resulting in a $3.5 million reserve deficiency.

Another example is when reserves are not established timely, especially after the 9-month terminal reserve (an exposure based reserve which represents what the claim facility would expect to pay on a claim at that point in time, based on what is known to date, either verbally or as actually documented). A claim is reserved at $50,000, yet the claimant attorney has a demand for the full policy limits of $1 million. The adjuster and claim manager do not believe the allegations of a traumatic brain injury with cognitive deficit because there has been no medical documentation submitted to date.

The claim continues to be open with no activity or receipt of additional documentation. The claimant attorney becomes uncooperative in providing any information or documentation, and ultimately places the claim in suit almost 3 years after the accident. Six months later, after initial legal discovery, defense counsel receives a medical report documenting the traumatic brain injury with cognitive deficit. The reserve is then increased to the policy limit of $1 million more than 3 years after the accident. Now we have a $950,000 reserve increase, resulting in a negative impact on rates and profit.

This type of problem is actually quite common and is caused not only by an overly optimistic outlook toward the claim value, but also potential pressure from the Underwriting Department, agent, or even senior management. The pressure may be ever so slight, yet enough for the claims manager to take inappropriate action. Sometimes, the wrong message gets circulated in a claim organization. On one hand, the reserve philosophy is documented and being followed, yet when a large reserve increase is submitted to the home office Claim Department, it is rejected, which instead requests a laundry list of investigation and additional documentation. The claim continues to be pending into subsequent underwriting years, waiting for the additional documentation. Ultimately, the reserve gets adjusted but is late.

Where was the problem? Was it an intentional delay by the home office? Was there a bonus pool that would have been adversely affected by the large reserve increase in a particular calendar or underwriting year? These issues are a reality and need to be addressed. This is another reason why a reserve philosophy should be clearly documented and used consistently throughout the year, even during the fourth quarter. Reserve adjustments in the fourth quarter get management's attention.

IBNR and Loss Development Factors (LDFs)

After adverse reserve development occurs, actuaries look at the historical results of the claims operation, project the results into future years, and may become concerned if the results are deteriorating. So, they increase the IBNR reserves,[2] further deteri-

[2]Incurred but not reported (IBNR) is an estimate of the amount of an insurer's (or self-insurer's) liability for claim-generating events that have taken place but have not yet been reported to the insurer or self-insurer. The sum of IBNR losses plus incurred losses provides an estimate of the insurer's eventual liabilities for losses during a given period.

orating profitability. These IBNR reserves are bulk reserves sometimes established to compensate for claims not yet reported and inadequate case reserves. These additional reserves may also be called incurred but not enough (IBNE) reserves.

There is a general upward trend in liability and workers compensation claim totals after the initial reporting period, called "loss development." Loss development simply means the claim is maturing toward the point where it has reached its full value, with increased reserve and payment activity. Loss development may not always mean there is a reserve problem, as reserve (loss) development is expected as the claim progresses. However, loss development is a problem when the reserves are adjusted late in the development of the claim file, when they should have been adjusted much earlier. This is called adverse loss development as it was not expected or planned for, resulting in the necessity to add reserve amounts. In an effort to disguise this problem, some companies may call it "reserve strengthening." An adjuster's goal should be to establish and adjust claim reserves within an appropriate amount of time to avoid adverse reserve development.

Loss development is the difference between the original loss as initially reserved by an insurer and its subsequent evaluation at a later date or at the time of its final disposal. Loss development occurs for three reasons:

- Inflation—both "social inflation" and inflation in the Consumer Price Index during the time period in which losses are reported and ultimately settled
- Time lags between the occurrence of claims and the time they are actually reported to an insurer
- Poor claims handling resulting in late increased reserve activity during subsequent underwriting years

To account for these increases, a loss development factor (LDF) or multiplier is usually applied to a claim or group of claims in an effort to more accurately project the ultimate amount for which they will be closed. A common method of adjusting losses for the growth in claims and IBNR losses is to apply LDFs. Loss development factors are used to arrive at the ultimate value[3] that can be expected for a claim. For example, an LDF of 1.50 means that for every $1 of current claims, the ultimate payout will be $1.50. A total of $50,000 in current claims would result in an ultimate payout of $75,000.

The historical results of the claims operation may cause an increase in the LDF factors. The LDFs are applied to the case reserves to account for the reserves as they would be projected until the claim is closed. This is called the ultimate net loss. The ultimate net loss is the total sum the insurer(s) and reinsurer(s) pay for a fully developed loss (i.e., paid losses plus outstanding reported losses and incurred but not reported losses). It may not be possible to know the exact value of ultimate losses for a long time after the end of a policy period. Actuaries are employed to assist with these projections for purposes of financial modeling and/or year-end reserve determinations.

New Claims Manager Effect

As discussed in Chapter 7, Claims Operations—Recruitment and Retention beginning on page 73, the new claims manager

[3]Ultimate value is basically the amount the insurer expects to pay on the claim.

Result Evaluation Methods

Insurance companies evaluate their results using several different methods, such as calendar year, underwriting or policy year, or accident year.

- **Calendar Year:** All claim transactions (reserves, payments, and recoveries) in a given 12-month calendar period (January 1 to December 31) are included in the profitability evaluation and results. It does not matter when the loss occurred.

- **Underwriting Year or Policy Year:** All claim transactions are included in the policy year, and it does not matter whether the transaction (i.e., reserve adjustment, payment, or recovery) occurs within the current calendar year. For example, the policy year is June 1, 2009, to June 1, 2010. The loss occurred March 1, 2010. The loss is placed back in the 2009 underwriting year results. (*Note:* The policy inception date drives the underwriting or policy year date.) If the reserve was adjusted in the 2011 calendar year, the adjustment will be evaluated in the 2009 underwriting year results. Results can deteriorate in subsequent underwriting years.

- **Accident Year:** Refers to all claim transactions within the accident year when the loss occurred, and it does not matter whether the transaction (i.e., reserve adjustment, payment, or recovery) occurs within the current calendar year. For example, the accident year is 2010. If the reserve was adjusted in the 2012 calendar year, the adjustment is actually evaluated in the 2010 accident year results.

Understanding these evaluation periods helps reveal the adverse impact of late or stepladder reserving,[a] as well as over-reserving. Many insurance companies use the underwriting year or policy year method. If a claim is initially reserved at $100,000 in 2010, which was in the 2010 underwriting year, and then increased it to $500,000 in 2013, the adjustment of $400,000 would appear in the 2010 underwriting year results. So even 3 years later, the results for underwriting year 2010 are adversely affected. This could have had an effect on pricing and a possible future increase in IBNR reserves. If the actuaries see late reserve adjustment for prior underwriting years, there may be a loss of confidence in the overall adequacy of reserves, necessitating an increase the overall IBNR reserves. Pricing is adversely affected as well.

[a]Stepladder or stair step reserving is the practice of frequently raising claim reserves to cover payments that come due. It is the process of a continuous change in reserves without properly evaluating the exposure up-front. For example, an adjuster is handling a PIP medical and wage claim. The adjuster establishes an initial reserve of $3,000. Thirty days later, the reserve gets adjusted by an additional $5000 due to additional wages to be paid and then 60 days thereafter, the reserve is adjusted again due to additional medical bills received in the amount of $8,000. If the adjuster had evaluated the claim properly from the outset, the initial reserve may have been $16,000, instead of $3,000.

effect refers to a situation when a new claims manager is assigned to an office, and the overall case reserves for the claims operation increase in a very short time period and continue to be higher than in prior years. This usually happens when a claims manager changes the reserve philosophy, even if it is a subtle change in the increased valuation of bodily injury liability claims.

For example, the claims manager consistently changes the adjuster's reserve recommendations, as the manager may not understand that in this jurisdiction, the settlement values are somewhat lower. The adjusters then modify their future reserve values by following the claims manager's reserve approach. This will eventually result in an over-reserving problem.

An over-reserving problem can be just as detrimental as an under-reserving problem. If the insurance rates are based on the historical claim data that has inflated case reserves, then the increased rates developed by the actuaries may have left the insurer in a less competitive position, reducing its ability to generate premium volume targets, adversely affecting profitability.

As can be seen from the above process, the overall effect of not following the reserve philosophy can be extremely detrimental to the insurance company and reinsurers.

Reserve Committees

Reserve committees are used as an internal method to discuss individual loss and expense reserves for particular claims. Generally, the reserve committees will include the handling adjuster, other co-adjusters, claims managers, defense counsel, and home office claims representatives. The underwriting staff may also be invited.

The purpose of the committee is to gain a consensus on the value of individual claims in terms of both reserve and settlement values. The adjuster usually presents the claim to the committee members in a predetermined format, discussing the investigation, adjustment, liability, compensability, damages, litigation management, and the future action plan. The use of reserve committees can minimize the new claims manager effect discussed above, and provide a more adequate claim reserve by applying a consensus methodology.

The Claims Reserve Process

The reserve process is sometimes a mystery to many people, especially the reserving of liability claims. Below are some instructional comments relative to the reserve process.

Bodily Injury (BI) Case Reserves

The reserving of BI liability claims is not a science. Values may differ considerably by a myriad of factors, including:

- The type of injury and treatment
- The claimant's preexisting health and prior illnesses or injuries
- The degree of disability and permanency
- The geographic location (cities, states, and counties)
- The venues and jurisdictions

- The socioeconomic conditions
- The type of risk insured

An example may help illustrate how these considerations come into play. Assume a BI claim is made involving a fractured arm. In a semirural area, such as Watertown, New York, this injury may be worth a lot less than the same injury in urban Brooklyn, New York. Why? A lot has to do with the socioeconomic and jury verdict climate for a particular location. If the jury verdicts are notoriously high for certain types of claims, then the settlements will be higher.

Some geographic areas that are economically depressed may have large jury verdict potential, due to the poor economic conditions of the location (such as the unemployment rate). Adjusters should recognize the different jurisdictions and their influence on claim evaluations. Also, if the insured is a target for large verdicts (i.e., a company accused of pollution, a cigarette manufacturer), the pool of jurors in nearby locales may not be very favorable to the insured.

To arrive at the reserve and settlement values for BI claims, adjusters need to research jury verdict results, seek defense counsel input, and rely on their own experience with similar prior claims as well as industry custom and practice. For example, a claimant's attorney is asking for $150,000 for a fractured ankle requiring surgery. The adjuster's last five fractured ankle cases during the past year, with similar claim factors, were settled at $85,000–$100,000. Therefore, the adjuster feels the settlement demand is excessive and the value should be in the $85,000 range. Who is correct—the adjuster or the claimant attorney?

The answer is, it depends. Adjusters become so accustomed to settlement ranges for various injuries, either through supervisor, defense counsel, or coworker input, or their own opinion, that they neglect to fully evaluate each bodily injury claim on its own merits, avoiding any type of pattern or custom. This is how claims end up in litigation.

Unfortunately, pattern and custom drive a lot of the settlement values. If a claim ends up in litigation, it's a good idea to ask the defense attorney for an analysis of the settlement value and the jury verdict exposure. They should be different. Then ask the attorney how many claims with similar claim factors has he or she tried to a conclusion to support the values provided.

Adjusters are seldom criticized for settling a BI claim for $15,000 when the value may be $12,000. No one has that type of knowledge to be so precise in this type of an evaluation. Let's face it, even the claimant's liability percentage (degree of fault) is often difficult to assess and is rarely agreed upon by the adjuster, claims manager, home office Claims Department, and defense counsel. The total value of a liability claim should be reduced or mitigated by the percentage of negligence on both parties.

For example, the claimant may have been found 10 percent negligent in the accident, and the full value of the injury would be reduced by that percentage of negligence. The bodily injury reserve evaluations illustrated in Exhibits 16.3 and 16.4, on pages 196–197, provide an explanation of the reserve process for a bodily injury liability claim. Notice that the two elements which are very subjective are the general damages (pain and suffering and permanency) component of the damage evaluation and the percentage of fault or negligence attributed to each of the parties involved. How can one accurately project for each individual claimant the monetary value of pain and suffering in each claim? How can a permanency rating be so precise that the physician applies an exact percentage? How can an adjuster accurately determine that the claimant is 25 percent negligent? These questions are rhetorical as it is impossible to be so completely accurate in projecting both.

Although the illustration in Exhibit 16.3 arrives at a net settlement value of $18,000, this value could vary significantly by claim. If it is determined that the claimant is 50 percent negligent, then the net settlement value is $12,000. If you only allocate $10,000 in general damages with 75 percent negligence, then the net settlement value is about $14,000. If the claimant had surgery, the calculation may look like the illustration in Exhibit 16.4. An adjuster needs to go through this exercise for each claim to arrive at a proper evaluation.

There are many variables to consider, such as the claimant's age, occupation, length of disability, medical and hospital treatment and bills, and other special damages. There are also other variables such as the payment of medical payments or personal injury protection (PIP) benefits provided under the automobile policy, which include medical, wage, and other benefits, depending on the jurisdiction. These special damages already paid may factor into the settlement calculation under the collateral source rule. This is a procedural rule followed by the courts in many states that prohibits informing the jury that the plaintiff has received money for his or her injuries from other sources, such as from his or her employer's workers compensation policy or an insurance policy covering another defendant.

Property Damage (PD) Case Reserves

Establishing individual case reserves on property damage claims is relatively straightforward. The extent of the damages is determined, and a monetary claim reserve is established. For example, assume a claimant has submitted an automobile estimate with a new claim report at $4,500. Although the investigation has not yet been initiated, it appears that the insured vehicle rear-ended the claimant's vehicle, according to the loss notice. The reserve evaluation would look like Exhibit 16.5. Keep in mind that the reserve recommendation may change with the assignment of an appraisal by a staff appraiser or independent appraiser as well as the results of the liability investigation.

If the initial accident facts were different, such as a left-turn claim, where the claimant made a left turn in front of the insured vehicle, the reserve would probably be at $1,275 which represents 25 percent liability [$5,100 × 25% = $1,275]. Ultimately, it may be determined that the claimant was 100 percent at fault, in which case liability on the claim would be denied and the claim reserve closed. Alternatively, the investigation could indicate that the claimant had a green left-turn arrow, and the insured was actually 100 percent responsible for the accident. This would result in an increase to the reserve of $5,100 (100 percent liability).

Automobile Collision and Comprehensive Case Reserves

Establishing individual case reserves on automobile collision and comprehensive

Exhibit 16.3: Bodily Injury Reserve Evaluation 1

Claimant Name: John Smith

Age: 45

Sex: Male

Occupation: Carpenter

Wages: $50,000 per year ($962 per week)

Injury: Fracture of the right femur

Treatment: X-rays; closed reduction with hard cast applied at hospital; emergency room hospital treatment; orthopedic treatment and evaluation; plus follow-up physical therapy.

Disability Period: 6 weeks

Special Damages:		**General Damages:**	
Medical:	$1,800	**Pain & Suffering:**	$10,000
Hospital:	$ 950	**Permanency:**	$ 5,000
Rx:	$ 28	**Total General:**	$15,000
Wage Loss:	$5,772		
Property Damage:	$ 0		
Other:	$ 0		
Total Special:	$8,550		

Gross Claim Value: $23,550 or $24,000 (special damages + general damages)

Insured's Negligence: 75% (Claimant is projected to be 25% negligent)

NET SETTLEMENT OR RESERVE VALUE: $18,000

Exhibit 16.4: Bodily Injury Reserve Evaluation 2

Claimant Name: John Smith

Age: 45

Sex: Male

Occupation: Carpenter

Wages: $50,000 per year ($962 per week)

Injury: Fracture of the right femur with open reduction and internal fixation

Treatment: X-rays; open reduction with rods and screws; hard cast applied at hospital; 4 days as inpatient in hospital; orthopedic initial and follow-up treatment and evaluation; physical therapy; x-rays; additional surgery and hospitalization to remove the hardware in the arm.

Disability Period: 12 weeks + 6 weeks (second surgery) = 18 weeks

Special Damages		**General Damages**	
Medical:	$ 6,500	**Pain & Suffering:**	$60,000
Hospital:	$10,000	**Permanency:**	$30,000
Rx:	$ 1,000	**Total General:**	$90,000
Wage Loss:	$17,300		
Property Damage:	$ 0		
Other:	$ 0		
Total Specials:	$34,800		

Gross Claim Value: $124,800 or $125,000 (special damages + general damages)

Insured's Negligence: 100% (Claimant is projected to be 0% negligent)

NET SETTLEMENT OR RESERVE VALUE: $125,000

Claims Process

Exhibit 16.5: Property Damage Reserve Evaluation

Claimant Name: Peter Jones

Damage: 2007 Toyota Corolla—Estimate at $4,500

Property Damage: $4,500

Other: $ 600 (Rental Reimbursement)

Total Specials: $5,100

Gross Claim Value: $5,100

Insured's Negligence: 100%

NET SETTLEMENT OR RESERVE VALUE: $5,100

Exhibit 16.6: Collision Reserve Evaluation

Insured Name: Martha Davis

Damage: 2008 Infiniti G35X, estimate at $8,700

Property Damage: $8,700

Other: $ 600 (Rental Reimbursement)

Total Loss: $9,300

Gross Claim Value: $9,300

Insured's Negligence: N/A

NET SETTLEMENT OR RESERVE VALUE: $9,300

claims is also relatively straightforward. The extent of the damage is determined, and a monetary claim reserve is established. For example, assume the insured submits an automobile estimate with a new claim report at $8,700. The reserve evaluation would look like that shown in Exhibit 16.6. Again, the reserve recommendation may change with the assignment of an appraisal by a staff appraiser or independent appraiser. Even though it is anticipated that a subrogation[4] claim against the adverse party will be successful, the claim is still reserved for the gross value. Any future subrogation return will reduce the incurred amount by the amount of the subrogation reimbursement.

First-Party Property Case Reserves

First-party property reserves are similar to the other case reserves discussed above; however, the various components of the claim need to be added. For example, a property loss may have building damage, business personal property damage, and a business interruption or extra expense claim too. Some insurance companies may reserve each component of the property loss as a separate feature, while others may reserve all the property loss components in one aggregate reserve.

Professional Liability Case Reserves

Professional liability reserve methodology will vary by company. Although a similar calculation methodology may be used, there are other components of the reserve process to take into consideration when arriving at a gross claim value. The damage aspect of these claims may be difficult to assess, and coverage issues may arise, with a portion of the damages not being covered. This makes the reserve evaluation more complicated.

To determine the reserve, an adjuster will break down the professional liability claim reserve by projecting the full damage value of the claim, then reducing the reserve by the noncovered allegations and damages as well as the liability apportionment on the claimant. A net claim reserve is then established. Professional liability reserves are difficult to evaluate, particularly when establishing the initial claim reserve, which may only be based on a review of a summons and complaint and receipt of the insured's records. After depositions are taken and legal discovery is underway, the reserve will need to be reevaluated and adjusted.

Also, there may be a significant allocated loss adjustment expense (ALAE) due to the pending litigation and need for discovery. Often, the expense costs far exceed the loss costs in professional liability claims. Defense counsel's input may prove very helpful in terms of the liability and damage evaluation. While defense counsel's input into any claim is always helpful—as it provides another opinion of the liability and damage exposures as well as potential jury verdict exposure—never rely exclusively on that opinion. Remember, a jury is not made up of adjusters, claims managers, home office claims examiners, and defense attorneys. It is usually a jury of the defendant's (the insured's) peers.

[4]After payment of a loss, the assignment to an insurer of the rights of the insured to recover the amount of the loss from one legally liable for it.

Workers Compensation (WC) Case Reserves

WC reserve descriptions differ from a typical general liability or automobile liability claim. WC reserve descriptions may be referred to as:

- WC indemnity or just indemnity
- WC medical or medical
- Vocational rehabilitation or voc rehab
- Expenses or ALAE

In a workers compensation claim, the indemnity reserve may involve a number of different types of indemnity payments. Indemnity reserves may, for example, consist of the following types of anticipated exposures:

- ***Temporary disability payments***—Wage benefits paid to the claimant for a specified temporary period. These benefits are typically paid in accordance with the established state rates for partial or total disability, as a percentage of the claimant's average weekly wage (AWW) (for example, 60 percent of the AWW).
- ***Permanent partial award payments***—Amounts paid to the claimant for any established permanency award by the state workers compensation commission or department. These awards can be scheduled loss awards for certain body parts or unscheduled loss awards for certain permanency ratings, potentially providing weekly benefits for the claimant's lifetime.
- ***Permanent total award payments***—Potentially providing weekly benefits for the claimant's lifetime.
- ***Fatality or death award payments***—Relating to the claimant's death payments to the claimant's spouse and/or dependants, providing weekly benefits.

The WC medical reserve may involve a number of different types of medical payments, including:

- ***Medical***—Physician, hospital, diagnostic, physical therapy, pharmacy, durable medical equipment, and other medical-related costs.
- ***Nurse case management***—The cost of a nurse, assigned by an adjuster, who goes on-site or telephones the claimant. In cases where a worker has injuries that complicate the recovery process, the nurse case manager will assist the injured worker in their progress toward recovery. Nurse case managers do not make diagnoses or treatment decisions.
- ***Transportation***—Expenses reimbursing the claimant for mileage or taxi expenses to and from medical providers.

Expenses or ALAE may include:

- ***Claim expenses***—Expenses related to adjusting and investigation.
- ***Legal expenses***—Attorney and other related legal costs.
- ***Medical bill review***—Fees to review medical bills to determine if they are in

accordance with the state fee schedule or based on usual and customary fees.

- ***Independent medical exam (IME)***—Expense of a physical examination conducted by a physician on injured workers to determine the diagnosis, prognosis, causal relationship of the injury to the accident, and future treatment. The IME can also provide a determination as to whether a worker has reached maximum benefit from treatment, the extent of any permanency, and a final determination of disability.
- ***Utilization review***—Expense to review the treatment regime to determine the reasonableness and appropriateness of medical treatment provided to a claimant.
- ***Vocational rehabilitation***[5]—Expenses related to rehabilitating a claimant toward other jobs and employment.

Bulk Expense Reserves

Most property and casualty claims will include an expense reserve. However, there are some insurance companies that do not establish individual case expense reserves. Instead, expense reserves are established in bulk, by line of business, based on an analysis of the historical paid expense amounts.

The loss adjustment expenses are composed of both allocated loss adjustment expenses (ALAE) and unallocated loss adjustment expenses (ULAE). Usually, the individual expense case reserve on a claim file is an ALAE. Exhibit 16.7 on page 202 outlines various ALAE claim expense categories. While adjuster and appraiser expenses are included in this category in the Exhibit, this may vary by company, as these expenses are often classified as ULAE.

ULAE reserves typically refer to those expenses associated with the overhead to operate a claim facility or Claims Department. They may also include adjuster and appraiser expenses. In the third-party administrator (TPA) environment, the client may request that the adjuster and appraiser expense categories be separately coded, reserved, and paid off the individual claim file as an ULAE, simply to track the expenses paid for the client's financial records.

Summary and Conclusion

Reserve management is a critical component of the adjustment process and one of the adjuster's primary responsibilities. Inadequate claim reserves can seriously affect the financial stability of an insurance company by not being able to meet its claim payment obligations and also its ability to price its insurance products competitively.

There is no exact science in establishing bodily injury case reserves. The adjuster must understand that similar injuries do not always translate into the same claim value for reserve or settlement purposes. Each claim should be evaluated on its own merits by analyzing the projected special damages and then applying an appropriate amount for general damages, keeping in mind that if a claim is decided by a jury, the general damage component would be calculated by a layperson. Differences in gen-

[5]Depending on the state, this may be considered an indemnity benefit.

Exhibit 16.7: Allocated Loss Adjustment Expense (ALAE) Examples

- Fees to attorneys for claims in suit or other matters requiring legal defense and/or representation
- Litigation management expenses, including costs incurred to audit outside legal bills by cost containment experts
- Fees for independent field adjusters and appraisers, surveyors, private investigators, reinspectors, rehabilitation nurses, and hearing representatives
- Fees to court reporters and the cost of transcripts
- All court costs, court fees, and court expenses
- Prejudgment and postjudgment interest paid as a result of litigation
- Fees for service of legal process
- Costs of surveillance expenses, undercover operatives, detective services, and fraud investigators
- Costs for employing experts for the preparation of maps, professional photographs and/or diagrams, accounting, engineering, chemical, or physical analysis
- Costs for employing experts for their advice, opinion, or testimony concerning claims under investigation or in litigation or for which a declaratory judgment is sought
- Costs of legal transcripts of testimony taken at coroners' inquests or at criminal or civil proceedings.
- Costs for all official reports and public records.
- Costs for ISO ClaimSearch® entries[a] (See Appendix B beginning on page 363.)
- Cost for witness fees and witness travel expenses
- Costs of asset search and verifications
- Costs of independent medical examinations and requests for medical, hospital, and wage records
- Fixed amounts for medical cost containment expenses, including medical bill review costs

[a]A TPA may code these expenses as ALAE; however, an insurance company may include these expenses as ULAE.

eral damage projections for pain and suffering or permanency and the liability apportionment based on contributory or comparative negligence can swing a claim value significantly to a lower or higher amount. Therefore, claim values should always be developed in ranges to account for any differences of opinion.

Property damage and physical damage reserves are much easier to calculate as the damages are fixed. Professional liability cases are more complex. Workers compensation case reserves have several different components, depending on the type of indemnity claim involved and at what stage the claim is in. For example, the initial indemnity reserve may be reflective of temporary total disability benefits; however, as the claim matures, and it is determined that the claimant may have a permanent injury and disability, the reserve will be changed to reflect the longer term projected indemnity payments and/or a permanency award.

FOR MORE INFORMATION ON:	GO TO:	PAGE(S):
Recruitment and Retention	Chapter 7	73
Claims Process	Chapters 10–17	105–220
Claims Process—Overview	Chapter 10	105
Investigation and Adjustment	Chapter 11	115
Claim Statements and Interviews	Chapter 12	127
Coverage Issues	Chapter 13	143
Evaluation and Resolution	Chapter 14	155
Going to Court	Chapter 15	173
Recovery	Chapter 17	205
Claims Handling Guidelines	Chapters 21–30	271–354
Litigation Management	Appendix F	421

Chapter 17: Claims Process—Recovery

Recovery is broad term that can include subrogation, salvage, third-party deductibles, contribution and indemnity, loss and expense refunds, workers compensation (WC) liens, personal injury protection (PIP) or no-fault liens, loss transfer, and second injury funds. This chapter discusses these various forms of recovery.

The primary reason why recovery is so important is that the funds which were previously paid out for claims are now being received back. Since recovery is a component of the incurred losses (paid + reserves – recovery = incurred losses), the receipt of recovery positively affects the loss ratio and the insurance company's results.

Recovery is also important to the policyholder. When an insured is paid a first-party loss, their deductible is applied to the loss. When an insurance company subrogates against a responsible party, the deductible is reimbursed to the policyholder and prorated based on the percentage of recovery received. For example, if a policyholder has a $10,000 loss with a $1,000 deductible, the $1,000 deductible will be included in the recovery claim. If the recovery claim is settled for 50 percent, the policyholder is paid their pro-rata reimbursement share of $500 or 50 percent of the deductible.

Subrogation

Subrogation is a principle of common law. It establishes that, when an insurer pays for a loss suffered by its insured, the insurer then acquires the insured's rights to recover for that loss from the third parties responsible for the loss. The theory behind this principle is that, absent repayment of the insurer, the insured would be unjustly enriched by virtue of recovery from both the insurer and the wrongdoer. Subrogation rights arise by action of law, regardless of whether they are provided for in the insurance contract or in any transactions between the insured and the third party.

The party whose debt has been paid or satisfied is referred to as the "subrogor." In the insurance context, then, the subrogor is usually the insured who has been paid by the

Exhibit 17.1: Commercial Auto Subrogation Provision

Our Right To Recover from Others:

If **we** make any payment, **we** are entitled to recover what **we** paid from other parties.

Any person to or for whom **we** make payment must transfer to **us** his or her rights of recovery against any other party. This person must do everything necessary to secure these rights and must do nothing that would jeopardize them.

insurer, the "subrogee," i.e., the party that has satisfied the subrogor's debt and that succeeds to the subrogor's rights against the third party responsible for the loss.

Subrogation is quite common in first-party automobile and property losses, such as collision/comprehensive claims, as well as building, inland marine, and contents losses. Subrogation can also exist in liability claims. Generally, insurance policies outline the insurance company's right of subrogation in the "Conditions" section of the policy. An example from the commercial automobile insurance policy is shown in Exhibit 17.1 above.

An example of a subrogation claim for an automobile collision claim would be the right of subrogation against the adverse vehicle operator who went through the red traffic light, striking the insured vehicle. If the insurer paid $5,000 to the insured, less the $500 deductible, then typically the insurer would file a subrogation claim against the at-fault driver or his insurer for the full amount ($5,000) and then reimburse the insured the full deductible amount (100 percent) or their pro-rata share if the full 100 percent of the paid loss was not collected.

A claim facility should always aggressively pursue subrogation against the adverse party and/or insurer. Although some claim facilities have a dedicated subrogation claim unit or department, many claim facilities may have the primary handling adjuster manage the subrogation component of the claim or have a recovery specialist position. The recovery specialist primarily handles subrogation claims and may at times co-adjust a claim with the primary adjuster to be sure the subrogation claim is handled and managed properly.

Upon recovery recognition, a file note or subrogation screen should be completed commenting on subrogation potential and identification of the responsible party (adverse party and/or adverse insurer). This should be clearly documented in the claim file. A dollar estimate for the estimated recovery amount should be established in the claim system to allow tracking of future estimated subrogation recoveries. As individual actual recoveries are received, the estimates should be reduced.

An initial subrogation letter should be sent to the responsible party or adverse insurer placing them on notice of subrogation interests. Exhibit 17.2 following provides a sample letter. Many claim facilities follow the 30/30/30 subrogation protocol. The handling adjuster should send the first subrogation recovery notification letter to the at-fault party or their insurer within 30 days of the claim report date. Thirty days later, within 60 days of the claim report date, a second letter should be sent to follow up. If a response is not received within 30 days, the claim should

Exhibit 17.2: Sample Subrogation Letter to Adverse Insurer

RE:	**Date of Loss:**	**02/03/10**
	Policy No.:	**AU-782349-01**
	Our Claim No.:	**45-NU-702345**
	Your File No.:	**NT978789**
	Our Insured:	**John Calabrese**
	Your Insured:	**Susan Armstrong**

Dear Mr. Jones:

We represent XYZ Insurance Company and are handling the above captioned property damage subrogation claim. We understand that XXX Insurance Company provides automobile liability insurance coverage to Susan Armstrong in this matter. Since payment was made by XYZ Insurance Company to its insured, John Calabrese, XYZ Insurance Company has rights of subrogation against the responsible party, Susan Armstrong.

We have enclosed a complete copy of all supporting documentation from our claim file, which includes an automobile appraisal, vehicle photographs, copy of issued claim check, policy record showing the deductible, and police report. Our records indicate your insured, Susan Armstrong, failed to yield right of way and was cited by the state police. The investigation indicates your insured was 100 percent responsible for this accident.

As a result of the accident, XYZ Insurance Company paid its insured, John Calabrese, $5,000. The policy carries a $1,000 deductible. Therefore, the total claim is for $6,000, which includes the deductible.

Kindly forward payment in the amount of $6, 000 payable to **XYZ Insurance Company as Subrogee of John Calabrese** as soon as possible.

Thank you.

be placed in arbitration or referred to a subrogation law firm (or subrogation/recovery company) to assist in the subrogation process. Before doing so, however, first determine whether there is any available insurance coverage on the part of the wrongdoer, i.e., tortfeasor. If there is no available insurance coverage, an asset check[1] should be conducted to determine whether it will be cost-effective to file litigation against the adverse party.

If there is no available liability insurance coverage for the tortfeasor, a decision will need to be made as to whether it is worth pursuing the responsible party. Filing litigation is costly, considering the filing fees and attorney fees. Typically, a subrogation attorney charges a fee equal to one-third of the subrogation recovery. Therefore, if the adjuster has a $1,500 claim where liability has been established at 50 percent, the net recovery claim is $750. If the recovery attorney takes one-third for the fee, plus a typical filing fee of $200, there is not much left to pursue.

Recovery adjusters will generally make the decision to not pursue recovery on a particular claim if the estimated recovery amount is within their claim authority. Just as an adjuster handing the underlying claim has claim authority to settle a claim, the recovery adjuster has authority to settle or adjust the recovery claim, making decisions on the percentage of recovery acceptable or closing the recovery claim without any recovery proceeds received. Recovery claim authority above the recovery adjuster's authority level would involve approval by a claims supervisor or manager.

If a recovery claim is closed either voluntarily or due to an unsuccessful arbitration hearing or trial, resulting in zero recovery, the policyholders should be advised of the results as they have an interest in the deductible reimbursement. The recovery claim file would then be closed, bringing the estimated recovery amount to zero.

To be successful with a subrogation claim, there are several important considerations:

- Investigation
- Use of experts
- Damages
- Legal liability
- Statute of limitations
- Forum for collection

These are discussed in more detail below.

Investigation

The underlying investigation is critical to support the subrogation claim against the responsible party. The extent of the claim investigation will depend on the accident details. For example, an automobile claim involving a question as to which vehicle had the green traffic light may require more investigation than a claim involving a rear-end accident, where the second driver is considered completely to blame, with the adverse driver not disputing how the accident occurred. The reason for this is that

[1]An asset check is a check performed by a third-party company to determine whether the responsible party has any viable assets to satisfy a claim or judgment. The asset check will include a determination as to whether the responsible party owns any property, such as houses, land, cars, or boats.

questions of fact require more investigation to support a liability position.

A claim investigation will usually involve statements being taken from the involved parties and witnesses. Statements can be taken by the adjuster in the field, as a signed statement or recorded statement, or a recorded statement can be taken by telephone. Statements are important as they support the primary evaluation basis for the subrogation claim. Scene photographs, damaged vehicle and property damage photographs, and diagrams are also important to evaluate both liability and damage exposures and should always be considered as part of the adjustment process. It is important to take such photos and diagrams early in a claim investigation when the accident scene and damages remain substantially unchanged from the accident date.

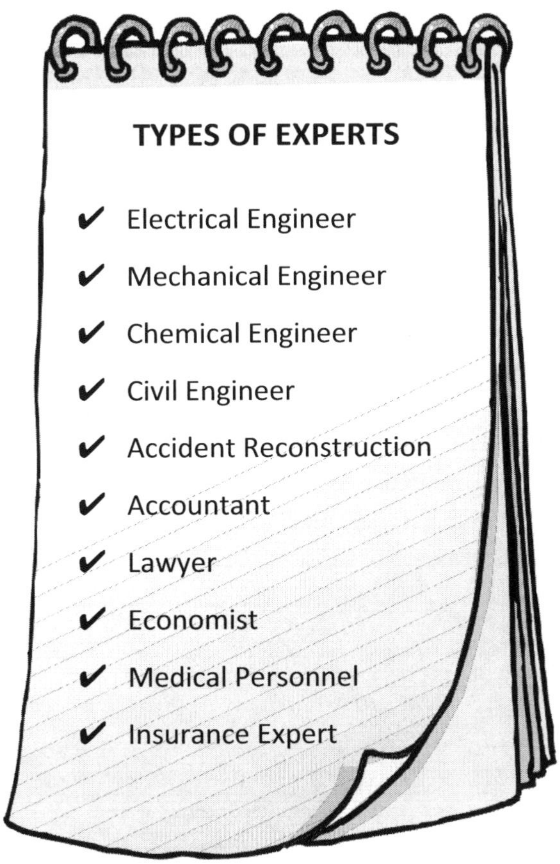

Copies of official reports should be requested to evaluate both liability and damage issues. These might include:

- Police accident reports
- Police statements
- Police photos
- Police accident reconstruction reports
- Fire reports
- Weather reports
- Traffic light sequence reports

Use of Experts

The initial investigation may include the prompt assignment of an expert, often referred to a cause and origin expert. The expert is retained to support any potential subrogation claim based on a defect, malfunction, recent work performed, etc. For example, a car may have caught fire as a result of recent service to the engine. The adjuster would retain an expert to inspect the vehicle and prepare a report providing an expert opinion as to whether the damages were causally related to the work performed prior to the loss, thereby supporting the liability position of the subrogation claim.

There are many different types of experts, and it is important to be sure that the most qualified expert is retained. It should be noted that experts can differ on their opinions and conclusions; therefore, adjusters need to research and retain a qualified expert who is experienced in the type of subrogation claim involved.

Damages

At the outset of a claims investigation, it is important to assess the damage potential. Damages can be in the form of property damage or injury damage. In an automobile claim, a subrogation claim for property damage arises out of the collision or comprehensive claim payment to the policyholder. For injury damages, a subrogation claim may be made based on the payment of medical and wage benefits paid under PIP or no-fault insurance coverage or some other type of lien, such as a workers compensation lien. Following are several examples of subrogation claims.

Automobile—The policyholder's vehicle is struck in the rear by the adverse vehicle. The insurance company pays the policyholder $2,500, which was reduced by a $500 deductible. The insurance company pursues the adverse insurer with a subrogation claim in the amount of $3,000, and is successful with 100 percent reimbursement. The policyholder is reimbursed her $500 deductible.

Property—The policyholder's home has a fire caused by a malfunctioning portable electric heater in the garage. The total damages were in the amount of $50,000 to the dwelling and contents, and there is a $1,000 deductible (net payment to the policyholder in the amount of $49,000). The adjuster assigns a cause and origin expert immediately after the claim was reported to determine whether there is any viable subrogation. The expert indicates that the electric heater has a product defect that caused the loss. The expert prepares a detailed report of his findings, which is provided to the electric heater manufacturer's insurer. After the adverse insurer investigates the claim, it is determined that there was a malfunctioning part in the heater, and this defect caused other losses in the past. After presenting all supporting documentation, including the appraisal documents, photographs, expert report, and issued check, the adverse insurer reimburses the subrogating insurer $50,000. The policyholder is reimbursed his $1,000 deductible.

Workers compensation—The employee claimant tripped and fell during a sales call at a client's location. The fall was the result of a defective walkway and had existed for over a year. The claimant had never been to the location previously. As a result of the accident, the claimant fractures her right arm, requiring surgery. The workers compensation insurer pays the claimant $5,000 in indemnity wage benefits and $15,000 in medical and rehabilitation benefits. At a final hearing, the claimant receives a scheduled loss award of $15,000. The total benefits paid to the claimant were $35,000.

The claimant retains an attorney to pursue the property owner at the client's location for negligent maintenance of the property. The workers compensation insurance company files a lien against any recovery the claimant may receive in the third-party claim. The claimant settles the claim for $100,000, which would mean that the workers compensation lien would need to be satisfied in the amount of $35,000. The claimant attorney is entitled to a one-third collection fee, so the workers compensation insurance company would receive a net recovery of approximately $23,300. It should be noted that workers compensation liens are often compromised, particularly if there are questionable liability issues.

Liability—A claimant slips and falls in a supermarket on a wet floor in the produce aisle. Liability is established as probable as there were multiple prior complaints throughout the day that the floor had been wet in the area where the claimant fell. The claimant fractured his ankle, which required a closed reduction (no surgery) and had medical and wage special damages in the amount of $5,000. The claim was brought against the building owner and the supermarket, but the supermarket never responded. The supermarket had a lease agreement with the building owner which includes hold harmless and indemnity provisions[2] favoring the building owner. The building owner's insurer tendered the claim to the supermarket on several occasions, but the supermarket never responded. It was discovered the supermarket had no liability insurance coverage due to policy cancellation for nonpayment of premium. Within the last letter, the building owner insurer indicated that if there was no response within 15 days, it would settle the claim with the claimant and then pursue an indemnity action against the supermarket for reimbursement. The supermarket did not respond. In an effort to avoid litigation, the liability insurer for the building owner settled the claim with the claimant, with a signed general release naming the supermarket and building owner, and then pursued a recovery claim against the super market for reimbursement.

[2]Indemnification is the promise to reimburse another party for damages. An indemnity provision specifies the indemnification agreed to in the contract. A hold harmless contractual provision states that one party will be held harmless by another party for any liability resulting from the activities in the contract, such as a lease agreement which may place responsibility for all interior building maintenance on the tenant. The tenant agrees to indemnify and hold harmless the landlord for damages resulting from poor or improper maintenance.

As these examples illustrate, to be successful in the pursuit of the subrogation claim, the damage aspect of the claim needs to be proven. All types of damages require supporting documentation to perfect the subrogation claim. For example, most subrogation claims arising out of a collision or comprehensive claim payment should have an appraisal done by a licensed automobile appraiser (with photographs), or in the alternative, some type of a desk review by a qualified damage appraiser.

In an arbitration proceeding, a qualified damage appraisal report will generally satisfy the necessary proof for the damage aspect of the subrogation claim. However, if a subrogation claim goes into litigation, an appraiser may need to testify as to the content of the appraisal report. Damage estimates (from a body shop or contractor) are sometimes used for the payment of smaller first-party claims (i.e., under $1,000), but this damage estimate amount could be challenged by the adverse insurer as being excessive by having its qualified appraiser perform a desk review of the repair estimate.

The subrogation claim may include indirect damages such as loss of use or rental reimbursement. Should the insurance policy provide coverage for indirect damages, the adjuster needs to be sure to control the rental process and payments and not overpay, or else the damages could be challenged in the subrogation claim. The process is controlled by providing specific rental reimbursement guidelines and instructions to the policyholder when acknowledging claim. This will help avoid any issues regarding excessive rental bills.

Direct damages are damages to the property itself. When handling vehicle claims, damage issues may involve both total losses and partial losses. A total loss is where the projected repairs or estimate exceeds the vehicle's actual cash value (ACV), i.e., replacement cost less depreciation. A constructive total loss is when the damages are estimated to be approximately 75 to 80 percent of the actual cash value of the vehicle, making the vehicle a total loss based on the potential for the repairs to exceed the actual cash value. When evaluating a constructive total loss, it is important to discuss the potential for supplemental damages—damages that are identified and estimated after repairs have been initiated or completed—with the assigned appraiser, as these may push the claim into a total loss category.

The adjuster may settle the claim based on a constructive total loss assessment, with the expectation that there may be future potential supplemental damages claimed during the repair process as repairs get underway, which may exceed the ACV. Since there will be potential salvage recovery[3] in a constructive total loss, the total loss payment, with the salvage recovery reimbursement, will reduce the overall total loss amount paid.

[3]Salvage recovery is the proceeds received from the damaged vehicle being sold for parts to a salvage company, which reduces the incurred loss.

Depending on the year of the vehicle, the policyholder may not be pleased with a constructive total loss assessment versus a partial loss, (i.e., the appraisal amount), as it may be difficult to replace the older vehicle with the current ACV valuation amount. It should be noted that some automobile policies have different settlement valuation provisions that are based on an agreed value or stated value, wherein the agreed or stated value amount is paid if the vehicle is deemed to be a total loss. These settlement valuation methodologies are common for classic or collector vehicles.

During the subrogation process, the adverse party or insurance company could challenge the total loss evaluation, claiming that the vehicle was not a total loss, or question the value of the salvage applied to the loss. A written damage appraisal report, total loss evaluation report, photos, and a proper evaluation and disposition of the vehicle salvage will typically avoid any of these issues.

Legal Liability

The subrogation claim is based on the legal liability of the responsible party. If the adjuster is unable to prove legal liability, then the subrogation claim will be unsuccessful.

Legal liability statutes and doctrines vary by state and jurisdiction; however, negligence—the degree of fault—is usually the primary liability issue. Negligence is basically a result of not using reasonable care. In many jurisdictions, liability is based on the percentage of fault or negligence by each party involved in the accident. Other states follow a modified comparative negligence law where, if one party is more than

51 percent negligent, they may be barred from recovery. Some states, such as New York, follow a pure comparative negligence law, where a party that is found to be 80 percent negligent could still pursue the other party for 20 percent of their damages. Theoretically, you could collect 1 percent of your damages in New York.

If the responsible party is a public entity, certain governmental immunities may apply that limit liability and damages. Public entities, such as a municipality or public school, have a formal notice of claim requirement that requires a formal pleading prior to litigation within a specified time frame (i.e., 90 days to 1 year from the accident date). After the notice of claim is filed, the public entity may be entitled to conduct prediscovery, including a deposition of the claimant.

For example, an adjuster investigates a claim where the policyholder's vehicle was damaged from a pothole in the road owned, maintained, and controlled by XYZ City, which is governed as a municipality in the state. After the claim is paid to the policyholder, the adjuster sends a subrogation letter to XYZ City. To pursue a claim against XYZ City, the City has certain statutory requirements which include filing a formal "notice of claim"[4] against the City within the prescribed time frame, which is 90 days from the date of the accident. The adjuster files the formal notice against the City 6 months after the accident, which is not in compliance with the statutory time frame. As a result, the subrogation claim is barred based on the 90-day statutory filing requirement.

Since municipalities may have statutory filing requirements within a specified time frame after an accident date, it is important for the adjuster to handle this type of claim in a timely manner and recognize the various jurisdictional requirements which can vary by municipality and state. These claims should be flagged by the adjuster with an appropriate diary date to file the notice of claim within that period.

Statute of Limitations

The statute of limitations is the time period within which a subrogation claim may be filed against the adverse party or insurance company. Typically, this time restriction applies to both claims filed in litigation and arbitration. The statute of limitations time period can vary from 1 to 6 years, depending on the state and the basis for the cause of action. The statute of limitations for actions based on contract law is usually longer than claims based on common law.

When handling a subrogation claim, the adjuster needs to be aware of the statute of limitations, as the adverse party can raise a defense that the statute of limitations has expired, thereby avoiding payment of the claim. When litigation is involved, the statute of limitations is protected by the filing of a summons and complaint before the statute of limitations expires. If the claim is going to be submitted to arbitration, arbitration must be filed before the statute of

[4] A notice of claim is a formal written claim presented to a municipality. Typically, the claim notice includes the basic claim details, such as the names and addresses of the parties involved; the date, time and place of the accident; the accident description; the damages being claimed; and the details of the claim against the municipality. Some municipalities have their own prescribed notice of claim form, while others use a format similar to a formal complaint filed in a litigation proceeding. When filing a notice of claim, it should always be sent certified mail, return receipt requested, as verification of timely filing.

limitations expires. If the adjuster is submitting the claim to arbitration, it is important to know in advance that the adverse insurer (or self insured) is a member of the arbitration forum. If they are not a signatory[5] to the arbitration agreement or a member, the statute of limitations will not be protected with the filing of arbitration in that forum.

Occasionally, the adverse insurer may waive the tolling of the statute limitations;[6] however, this course of action would be an exception. This may be done in situations where settlement negotiations are underway, with a settlement disposition expected in the near future.

There may be situations when the adverse insurer is defending a liability claim presented by two claimants involved in the same accident. If the statute of limitations is approaching, the insurer or claim facility presenting the subrogation claim will file for arbitration to protect the statute of limitations. A request may be made by the adverse insurer to the arbitration committee requesting that the claim be deferred until the liability claim has been resolved by settlement or tried to a conclusion. The primary reason for deferring the arbitration process for the subrogation claim is that the liability insurer does not want a potentially adverse subrogation arbitration award affecting the defense of the liability claim.

[5]Many insurance companies are signatories to arbitration agreements (such as Arbitration Forums, Inc.), which requires them to sign and be bound by the arbitration rules and procedures. Being a signatory typically means that they are members of that arbitration forum.

[6]Tolling of the statute of limitations means that the time period allowing a claim has expired, precluding the claim from being presented.

It is very important to protect the statute of limitations during the subrogation claims handling process. If the statute of limitations expires, the claim will be barred from recovery, and this will have a financial impact on the insurer, as it will not be able to pursue the subrogation claim.

Forum for Collection

There are various methods of subrogation collection, ranging from voluntary settlement to litigation. There are several arbitration forums to arbitrate subrogation matters. One such forum is called Arbitration Forums, Inc. (www.arbfile.org) which provides a venue for all types of claims, including auto physical damage, personal injury protection, and property claims. Most insurance companies and many self-insured entities are members of arbitration forums resulting in mandatory arbitration, versus costly litigation. The decisions are typically binding on both parties involved.

Salvage

Salvage is another form of insurance recovery. Salvage basically refers to the undamaged, or sometimes damaged, portion of a loss. For example, if a vehicle is declared a total loss, the vehicle still may have undamaged or damaged parts which can be sold (i.e., engine, tires, steel frame). Automobile salvage handling is further explained in Chapter 22, Claims Handling Guidelines—Auto Physical Damage beginning on page 273.

Salvage also exists in property, cargo, and marine losses. For example, a manufacturing facility may have sustained a fire loss. The warehouse contains damaged goods that cannot be sold in the insured's market, but may have salvage value in some secondary market. During the adjustment of these types of losses, it is recommended that a salvor or salvage company be retained to assess the salvage value and make an offer to purchase and take it away. Remember, the salvage value will reduce the gross claim loss, and any payments made to the claim facility for the salvage value will reduce the overall incurred loss. The incurred loss is equal to reserves + payments – recoveries.

Should the insured wish to retain the salvage, the salvage value should be determined by the appraiser based on the salvage bids. When negotiating vehicle salvage value, keep in mind the processing charges anticipated if the vehicle is to be picked up by a salvage vendor and delivered to an auction facility. There may also be storage charges and dismantling charges. All of these charges should be considered when evaluating the full exposure of the vehicle total loss and salvage value. When a salvage vendor picks up vehicle salvage, they prepay all outstanding charges (storage fees, towing, etc.) and deduct the charges from the gross salvage return. Should the expenses exceed the gross salvage recovery, the adjuster will receive an expense invoice. All of these costs may be included in the subrogation claim.

Third-Party Deductibles

Yet another form of recovery is the third-party deductible. Insurance policy deductibles may include loss and allocated loss adjustment expenses (legal and adjuster expenses). Third-party deductibles, a form of retention, are used to retain the smaller losses and/or reduce the premium by absorbing a frequency layer. The frequency layer is where most losses occur, which can be absorbed under a self-insured retention, as the frequency may be predicted.

Some deductible programs include expense payments as well. Typically, the insurance company pays the loss and expenses, and then requests reimbursement from the insured. Depending on the premium and the size of the deductible, the insured may be required to post collateral or security to be sure the deductibles will be collected and reimbursed.

There are different ways to collect third-party deductibles. After any payment is processed—loss or expense—a deductible recovery letter should be sent to the insured for reimbursement. Alternatively, after the total deductible limit is met, an itemized invoice is sent to the insured. The deductible recovery letter should attach a copy of the expense invoice or release and discontinuance as well as the check issued. Deductible reimbursements outstanding beyond 60 days are usually brought to management's attention for referral to the agent, broker, or general agent/program administrator for assistance.

Some policies have third-party deductibles per loss as well as aggregate deductibles. Aggregate deductibles represent the total retained limit during a given policy period. For example, an insured may have a per-occurrence deductible of $50,000 and an aggregate deductible of $250,000. This means that the insured can have five losses at $50,000, and then will no longer have any per-occurrence deductibles for the remaining policy period.

Contribution and Indemnity

Contribution and indemnification are two other forms of recovery. They occur in situations where a third-party defendant, codefendant, or responsible party is found to be either partially or fully responsible for a loss.

Contribution is the principle holding that two or more defendants may be liable in a loss. During the claims handling process, contribution applies when there are codefendants in a lawsuit or an arbitration proceeding, with each defendant responsible for a portion of the damages. In this situation, there are claims among the codefendants in the form of cross-claims, or claims against one another, or third-party claims, where a defendant brings in a third party to the action. If a codefendant or third-party defendant is responsible for damages and refuses to contribute to the payment of the loss, the other defendant may pay the loss and then file a claim against the offending codefendant for contribution toward the settlement payment.

It should be noted that contribution is also the principle holding that two or more insurers each liable for a covered loss should participate in the payment of that loss. Having paid its share of a loss, an insurer may be entitled to equitable contribution—a legal right to recover part of the payment from another insurer whose policy was also applicable. Many insurance policies stipulate the formula under which contribution among multiple insurers will take place. Two standard methods are contribution by limits and contribution by equal shares.

Under contribution by limits, any participating insurer's share of the total loss is the percentage of that loss that the insurer's policy limit represents as part of all insurers' applicable limits. Under the contribution by equal shares apportionment method, the loss is shared equally among all the insurers who have valid insurance on the risk, up to the limit of liability of the insurer with the lowest limit of liability. After that, if the judgment or settlement has not been satisfied, all insurers that still have unexhausted limits will split the loss equally until the next insurer exhausts its limit or the loss is paid. This will continue until the judgment or settlement is fully paid or all insurers exhaust their limits.

Indemnification refers to the agreement of one party to assume financial responsibility for the liability of another party, which would be found in a contract or agreement. Indemnity and hold harmless agreements are used to impose this transfer of risk. They are written to protect one party against claims, litigation, and other losses as a result of another party's negligence. Recovery for indemnification, therefore, typically refers to those situations where the contribution toward the claim is after settlement or a jury verdict. The defendant will file a separate or third-party action against the at-fault party, shifting the responsibility to pay judgments or damages to that party, and attempt to recoup any dollars paid or to be paid to the plaintiff.

Contribution and indemnification are very common recovery tools in liability claims handing. The claim investigation should always include exploring whether there are any potential third parties to shift responsibility either prior to or during the litigation stage of the claim. All contribution and indemnity issues should be addressed with written notification to the responsible party.

For example, assume that ABC, Inc., owns a building where a claimant fell down. XXX, Inc., is a tenant of the building, and the claimant fell in the tenant's office space, slipping on liquid left on the floor. The building owner (ABC) has a lease agreement with tenant XXX. Within the lease agreement, the tenant assumes responsibility for the maintenance of the interior of the premises. There is also a provision that states that in the event of a claim resulting from the tenant not maintaining the premises properly, and resulting in an accident, the tenant will assume the defense of the claim and indemnify the landlord or building owner for related costs. This claim and lease have triggered both a contribution and indemnity claim by the landlord against the tenant. Sample lease agreement language is shown in Exhibit 17.3 below.

During the course of the investigation or through the legal discovery process, information or documentation may arise indicating that another party may be responsible for payment of the claim. In this instance, the adjuster is said to tender the claim to another party. Therefore, a tender is an act in which one party demands defense and indemnification in a claim or litigation pursuant to the provisions in a contract or agreement. This request to the responsible party or its representatives specifically outlines the reasons supporting demand for defense and indemnification.

Most often, a tender is in the form of letter sent certified mail, which provides an overview of the claim or litigation, including the accident and damage details, its current status, the specific reasons for the demand for defense and indemnification, including any relevant language from a contract or agreement. The tender letter will request a response within a specific time period and may threaten litigation if the tender is not honored.

The party demanding defense and indemnification may also be named as an additional insured on the responsible party's liability insurance policy, pursuant to the same con-

Exhibit 17.3: Lease Agreement Hold Harmless Language

The Tenant, shall keep the Leased Premises neat and clean, in good repair, order, and condition and make all necessary internal and nonstructural repairs thereto …

The Tenant shall *defend, indemnify,* and *hold harmless the Landlord* and its agents and employees against and from all liabilities, suits, actions, damages, liability and expense, penalties, claims, and costs which may be imposed upon or incurred by or asserted against the Landlord or its agents or employees by reason of, or in any way *arising out of the Tenant's use or occupancy of the Leased Premises* or any part thereof after the execution of this Lease or occasioned wholly or in part *by any act or omission of the Tenant,* its agents, contractors, employees, servants, invitees, licensees … *excluding any damage or injury resulting from any negligence act or omission of Landlord….*

tract or agreement that provided for defense and indemnification. An additional insured is a person or organization not automatically included as an insured under an insurance policy, but for whom insured status is arranged, usually by endorsement. A named insured's impetus for providing additional insured status to others is typically to comply with a contractual agreement requiring the named insured to do so (e.g., customers or owners of property leased by the named insured). In the case of the tender letter indicated above, the tender letter will also cite the additional insured status and request that coverage be provided pursuant to the endorsement or coverage.

Part of the claims adjuster's responsibility is to search for any potential for recovery where the insured has the benefit of additional insured status on another responsible party's liability insurance policy. As part of the investigation, copies of the applicable insurance policies and any additional insured endorsements are critical, as well as certificates of insurance which provide all the necessary insurance policy information, including the insurance company name, policy number, effective dates, policy limits, and other pertinent information.

Contribution and indemnification are very common in liability claims handling. It is important to secure all the applicable contracts during the investigative process to analyze the agreements for potential recovery.

Loss and Expense Refunds

Loss refunds and expense refunds are another form of recovery and basically are reimbursements as a result of overpayments, improper payments being returned, and any other payment that is unnecessary or improperly made and which should be deposited back into the loss fund account. Loss and expense refunds may result due to an error in check issuance or possibly payment to the wrong party.

Workers Compensation and PIP Liens

Often, in claims involving employers and employees, there is a workers compensation lien or personal injury protection (PIP) lien that allows the insurance company or claim facility take an offset against the claimant's total recovery. For example, consider the situation where the claimant fell down during work and filed a legal action against the landlord. The insurer that paid workers compensation benefits to the claimant will have a lien against the claimant's third-party recovery and settlement against the landlord. So, if the claimant recovered $10,000 for the liability or tort claim, and the total paid workers compensation benefits came to $2,500, then the claimant would ultimately be paid $7,500, with the $2,500 paid to the workers compensation insurer to satisfy its lien. The claimant's attorney will usually take a percentage of the lien recovery as a contingency fee, with the workers compensation insurer only receiving two-thirds of the lien recovery.

A PIP lien is similar to the workers compensation lien and sometimes applies to no-fault or PIP benefits paid to the claimant. It should be noted that these liens generally only apply to additional PIP benefits that are over and above the statutory PIP benefits.

Claims involving medical and wage benefits require documentation to support the payments made. For example, if an adjuster paid PIP benefits to a claimant who was treated excessively, made overpayments of the wage loss due to a calculation error, or failed to take various statutory offsets, such as Social Security benefits or workers compensation benefits, this could result in the damage aspect of the subrogation claim being challenged. This emphasizes how important the underlying claims handing is to the subrogation claim.

Loss Transfer

Some states allow for the recovery of statutory PIP benefits paid by an insurance company in the form of loss transfer. The recovery claim is brought by the insurance company paying the PIP benefits directly against the insurance company providing liability coverage for the responsible party. This is called loss transfer, as the claim is between the insurance companies and does not directly involve the insured or claimant. Loss transfer allows for the shifting or transfer of the PIP payments to the insurer for the responsible party under certain circumstances. The determination of responsibility follows the same negligence standards as in liability claims handling, and may involve partial recovery if comparative negligence applies.

Loss transfer is a recovery transaction between insurance companies and is subject to an arbitration agreement. PIP loss transfer may only apply in certain circumstances. For example, in New York, a loss transfer claim can only be brought if one of the vehicles in the accident is 6,500 pounds or over, or is a vehicle for hire.

The loss transfer claim may be set up as a separate claim feature for tracking purposes. There are no policy limits on an automobile policy for loss transfer. The policy limit typically equals the statutory limits for the state-mandated PIP coverage. Loss transfer is generally mandated in the insurance law or regulations for the state involved, outlining its applicability and process.

Second Injury Funds

Yet another source of recovery is a second injury fund. In workers compensation insurance, claim apportionment between insurance companies may apply in situations where there are preexisting injuries or illnesses to an employee who has now presented a claim under the current policy. This may trigger more than one policy applying to the claim under certain situations in some states. Usually this means dividing the claim exposure among a group of employers—the employers the employee worked for when exposed to the conditions that contributed to the illness. It can also mean division of liability between an employer and a fund, such as a second injury fund, that pays for the portion of a claim attributable to preexisting conditions.

Certain states have implemented second injury funds to encourage employers to hire disabled employees. An example of a second injury fund would be the insurance company only being responsible for the first 104 weeks of workers compensation benefits. Thereafter, all future payments are reimbursed by the second injury fund. Second injury funds are typically subsidized from the premium on every workers compensation insurance policy issued in a particular state. Many states have eliminated or are phasing out second injury funds due to a lack of funding.

The second injury fund potential is often part of the initial claim investigation. If it is determined that the claimant had a preexisting injury or illness, then a written knowledge statement would be secured from the employer along with an authorization to secure the medical records. A formal submission, with the knowledge statement and second injury fund application, are submitted to a separate department at the state workers compensation commission or department.

Summary and Conclusion

Recovery is critical to any claim organization, but its financial impact on the insurance company or self-insured is often overlooked. Every dollar recovered goes right to the bottom line of the insurer's or self-insured's financial results. For example, if an insurance company paid $2.5 million in incurred losses in a given calendar year, with premium at $5 million, the loss ratio would be 50 percent. If the Claims Department was able to recover $500,000 in the same year, the incurred losses would be reduced to $2 million, bringing the loss ratio down to 40 percent. The reduced loss ratio improves the financial condition of the company.

Recovery, particularly recovery involving subrogation or contribution from a responsible party, should not be an "after thought" once the claim is paid. Recovery should be part of the initial investigation and pursued aggressively so that when payment is made, all the necessary supporting documentation and investigation results are available to pursue the subrogation claim without delay. As time passes, evidence gets stale, including the availability of witnesses. It is important to focus on the recovery aspects of the claim at the outset.

FOR MORE INFORMATION ON:	GO TO:	PAGE(S):
Claims Operations	Chapters 2–9	5–104
Claims Process	Chapter 10–17	105–220
Claims Process—Overview	Chapter 10	105
Investigation and Adjustment	Chapter 11	115
Claim Statements and Interviews	Chapter 12	127
Coverage Issues	Chapter 13	143
Evaluation and Resolution	Chapter 14	155
Going to Court	Chapter 15	173
Reserve Management	Chapter 16	183
Litigation Management	Appendix F	421
Legal Theory and Doctrines	Appendix G	427

Chapter 18: Third-Party Administrators—Overview

This section of *Claims Operations: A Practice Guide* focuses on third-party (claim) administrators (TPAs). An overview of TPAs, the typical TPA's functional departments and operations (Chapter 19, page 229), and the legal and regulatory environment within which they operate (Chapter 20, page 253) are discussed in this section. Although there are several types of TPAs in the insurance industry, this section primarily focuses on property and casualty TPAs, including TPAs handling workers compensation claims. The development and different categories of TPAs are the focus of this chapter.

TPA Development

Historically, the need for the TPA developed as the industry began to use more alternative market structures rather than a traditional insurance arrangement. The insurance customer, particularly large companies and public entities, became more sophisticated in terms of risk management and began to utilize risk retention, including the formation of captives, pools, and reciprocals, as an alternative to traditional insurance. These companies required a claims administration alternative to protect their interests within the retained layer. The alternative included an unbundled claim solution by contracting with a TPA to manage the claims process. TPAs developed experience in specialty markets, and the number of TPAs in the marketplace expanded.

At the same time, program business took off. Program business is a controlled homogenous or heterogeneous group of insurance business that involves a block of insurance premium. Typically, program premium volume will start at $2 to $5 million and can go up to hundreds of millions. The business may be written through an insurer, risk retention group (RRG),[1] or other risk-bearing facility, typically with a portion of the business reinsured through a reinsurer. Program business became very attractive to specialty insurance companies and reinsurers with the ability to increase premium volume with reduced acquisition costs. The specialty insurance companies were able to increase premium volume and maintain limited internal resources, as many of the functions normally handled by the insurer were being handled by a man-

[1] An RRG is a group self-insurance plan or group captive insurer operating under the auspices of the Risk Retention Act (RRA) of 1986 that can cover all the liability exposures, other than workers compensation exposures, of its owners. RRGs are not subject to the individual state laws that would otherwise prohibit the formation of group captives or make it difficult to form or operate them. RRGs are discussed in Appendix A, beginning on page 355.

aging general agent (MGA)[2] or program administrator. Often, the claims handling function would be outsourced to a TPA. The specialty insurance company would utilize high-level staff resources to manage those services being outsourced through the use of audits and other controls.

In a program business arrangement, commonly called a "program," retail agents or producers are utilized as a distribution mechanism but are controlled by the program administrator. The program administrator may underwrite the business, issue policies, and collect premium, functions which would normally be handled by the insurance company. A program administrator usually has a special expertise in a class of business, such as tow trucks, trash haulers, trucking, ambulances, new car dealerships, mental health facilities, etc. This expertise may translate into an improved loss ratio by implementing risk management programs, special policy forms, association sponsorships, and other special programs to make the program unique and profitable.

As with the traditional insurance market, TPAs' use of technology has developed over the years. Systems technology is critical to operate effectively, particularly when handling a large volume of claim transactions. Advanced claims systems are necessary to track individual claims, generate comprehensive claims management reports, allow clients to access their claim records, and properly manage loss fund bank accounts. (See Chapter 9, Claims Operations—Technology, beginning on page 93, for more information on these systems.)

Some TPAs have developed a poor reputation in the industry. TPAs may underprice their service fees in an effort to gain market share and remain profitable. The underpricing results in staff resource restrictions, which ultimately affects claim workloads, resulting in poor quality and employee turnover. As employees leave the company due to excessive workloads, turnover continues, with the remaining staff becoming dissatisfied with the work environment. As employee turnover continues, the claim files do not receive the required attention, and problems with service and claim results arise.

A TPA operating in a virtual environment has resolved many of these issues, improving both profit margins and more importantly, the quality of claims handling. A virtual TPA reduces its operating costs by eliminating traditional "brick and mortar" expenses (i.e., physical plant, furniture). These reduced costs allow for proper staffing and investment in improved technology. For TPAs to be successful in the future, they must operate in a virtual environment to control expenses and avoid underpricing service fees to achieve market share.

Moving toward a virtual business model is not an easy task and requires a management team that embraces the virtual concept, including its positive impact on the environment (i.e., eliminates gasoline consumption by employees with reduced auto emissions, elimination of paper). Changing the current

[2]An MGA is a wholesale insurance intermediary with the authority to accept placements from (and often to appoint) retail agents on behalf of an insurer. MGAs generally provide underwriting and administrative services on behalf of the insurers they represent. These arrangements are most common in the surplus lines marketplace. Typically, MGAs market more unusual coverage for which specialized expertise is required to underwrite policies. MGAs benefit insurers because such expertise is not always available within the company and would be more costly to develop on an in-house basis.

business model does not just mean utilizing a paperless claims management system; there needs to be a complete change in how the business operates, including the utilization of advanced technology as well as the decentralization of staff with remote employees. Videoconferencing, voice recognition software, Voice over Internet Protocol (VOIP) telephone systems, and other technological advances will contribute to a more cost-effective business environment, improving profit margins, and, at the same time, maintaining a quality work product with adequate claim staff resources.

TPA Categories

As the need for different types of claim facilities developed, various categories of TPAs evolved. Clients, including self-insureds, program business companies, and public entities began to need an unbundled claim arrangement involving a TPA. Such unbundling of claim services allowed clients to pick and choose the type of claim services provided by TPAs.

To fully understand the TPA environment, it is important to differentiate between the various types of TPA companies or firms. TPAs can vary by the type of firm, specialty, claim services provided, and the resources utilized to handle claims. TPAs fall into four categories:

- Traditional TPAs
- Adjuster TPAs
- Captive TPAs
- Recovery TPAs

Each is discussed in more detail below.

Traditional TPAs

A traditional TPA primarily provides claims administration services. Although claims administration services may be its primary source of income, other ancillary claim services may be provided, such as claim consulting, auditing, and recovery services. Claims administration and other services are provided to insurance companies, reinsurers, self-insureds, and various alternative risk financing vehicles, such as captives and risk retention groups. (See Appendix A, beginning on page 355, for more information on the alternative market.)

The primary department within a traditional TPA is the technical claims operation. Technical claims handling involves the claims process activities of the adjuster, supervisor, or manager, and basically includes the entire claims process, except for the support tasks. Most of the staff resources are involved in the technical claims operations; however, there are other departments within the operation, including Financial, Operations, Information Systems, Human Resources, Sales and Marketing, and Legal.

A traditional TPA operates very similarly to an insurance company Claims Department, with adjusters, claim managers, and claims support staff. TPA claims staff does not generally handle field adjusting assignments other than perhaps attending a mediation, arbitration, deposition, or trial. Employees are recruited from insurance companies, reinsurers, and other TPAs. They will need experience in managing the claims process as a desk adjuster or claims examiner.

Traditional TPAs maintain physical office space, either centralized with one or two main offices, or decentralized with various branch offices. Innovative traditional TPAs have utilized technology to eliminate physical office space and other brick-and-mortar expenses. This type of TPA can vary in size from 5 to 10 employees, up to 1,000+ employees, depending on whether the TPA is a small, regional, or national company.

Traditional TPAs may handle only one line of business, such as workers compensation, or handle multiple lines of business, such as automobile, property, general liability, and professional liability insurance. Traditional TPAs may also offer managed care services that are integrated into workers compensation claims handling. Many larger TPAs have entire managed care divisions or subsidiary companies operated by a national managed care company under "private label" arrangements. Essentially, a private label arrangement is where the managed care company provides services to the TPA's clients under contract. The managed care company actually operates under the TPA's name, and the TPA receives a portion of the managed care fees. This benefits the managed care company through an increased volume of business, and the TPA benefits in that it has expanded its services, making it more marketable.

Adjuster TPAs

The adjuster TPA offers both general adjusting services as well as claims administration services. However, their core services and income are primarily driven by general adjusting services conducted in the field. Some adjuster TPAs may provide recovery services as well. Small, regional, and national adjusting companies, providing both adjusting and claims administration services, fall in this category.

Adjuster TPAs initially provided general adjusting services to insurance companies, self-insureds, and TPAs. These companies expanded their market by maintaining a separate TPA claims division. This increased competition in the TPA market with many adjusting companies bundling general adjusting and TPA services. The adjuster TPA competes for TPA business with the traditional TPA as well as other categories of TPAs.

Claims services are provided to insurance companies, reinsurers, self-insureds, and various alternative risk financing vehicles. In an adjuster TPA, the technical claims operation looks more like a general adjusting company where field adjusters and additional TPA desk claim resources handle claims. Adjuster TPAs manage multiple lines of coverage and may offer claims administration services in addition to field adjusting. The availability of a quality claims management system to handle these services is critical to providing comprehensive reports and data interfaces.

Successful adjuster TPAs have separated their general adjusting and claims administration services as either individual divisions or even as separate entities. As the adjuster TPAs competes with the traditional TPAs for claims administration services, separate divisions or separate entities may allow the adjuster TPA to continue to provide general adjusting services and at the same time operate as a TPA for those same companies.

There are distinctions between a traditional TPA and an adjuster TPA. In an adjuster TPA, the field adjuster may have a different role in the adjusting process as compared to the desk adjuster. For example, an adjuster with experience in field adjusting activities may be more focused on completing task assignments, which may include taking statements and photographs, making diagrams, and canvassing for witnesses, as well as preparing appraisals. The field adjuster may not be responsible for managing the overall claims process and routinely may have to request authority or take direction from a desk adjuster or claims supervisor.

A desk adjuster working in a traditional TPA environment may manage a large volume of claims, outsourcing field task assignments to field adjusters, and be responsible for the entire claim process. This would include coverage analysis, investigation, reserve management, litigation management, and settlement resolution. As a result of these distinctions, some adjusting companies that have added claims administration services may find that the staff resources and processes in place are very different than in a traditional TPA environment. This is why adjusting companies tend to either eliminate claims administration services or create separate divisions with different resources, systems, and processes in place.

The adjuster TPA has the ability to manage the claims administration activities and also outsource or assign its own field adjusting staff. Often, the adjuster TPA's pricing may be lower for the core claims administration activities (unallocated loss adjustment expense) than a traditional TPA; however, it recoups the additional income by using its own field staff to conduct many of the adjusting activities, including those adjusting activities that a desk adjuster would generally be responsible for at a traditional TPA. The field adjusting activities are charged to the claim file as an allocated loss adjustment expense. When a TPA provides both adjusting activities and core claims administration activities, with both components included in its fee structure, the pricing is called a bundled fee structure.

When a TPA client is comparing proposals from an adjuster TPA and a traditional TPA, there needs to be not only a comparison of the unallocated loss adjustment expense component for the core claims administration activities, but also the field claims adjusting activities to be performed. In addition to a flat-rate claims service administration fee, the adjuster TPA will charge for field adjusting activities on a time-and-expense or flat-rate basis. The traditional TPA will charge a flat-rate claims administration service fee and may outsource the field adjusting activities as task assignments, paid as an allocated loss adjustment expense. If the adjuster TPA utilizes its field adjusting staff to handle claims that would normally be handled by a desk adjuster at a traditional TPA, the overall adjuster TPA claim service fees may be higher. The client will be paying more time-and-expense service fees on adjusting activities than would have normally been included in the traditional TPA's flat-rate claim service administration fee.

Captive TPAs

Captive TPAs are formed to provide TPA services to a specific company or client, and may be owned by the company that generates the claim activity. Captive TPAs are formed for a variety of reasons: better claims control, opposition to or dissatisfaction with outsourcing, lower costs, and improved customer (i.e., company or owner) satisfaction. These TPAs evolve because the organization wants to provide its own claims services internally as opposed to outsourcing these services to another type of TPA.

There are different types of captive TPAs. For example, a captive TPA may include:

- An MGA or program administrator with its own claims administration division or separate company
- A law firm providing claims administration services for a particular client
- A captive insurance company[3] or RRG forming its own internal claims administration division or department
- A self-insured organization with its own internal claim facility or department

An MGA may form its own internal TPA to service its program business. By forming and managing its own TPA, the MGA will be able to develop a focused claim facility handling the MGA's business. The claim facility becomes very skilled at claims involving the MGA's book the business, thereby contributing to the MGA's results through effective claims handling.

This type of facility will only be successful and contribute positively toward the MGA operation if the proper experienced claims personnel are recruited. If the MGA attempts to operate a claim facility with inexperienced staff, the opposite may occur, negatively affecting the MGA's book of business. In an MGA-TPA business environment, it is critical that the underwriting/marketing authority functions remain separate from the claim function to avoid any influence on the TPA to reserve claims improperly.

A law firm may represent a large self-insured entity or provide legal services on a book of business that places heavy emphasis on legal services integrated into the claim activities. For example, a large self-insured entity may feel that a law firm handling the claims administration activities may be more effective as many of the claims involve litigation. Routine claims adjusting activities would be assigned to an internal paralegal or an independent adjuster. Providing TPA claims and legal services on a specialty book of business may involve the handling of professional liability claims or medical malpractice claims, which involve comprehensive coverage issues, discovery, and litigation.

A captive or RRG may form its own internal claims administration division or department for the same reasons as the MGA. The captive will typically be formed to handle a specific class of business or program, which will require specialized claims handling. By creating its own claim facility, the captive will develop the necessary specialized claims handling ability, such as proper reserve management, that will result in a positive impact on the captive's financial results.

A self-insured organization may develop its own internal claim facility or department to reduce costs and improve claim results. A self-insured may have a large volume of

[3]A captive insurance company is generally defined as an insurance company that is wholly owned and controlled by its member insureds. Its primary purpose is to insure the risks of its owners, and the primary beneficiaries of its underwriting profits are its insureds. (For more information on captives, see Appendix A, Alternative Market, beginning on page 355.)

high frequency/low severity claims in a given period of time. The higher exposure (low frequency/high severity) claims may be referred to the excess insurance company for handling, with the routine high frequency claims being handled by its own internal or captive TPA. By handling its own claims, the self-insured will develop consistent claims handling, reduce costs, and be more involved in the claim decisions, with the goal of improving its overall claim results in the retained layer.

Captive TPAs are comparable to a traditional TPA, but their systems and resources may be limited, depending on the size and resources of the organization. These types of TPAs may also lack the comprehensive advanced claims management systems (i.e., Web-based paperless technology) maintained by a traditional TPA.

Recovery TPAs

A recovery TPA, sometimes called a "subrogation recovery company," primarily provides subrogation and recovery services for insurance companies and self-insured clients on a contingency basis. (See Chapter 17, Claims Process—Recovery, beginning on page 205, for more information on subrogation and recovery.) For example, as a fee for service, the recovery TPA may charge 15 percent of the gross recovery proceeds. This type of fee arrangement is an incentive for the TPA to aggressively pursue recovery dollars.

Recovery TPAs typically are not involved in the underlying claims handling activities. The claim files are already investigated and adjusted, with recovery being the only remaining activity. Often, insurance companies or self-insureds will forward recovery claims to a recovery TPA because they have been unsuccessful in their attempt at recovery. Alternatively, the TPA may be retained to service all of the recovery activities for a particular company. In this arrangement, as claims with identified recovery potential are closed, they are automatically referred to the TPA for review.

Recovery TPAs may agree to review blocks of open and closed claim files to identify claims with recovery potential at no charge to the client unless they are successful with a recovery. The TPA's incentive is to uncover as many recovery dollars as possible. The company's incentive is to identify any recovery potential that has not been identified or is otherwise missed by their handling adjusters.

Recovery TPAs generally hire experienced recovery adjusters or individuals experienced in collection activities. Claim recovery is a subset of adjusting activities, but not every adjuster is experienced in handling claim recovery. This type of position is very specialized with limited resources in the industry.

A recovery TPA may not need a typical claims administration system. However, a recovery TPA has to track client information, financial transactions, identification and tracking of files by recovery potential percentage, and develop recovery estimates and recovery amounts. The system also has to offer letter generation, e-mail integration, imaging interface, arbitration referral interface, ability to track subrogation payment schedules with promissory notes, productivity reporting, cost savings analysis, diary management, interface with third-party databases, and other functions.

Summary and Conclusion

Although there are different categories of TPAs, they all operate to provide claim-related services. Even though there are differences in how each TPA may be structured, the staff resources and fundamental technical claims handling activities are common denominator to all TPAs.

TPAs need to embrace advanced technological solutions and move toward a virtual business model to reduce costs. If claim services continue to be price-sensitive in the marketplace, higher workloads to improve profit margins will only tarnish the reputation of the TPA and the industry. The TPA is a viable solution in the unbundled environment and a necessary service for many companies. However, there must be a balance between profitability and quality results for TPAs to thrive as a cost-effective and quality-driven unbundled solution.

FOR MORE INFORMATION ON:	GO TO:	PAGE(S):
Claims Operations—Technology	Chapter 9	93
Third-Party Administrators	Chapters 18–20	221–270
Operations	Chapter 19	229
Legal and Regulatory Compliance	Chapter 20	253
Alternative Market	Appendix A	355
Ethics in Claims Handling	Appendix E	409
Litigation Management	Appendix F	421
Legal Theory and Doctrines	Appendix G	427

Chapter 19: Third-Party Administrators—Operations

In some respects, third-party administrator (TPA) claims operations may resemble an insurance company Claims Department.[1] However, the primary difference is that a TPA is in business to earn revenue and income, whereas the insurance company's claims section is a function of customer service and does not directly earn revenue for the company. Without revenue and income, there is no reason for the TPA to continue its operations, unless the owners utilize the TPA to service another business that generates enough income to make up for the TPA's loss.

This chapter reviews a standard TPA's functional departments, which are illustrated in the TPA Claims Operation Exhibits 19.1 and 19.2. A TPA maintains functional

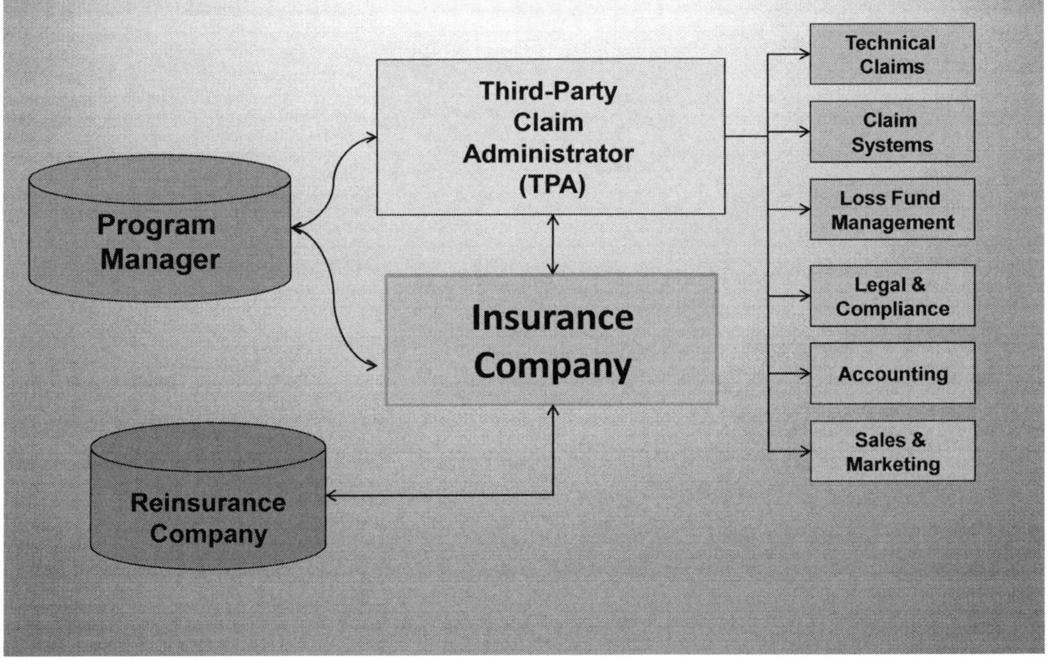

Exhibit 19.1: TPA Claims Operation
Program Business

[1]Refer to the chapters in the Claims Operations section of this *Guide*, beginning on page 5, for more explanations of operational issues, many of which are faced by both insurer claims personnel and TPAs.

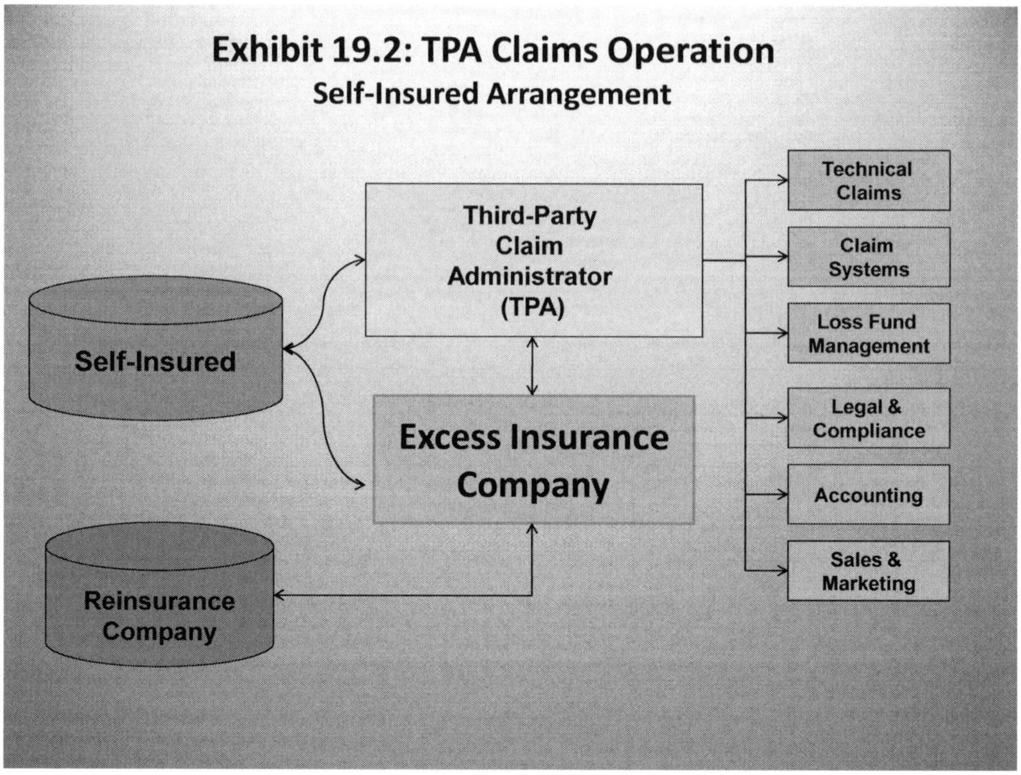

departments, as in any other business. These departments may include:

- ***Technical Claims Operations***—As the core function of the business, this department is primary and interfaces with TPA clients, including handling and managing individual claims and litigation.
- ***Finance and Accounting***—Provides services such as general ledger accounting, budgeting, cash flow analysis, client billing, banking, loss fund account management, and other general financial matters.
- ***General Operations***—Handles various operational issues including maintenance of the physical plant, furniture, and equipment, and business continuity.
- ***Legal and Compliance***—Assists in licensing, regulatory, and compliance matters, and other legal issues requiring general counsel.
- ***Human Resources***—Provides general personnel services, including recruitment, interviewing and hiring, and benefits.
- ***Technology and Systems***—Maintains a comprehensive claim management system, as well as other IT-related services, such as e-mail, telephone systems, disaster recovery, data management and data interfaces, personal computer applications, and video conferencing.
- ***Sales and Marketing***—Promotes TPA services.

- ***Executive Management***—Provides high level management and leadership of the organization, including planning and organizing, development of company culture, company direction, oversight of financial matters, reports to the board of directors (if applicable), and may participate in client interaction.

These are discussed in more detail below.

Technical Claims Operations

The technical claims operation, the core operation within a TPA, must provide quality claims services or the TPA will not survive. Although some TPAs may vary in their operational structure, most TPAs will maintain a technical claims operation similar to that of an insurance company.

The technical claims operation primarily refers to staff and other resources handling the investigation, adjustment, and management of clients' claims. A typical TPA may have adjusters reporting to a claims supervisor or manager, a manager reporting to a director, and a director reporting to a claims officer. Depending on the size of the TPA, there will be multiple units of adjusters and claims supervisors or managers. If a large client is involved, dedicated units of adjusters and managers may handle only that one client's claims.

The technical claim activities provided by the TPA staff are no different than the fundamental claim activities discussed in previous chapters. An important factor in a TPA claims operation is that an error or mistake in technical claims handling situation will adversely impact not only the client relationship, but also potentially generate an errors and omissions claim.[2] The errors and omissions claim would be brought by the client against the TPA based on the breach of certain contractual provisions (i.e., requirement to provide proper claim handling and a "bad faith claim" result). The TPA's client must be satisfied with the technical claims handling or the contract could be canceled or nonrenewed. The client's dissatisfaction with claims handling can also be devastating to a TPA's reputation in the industry.

Since the technical claims operation is the core operation within a TPA, it is also where the TPA maintains most of its staff resources. Therefore, the technical claims operation is the most costly department within a TPA. If a TPA is not meeting its profitability target, a reduction in the technical claims operation staff resources will be necessary. If the adjusters and claim managers maintain higher workloads, the TPA will be able to reduce salary expense, which represents over 50 percent of the TPA's annual budget. However, the corresponding reduction in staff increases staff workloads, causing several other problems.

These problems include poor quality results because the adjuster's workload is too high to manage both new incoming claim assignments and pending workloads. Quality suffers in terms of customer service, claim results, reserve management, and other technical claims handling issues. Adjusters become dissatisfied with the high

[2]An errors and omissions claim results from a mistake, error, or omission on the part of the TPA, which is typically covered under an errors and omissions insurance policy—an insurance form that covers liability for committing an error or omission in performance of professional duties. Generally, such policies are designed to cover financial losses rather than liability for bodily injury and property damage.

workloads, and a wave of turnover can result. The turnover problem continues as workloads from adjusters leaving the company are reassigned to the remaining adjusters, exacerbating the problem even further. Generally, this type of problem can occur pretty quickly; however, it may take years to correct. On the other hand, if a TPA prices its services properly, and maintains proper workloads, the operation will produce quality results, allowing it to maintain client satisfaction, client retention, and attract new business opportunities.

Finance and Accounting

The Finance and Accounting Department handles a variety of functions, including general accounting, service fees and pricing models, billing, investments, banking, and loss fund account management. It provides the necessary support to manage the finances of the TPA as well as its clients' loss fund accounts. This department may have subdepartments to handle specific responsibilities within the department.

The general ledger is the primary accounting record for most businesses. Basically, the general ledger is the group of accounts where debits and credits are posted. Debits include accounts payable, which are the expenses or bills received that require payment, and accounts receivable, which is the revenue invoiced to clients. The general ledger typically includes accounts grouped as assets, liabilities, revenue, expenses as well as gains (profit) and losses. These accounts are detailed in the chart of accounts, which, for example, may include specific categories such as cash, credit cards, and revenue as assets; and telephone, payroll, and automobiles as expenses.

The balance sheet and income statement are generated from the general ledger. The balance sheet can be generated on a summary or detailed level and includes assets, liabilities, and the owner's equity in the business. The owner's equity, sometimes referred to as net worth, is basically the difference between assets and liabilities. The income statement, sometimes called a profit and loss (P&L) statement, provides an indication of how revenue and expenses are compared.

Revenue is sometimes referred to as "top line." After expenses are applied to the revenue, the result is the "bottom line." The primary purpose of the income statement is to compare profit and loss, on a detailed or summary level, for a specific time period. Most income statements illustrate monetary values and percentages for comparison purposes. In a TPA operation, after all is said and done, the objective or goal is to generate an acceptable bottom line net income, or profit margin, and an acceptable return on equity (ROE). The ROE is the amount of income returned, expressed as a percentage of the shareholders' or owners' equity. Earnings are also described as earnings before interest, taxes, depreciation, and amortization expenses (EBITDA). EBITDA may also be used as one financial indicator to measure profitability.

Common financial statements include the balance sheet, income statement, and cash flow analysis. There are several different ways of presenting financial statements. The compiled financial statement is a basic financial statement provided by a certified public accountant (CPA). The financial statement is prepared in accordance with Generally Accepted Accounting Principles

(GAAP) and is typically used by privately held companies.

Reviewed financial statement requires the CPA to perform more inquiry and analytical procedures than simply compiling financial statements. In an audited financial statement, the CPA verifies and substantiates its content. This is the most expensive financial statement given the amount of labor required on the part of the CPA during the preparation process.

Every business should have an operating budget broken down by individual department and company. The operating budget categories typically match the chart of accounts. The operating budget starts off with revenue projections and then includes expenses in detail. The primary objective of the operating budget is to manage revenue and expenses for a given time period. At the departmental level, the budget will generally include expense categories only associated with that particular department. The company operating budget specifies types of revenue in the top-line part of the budget, and then details each expense category. Although expense categories are usually the same from company to company, a TPA operation may have expense categories specific to the operation that need to be tracked separately, such as professional licensing or E&O deductible expense accruals.

The absolute key component of the TPA's operating budget is the revenue projection. When projecting the expense component of the operating budget, management uses the revenue projection as the basis for profitability. Revenue should be projected conservatively as expense projections are fixed, and results depend on the revenue targets being met.

If actual expenses exceed the expense budget projection, and the revenue projection is achieved, profitability will be adversely affected. If the revenue projection is not achieved, and the expense projection is achieved, profitability may still be adversely affected. The best result is for the revenue and expense projections to be accurate. If the TPA does not achieve the operating budget projections—either in the expense or revenue categories—the TPA will need to take action either in the form of reducing expenses or aggressively generating additional revenue. Aggressively generating additional new revenue can be very difficult for a TPA for the following reasons:

- Lack of prospects in the sales pipeline
- Ramp-up time for revenue to actually generate for a new client
- The time necessary to complete or finalize the TPA contract and complete the implementation and set up process
- The need for a TPA to fully earn revenue over a period of time

Therefore, to quickly improve operating results, the TPA will need to aggressively slash expenses. When this situation occurs, it can have an adverse effect on the organization, which was discussed above in the technical claims operations section.

Cash Flow Analysis

The Finance and Accounting Department controls cash flow in the organization. Cash flow is generated from revenue being booked so that expenses can be paid. Most organizations generate cash flow analysis reports to monitor cash flow so that expenses can be paid timely.

The cash flow analysis is only as good as the revenue projection is accurate and the receipt of payment from accounts receivable (invoiced service fees) is timely. If several large clients do not pay service fees when due, cash flow may be restricted for a period of time. If cash flow is severely restricted, it may impact the ability to meet payroll and other key expense categories. This could have a detrimental effect on the company's reputation and an employee's perception of the financial stability of the company, potentially contributing to employee turnover. Also, if a company cannot meet its cash flow obligations, it may require an employee layoff or even a shutdown.

Claims Service Fees

Within claims service agreements or TPA contracts, client service fees are outlined in detail. The bill or invoiced service fees represent the TPA's accounts receivable and revenue when actually received. Service fee categories are usually developed by using various pricing models, including:

- Percentage of premium
- Fixed fee
- Annual fixed contract fees
- Cost-plus-fee structure
- Percentage of the incurred losses
- Time-and-expense fees
- Contingency fees
- Administrative fees
- Managed care fees

Underpriced service fees yield reduced revenue while expenses, or the cost of doing business, may remain the same. This results in restricted cash flow and potential problems as illustrated above. If the profit margin is thin, then the possibility of a financial loss may occur. The only way to increase the profit margin on thinly priced business is to reduce expenses, which brings us back to high workloads, poor quality, and employee turnover.

The different TPA pricing methods are discussed below.

Percentage of Premium

The percentage of premium pricing method is very common in program business. Using this method, the TPA receives a percentage of the gross written premium or collected premium monthly. The managing general agent (MGA) or program administrator generates premium for policies sold in a given month. The policies are either sold through a distribution mechanism, such as retail agents, or directly by the MGA. At the end of each month, the MGA or program administrator provides a monthly statement to the insurer listing each policy sold along with the policyholder name, policy numbers, premiums written, effective dates, return premiums, commissions, and net amount due to or from the insurer. This is called an "account current." The MGA or program administrator provides a copy of the account current to the TPA. The TPA utilizes the account current as a mechanism to issue its invoice for claims services.

The actual percentage of premium received will depend on a number of variables, including the line of business, class of business, historical claim volume, and the extent of the claims services provided by the TPA. The percentage of premium in property and casualty business usually varies from 2 to 8 percent, and the percentage should be directly related to the claim volume to be serviced. Even if no claim activity occurs, the TPA still earns service fees with this pricing methodology.

There are insurance companies that allow only a certain percentage of the premium for claims handling without regard to any of the issues indicated above. For example, some insurers automatically include 4 percent of the gross written premium as the TPA's service fee. Depending on the type and volume of claims being handled, the 4 percent fee will either be appropriate, underpriced, or overpriced.

For the TPA to properly price its services, it is necessary to not only know the premium volume but, more importantly, the historical loss ratio, claim volume by line, and class of business as well as frequency and severity. Changes in the premium pricing or rating structure will also determine if there are going to be premium fluctuations. The percentage of premium service fees is affected by the insurance market cycles. During a soft market, when rates are lower, the overall premium volume may be lower on the same book of business, resulting in lower fees. In a hard market, when rates are higher, the overall premium volume may be higher on the same book of business, resulting in higher fees. During these two market cycles, the claim volume may remain the same, but the service fees will fluctuate with the premium.

If a TPA enters into a contract during a hard market cycle, expecting a 10 percent profit margin, the margin will be eroded in a soft market if the same volume of policies were written with reduced premium. In contrast, if the TPA enters into a contract during a soft market cycle, expecting a 10 percent profit margin, the margin will be more favorable in the hard market, with increased written premium resulting in the TPA making more money. To resolve this market cycle pricing fluctuation, both the client and the TPA need to understand its impact. If the TPA is not making a profit, the client should beware as financial difficulties may be around the corner. A periodic profitability analysis and open communication between the TPA and the client relative to changes in premium volume, rates, and claim counts are imperative.

If the TPA and the client do not communicate, the impact of these pricing issues may be subtle and not be initially recognized. For illustration purposes, let's look at a hypothetical example illustrated in Exhibit 19.3 on page 236.

Assume that in Years One, Two, and Three, the client wrote $10 million of transportation premium in each year. In Year Two, the insurance market cycle is moving from a hard market to a soft market, with insurance rates reducing from an average premium per policy of $25,000 to $18,000 over a 3-year period. In Year Three, the market cycle continues to be soft. By the time we get into Year Three, the loss ratio changed and has matured toward ultimate at 69 percent, the premium remained the same at $10 million annually, however, at lower rates with an increased policy count. Correspondingly, the claim counts increased, and in the Year Three, the TPA may need two

Exhibit 19.3: TPA Pricing Example

Year	Year One	Year Two	Year Three
Total Premium	$10,000,000	$10,000,000	$10,000,000
Policy Count	400	500	555
Average Premium Per Policy	$25,000	$20,000	$18,000
Incurred Losses	$5,000,000	$6,000,000	$6,900,000
Loss Ratio	50%	60%	69%
New Claim Count Per Year	1,430	1,715	1,971
Average Claim Cost	$3,500	$3,500	$3,500
# of Adjusters Needed	4	5	6
Service Fees @ 5% of gross written premium	$500,000	$500,000	$500,000

additional adjusters, with the claims service fees remaining the same as in Year One. The TPA's profit margin has now reduced, and it may not want to or financially be able to increase its staff resources.

The increased workloads can potentially cause poor quality resulting from turnover, a slower disposition rate of claim closures, and potentially an increase in the average claim cost, which will result in a higher loss ratio. If a TPA has this same problem with multiple clients, the overall impact is obvious. As the claim volume increases across the organization with a slower claim disposition rate, the pending claim base becomes larger each year. As a result, the TPA may need to increase the amount of revenue it defers to handle future pending claims, eroding profitability even more.

Both the TPA and the client should understand how the TPA earns its fees before coming to a conclusion that the TPA is being overpaid. When the account current is received by the TPA, the TPA applies the agreed-upon percentage toward the actual premium written in the prior month. If the policies are written on a 12-month basis, the TPA will have been paid in advance for 12 full months; therefore, the fees received are not actually earned at that point in time.

For example, if a policy was written for $12,000 in January, the TPA would invoice the client in February, and be paid its percentage of premium in March. Since the policy was written on a 12-month basis, the premium is earned at $1,000 per month. If the policy was canceled for nonpayment of premium during the ninth month, the account current would reflect a credit, which would mean the TPA would be required to reimburse a portion of its fees, even if claims occurred during the first 9 months.

The calculation gets even more complicated because during a 12-month period, policies have different inception dates, with policy periods rolling into the following year. If the program is discontinued or terminated, the TPA would have to handle claims during the 12- to 24-month period. This is further compounded by another fee earning issue referenced below, called the service fee earning schedule.

Service Fee Earning Schedule. Although the issue of earning fees referenced above affects the TPA, a more important issue is how the TPA manages the overall service fee earning schedule. If the TPA is paid a percentage of premium in January 2011, typically the payment represents service fees for the life of the claim.[3] Therefore, a TPA must defer revenue over a scheduled period of time and maintain a revenue deferral account on its balance sheet. For example, a typical automobile or general liability bodily injury claim could be pending from a period of 12 months to 36 months. It would be prudent to earn these fees over a 36-month period.

Some TPAs develop earning schedules by line of business. In the automobile or general liability bodily injury claim indicated above, the TPA may earn 50 percent of the service fee in Year One, 35 percent in Year Two, and 15 percent in Year Three. If the line of business involved automobile physical damage, the TPA may earn 100 percent of the service fee in Year One, without any revenue deferral. In a first-party property line of business, the earning schedule may be 50 percent in Year One and 50 percent in Year Two. However, in workers compensation claims handling, the earning schedule may be over a 48-month period with 35 percent earned in Year One, 35 percent earned in Year Two, 15 percent in Year Three, and 15 percent in Year Four.

This explanation of the service fee earning schedule is just an illustration. The process may be more complicated and requires an annual audit to determine the number of claims actually closed in any given line of business schedule. This annual audit process allows the TPA to debit and credit the revenue deferral account by converting projections to actual numbers. Often, this process is completed with management and the Accounting Department, as well as external auditors. Some companies may accrue an expense category for the same purpose instead of a revenue deferral account. In the end, the result is generally the same.

The earning fee schedule applies to the percentage of premium and fixed-fee pricing methodologies, particularly if the fees are based on life of claim. However, there are pricing methods that may eliminate or reduce the duration of the earning schedule when utilizing fixed-fee pricing by applying maintenance service fees either annually or biannually. The annual fixed contract fees, time-and-expense fees, contingency fees, cost-plus fees, and administrative-fee pricing methodologies generally do not require an earning schedule.

Fixed-Fee Pricing Method

The fixed-fee pricing method is very common with all types of property and casualty TPA business. There are various types of fixed-fee pricing methods. For example, fixed fees may be based on a per claim feature, per claim occurrence, per claimant, or per insured. If fees are based on a per claim

[3] *Life of claim* means that the TPA is required to handle all claims until closed, even if income is not currently being earned, or if the contract has been canceled.

feature, the fee structure may be much higher, particularly in an automobile line of business. Each automobile claim occurrence could have several claim features involving bodily injury, property damage, collision, and personal injury protection (PIP). However, in a general liability claim, there may only be one or two claim features, which may be more suitable to a per claim occurrence fee structure. The per claimant and per insured fee structures include one fixed fee for each party presenting a claim. Under this fee structure, it would not matter how many features apply to each claimant or insured.

There are some types of claims that have the propensity to have a long tail, meaning they could be pending for many years before resolution. These types of claims could involve professional liability, medical malpractice, product liability, or workers compensation. Because of the long tail, it may be difficult for a TPA to quote service fees for the life of the claim without losing money. These classes of business would require a longer service fee earning schedule, which would mean that service fees would have to be earned over a longer period of time.

There are only two ways to resolve this issue. One method is to charge a higher fee structure up-front, spreading out the earning schedule over a period of years. Another method, which is fair to both the client and the TPA, is to charge a certain fee structure for the first year or two, and then charge an annual maintenance fee for every year or two thereafter until the claim is closed. This fee structure would have a lower earning fee schedule and the initial fee in the first year would be lower than paying the total fee up-front.

To be competitive, a TPA may need to be creative in how it approaches the fixed-fee pricing method. For example, a TPA may charge a certain fixed fee for the first two claim features, and then a lower fee for each claim feature thereafter. This approach may only work in situations where multiple claim features for each claim occurrence are expected. Bundling service fee categories and discounting is quite common in fixed-fee pricing.

Generally, fixed service fees range from \$200 to \$1,800 per claim. The lower claim fee range applies to physical damage and property damage claims, and the higher fee range applies to bodily injury, workers compensation indemnity, and professional liability claims. Ranges can also be affected by other factors, including geographic location, line of business, class of business, and volume. A workers compensation indemnity claim involving a construction worker may be pending for a much longer time than a workers compensation indemnity claim involving an injured office worker. The claim involving the construction worker may have increased injury severity due to the work environment, a longer disability period due to the labor-intensive job responsibility, and a higher permanency rating and award. The injured office worker may have sustained a less severe injury with a shorter disability period. An automobile claim in New York State may be more labor-intensive than an automobile claim in Maine. The New York State claim may have additional exposure involving no-fault or PIP coverage as well as loss transfer for PIP benefits between claim facilities.

A TPA may also charge a monthly or annual administrative fee for other ancillary services such as loss fund account maintenance, claim management reporting, and other services. If the claim frequency per year is low, the TPA may charge an annual administrative fee to cover its costs as a lower claim frequency will produce lower service fees.

Annual Fixed Contract Fees

Annual fixed contract fees are annual fees that include all claims handling activities for 1 year, paid monthly or quarterly. Annual contract fees do not have an earning schedule, as the annual fee is renewed each year; therefore, there is no need to defer revenue. These fees are typically calculated by projecting the claim volume for a given year, applying the cost of labor and other fixed costs, arriving at an annual fee, adding a profit margin and possibly a discount to be competitive. This type of fee structure is common with self-insured and public entity business. Sometimes, there is a percentage threshold of annual claim volume that may necessitate a cost increase or decrease. For example, the annual claim volume may be projected at 500 claims per year with a 10 percent swing. If the annual claim volume is 10 percent more than projected, the TPA may receive additional fees. If annual claim volume is 10 percent or less than projected, the TPA may credit fees to the client.

Cost-Plus-Fee Structure

Cost-plus-fee structures are used when it is difficult to project accurate pricing due to the duration that certain claims may be pending. This type of fee structure is common when handling claims in run-off (discussed below). The fee structure is calculated by projecting the TPA's costs, including labor, overhead, and administrative costs, and then adding a profit margin. The structure may also be calculated by using a factor or multiple of the annual salaries of the claims support, adjuster, and management staff handling the claims. For example, the fee structure may be based on 2.5 times the salaries of the claim staff involved. The salary multiple pays the TPA's costs and includes a margin. Cost-plus-service fees are fully earned and do not require any revenue deferral. As the claim volume increases or decreases, so does the claims service fee. Increased claim volume results in additional staff and expense with increased fees. Increased fees and decreased claim volume results in a reduction in staff and expense, with corresponding reduced fees.

Percentage of the Incurred Losses or Funding Level

Occasionally, you will see a fee structure based on a percentage of incurred losses. This type of fee structure may be used in workers compensation. The method of calculating the fee structure presents a problem in that a TPA could maintain higher claim reserves, thereby increasing the incurred losses, which will increase the service fees. The percentage of incurred losses is easy to calculate as the information is typically indicated in many claim management reports.

In a pool or a similar risk facility, the claims service fee may be tied to the annual funding level of the risk facility, as a percentage of funding. If incurred losses increase due to severity or frequency, the TPA fees may increase as a percentage of the funding set aside by the risk facility to pay losses.

Time-and-Expense Fees

The time-and-expense fee structure is not common in the traditional TPA environment. However, it is prevalent in the adjuster TPA environment. Basically, a time-and-expense fee structure utilizes an hourly rate for adjuster and management staff, with reimbursement for expenses incurred. This type of fee structure can be very costly to a client, depending on the claim volume and the amount of time necessary to investigate and adjust claims. Generally, each individual claim file has a detailed invoice with a time sheet for the services rendered.

The time-and-expense fee structure is often used by adjusters handling a small TPA program. It is also used by TPAs handling professional liability claims that may be pending for a long time period, to eliminate the need to apply an earning schedule and defer revenue. Time-and-expense service fees are fully earned and do not require any revenue deferral.

An important point about time-and-expense service fees is that the activities of each employee need to be recorded by claim file and client. Some adjusters still use a manual time sheet; however, automated claim management systems now have a component that includes the ability to track time-and-expense entries. Additionally, there are various software programs available that serve the same purpose.

Contingency Fees

Contingency service fees are paid as a percentage of the gross recovery proceeds. When contingency service fees are utilized, the client only pays service fees when the TPA is successful with recovery. The service fees are paid when the recovery claim is closed.

Contingency service fees are fully earned and do not require any revenue deferral. A TPA managing recovery claims and utilizing a contingency service fee arrangement will need to be sure the volume of recovery claims has the potential for recovery to sustain the operation and yield a profit. Revenue will only be generated when recovery claims are successfully closed, generating a contingency fee. If recovery workloads are too high, slowing down the closure process, it could be very detrimental to the TPA as well as the client.

It is important to note that contingency fees typically do not include the expenses incurred during the collection process, such as litigation filing fees, investigative costs, official reports, etc. The recovery payment is paid off the gross recovery amount and not the net amount.

Contingency fees are usually separated into (1) claims handled without an attorney or litigation involved or (2) claims with an attorney or litigation involvement. The second situation will naturally result in higher contingency fees. This is primarily due to the need to pay the cost of the attorney retained to litigate the claim.

For example, a recovery adjuster may settle a $10,000 claim with the adverse insurer and bill the client at 15 percent of the gross recovery proceeds. If the full $10,000 is recovered, the TPA retains $1,500 as its collection fee and remits $8,500 to the client. If the same claim has reached the litigation stages with suit filed, the client may be billed 30 percent of the gross recovery proceeds plus expenses. The same $10,000 claim in litigation may result in 8 percent to the TPA and 22 percent to the handling subrogation attorney. With a $500 litigation filing fee, the client would receive $6,500 ($10,000 gross recovery, less $800 (8 percent to the TPA), less $2,200 (22 percent to the handling attorney), less $500 (litigation filing fee) = $6,500].

Administrative Fees

Monthly or annual administrative fees may be charged for various ancillary services, such as loss fund account maintenance, claim management reporting, client system access, travel expenses for client meetings, and other services. The administrative fee is commonly used when the expected claim frequency per year is low. Often, an administrative fee is used in conjunction with fixed service fees, as the administrative fee covers the TPA's costs with a lower claim frequency generating lower fixed service fees. The administrative fees may also be used in conjunction with time-and-expense fees.

The use of monthly or annual administrative fees is common in self-insured and captive insurance company TPA arrangements, particularly when the projected claim volume is low.

Managed Care Fees

Some TPAs, particularly the larger national TPAs, develop private-label arrangements with managed care vendors or form their own managed care facility. Managed care vendors provide a variety of services including medical bill review, utilization review, nurse case management, and pharmacy benefit programs. The managed care vendor provides services for the claims being handled by the TPA. These services are billed to the TPA based on a wholesale rate, and the TPA bills its client at a retail rate. When quoting on workers compensation claims handling, a TPA with this arrangement may intentionally underprice the claims handling fees, making up the difference with managed care service fees. These service fees are not subject to any revenue deferral calculation.

LIFE OF CLAIM VERSUS LIFE OF CONTRACT SERVICE FEES

Claims service fees can be structured as life of claim or life of contract. Service fees based on the life of the claim will include all claim activities until the claim file is closed. Life of contract refers to all claim activity within a particular contract period, which is typically 1 to 3 years. Claims service fees involving the life of a claim may be higher than claims service fees involving the life of a contract, as the duration of claims handling may be longer in the life-of-claim fee structure. Some pricing methodologies are not conducive to a life-of-contract fee structure, e.g., percentage of premium fee structures. The life of contract fee structure is more favorable to the TPA as it limits the run-off exposure and the need to establish any lengthy earning fee schedule.

Pricing Models

During the sales and marketing process, the TPA will need to submit a written proposal in response to a formal bid (also known as a request for proposal (RFP)) or upon a client's request. Within the written proposal, the TPA must quote a fee structure. To arrive at a fee structure, the TPA will require certain information, such as class of business and lines of business, claim frequency and severity, historical claim information, loss ratio, premium volume, geographic location, investigation and adjusting requirements, and the definition of allocated loss adjustment expense (ALAE). The definition of ALAE is important as this will define whether field adjusting, appraisal, and investigative expenses[4] are included or excluded from the TPA service fees (unallocated loss adjustment expenses). It is also important to determine whether the TPA will be receiving any monetary benefit from managed care expenses relating to workers compensation claims.

To provide consistent pricing and protect the company from underpricing, most TPAs have developed pricing models. A pricing model can be as simple as formulas within a spreadsheet or be developed from very comprehensive actuarial-based formulas.

A fixed-fee pricing model utilizes fixed-fee rates and claim counts—along with any annual maintenance fees, administrative fees, or contingency fees—and compares it against the cost of labor and earning schedule. In any pricing model, the cost of labor and the projected workloads drive the TPA's costs and the service fees. For example, the typical pricing model will include the line of business (i.e., physical damage or bodily injury), the type of adjuster and salary required to handle the claims, the projected claim count for the business opportunity, the maximum annual and monthly claim capacity for the position, and the number of adjusters needed for each line of business by comparing the projected claim count with the monthly capacity and arriving at a pure salary cost.

After this calculation is completed, the costs of claims support and management positions are added. This is calculated by utilizing the annual salary for each position multiplied by the necessary annual capacity, yielding a pure salary cost. The annual capacity is driven by ratios of the number of adjusters each position can service. For example, one processor may be able to provide support services to seven or eight adjusters.

Other ancillary costs are then added, such as data interfaces and the salaries and administrative costs for the operation other than the pure salary costs indicated above for adjusters, claims support, and management. Lastly, the future liability of the runoff expense is projected, as service fees are being earned over the period of the service fee earning schedule. This last item is probably the most difficult to project and has a very large impact on the adequacy of the pricing and profitability.

There are a variety of pricing models, and each pricing model will need to be specifically adapted to the TPA's operation. Always remember the cost of labor and the projected adjuster workloads are based on established workload standards compared against the projected claim volume count. If the claim volume count is higher than expected, the pricing may be inadequate if

[4] Some insurance companies require that adjuster and appraisal expenses be coded as an unallocated loss adjustment expenses.

additional staff resources are necessary to service the client, particularly when the service fees are based on a percentage of premium. If the TPA prices the services aggressively, and does not use the pricing model properly, the service fees may end up being underpriced. For example, the pricing model established workload standards is modified to increase workloads so that the pricing may be competitive. When this happens, even though the pricing may be more aggressive, the quality of the services to be provided may be adversely affected with increased workloads.

Another example is allocating certain positions and salary levels to a particular account or program, which results in paying higher salary levels than contemplated in the pricing model. This will adversely impact the expense structure. The pricing model can also be affected if the service fee earning schedule for a particular line of business is improperly projected. The pricing model has many variables, and a slight change in one variable could cause the service to be underpriced.

Within the industry, there are many TPAs with underpriced business. The result of the underpricing is that there are large volumes of claims outstanding with no corresponding revenue. This results in higher workloads, poor quality, and employee turnover. When this happens, it's important to determine what caused the business to be underpriced in the first place. When the service fees were being negotiated, was immediate cash flow more important than profitability? From either the client or TPA perspective, the TPA service fees should never be underpriced. Both the client and the TPA will be adversely affected if they are.

Client Diversification

For a TPA to maintain financial and operational stability, it is important that the client base be diversified. Diversification can include the type, size, and fee structure. For example, a TPA may want to diversify its client base with a balance of program business accounts and self-insured accounts. The reason is that many program business accounts are priced as a percentage of premium, while self-insured accounts are priced at a fixed fee per claim or based on an annual contract price. The percentage of premium pricing method may result in increased cash flow; however, if the program is terminated, the TPA will be required to service the pending claims until closed (i.e., in run-off), which could take several years. During that time period, the TPA will not be receiving income. The percentage of premium method may also result in underpricing with difficulty in getting a price increase, particularly in a soft market cycle when rates are lower resulting in lower premiums and lower service fees.

In a fixed-fee-per-claim arrangement, the TPA will continue to be paid as new claims are received,[5] or in the case of a contract price, the TPA would be paid annually or in

[5]In a fixed-fee-per-claim arrangement, the TPA may be paid up-front, but will still be responsible to handle the claims for either the life of the contract or the life of the claim. Generally, the financial impact of the life of the claim in a fixed-fee arrangement is more favorable than in a percentage-of-premium fee arrangement. In a fixed-fee-per-claim arrangement, the TPA is paid as claims are reported, providing current revenue to pay expenses. In a percentage-of-premium fee arrangement, there is the potential for claim activity during the 12-month period of a policy. Claims could be reported in the twelfth month, when payment was actually received 11 months earlier.

12 monthly installments. Also, it is important to note that program business is not typically subject to the RFP process as much as self-insured business. Therefore, self-insured business may be subject to a change in TPA selection more readily than in program business.

A diversification of the size of an account is very important for several reasons. If a TPA has several large accounts, with only a few small accounts, its financial stability is at risk if one large account is terminated. The termination of the large account will also result in employee layoffs and drastic expense reductions. The termination will also result in a TPA potentially having to service the remaining open claims (i.e., run-off) over the next several years with no corresponding income generated. The TPA should have a balance of small and large accounts, and no single account should represent more than 5 to 10 percent of the TPA's annual revenue. The balance of small and large accounts will allow the TPA to maintain financial and operational stability even if a large account is terminated.

A TPA should also balance the fee structures being utilized for its client base. As indicated above, using a percentage of premium may result in increased cash flow initially; however, the terminated program may adversely impact the TPA financially. A balance of fixed fees per claim, percentage of premium, and contract pricing provides more financial stability.

Managing Run-Off Claims

If a client relationship no longer exists, and/or a program is canceled, the TPA will have run-off claims. If the existing TPA continues to handle the claims in run-off, there is a chance that the claim files will not receive the proper attention. If the TPA is no longer receiving income from the claims in a run-off situation, the claim files may not be a priority and assigned to unqualified and inexperienced resources. Unfortunately, the remaining claims in run-off may include the more difficult and high exposure claims. If the claims are not receiving the required attention, the "tail" may become longer and longer, with the claim files closing at a very slow pace. The remaining claim reserves will continue to develop with reserve adjustments and deteriorate the results, costing the client money.

Even a quality TPA can put run-off claims on the "back burner" or assign them to claim professionals who lack the necessary skill level to protect the client's interests. Why does this happen? The TPA pricing may have been inadequate from the outset. If the pricing did not properly contemplate handling the tail, the client may have thought they had a "good deal" up-front, but in the end, everyone loses: the client, the policyholder, the claimant, and the TPA.

Even if the claim facility properly deferred its service fees to "earn" the fees over time, those remaining nasty claims still cost money to handle. New programs and new claims get priority as they are generating income. It doesn't matter how large the TPA is, it faces the same problem. The run-off issue gets further compounded by high employee turnover and the inability to find replacement claim resources quickly enough. The remaining staff needs to handle the new claims to keep the current clients happy, and the run-off claims get even less attention. The remaining staff become disenchanted with their jobs because of the high workloads (and potential job elimination as the run-off claim volume reduces) and end up leaving, perpetuating the problem. In the meantime, the TPA has poor claims service, poor quality issues, and mounting financial costs.

It has, and always will be, an industry problem, but here are some recommendations for the client to minimize the problem:

- Incorporate contractual provisions that address future run-off issues and consider holding back a percentage of the claim fees as collateral. This will reduce the amount of service fees in the TPA's revenue deferral account, and leaves the option of using the hold-back fees to take back the remaining run-off claims and outsource them to another TPA that has the incentive to handle them properly. In the long run, this will save a lot of loss and expense dollars, even if it costs a little more up-front.

- Contract with a TPA to handle the run-off claims that can assign experienced resources without geographic limitations to tap into a huge pool of qualified claim resources across the country. A virtual TPA will have this capacity.

- Manage the run-off process using skilled claim management resources and business rules-based technology with close supervision.

- Build in incentives to manage the run-off process timely and effectively.

- Demand agreed upon adjuster caseloads and adjuster to claims manager ratios, and monitor them closely.

- Insist on mandatory adjuster and manager diary review intervals to improve closing disposition ratios.

Pricing is so important, and unfortunately, the same mistakes are often made. A sophisticated client should ask the TPA executive, "What will it cost me to have my claims handled properly and timely, with qualified and experienced resources, until all claims are closed, with an agreed upon profit margin?" This levels the playing field, opening up honest pricing discussions.

Remember, a quality claim organization can improve the overall claim results, and it's not an area where a client should be cutting costs. In the author's opinion based on 30 years of claim and insurance operational experience, the loss ratio can improve up to 4 points with a properly staffed quality claim operation. If the program generates $5 million in premium with a 50 percent loss ratio, a quality claim operation could reduce the loss ratio to 46 percent, saving up to $200,000 (4 percent of $5 million) annually. If $50,000 is saved on claims service fees up-front, and a poor quality claim results, the TPA could lose it in its loss ratio.

Banking and Loss Fund Accounts

Within a TPA, there are two primary types of bank accounts managed by the Finance and Accounting Department: operating accounts and loss fund accounts. Operating accounts are used to manage financial resources, including the payment of expenses and receipt of revenue. Some TPAs may have several operating accounts, including checking accounts, saving accounts, and other cash management accounts.

Loss fund accounts are bank accounts that may or may not earn interest. They are used to manage the client's funds and pay claims. These funds, maintained in a trust or fiduciary account, are owned by the client or the TPA, and are managed by the TPA. Loss fund accounts are funded to pay claims and process any reimbursements or recoveries. As discussed in Chapter 8: Claims Operations—Financing and Banking, beginning on page 87, there are several different types of bank accounts, including zero balance checking accounts (ZBA), positive pay accounts, and demand deposit accounts. The bank account may be set up as "XYZ Claims Services Company, Inc., FBO Baker Insurance Company." FBO means "for the benefit of."

Loss fund accounts may be maintained and owned by the client or the TPA; however, the client is usually a signatory on the account. The party that owns the account is responsible for reconciling the account and process Internal Revenue Service (IRS) 1099 forms at the end of each calendar year. The party that owns the account will also sign the bank corporate resolution and utilize its IRS federal tax identification number (FEIN or TIN) to set up the account. Typically, the bank corporate resolution is provided by the bank; however, some companies will provide their own tailored corporate resolution. The corporate resolution is basically a resolution by the company providing authority to establish the bank account and listing account parameters as well as to name the officers and signatories on the account.

Within a corporate resolution, the primary corporate signatories will be listed. As additional signatories are added to the account, the bank provides signature documents for each person so authorized. Every authorized person on the account will need to provide their Social Security numbers, home addresses, and titles with the company, as well as a copy of their driver's licenses or passports. Banks are now required to utilize the U.S. Treasury Department's Office of Foreign Assets Control (OFAC) screening processes for each authorized signatory on the account.

In terms of check authority amounts, banks are usually reluctant to be responsible to screen the amount of the check and the signature required. This process is usually controlled internally by the TPA through its claim management system and other management controls. Checks over certain monetary levels may require dual signatures. Also, TPAs may use a Magnetic Ink Character Recognition (MICR) signature process where payments under a certain monetary level have an automatic signature applied to each check.

The management of loss fund accounts includes control of the check issuance process and reconciliation of the loss fund accounts. Chapter 8 provides detail concerning the various loss fund account processes including OFAC compliance, escheatment, and the issuance of IRS 1099 forms. A key function of the Accounting Department is to monitor balances in the loss fund accounts, making sure funds are available to pay claims. Signature documents are maintained along with check stock, online banking access, deposit slips, and deposit stamps. TPAs using current technology are able to scan checks directly to the bank for deposit, eliminating the need to mail or deliver deposits to the local bank branch.

Generally, the client will fund the account utilizing either an Automated Clearing House (ACH)[6] or wire transfer[7] transaction. At the inception of the new contract, the client will initially fund the account with an amount mutually agreed on by the TPA and client. This amount may be projection or established based on the historical average paid claims per month. The initial funding will include funds available to pay claims for the first 90 days. Each month, the client receives a complete bank reconciliation report, bank statements, and check register. The TPA will request that the client fund the account with an amount equivalent to the prior month's paid losses and expenses. If there are unusually large checks to be written, the TPA may request a cash call, which is an individual funding request attributed to one or several claim payments.

Occasionally, a client company may fail to fund the loss fund account with a sufficient amount of funds to process all outstanding checks to be issued. This can be a real problem for a TPA in terms of responding to the claimant or insured, and the potential involvement of an insurance regulator. It can have an adverse effect on the TPA's reputation as well. If a claimant calls the TPA adjuster inquiring as to why they have not yet received their settlement, how does the adjuster respond? In all cases, the adjuster should respond truthfully and indicate they are waiting for the loss fund account to be funded by the client. Many TPA contracts will include a provision indicating that a lack of funding by the client to pay outstanding checks will result in discontinuance of all claims handling.

[6]An Automated Clearing House (ACH) is an electronic system used to transfer funds between banks, a service usually offered by the cash management division of a bank.

[7]A wire transfer is an electronic transfer of funds. A bank wire transfer is a message to the receiving bank requesting them to process payment in accordance with the settlement instructions provided.

TPA General Operations

The General Operations Department of a TPA is responsible for business and operational planning, physical plant (including office space, lease arrangements, signage), telephone systems, office services, equipment, and furniture. The size of a General Operations Department, or even its existence, will depend on the size of the TPA.

The General Operations Department also has the responsibility to make sure employees follow procedures and processes, and takes part in the development of operational and procedural manuals. The Information Technology (IT) Department may report directly to the General Operations Department. Responsibilities also include the development and maintenance of a business continuity plan, including a disaster recovery plan. Depending on the size of the TPA, the Operations Department may designate a senior officer as the chief risk officer responsible for risk-related activities.

Another responsibility of the General Operations Department is to develop and manage business controls within the organization. Some of these controls may be technology related or operationally monitored by management. Given the fiduciary environment of a TPA, financial and operational controls are vitally important. Most TPAs have established comprehensive operational controls, including system technology and management controls. These controls are usually documented in technical, procedural, and processing manuals. Some larger TPAs may undergo a Statement on Auditing Standards (SAS) No. 70 for Service Organizations review. An SAS 70 report outlines the professional standards that a service organization should meet. There are two types of reports. A Type I service auditor report addresses the suitability and fairness of the internal controls. The Type II report goes further, including the auditor's opinion and the effectiveness of the controls during the period being considered.

The Operations Department also has the responsibility to place insurance coverage for the TPA. Generally, the insurance required consists of the following:

- Errors and omissions (E&O)
- Crime and fidelity bonds
- General liability
- Automobile liability
- Umbrella liability
- Property
- Inland marine
- Electronic data processing
- Computer fraud
- Workers compensation
- Adjuster or TPA license surety bonds
- Employment practices liability (EPL)
- Directors and officers (D&O) liability

For a TPA, the most important insurance coverages are the E&O and fidelity bond coverage. Both are required by the client or insurance company in a TPA contract. A TPA needs to be sure it has adequate policy limits for errors and omissions coverage. Generally, policy limits should be at a minimum of $5 million per claim and $5 million aggregate for errors and omissions. Deductibles can range from $10,000–$50,000; however, for larger TPAs, the deductibles may be much higher, in the $100,000–$500,000 range. Deductible levels should be consistent with the TPA's ability to financially absorb the payment of a deductible throughout the year.

E&O insurance provides coverage for loss and expense as the result of the negligent handling of claims, bad faith allegations, or some other claim-related mistake. There are many exclusions, limitations, and requirements in an E&O policy with regard to both the reporting of losses and coverage application. The policy is usually written on a claims-made basis, which means that the coverage only applies to losses and claims reported during the policy period.

Crime coverage for the TPA usually has eight sections, each with a separate limit and deductible:

- Employee theft (fidelity bond)
- Forgery or alteration
- Inside the premises—theft of money and securities
- Inside the premises—robbery or safe burglary
- Outside the premises

- Computer fraud
- Funds transfer fraud
- Money orders and counterfeit money

The employee theft (or fidelity bond) coverage, forgery and alteration, computer fraud, and funds transfer fraud are important coverages for a TPA. The fidelity bond limits should be a minimum of $1 million, and upward toward $5 million, depending on the TPA services and the size of loss fund accounts, with deductibles ranging from $5,000 to $25,000. Electronic data processing (EDP) coverage provides hardware, software, and extra expense coverage for various computer-related claims. Adjuster or TPA license surety bonds are generally required for adjuster and TPA licensing in certain states.

Legal and Compliance

Chapter 20: Third-Party Administrators—Legal and Regulatory Compliance, beginning on page 253, provides an overview of various legal and compliance issues relating to TPA claims operations. Regarding the TPA legal staff, TPAs usually have a general counsel on staff or outsource the general counsel function to an external law firm. The general counsel is involved in all corporate activities, including entity formation and filings, legal actions, employee-related legal issues, corporate resolutions and other corporate documents, shareholder and board of director meetings, and contract preparation and review. The general counsel is also typically involved in the development or review and maintenance of various corporate policies, such as a privacy policy.

The general counsel position usually reports to executive management. In the TPA environment, there are many legal issues that develop, including situations involving errors and omissions claims. The general counsel should be involved in all legal issues that may have the potential to impact the organization.

The general counsel may also be involved in regulatory compliance issues within a TPA. Regulatory compliance issues may involve market conduct reviews by state insurance departments pertaining to technical claims handling issues as well as professional licensing requirements. TPAs and their professional staff are often required to be licensed by the states in which they operate; therefore, it is very important that the TPA and its staff maintain proper and current licensing. If a problem develops, general counsel may need to be involved on behalf of the TPA.

Human Resources

Chapter 7: Claims Operations—Recruitment, beginning on page 73, and Retention detailed human resource issues that also apply to a TPA operation. These human resource issues include recruitment, hiring and firing, employee turnover, training and development, job environment, and performance management.

Technology and Systems

Chapter 9: Claims Operations—Technology addresses informational requirements that also apply to TPAs. See page 93 for this important discussion.

Sales and Marketing

The Sales and Marketing Department of the TPA is critical for its survival. The TPA needs to continuously market and sell its services. If a client terminates its services, the TPA should have other sales opportunities pending in the sales pipeline taking the place of the terminated client.

The Marketing Department develops and maintains marketing resources for the company. For example, the company may have trade booths, product and service brochures, and tradeshow giveaways. The company may also sponsor various activities at trade shows that require coordination and management. The Marketing Department basically supports the Sales Department in its effort to develop new business opportunities, including telemarketing activities.

The Marketing Department will also facilitate the branding and advertisement of the company through trade magazines and trade websites. It will facilitate public relations through various press releases and trade articles. The Internet has become a primary resource to support the marketing effort. The use of e-mail blasts and other methods capturing many prospects at one time are utilized.

Most TPAs maintain sales resources. The Sales Department develops sales leads, facilitates the sales process through the various sales stages or phases, and ultimately closes the sales opportunities. During the sales process, the sales staff may engage others in the firm to assist, such as senior management, finance and accounting personnel, and systems and the technical management staff.

The sales function is usually conducted by an individual with both sales experience and insurance industry experience, preferably in a claims environment. A person who understands the claims administration process, and who also has solid sales skills, will make an excellent sales candidate for a TPA.

The TPA sales force is involved in business opportunities from the point where the sales lead is developed up until the contract signing stage. Sometimes, the sales force will be involved in continued client maintenance, depending on how commissions are paid. The TPA salesperson is responsible to develop business opportunities and also prepare proposals. The proposal preparation process can often be time-consuming and will involve the utilization of pricing models and management approval of the proposal before it is released. A successful TPA salesperson networks among industry professionals and maintains a thorough understanding of industry events and the competition.

The TPA sales staff is generally compensated with a base salary, possibly a company car, and a percentage of the revenue generated. The percentage of revenue, as a commission, will vary depending on the size of the TPA and the base salary level. The duration of the commission will depend on the company and the size of the account, and is typically paid from 1 to 3 years.

Executive Management

In a small to midsized TPA, the Executive Management Department may consist of senior officers, or owners, who are involved in all aspects of the company operations, including the daily activities of the company. In a larger TPA, the department may involve executives who are far removed from the daily management activities.

As in any business, executive management is charged with the responsibility to facilitate business planning including organizational strategy. Short-term and long-term planning is essential in a TPA environment. There are so many variables that can occur which can adversely impact the operational or financial stability of the company. Therefore, a TPA should have contingency planning in place in addition to business and marketing plans.

A TPA executive who understands the technical aspects of the claims process, who is trained in management, and embraces advanced technology, will be the most successful. The TPA operation cannot run effectively and be profitable without human resources and technology. Executive management needs to understand the human element of the operation as well as technology and how it affects the services provided. When management empathizes with the human element, the result is a workforce that enjoys working for the company and produces a quality work product with minimal turnover.

Summary and Conclusion

In this chapter we discussed various TPA operational issues. The primary department in any TPA is the technical claims operation. It is comparable to the products manufactured and sold by a business making widgets. Without the widgets, there is no business. In a TPA, without the technical claims operation, there is no TPA. The quality of the technical claims operation drives its ability to sell the TPA services. If the TPA has poor quality, or an inexperienced technical claims staff, it will not be able to sell its services to clients and sustain the operations.

Although the technical claims operation is the primary functional department, the TPA would not be able to function without the other departments: Finance and Accounting, General Operations, Legal and Compliance, Human Resources, Technology and Systems, Sales and Marketing, and Executive Management. Since the TPA is a business, it needs to earn revenue and make a profit. If is not profitable, the business will not survive. If you are a client contracting with a TPA to provide claims services, it is important to be sure that the TPA will be making a profit on the service fees quoted. If not, problems will surely develop.

Should the operational management of a TPA have technical claims and management experience? Some may feel that a strong management background would allow any experienced manager to manage a TPA. In the author's opinion, a strong management background is important, but so is the experience of managing a claims operation—either for a TPA or an insurance company or reinsurer. There are so many technical claims operational issues that affect a TPA, that a strong background in technical claims operations and management is a real asset when managing a TPA.

FOR MORE INFORMATION ON:	GO TO:	PAGE(S):
Claims Operations	Chapters 2–9	5–104
Recruitment and Retention	Chapter 7	73
Financing and Banking	Chapter 8	87
Technology	Chapter 9	93
Claims Process	Chapters 10–17	105–220
TPA–Legal and Regulatory Compliance	Chapter 20	253
Claims Handling Guidelines	Chapters 21–30	271–354
Statement Guides	Appendix C	369
Ethics in Claims Handling	Appendix E	409
Litigation Management	Appendix F	421
Legal Theory and Doctrines	Appendix G	427

Chapter 20: Third-Party Administrators—Legal and Regulatory Compliance

Legal issues are common during the claims handling process for a variety of reasons. One important reason is the inherent nature of the claims process and its propensity for mistakes or noncompliance with laws and regulations. For example, if a claimant is dissatisfied with a settlement offer by an adjuster, the claimant may decide to retain an attorney. During the continued claims handling process, while working with the claimant attorney, the adjuster makes a mistake and violates certain state unfair claim practices regulations. As a result of such a mistake, a legal action may be brought against the adjuster and claim facility, whether it is a third-party administrator (TPA) or the Claims Department of an insurance company.

This type of legal issue can be avoided with proper training and development, as well as appropriate management and business controls. Excessive employee workloads can result in mistakes and errors that could prove costly for the company.

During the normal course of business, a TPA may encounter many legal issues, including:

- Litigation filed against the insured
- Bad faith and errors and omissions regarding claims against the TPA or the insurance company it represents
- General corporate problems pertaining to the TPA or insurance company, including TPA contractual issues

These situations may be handled by assigned defense counsel, E&O insurer counsel, or by the company's in-house general counsel. This chapter will focus on bad faith and unfair claim practices, and E&O and general corporate legal issues. Appendix F, beginning on page 421, focuses on litigation management handling pertaining to legal actions against the insured or policyholder, so it will not be discussed in this chapter. Appendix G, beginning on page 427, deals with legal theory and doctrines, which may prove helpful to the reader.

Errors and Omissions (E&O)

A TPA has liability exposure from errors or mistakes made during the claims handling process. In an insurance company Claims Department, errors or mistakes are absorbed in the operating budget as the cost of doing business or are paid as a loss or expense off the claim file. Depending on the size and severity of the mistake, senior management may never be aware of an individual mistake or even the frequency of other minor mistakes. It's only when a mistake results in damage that severely affects the company that the insurer's senior management will likely become involved.

In a TPA environment, errors or mistakes may be covered under an E&O insurance policy. This coverage provides protection in the event of a wrongful act, an omission, or mistake is made by the claim facility within the course of performing professional services. E&O coverage may be written for a risk management company or TPA, but not usually for an insurance company, unless it will be covering a subsidiary claim facility. As with all insurance, not all TPA errors will be covered under an E&O policy. That said, it is recommended that a TPA always maintain proper E&O coverage with adequate limits.

A TPA enters into a contractual agreement with its client. (These contracts are discussed in more detail later in this chapter.) Within the agreement, the TPA agrees to assume the responsibility for all damages resulting from its errors, mistakes, or omissions. If the TPA has a large deductible, the damages resulting from mistakes or errors may need to be absorbed within the operating budget as an expense. If there is a large volume of E&O claims, it could affect the company's reputation and profitability.

If an adjuster is unfamiliar or not trained properly in a particular jurisdiction, a costly mistake could be made. Also, if an adjuster pays the wrong party and is unable to get that money back, the TPA will need to reimburse the client. There are many other situations that could result in an error, including duplicate payments, overpayment of benefits which should have been covered under a fee schedule, interest on late payments, administrative or regulatory fines, or the blatant overpayment of a claim.

One of the most costly errors or mistakes a TPA can make is improper management of an incoming lawsuit, resulting in a default judgment. A default judgment is the result of an answer or appearance not being filed timely in accordance with the jurisdiction's requirements. Default judgments can occur as a result of an insured not referring the pleadings to the claim facility in a timely manner (which is not the fault of the TPA), or as a result of an error on the part of the claim facility. Proper management control of incoming and outgoing lawsuit activity is critical for a claims operation, including date stamping pleadings as received.

If a default judgment is received, some states are not lenient in vacating or voiding the judgment, which could result in a substantial judgment with no ability to challenge it. A mistake of this nature could cost several million dollars. The same situation, although to a lesser degree, can occur when an adjuster fails to timely respond to an arbitration proceeding or fails to pay the arbitration award timely.

Many of these errors and mistakes are avoidable, and the most effective way to control these exposures is to implement an effective risk management program, taking into consideration both risk avoidance and loss mitigation. Listed below are events that may involve exposure to errors and omissions claims. It is recommended that the following circumstances be immediately referred to claims management upon recognition:

- Any alleged or actual default judgment
- Any allegations of failure to respond to an arbitration proceeding timely, resulting in an adverse award
- Any and all litigation, administrative proceedings, and declaratory judg-

ment actions naming the client or TPA as a defendant

- Any and all litigation, administrative proceedings, and declaratory judgment actions naming the insured or policyholder, wherein there are allegations of improper claims handling, even if the TPA is not directly named in the litigation
- Any verbal or written allegation of bad faith, unfair claim practices, or deceptive trade practice regulations or statutes, or consumer protection acts, even if the allegations are unfounded
- Demands for punitive damages, exemplary damages, or treble damages against the client or TPA involving both litigation and nonlitigation claims
- Unresolved regulatory or consumer complaints with allegations of improper claims handling.
- Allegations of failure to adhere to state adjuster licensing requirements
- Accusations of theft, mismanagement, or misuse of funds held in a client loss fund bank account
- Suspected misapplication of coverage, including misinterpretation of policy language and payments outside the policy period, or an improper coverage position letter
- Allegations of improper claims handling or failure to follow client procedures, including the failure to follow established claims and litigation management procedures.
- Accusations of improper reserve management
- Charges of breach of claim authority
- Allegations of improper or untimely claim payments including the failure to name a loss payee or mortgagee on a claim check
- Fines, penalties, and interest imposed as a result of improper or delayed claims handling
- Adverse client claim audits, where the final results are unacceptable or unsatisfactory, there are allegations of improper claims handling, or fines are imposed on the client based on the audit results
- Any other issue, situation, event, error, or omission that has the potential to result in a claim against the company

Obviously, risk avoidance—avoiding the potential error or mistake—is the most acceptable risk management technique. However, when errors or mistakes do occur, loss mitigation is the best practice. The key to controlling E&O exposure and damages is early identification and recognition of the potential for a claim. Proper supervision and management of the claim file, as well as manageable workloads, will reduce the frequency of E&O claims. If an adjuster does not recognize the potential for an E&O claim, and a time-sensitive issue is not addressed, a costly claim may develop.

E&O claims will typically be forwarded to the E&O insurer for handling. Timely and accurate reporting of claims is important, as most E&O policies are written on a claims-made basis. This means that, to be covered, the E&O claim or potential claim must be reported to the insurer during policy period. The larger a TPA becomes, the greater the potential for E&O claims. It is recommended that E&O claims be tracked monthly with documented status reports. This documentation will also assist when auditors require information concerning pending claims or legal action against the company.

It is recommended that all potential or actual E&O claims be referred to general counsel for review and monitoring. As the claim progresses, general counsel should be advised with regular updates.

Bad Faith

"Bad faith" is a term used to describe blatantly unfair conduct that exceeds mere negligence by an insurance company or TPA. For example, a bad faith claim may arise if an auto liability TPA arbitrarily refuses to settle a claim within policy limits, where an insured's liability is incontrovertible. Bad faith damages are often substantial and frequently exceed the limits of the insurance policy that is the subject of the claim.

Bad faith claims can result from action or inaction on the part of an adjuster or claims manager. Many states have enacted bad faith statutes that impose liability on a claim facility or an insurance company Claims Department for its improper actions during the claims handling process. The damages sought in bad faith actions typically exceed the damages claimed in the underlying action, including punitive damages, which serve to punish the defendant for the alleged wrongdoing. Generally, punitive damages are awarded when the defendant commits acts that are grossly negligent, intentional, or egregious. Punitive damage awards can far exceed general damage awards. In some jurisdictions, a plaintiff may receive treble or triple the general damages.

Bad faith claims handling has developed into its own subcategory of claims handling and litigation. Both plaintiff and defense firms have established special legal expertise with services exclusively devoted to the handling of bad faith claims. There are many legitimate bad faith claims, where the claim facilities have committed wrongs or violated unfair claim practice statutes. Claimants and policyholders retain counsel to protect their interest and litigate the claims. Unfortunately, there have been situations where an adjuster is set up for a bad faith action, often at the behest of plaintiff law firms specializing in bad faith actions. Although this may be unethical, an adjuster needs to recognize when this occurs. This is why it is absolutely essential that all adjusters and claims managers thoroughly understand the jurisdiction within which they work, including its requirements for various time-sensitive filings as well as its overall unfair claim practices regulations.

Below we will examine extracontractual liability claims and excess of policy limit (XPL) claims, which are the basis for many TPA errors and omissions claims. When a TPA contracts with an insurance company, program administrator, or reinsurer, it contractually agrees to manage the claims properly and defend and indemnify the insurance company (or other clients) for any errors, omissions, or mistakes made by the TPA during the claims handling process. Even though the TPA is not the insurance company that wrote the policy and sold it to the policyholder, the TPA directly handles the claims. Therefore, the TPA can be held liable for the claims brought against the insurance company by claimants and policyholders.

Typically, if the TPA represents an insurance company, and a bad faith claim is presented, the insurance company will tender the bad faith claim to the TPA, requesting defense and indemnification pursuant to the TPA contract. Although the insurance company may have coverage for the bad faith claim within its reinsurance agreements, it will make every effort to refer the claim to the TPA's E&O insurer for handling.

Extracontractual Obligations (ECO)

Extracontractual damages is a generic term that refers to damages awarded by a court against an insurer or reinsurer that are outside the provisions of the insurance policy, due to the insurer's bad faith, fraud, or gross negligence in the handling of a claim. They are a form of punitive damages, intended to punish extreme insurer conduct. Extracontractual damage awards most frequently arise from unfair claims handling practices (e.g., unjust denial of coverage, failure to settle a claim within policy limits).

Let's look at an example of claim involving an ECO bad faith exposure. Assume an adjuster is assigned to investigate a claim involving an elderly woman who slipped and fell at the insured premises. The claimant sustained a fractured arm and was hospitalized for 2 days. The investigation indicates that the insured is liable for the accident.

In an effort to reduce costs and save loss dollars, the adjuster decides to offer medical payments coverage only. The claimant questions whether there is any other coverage available, feeling that the insured is responsible. The adjuster simply indicates that medical payments coverage at $1,000 is only available, and to either accept it or the claim will be denied. The adjuster knows that the liability coverage limit of $100,000 would be available to the claimant, and the claim has a value of $15,000–$20,000, yet fails to disclose the coverage.

The adjuster not only violated unfair claim settlement practice laws but was also unethical. The adjuster took advantage of an elderly person who had limited knowledge of the claims handling process, being advised by the adjuster that the only recourse for compensation would be medical payments coverage, which may have been inadequate to pay all the medical bills.

ECOs can involve both the insured and the claimant. For example, an adjuster could misrepresent insurance policy provisions to the insured during the course of the claims handling process. This type of misrepresentation may not have been intentional; however, after recognizing the error, the adjuster does not go back and remedy the issue for fear of being criticized in making an error or mistake. In this situation, the adjuster has not only misrepresented the policy provisions, but also could be held in bad faith for attempting to hide a mistake.

In recent times, extracontractual damages involving claimants have increased dramatically. Many times, an extracontractual claim is the result of an adjuster either being inexperienced or not properly trained in a particular jurisdiction. An example of an adjuster being inexperienced may involve an adjuster not understanding how to handle demands for policy limits in advance of litigation. In some jurisdictions, this may need to be done within a specified time, and the response may need to be in a specific format. If the adjuster does not respond properly, and within the statutory time frame, the result is an extracontractual claim that may exceed the damages claimed in the underlying action.

Occasionally, extracontractual claims result from a culture that has developed within the claims organization relating to claims handling processes. For example, standard operating claim procedures may include an intentional delay in the claim investigation and limited contact with the parties involved in the claim to avoid or delay claim payments. Claims may be denied with limited investigation, hoping that the claimants will get frustrated and abandon their claims. Although this type of claims handling may not be condoned by senior management, line management permits it. This type of claims handling is unacceptable, unethical, arrogant, and in violation of the law.

Excess of Policy Limits (XPL)

XPL refers to damages awarded that would normally be covered under the insurance policy but which exceed the policy limits due to an error or poor judgment in the claims process. The insurance company's reinsurer may provide coverage for these types of claims within the reinsurance agreement.

Let's look at an example of bad faith involving XPL. The claimant sustains a fracture of the right hip which requires an open reduction with surgery. Liability is clear on the insured. Medical damages are $35,000, and disputed wages are $50,000 (total special damages are $85,000). The adjuster and claims manager both evaluated the claim at $150,000, and a settlement offer is extended to the claimant but is refused. The adjuster and claims manager agree the settlement offer was low, but the claimant was unrepresented. Negotiations discontinue.

The claimant hires an attorney. The insured has a $500,000 liability policy limit and no umbrella liability coverage. Prior to litigation, the claimant attorney demands $350,000. An offer of $225,000 is extended, which is refused, and suit is brought for $1 million. During trial, the adjuster and claims manager increase the offer to $275,000, which is refused. The demand is still at $350,000.

During the course of the litigation handling, the adjuster and claims manager send an excess letter to the insured stating the policy's coverage limits and advising that the amount sued for exceeds the policy limits. The insured demands in writing that the claim be settled immediately at the $350,000 demand.

While attending the trial, the insured becomes increasingly nervous about an adverse verdict and again demands in writing that the $350,000 be offered, fearing that the verdict will exceed the policy limit of $500,000. The adjuster and claims manager will not increase the settlement offer. The settlement negotiations discontinue; the jury awards the claimant $600,000, which exceeds the policy limit. This is an example of an XPL judgment. What happens next? More than likely, the insured assigns a bad faith claim to the claimant attorney in exchange for a release for the full $600,000. The claimant attorney then pursues the insurance company for an XPL bad faith claim.

Unfair Claim Practices Regulations

Complaints or lawsuits in the situations addressed above usually allege not only bad faith, but also violations of unfair claim practices, trade practices, and consumer protection acts as well. These are statutes enacted to protect the claimant and insured, and are available from several sources, including the state insurance department, local defense counsel, and various insurance industry organizations. Although each state may have its own unfair claim practices act, generally, they are very similar from state to state.

It is adjuster's obligation, both ethically and legally, to comply with these statutes and regulations. It's also the TPA's and insurance company's responsibility to be sure that all claim employees are trained to comply with these regulations in all states where business is conducted. Training should never simply be the referral of a voluminous unfair claim settlement practices act to an adjuster for review. The adjuster will either not take the necessary time to review the document or will conduct a cursory review, resulting in limited understanding and retention of the material.

Training needs to be in-depth with an analysis of state regulations as well as the development of abbreviated compliance points, so that an adjuster has a reference resource during the claims process. The TPA and insurance company also have a duty to make sure that all claim forms and letters used during the normal course of business have appropriate language to comply with various state regulations. Lastly, workloads need to be manageable so that adjusters do not take shortcuts or mishandle claims because the volume of work is excessive. As indicated in other chapters, excessive workloads negatively impact many aspects of the claims handling process, including the potential for bad faith legal action.

Claims involving extracontractual damages are very costly to an organization. If a TPA does not maintain adequate E&O coverage, a sizable extracontractual claim could potentially cause bankruptcy. Still, even with the damage potential indicated above, some adjusters and companies may not comply with unfair claim practices regulations, and consider the fines and reprimands by insurance regulators as the cost of doing business. This cost of doing business (unless a huge bad faith claim develops) may be less than an increase in staff resources to allow for full compliance. The unfair claim practices regulations were enacted to protect the citizens of each state. Noncompliance not only causes damage exposure, but also contributes to a poor reputation in the industry.

TPA Contracts

The utilization of claims service agreements or contracts is very common in third-party claims administration. These agreements are typically negotiated and executed prior to the inception date or start date of a claim program. The negotiation of the claims service agreement involves senior management at the TPA and client, as well as attorneys representing both parties.

TPA language and provisions are very similar from contract to contract. The type of

TPA client will determine whether the claims service agreement is authored by the TPA or the client. For example, when handling program business, it is not unusual for the specialty insurer or reinsurer to provide a template claims service agreement that must be utilized or the TPA will not be granted the business. However, when handling self-insured business, the TPA typically authors the claims service agreement, which may or may not be modified by the self-insured client's legal counsel.

There are certain contractual provisions that must be included in a claims service agreement to protect both the TPA and the client. The relevant important provisions are detailed below. Maintaining proper and in-force claims service agreements is an important function of the Legal Department for a TPA. If there is a change in how services are being provided, the structure of the program, or some other issue involving the contract, the claims service agreement should be modified by amendment or addendum, signed by both parties.

If there is a violation of the claims service agreement by either party, the issue should be reduced to writing with notification to the party violating the agreement. These issues should be addressed promptly and timely.

Contract Term

The claims service agreement will state the period during which it applies. This may be a specific time period or continuous until terminated.

Fees and Charges

Service fees are set forth in this section, or are referenced as an exhibit, and outline in detail the agreed upon pricing. This section or the exhibit will include service fees, provisions for annual fee adjustments, TPA invoice procedures, and payment terms, including a monthly interest rate for unpaid balances.

Definitions

This is an important section that clearly describes certain terms in the agreement. For example, this section will most likely include the definitions of "allocated loss adjustment expense," "authority," "territory," and "claims services," as well as others. Definitions serve to explain the term so that there is no confusion by either party as to the meaning and interpretation of the term when it is being used in the contract.

Service Company Duties

This section sets out what activities the service company will perform under the agreement. In some claims service agreements, the provision may simply state the service company agrees to provide claims services as detailed in an exhibit. The attached exhibit then outlines what activities will be provided. Typically, this section will include technical claims handling and documentation requirements, reporting requirements, reserve and litigation management requirements, and quality assurance mechanisms. This section also includes reference to compliance with unfair claims practices statutes and other regulations, statutes, and regulatory complaint handling and response authority. It also includes provisions concerning insurance and indemnity provisions. This section generally also indicates that the client owns the claim file data and has the right to audit and access the data with reasonable notice.

A sample TPA contract insurance provision is shown in Exhibit 20.1 below. A side-by-side comparison of a sample contractual indemnity provision favoring the client and the TPA is shown in Exhibit 20.2 on page 262.

Claim Authority

Claim authority for the TPA will be documented in a separate exhibit or schedule, or may be included in the Service Company's Duties. Typically, claim authority extended to the TPA will be expressed in terms of settlement authority, reserve authority and check signing authority. The claim authority will apply to the TPA, which will delegate the claim authority at various levels to its adjuster and management staff, based on experience and management authority.

Client Duties

This section details the client's duties under the agreement. In this section, it states that the client will pay the service fees timely and also provide adequate funds for the loss fund account for the payment of loss and expense payments. It further states that the client will cooperate with the service company and provide the necessary information for the service company to provide its services.

Claim Management Reporting

This section of the claims services agreement outlines the claim management reports and data to be provided to the client on a periodic, typically monthly, basis. Sample language may include:

> The Service Company shall provide the Client with monthly claim management reports electronically, no later than the 15th day following the close of each month. Claim management reports will include loss runs, production reports, recovery reports, financial reports, bank statements and reconciliation reports, and financial and check registers.

Exhibit 20.1: Sample TPA Contract Insurance Provision

The Service Company will provide the Client with Certificates of Insurance, evidencing Professional Liability—Errors and Omissions Insurance with annual limits of $5,000,000 for any one event or occurrence and in an amount not less than $5,000,000 in the aggregate, underwritten by insurance carriers rated "A-" or better by A.M. Best Company. The Service Company warrants that, as of the date of this Agreement, it has and shall maintain throughout the term of this Agreement a fidelity bond in an amount of $1,000,000 with an insurer rated "A-" or better by A.M. Best Company. The Service Company also warrants that it will maintain General Liability and Automobile Liability coverage with minimum liability limits of $1,000,000, and statutory Workers Compensation Insurance coverage.

Claims Account

This section outlines provisions for the claims account or loss fund account. In situations where the TPA is not maintaining the loss fund account, this provision may not be included in the claims service agreement. Also, this provision may be modified depending on responsibilities for the loss fund account. Sample language is shown in Exhibit 20.3.

Confidentiality and Privacy Policy

A TPA contract may include provisions for confidentiality in the agreement, mutually protecting the client and the TPA. Also, given the information, documentation, and transaction exchanges with the public, privacy policy language may be included in the agreement as well. The agreement may state:

> The Service Company shall not disclose or use any nonpublic personal financial information or nonpublic personal health information related to any claimant or policyholder, or to any consumer or customer (as such terms are defined under applicable state and federal privacy laws), except as necessary to carry out its duties and obligations under this Agreement or as otherwise permitted under applicable state or federal law.

The agreement should also indicate that the TPA must develop and maintain an information security program and privacy policy to ensure security and confidentiality in accordance with state and federal statutes.

Exhibit 20.2: Sample Contractual Indemnity Provision

Favoring the Client

The Service Company agrees to indemnify, defend, and hold harmless the Client with respect to any claim, demand, action, damage, cost and/or expense to which the Client may be subject as a consequence or result of any intentional tort, wilful misconduct, or negligence on the part of the Service Company and/or its employees pertaining to this Agreement, unless the complained action of the Service Company was taken at the specific direction of the Client or as a consequence of the Client's failure to act within statutory or regulatory time limits.

Favoring the TPA

The Client shall indemnify, defend, and hold harmless the Service Company with respect to any claim, demand, action, damage, cost, and/or expense to which the Service Company may be subject to as a consequence or result of any intentional tort, wilful misconduct, or negligence on the part of the Client and/or its employees pertaining to this Agreement, unless the complained action of the Client was taken at the specific direction of the Service Company or as a consequence of the Service Company's failure to act within statutory or regulatory time limits.

Termination

The termination provision is very important in the claims service agreement. Naturally, it states when the agreement can be terminated; it also specifies how claims are handled upon termination. This section typically addresses life of claim (all claim activities until the claim file is closed) or life of contract provisions (all claim activity within a particular contract period, typically 1 to 3 years), as well as voluntary termination and termination for cause in the event claims are mishandled. Some claims service agreements include a provision to allow each party an opportu-

Exhibit 20.3: Sample Loss Fund Account Provision

For the term of this Agreement, the Service Company shall separately account for, maintain, and disburse funds remitted to the Service Company by the Client as provided herein for the purpose of paying losses and Allocated Loss Adjustment Expenses. Such funds, as separately accounted for by the Service Company, shall be referred to as the Claims Account, to be established and maintained at the level necessary to pay loss and loss adjustment expenses in a timely manner from funds provided by the Client. The Client shall promptly make arrangements to fund the Claims Account in order to pay losses on Self-Insured Retention (SIR) Claims and Allocated Loss Adjustment Expenses on a timely basis. It is further agreed that the Claims Account will continue to be funded monthly, at a minimum, with amounts necessary to pay loss and loss adjustment expenses in a timely manner.

The Service Company shall hold all Claims Account funds in a fiduciary capacity and maintain such funds in a separate bank or trust account. The Service Company shall be entitled to all interest income earned on the Claims Account, and is responsible for all bank service fees and charges in connection with the Claims Account. The Service Company shall perform all necessary bank reconciliations of the Claims Account, which shall be subject to periodic audit by the Client or its auditors, Insurance Company, or Reinsurer.

The Service Company shall have the authority to disburse funds from the Claims Account in such amounts as are necessary to process claim and/or loss payments and payments of Allocated Loss Adjustment Expenses as provided in this Agreement. Claims and/or loss payments and Allocated Loss Adjustment Expenses shall be deducted from the Claims Account on the date payment is issued.

The Client shall have full access to the Claims Account and be designated as a signatory on the account with full signatory authority, including access to all bank account records.

The Service Company shall be held harmless and indemnified by the Client from any failure of the Client to fund the Claims Account so as to enable loss or expense payments to be made within statutory or regulatory time frames.

nity to cure a material breach of the contract before the termination for cause goes into effect.

Sample language is presented in Exhibit 20.4 below. The TPA contract may be terminated for material breach, insolvency, or bankruptcy by either party, sale of the company, its assets or its controlling interests, failure to staff properly, or engagement in fraud or other illegal activities. An example of a material breach may be an unauthorized payment of claims or failure to provide proper bank reconciliations of the loss fund account.

It should be noted that some TPA contracts include an option to terminate if there is an ownership change or any substantial management change that could adversely impact the account or program.

Disputes

This provision outlines how disputes will be resolved, either by litigation or arbitration. It also provides for temporary restraining orders or injunctions, if necessary. Some clients may not want an arbitration provision within the claims service agreement. If the arbitration provision is removed, litigation will be the sole remedy for both parties to resolve contractual issues.

Independent Contractor

This provision confirms that the service company is an independent contractor. Sample language may include:

> The relationship under this Agreement of the Service Company is that of an in-

Exhibit 20.4: Sample Termination Provision

This Agreement covers the period stated in ARTICLE I herein. In the event that this Agreement is terminated, subject to the terms, conditions, and limitations of this Agreement, the Client may require the Service Company to continue to handle to conclusion all claims reported and assigned prior to the date of the termination notice.

This Agreement may be terminated by either the Client or the Service Company with or without cause and for any reason whatsoever upon ninety (90) days' prior written notice.

This Agreement may be terminated by either the Client or the Service Company upon material breach of its terms and conditions by the other, upon thirty (30) days' prior written notice. In such event, the terminating party shall specify in the written termination notice the breach(es) of this Agreement upon which its action is based.

Any indemnification provision in this Agreement shall survive termination of this Agreement.

> dependent contractor to the Client. Neither party to this Agreement is responsible for the debts and liabilities of the other. Nothing shall be deemed to create any form of principal-agent relationship, partnership, or joint venture between the parties. Neither party shall have any participation, by way of management or otherwise, in the operations of the other, other than as provided for in this Agreement, and nothing shall be deemed to create or recognize any relationship other than that expressly described in this Agreement.

Controlling Laws

This section determines in what jurisdiction both parties agree to interpret and litigate issues under the contract. Sample language may include:

> It is hereby agreed that this Agreement shall be interpreted and construed in accordance with the laws of Connecticut and the proper venue for any action shall be in the State of Connecticut. The Service Company hereby consents and agrees to submit itself to the jurisdiction of any court of competent jurisdiction in the State of Connecticut and shall comply with all requirements to confer jurisdiction upon itself by such court.

Nonwaiver of Rights

This section states that any neglect or failure by either party to enforce any of the contract provisions does not mean that either party has waived any rights or privileges under the agreement. Sample language may include:

> Forbearance, neglect, or failure by the Client or the Service Company to enforce any or all of the provisions of this Agreement or to insist upon strict compliance by either party shall not be construed as a waiver of any rights or privileges of either party. A waiver of a past act or circumstance shall not constitute or be a course of conduct or waiver of any subsequent act or circumstance.

Basically, this means that even though the client may not enforce all the provisions of the contract it does not waive any rights to enforce them in the future.

Notice

This provision determines where all notices should be forwarded and includes the required format of the notice. The notice provision provides an address and a person's name where all relevant contractual documents should be sent. For example, all proposed amendments, addendums, revised schedules, and termination notices must be sent to the contact information in the Notice section. Sample contractual language may include:

> Except as otherwise set forth herein, any notice required under this Agreement must be in writing and either sent by first class mail, facsimile, certified mail, or personally delivered. Notice shall be effective five (5) days after the date of mailing or upon receipt, whichever is earlier. Unless changed, the addresses of the respective parties are: (list).

Assignment

This provision indicates that the agreement cannot be assigned to another party. Sample language may include:

> This Agreement and all provisions herein shall be binding upon, and in-

> ure to the benefit of, the parties hereto and their permitted assigns and successors. The Claims Services to be provided by the Service Company under this Agreement may be provided, in whole or part, by any affiliated entity of Service Company, at the sole discretion of Service Company. In such event, the terms of this Contract shall also be binding upon and inure to the benefit of such affiliated entity. Neither this Agreement nor any of the rights, title, or interest hereunder shall be otherwise assigned by either of the parties hereto without the prior written consent of the other party, such consent not to be unreasonably withheld.

This provision is important. The first section states that the contract is binding on any successor company (i.e., if the TPA is sold) or if the contract is assigned to another company (with permission). The second section indicates that the TPA may use an affiliate company for services; however, the affiliate company is bound by the contract. The last sentence indicates that the contract may not be assigned without prior written consent of the other party. For example, the business assets of the TPA may be sold to another entity (see below). If the client does not want to work with the new entity (TPA), it could terminate the agreement and refuse the assignment of the contract to the new TPA.

When TPA's are sold, it may be a stock sale where the company's shares of stock are sold outright to other shareholders or another entity. Typically, this would not cause a problem with assignment as the corporate name and legal structure remains intact, but with different shareholders.[1] However, when there is an asset sale where the buyer only purchases the business assets and limited liabilities of the TPA, an assignment may be necessary, as the TPA will operate under a new entity. The primary asset of the TPA is the contracts it has with the clients. This asset may need to be transferred or "assigned" if the TPA is sold. Not all clients will agree to the transfer of the TPA contract to another entity. If the contract is assigned, the claim liabilities associated with the contract (past, present, and future) will be assumed by the new entity.

Entire Agreement

This provision provides for protection that the claims service agreement is the entire and final agreement between both parties. It eliminates disputes concerning other oral or written documents agreed upon prior to the execution of the contract. Following is sample wording:

> This Agreement supersedes all previous oral or written agreements on the same subject matter between the Client and the Service Company, and constitutes the entire and sole contract between the parties. No change, alteration, or modification hereof may be made except in a writing that expressly refers to this Agreement and is signed by both parties.

[1] See the "Termination" section beginning on page 263. Some TPA contracts may include an option to terminate if there is an ownership change or any substantial management change that could adversely impact the account or program.

Exhibits

Generally, exhibits include details regarding claims service fees, a detailed outline of claims services to be provided, and other documentation relevant to the claims service agreement such as data interface specifications and claims handling and litigation management guidelines.

Regulatory Compliance

For this discussion, regulatory compliance can be divided into four major categories: financial regulatory compliance, insurance regulatory compliance, other regulatory compliance, and professional licensing. These are discussed in more detail below.

Financial Regulatory Compliance

Financial regulatory compliance refers to compliance required by regulatory agencies such as the Securities and Exchange Commission (SEC) or various federal statutes and laws. An example of a regulatory compliance requirement, and federal law, is the Sarbanes-Oxley Act, which established that publicly traded companies must establish internal controls and procedures to ensure accurate financial reporting and disclosures. An important aspect of the Act is that corporate officers must certify that the internal controls are in place and effective.

Insurance Regulatory Compliance

Claim professionals are required to adhere to all insurance regulations, including state unfair claim practices regulations. All claim staff members should familiarize themselves with regulations pertaining to the states where claims are being handled. Copies of all state unfair claim practices regulations should be available for review at any time. The Department of Commerce and Insurance Division, Consumer Protection Act, and related laws also protect consumers and businesses from unfair business practices. Some states (i.e., California, New York, and Florida) require that specific time-sensitive letters, as well as state specific forms, be sent to the claimant and insured during the claims process.

Noncompliance with state regulations may result in the claim facility undergoing a market conduct review by a state insurance department. This is an investigation by insurance regulators to determine if an insurer or TPA has followed laws relating to the distribution of products to consumers and settlement of claims. The state auditors will review individual claim files, as well as Claims Department operational records, to confirm that the claims facility is complying with all insurance department regulations and unfair claim practices acts.

Individual claim files are reviewed to determine compliance with time-sensitive dates, proper use of state-specific form letters and claim forms, adjuster licensing requirements, coverage applications, and consumer complaints. If the state auditors determine there has been noncompliance within a certain percentage of the files reviewed, administrative fines may be levied against the claim facility, or the insurance company client. Sometimes the administrative fines can be high, especially if there is an excessive volume of noncompliance.

Other Regulatory Compliance

Other regulatory compliance may include Office of Foreign Assets Control (OFAC) concerning all claim payments being issued, discussed in Chapter 8. It may also include compliance with state escheatment requirements, discussed in Chapter 8. Escheatment is the remittance of abandoned/unclaimed property to the state of an owner's last known address after a time period established by each state has elapsed. As a claim facility, escheatment primarily pertains to unclaimed claim checks issued to claimants and policyholders.

Professional Licensing

Professional licensing pertains to individual adjuster licensing, adjuster licensing for the firm or company, administrative licensing required by some states for workers compensation, and licensing for third-party administrators (TPAs).

Most states require individual adjuster licensing and the 14 states shown in Exhibit 20.5 require corporate/firm adjuster and/or TPA licensing. As indicated above, before handling claims in any given state, a thorough review of the relevant insurance statutes and regulations should be conducted before engaging in any adjusting activities. Licensing requirements are subject to change in each state.

It should be noted that some states only require that independent adjusters be licensed, as well as independent adjuster companies and third-party administrators, exempting insurance company staff claim adjusters.

To control and monitor the adjuster licensing process, many companies have a License Compliance Department. License databases may be used to track employee adjuster licensing and corporate licensing, including expiration dates and continuing education requirements. If claims are handled by an unlicensed adjuster, both the adjuster and the company may be subject

COMMON STATE ADJUSTER REQUIREMENTS

- ✔ Completion of license application
- ✔ Payment of annual or biannual license fees
- ✔ Satisfactory completion of a prelicensing course
- ✔ Passing a state licensing exam
- ✔ Fingerprints by a local or state police department
- ✔ License surety bonds
- ✔ Letter of certification from resident state
- ✔ Annual or biannual continuing education requirements
- ✔ Satisfying the residency requirement
- ✔ Submission of certificates of character

to administrative fines. Also, the administrative action would need to be disclosed within all future license applications. It is very important for the TPA to control this process. Any fines or poor publicity as a result of unlicensed adjusters could adversely affect a client relationship and the company's reputation. If a company handles multistate jurisdictions, claims should only be assigned to adjusters who are properly licensed. By automating the adjuster license verification process, a claims manager can quickly identify if a particular adjuster is unlicensed.

Summary and Conclusion

This chapter focused on the legal and regulatory environment for a TPA. Since the TPA is a claim facility, various sections of the chapter also may apply to an insurance company Claims Department or other types of claim facilities.

As indicated in this chapter, there are many exposures the TPA encounters on a daily basis which involve the potential for monetary damages. Some of these exposures are insurable and others are not. The key to controlling E&O exposures is to maintain proper staffing and workloads as well as making sure the adjusting and management staff is properly trained and licensed in jurisdictions where claims are being handled.

A contract should be used on all TPA business. The contractual provisions protect both the TPA and client. If you are a TPA, when negotiating a TPA contract, be sure you are able to "deliver" what you have contracted for. If the contract is breached, the TPA may be held liable. For the client, make sure the service fee structure, termination provisions, and how the run-off claims will be handled and paid for after termination are clearly outlined in the contract.

Exhibit 20.5: States Requiring Corporate/TPA Licensing

Alabama	Michigan (WC only)
Alaska	Minnesota
Arizona	Mississippi
California	Nevada
Connecticut	New York
Kentucky	Utah
Maine (WC only)	Washington

Note: This is as of January 2010. Be sure to verify.

CHAPTER 21: CLAIMS HANDLING GUIDELINES—OVERVIEW

This section of *Claims Operations: A Practical Guide* provides various claims handling guidelines for specific types of claims. The claims handling guidelines provide some basic methodologies in how to handle a variety of property, casualty, professional, and management liability claims. Claims handling guidelines and requirements can vary by company, but the fundamental elements of handling are similar from company to company.

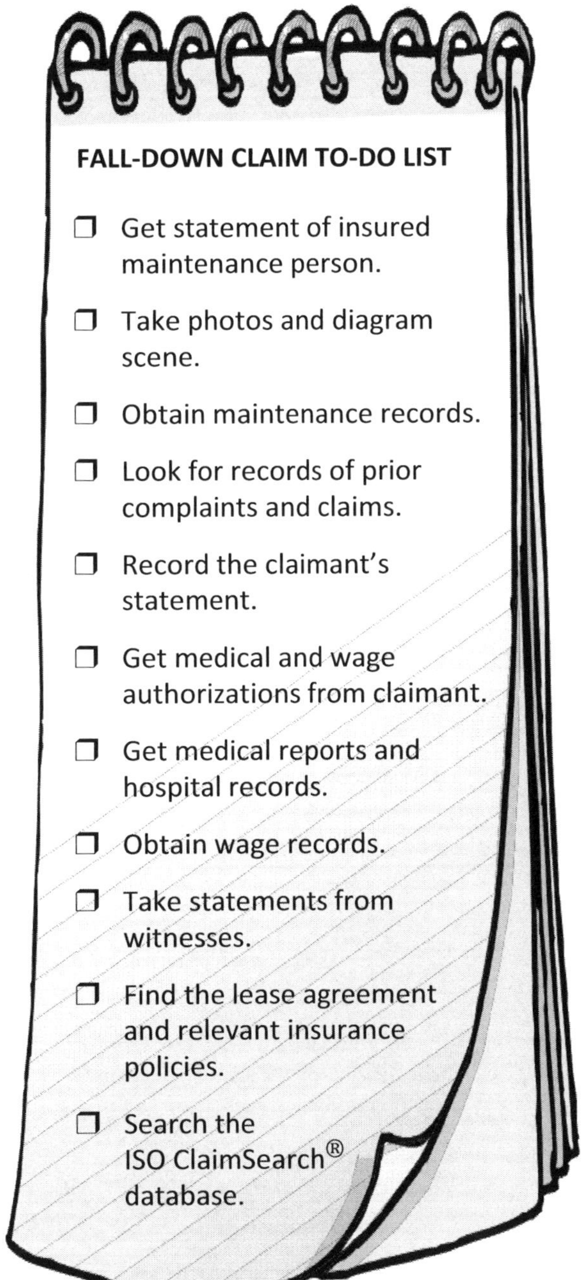

As in any occupation or profession, there is no substitute for experience. As adjusters become more proficient and experienced in handling certain types of claims, the handling becomes routine and the adjuster is more confident in the individual claim requirements. These guidelines simply provide basic claims handling instructions, as well as an explanation of certain issues that may apply to that particular line of business. These guidelines should be supplemented by any other available claims handling manuals or reference material.

In previous Chapters 10–17, we discussed the claims process and the various stages of activities. A review of these chapters at the outset of the initial investigation will serve as a reminder or outline of the basic claims handling and investigative requirements. Remember, not every claim will require all of the investigative items listed, or additional investigation may be required and not be listed. Adjusters need to learn how to frame their investigations by reviewing the initial loss notice and determining what is necessary for the claim to be handled and managed properly. The most effective method of framing an investigation is to develop a list of what needs to be done. For example, an initial investigative list for a general liability fall-down claim at the insured's premises is shown on page 271.

As the claim progresses, the list may be modified. For example, if the claimant retains an attorney, attorney allegations will need to be secured. Or if the medical records indicate a prior injury, additional medical records will need to be obtained to determine if the current treatment is causally related to the accident.

During the investigation, be prepared to change course, depending on how the investigation develops. While an adjuster may go into an investigation with the notion that the insured is responsible based on the insured owning, maintaining, and controlling the premises, developments may occur to change that initial impression. However, if it is learned that a third party maintains the premises, this will now require securing a statement from the third party as well as all the contract and records pertaining to the work performed. If the claim is tendered to the third-party insurer, and it accepts liability, the need to conduct any follow-up investigation may be eliminated, but the opposite could also occur, requiring a comprehensive investigation after determining that the insured is in fact responsible for the accident. Adjusters need to remain flexible and adapt their claims handling based on the claim development.

The guidelines provided in this section are listed below. Also see Appendix F for litigation management guidelines for property and casualty claims. It includes an instruction memo format that can be included in a litigation referral to defense counsel.

Chapter 22: Auto Physical Damage Claims Handling Guidelines

Automobile claims that involve physical damage to owned automobiles are probably the most common insurance claim situation an adjuster will face. If liability is involved, things tend to get a bit more complicated. That's why auto liability is addressed separately in Chapter 23 (see page 279). Personal injury protection (PIP) or so-called no-fault claims are another situation altogether, which is why they are also separately addressed in Chapter 24 (see page 289).

To maintain continued quality service, the following guidelines are recommended for automobile physical damage claims handling. Automobile physical damage claims should be handled promptly, fairly, and in accordance with state regulations. The guidelines below reflect basic claims handling procedures. Procedures may vary depending on the insurer, a particular client, and any special claims handling requirements. State regulations may also modify these guidelines.

Assignment of [Independent] Appraisers

During the automobile physical damage claims handling process, appraisal assignments should be assigned to an internal staff appraiser or an independent appraiser, depending on the company procedures and requirements. Some insurance companies have an appraisal dispatcher who coordinates the appraisal process, including arranging for appointments in the field and at any available drive-in appraisal service location.

When establishing initial contact with the insured, the handling adjuster should determine the extent of the damages to the insured's vehicle. The handling adjuster should request an estimate be prepared by the body shop where the insured intends to have the vehicle repaired. The adjuster should not usually recommend body shops to an insured; however, some insurance companies have programs permitting the recommendation of body shops or have designated repair facilities.

At the point of initial contact with the insured, the handling adjuster should utilize his or her judgment as to whether an appraiser should be assigned based on the extent of the damages indicated by the insured and the appraisal requirements as outlined in the insurer's claims handling guidelines or other special claims handling instructions. Some companies use $500 or $1,000 as the vehicle estimate threshold before assigning an appraiser. When in doubt as to the extent of damages, an appraisal should be assigned.

The handling adjuster should provide specific written instructions to the appraiser concerning the appraisal assignment, either via fax, e-mail, or other internal communication. The instructions should include copies of any estimates in the file, the claim details, contact information, and special handling instructions. The appraiser should be requested to complete the assignment within the required specified time period, such as in 2–5 days, and forward the appraisal report to the adjuster's office via e-mail along with digital photographs. *Note:* The required time period for the return of the completed appraisal report will vary by the claim facility and the type of claim involved. For example, a commercial truck appraisal may take longer than a personal auto appraisal. Appraisals may also be delayed by the insured who is making arrangements for the inspection, e.g., the insured may have difficulty selecting a body shop.

All appraisal assignments should be e-mailed or faxed to the appraiser to expedite handling. On routine cases, the appraiser should be able to complete the appraisal assignment in 2–5 days, including e-mailing or faxing a copy of the appraisal report to the handling adjuster. After the initial vehicle inspection by the assigned appraiser, the appraiser should telephone the claims office immediately if the vehicle is deemed to be a total loss. Prompt contact by the assigned appraiser regarding a total loss will reduce storage and rental charges, overall loss costs, and will enhance claims service.

Due to the variety of different types of personal and commercial vehicles, it is very important that the appropriate appraiser be assigned to an individual claim based on his or her experience and knowledge. Questions concerning which appraiser should be utilized should be directed to the claims handler's immediate supervisor or manager. It is the handling adjuster's responsibility to be sure automobile appraisers handle the claim timely; therefore, the adjuster's initial diary date on an automobile physical damage claim should be no later than 5–7 days from the report date to the claims office. A copy of the appraisal report should always be provided to the insured with either the proof of loss or under separate cover when the final settlement check is issued, unless the assigned appraiser has already provided it at the time of inspection.

Upon receipt of an appraisal report, the physical damage claim reserve should always be reviewed for adequacy.

Vehicle Total Losses

Vehicle total losses should be handled promptly to avoid unnecessary storage charges. The appraiser should always be instructed to immediately advise the claims office in the event of a total loss. The total loss investigation should include the information outlined in Exhibit 22.1.

Typically, a vehicle is considered to be a constructive total loss if the written appraisal is at 75 to 80 percent of the actual cash value. When evaluating a constructive total loss, discuss the potential for supplemental damage with the assigned appraiser. It may be more prudent to have the vehicle declared a total loss in lieu of multiple supplemental damage claims.

Should a potential subrogation claim exist involving mechanical or service repairs to the insured's vehicle prior to the accident, the adjuster should consider assigning a cause-and-origin expert and retain the salvage as evidence.

An adjuster should consider making a partial payment (i.e., 75 percent) to the vehicle owner if the lienholder needs to be satisfied first to complete the adjustment of the claim. Upon receipt of the vehicle title, lien release, and proof of loss, the balance of the claim proceeds for the vehicle are issued to the owner.

Coverage verification should include a determination as to whether the policy is written on an actual cash value, stated

Exhibit 22.1: Total Vehicle Loss Claims Handling

- Obtain a detailed written appraisal with a total loss evaluation sheet.
- Take at least four vehicle digital photographs.
- Develop an estimate of the salvage value, preferably using three salvage bids if the salvage is going to be disposed of through a competitive bid process.
- Get a referral to the appropriate salvage auction facility should the vehicle salvage not be retained by the insured.
- Make a completed ISO ClaimSearch® Salvage entry in the event the insured retains the salvage. (*Note:* Some salvage vendors may file the ISO ClaimSearch® Salvage entry.)
- Complete an Affidavit of Salvage Retention form if the insured is retaining the salvage.
- Secure a signed and notarized proof of loss form should the claim value meet the claim facility's proof of loss requirements.
- Obtain the original vehicle title, signed by the vehicle seller, any applicable lien satisfaction, and the vehicle keys. Please note that these items will normally be requested by the salvage vendor handling the processing of the vehicle salvage. The adjuster may assist the salvage vendor in securing these items when necessary. Should the insured retain the salvage, these items are not required. However, some states require the vehicle title to be reprocessed as a vehicle salvage title at the Department of Motor Vehicles.
- A completed odometer statement, bill of sale, and power of attorney may be needed from the vehicle owner as part of the total loss claims handling process.
- The vehicle title transfer should be processed in accordance with state requirements and usually is transferred to the client insurer's name. Titles should always be sent via certified mail with specific handling and transfer instructions.

value, or agreed value basis. The information will be very important if the vehicle is deemed to be a total loss as the settlement amount could vary depending on the valuation method.

Vehicle Salvage

Although most automobile policies state the insurance company is to retain the salvage in a total loss, sometimes an adjuster may allow the insured to retain the vehicle salvage. In this situation, the adjuster calculates the total loss payment and reduces the payment by the vehicle salvage amount, leaving the handling of the salvage with the insured. This eliminates the need for referral of the salvage to an auction facility and payment of the storage costs.

On the downside, however, allowing the insured to retain salvage may create other problems, which is why it is not recommended as a regular course of handling. For example, the insured may repair the vehicle and put it back on the road in an unsafe condition. Unprocessed salvage could also create the potential for fraud in the future by using the vehicle title information to register a vehicle that does not exist. An ISO ClaimSearch® entry should always be made when the insured retains the salvage to avoid the potential for fraud. If the vehicle owner retains the vehicle salvage, an Affidavit of Salvage Retention should be requested.[1]

Although not the preferred method, should the vehicle owner (insured or claimant) want to retain the vehicle salvage, using a competitive bid process is recommended. The assigned appraiser should request three written bids and accept the highest salvage bid, unless there are unusual circumstances or state regulations that dictate otherwise. The salvage value should be determined by the appraiser's estimated value based on the highest salvage bid.

When negotiating the vehicle salvage value, keep in mind the processing charges anticipated if the vehicle was picked up by a salvage vendor and delivered to an auction facility. There may also be storage charges as well as dismantling charges. All of these charges should be considered when evaluating the full exposure of the vehicle total loss and salvage value. When a salvage vendor picks up the vehicle for salvage, it prepays all outstanding charges (storage fees, towing, etc.) and deducts the charges from the gross salvage return. Should the expenses exceed the gross salvage recovery, an expense invoice will be issued.

While it is advisable to consider competitive bids (three written, legitimate bids), the sale of vehicle salvage at an auction, using regional or national salvage companies, is often the preferred approach. The vehicle auction process involves the retained vehicle salvage company picking up the total loss vehicle where it is currently being stored (i.e., at the service station, body shop, impound), paying the applicable storage costs, storing the vehicle on its own site, and then placing the vehicle up for auction along with other vehicles. After the vehicle salvage is sold, the salvage company processes the title transfer and then remits the net salvage proceeds to the claim facility. The gross salvage proceeds will be reduced by storage fees, towing fees, and any dismantling or other salvage pro-

[1]Sample Affidavits of Salvage Retention and other claims forms can be found at http://www.claimspages.com.

cessing fees, arriving at the net salvage proceeds.

Total Vehicle Thefts

Total vehicle thefts require a comprehensive claim investigation and may not necessarily be concluded within 7 to 10 days from when the claim is first reported to the adjuster's office. The insurance policy should be reviewed to determine when payment is required. Some automobile policies indicate vehicle thefts are not paid until 30 days from the date the claim is first reported to the company. The insurance policy should also be reviewed to determine whether there is any applicable rental reimbursement coverage for vehicle theft claims.

When handling a vehicle total theft, the minimum investigation should include performing the tasks shown opposite. All suspicious vehicle thefts should be immediately reported to the Special Investigative Unit (SIU). Further investigation may be required, including an interview with the law enforcement agency, an examination under oath, assignment of an SIU investigator, and/or a financial background check.

Loss of Use/ Rental Reimbursement

Should the insurance policy provide coverage for loss of use or rental reimbursement coverage, the policy form should be reviewed for coverage limits and details. Generally, reimbursement is made for loss of use at a reasonable daily rate (plus tax), excluding costs associated with mileage, gasoline, and insurance. All loss of use arrangements should be confirmed in writing and include any state-mandated language along with an explanation as to the loss of use details and parameters. Some claim facilities have direct payment arrangements with rental car companies.

VEHICLE THEFT TO-DO LIST

- ❒ Secure a recorded statement from the named insured and any witnesses.
- ❒ Obtain a copy of the vehicle police theft report.
- ❒ Make an ISO ClaimSearch® Vehicle Theft entry.
- ❒ Obtain a signed and notarized Vehicle Theft Affidavit with the appropriate state fraud language, if applicable.
- ❒ Secure a total loss evaluation report prepared by the appraiser.
- ❒ Obtain a signed and notarized automobile proof of loss at the conclusion of the claim.
- ❒ Get the original vehicle title (signed at the Seller's section), any applicable lien documentation, and the vehicle keys.
- ❒ Process the vehicle title in the insurance company or client's name.

Vehicle Title Processing

All original vehicle titles should be referred to the appropriate claims person responsible for this important process. They should be logged in the vehicle title log and filed in a locked cabinet or safe. The claims support staff may photocopy the vehicle title or scan a copy to the claim file, with the date received and initialed.

Vehicle title processing will be necessary when the claim is a total vehicle theft or the insured does not retain the vehicle salvage. When a salvage company is used to sell the vehicle salvage, the salvage company normally processes the vehicle title transfer documents as part of its service. If vehicle keys are received, the keys should be placed in an envelope identifying the insured by name and claim number, and be retained with the original vehicle title.

It is particularly important that, in its processing of vehicle titles involving vehicle total losses, the claims operation comply with all state statutes as well as the Department of Motor Vehicle Regulations pertaining to title processing. For example, some states require a salvage title even if the insured has retained the salvage during the adjustment process.

Specific written instructions should be provided to the vehicle owner when requesting a vehicle title. Upon receipt of the original signed title from the vehicle owner, the vehicle title is transferred to the name of the insurance company. Again, the vehicle keys should be retained with the original title documents.

FOR MORE INFORMATION ON:	GO TO:	PAGE(S):
Claims Process	Chapters 10–17	105–220
Claims Handling Guidelines	Chapters 21–30	271–354
Auto Liability	Chapter 23	279
Auto PIP/No Fault	Chapter 24	289
First-Party Property and Inland Marine	Chapter 25	295
Cargo	Chapter 26	305
General Liability	Chapter 27	311
Professional and Management Liability	Chapter 28	323
Public Entity	Chapter 29	331
Workers Compensation	Chapter 30	337
ISO ClaimSearch®	Appendix B	363
Ethics in Claims Handling	Appendix E	409

Chapter 23: Auto Liability Claims Handling Guidelines

Auto liability claims involve financial loss to a third party due to legal liability which results in injuries to the third party or damage to their property caused by an automobile. Automobiles present a number of liability loss exposures, including the following:

- Liability for injury or damage caused by the ownership, maintenance, or use of:
  - Automobiles owned by the named insured
  - Automobiles leased, hired, rented, or borrowed
  - Automobiles that are sponsored (e.g., carpools, vanpools)
  - Nonowned automobiles used in connection with the insured's business (e.g., employee-owned or borrowed automobiles and automobiles rented by employees, partners, and members of a limited liability company on business) and nonowned automobiles in the insured's custody.
  - Liability for pollution damage caused by the overturn of cargo or the automobile, or pollution damage caused by a collision.
  - Liability for injury or damage caused by wrongful delivery of a liquid product (e.g., delivering gasoline to a diesel tank).

The investigation and documentation necessary in handling a liability claim may vary depending on the type of claim as well as the complexity and severity of the claim. While claim guidelines may vary depending on individual company or client requirements, the following are third-party automobile claims handling guidelines for claims staff or third-party administrator (TPA) adjusters and claims attorneys. It is the adjuster's job to effectively handle liability claims through proper coverage analysis, appropriate claim investigations, and effective litigation management.

Investigation

As with all claims, conducting a proper investigation, evaluating liability, and assessing the full damage exposure are critical. The investigation is crucial to determine whether a liability claim will be settled or prepared for defense. The results of the claim investigation are also the basis for evaluating and establishing the claim reserves.

Liability claim investigations are the foundation for the ultimate disposition of each claim; therefore, the investigation must be timely and complete. When a liability claim is assigned to the handling adjuster, the adjuster should prepare an action plan and document it in the claim file notes, outlining the elements of the claims investigation to be completed.

At times, the independent adjuster may assist in the investigative process and report directly to defense counsel to protect the adjuster's work product as being attorney client privileged. Attorney-client privileged information and documents are protected from discovery as they represent a confidential information exchange or communication between attorneys and their clients for preparation of a defense. The legal doctrine or concept fosters open and honest communication between attorneys and their clients.

Statements

For the portions of the liability investigation conducted by telephone, recorded statements should be secured from the interviewed parties involved in the loss as necessary and appropriate. When working in the field, the adjuster should secure either secure recorded or signed statements from the insureds, claimants, and any witnesses. Statement guides can help. These are generally a series of questions that adjusters should ask to achieve the full picture of the automobile accident and claim See Appendix C for various statement guides.

Many insurers have developed their own statement guides. Another source of online statement guides for use by adjusters can be found at www.claimspages.com. These statement guides include claims involving animal bites, product liability, slip and falls, vehicle accidents, swimming pool accidents, workers compensation, and many others. The website is an excellent resource, and many claims people bookmark the site for daily use and reference.

Independent adjusters take both recorded and signed statements. Signed statements are typically more costly and should be reserved for those claims where securing a signed statement is appropriate (i.e., serious injury, subrogation potential). Recorded statements taken by an independent adjuster are faster to secure but may need to be transcribed. The independent adjuster should provide the statement in a computerized digital format for storage in the electronic claim file. The independent adjuster should provide a summary of the recorded statement or summarize it within the independent adjuster's report.

Some claim facilities may also utilize an automobile driver's statement and other accident reporting forms (for claimants, insureds, and witnesses) when handling liability property damage claims that require statements from the parties to a loss. This type of an investigation technique can be appropriate in the handling a small claims or lower value claims.

Attorney Allegations

Auto liability claims are much more likely to involve an attorney than basic property damage auto claims. When contacting a claimant attorney, secure as much information as possible to properly evaluate the claim exposure. Always request that the claimant attorney allow statements to be taken from the claimants. Occasionally, claimant attorneys do allow statements that will assist the adjuster in evaluating the claim. The primary reason claimant attorneys will not allow statements from their client, or the claimant, is that they do not want their client disclosing information that may be detrimental to their claim. Most claimant attorneys prefer that their client provide a statement prepared by the attorney or wait for legal discovery and a formal deposition. The information in Exhibit 23.1 on page 282 provides basic information that should be garnered from the attorney during the initial contact.

Note that some states require a written disclosure of policy limits in a state specific format when contacting or requesting information from the claimant attorney (i.e., Florida). This emphasizes the importance of becoming familiar with the jurisdictions where claims are handled to avoid costly errors.

Authorizations

For every injury claim presented, be sure to request and receive signed medical and wage authorization forms. Most claim facilities have various template authorization forms for the release of medical and hospital records, wage and salary information, and release of the no-fault or workers compensation claim file information from the insurer. It is important that the authorizations contain any necessary required language to comply with state and federal laws, e.g., the Health Insurance Portability and Accountability Act (HIPAA). HIPAA provides protection to an individual's personal and confidential information from being used inappropriately or disclosed illegally to third parties.

According to the U.S. Department of Health and Human Resources:

> The HIPAA Privacy Rule provides federal protection for personal health information held by covered entities and gives patients an array of rights with respect to that information. At the same time, the Privacy Rule is balanced so that it permits the disclosure of personal health information needed for patient care and other important purposes.

Information on HIPAA can be found at http://www.hhs.gov/ocr/privacy/hipaa/understanding.

When an attorney represents the claimant, acknowledge the claim in writing and attach authorization forms to be signed and returned. Although some attorneys may not want to provide authorizations, they should always be requested by the adjuster since it will accelerate the claims handling process. Often, the claimant attorneys will provide their own signed authorizations or copies of the hospital and medical reports along with itemized bills.

Upon receipt of the signed authorizations, request the appropriate records from the medical providers and employers. Most claim facilities generally have various forms on file to be completed by attending physicians and employers. Hospital records should always be requested as well. When requesting hospital records, be sure to indicate whether the treatment was on an emergency room basis or as an inpatient. If the claimant was an inpatient, indicate the dates hospitalized and the discharge date, and specify whether the entire hospital record is requested or simply the hospital discharge summary.

Special Damages

Special damages are objectively assessed monies awarded to an injured party for tangible losses, such as wage loss and medical, hospital, diagnostic, and nursing care

Exhibit 23.1: Attorney Allegations

Secure the following information from the claimant's attorney as soon as possible after a claim has been made:

- Attorney and law firm name, business address, telephone and fax numbers, and e-mail address
- Claimant(s) full name, permanent address, age, date of birth, and marital status
- Date and time of accident, description of accident scene, and weather conditions
- Attorney's theory of liability, i.e., who is to blame, degree of fault
- Claimant occupation, employer name and address, wage rate, and disability period
- Physician names, addresses, and specialties; injuries, diagnosis, treatment, and prognosis
- Hospital name and address with inpatient or service dates
- Itemized special damages (objectively assessed monies awarded to an injured party for tangible losses), including wage loss, loss of use, nursing care, hospital and medical expenses, property damage, etc.
- Third-party involvement/other parties on notice, including contact information, insurer, and attorney information
- Witness names, addresses, and telephone numbers
- Responding police agency and/or ambulance company
- Claimant vehicle make, model, and year; claimant vehicle damage and any available estimates.
- Photographs of accident scene and vehicles
- Workers compensation and no-fault insurer and claim reference numbers
- Litigation: yes/no (If yes, consider securing an extension of time to answer without waiving any defenses.)
- Names of any experts retained

Exhibit 23.2: Special Damages Documentation—Injury Claims

- Attending Physician Reports
- Medical Narrative Reports
- Diagnostic and Radiology Reports
- Physical Therapy Reports
- Hospital Emergency Records
- Hospital Records (Full Record and Discharge Summary)
- All Medical and Hospital Bills
- Dates of Disability Confirmation
- Employer Wage Loss Records
- Claimant Tax Returns (If Self-Employed)

expenses. To properly evaluate bodily injury claims, the investigation needs to include copies of all itemized special damages, including all hospital, medical, and physician reports, diagnostic reports and records, and itemized bills. The records will provide a detailed analysis of the claimant's diagnosis, prognosis, treatment regime, disability periods, and other information necessary to evaluate the claim. It is important to include itemized medical and hospital bills in the analysis or evaluation of the claim. A list of such damages is shown in Exhibit 23.2 above.

In addition, an independent medical examination by the insurer's own physician, expert, or consultant should be considered if the claim so merits. Physical examinations are usually assigned by specialty. For example, if a clamant is treating with an orthopedic surgeon, the physical exam, commonly referred to as an independent medical exam (IME), should be assigned to an orthopedic surgeon as well. If the claimant is treating with multiple specialties, multiple IMEs may be necessary.

Bodily Injury Claim Evaluation

All bodily injury claims require an evaluation, and the evaluation must be documented in the claim notes. Items to include in the evaluations are:

- Claimant name, age, and occupation
- Brief summary of the claim facts
- Theory of liability alleged
- Defenses available
- Third-party involvement
- Summary of special damages (medical, hospital, wage loss/disability period, etc.)
- Gross damage exposure of claim
- Liability percentage on the insured
- Claim value calculation (i.e., \$100,000 gross value X 50% liability = \$50,000)

A bodily injury claim evaluation will assist the adjuster and manager in establishing an accurate claim reserve. Remember, bodily injury claims can vary widely in value depending on a variety of circumstances. Try to avoid the use of pattern injury claim values; that is, claim values established based on the handling of prior claims, which may or may not have similar circumstances or damages. While it may seem that auto liability claims are similar enough to replicate the outcome, each must be evaluated on its own merits.

Photographs and Diagrams

Scene photographs, vehicle photographs, and diagrams are very important to evaluate both liability and damage exposures and should always be considered as part of the adjustment process. Photographs and diagrams should be taken and made early on in a claim investigation so that the accident scene remains substantially unchanged from the accident date.

Diagrams are very helpful in understanding how an accident happened and in ascertaining which vehicle is responsible. Adjusters should consider using diagrams when taking statements, particularly if the statement is being taken in person. The diagram also assists the witness in recollecting the accident details and position of vehicles. It is not unusual for the adjuster to ask the witness to sign and date the diagram as further confirmation of the accident description.

Diagrams also help assist in viewing the photographs of the accident scene, providing measurements, compass direction, and an overall simulation of the accident with the placement of vehicles on the diagram showing travel direction and vehicle impacts. Every automobile liability claim should have a diagram of the accident scene to assist the adjuster in evaluating the liability issues.

Official Reports

Copies of official reports should always be requested to evaluate both liability and damage issues. The following is a list of some available official reports and where they can be secured:

- ***Police accident reports***—Police reports can be secured from the police precinct or trooper barracks, by making a formal request to the police agency records department, or by using a third-party company which requests police reports for claim facilities and insurance companies, such as ISO ClaimSearch.®
- ***Police statements***—Generally, in serious accidents, the police agency will take written statements from witnesses and other parties to a loss. The police report will indicate if statements were taken by the responding police officers. These statements should be specifically requested from police agency records department, providing the police accident report reference number(s).
- ***Police photos***—In serious accidents, the police agency will often take photographs of the accident scene and the vehicles involved. The police report will indicate if photographs were taken by the responding police officers at the accident scene. The photographs should be specifically requested from police agency records department, providing the police accident report reference number(s).

- ***Police accident reconstruction reports***—In serious accidents, the police agency will complete an accident reconstruction and prepare a written report. The accident reconstruction is made by specially trained law enforcement officers and includes measurements, video, photos, and compilation and analysis of other evidentiary documentation and information. The purpose of the report is to support the police agency's findings with regard to the persons or conditions deemed responsible for the accident and whether any criminal charges will be brought. The accident reconstruction report will typically include photographs taken by the responding police officers at the accident scene. The report should be specifically requested from police agency records department, providing the police accident report reference number(s).

- ***Fire reports***—Fire reports can be secured from the local fire department responding to the fire (particularly immediately after a fire occurs) or by making a formal request to the fire department records department. A third-party company can sometimes be used, which requests fire reports for claim facilities and insurance companies.

- ***Weather reports***—Weather reports can be very helpful in documenting the weather on a specific date, such as whether it was raining or snowing, indicating the specific accumulation, etc. Weather reports can be secured from the National Climatic Data Center (NCDC) at http://www.ncdc.noaa.gov/oa/ncdc.html.

- ***Traffic light sequence reports***—Traffic light sequence reports can be secured from the local municipality, county, or state facility responsible for maintenance of the traffic lights, such as the local municipality department of public works. These reports are helpful to determine if the traffic light sequence was accurate, particularly in accidents involving left-turn claims.

- ***Death certificates***—Death certificates can be requested from local municipality or county offices which retain these records, such as a county clerk's office.

- ***Medical examiner or autopsy reports***—These reports can be requested from the local municipality or county medical examiner's or coroner's office.

Experts

Experts should always be considered during the adjustment process. The following is a list of some expert types that might prove useful in evaluating an auto liability claim:

- Medical (e.g., doctors)
- Engineers
- Accident reconstructionists
- Economists

The assignment of experts should be reserved for serious claims or to support a subrogation claim, given the cost involved. Locating experts can be accomplished by consulting with defense counsel, other claim professionals, or through various outside firms that provide experts for a variety of claims, such as the Technical Advisory Service for Attorneys (TASA) at http://www.tasanet.com/.

When considering an expert, be sure to request a detailed curriculum vitae (or résumé), references, and fee schedule. Determine if the expert has testified in the past and whether their expert services have been provided primarily to plaintiffs or defendants, or both.

ISO ClaimSearch®

All bodily injury claims should be entered electronically in the ISO ClaimSearch system within 10 days from the claim report date and every 6 months thereafter, or in accordance with the claim facility's claims handling guidelines. The ISO ClaimSearch system (discussed in more detail in Appendix B, page 363) is an all claims database utilized for property, casualty, and automobile claims. It is the industry's most comprehensive resource for claims professionals. The ISO ClaimSearch database contains information from the former Property Insurance Loss Register (PILR), the former Index System (CIB) for bodily injury claims, and the vehicle information databases formerly administered by the National Insurance Crime Bureau (NICB). Today, all of those claims are part of a single database that lets adjusters search all lines of business and all types of claims simultaneously.

Property Damage Liability Claims

When presented with a property damage liability claim, always request a damage estimate from the claimant or assign an appraiser to reach an agreed price with the claimant's choice of repair facility. An agreed price is when the appraiser meets with the body shop which provided the estimate and agrees on the repair costs, so that a settlement offer can be extended to the claimant for an amount to cover those costs. An appraisal review service, such as American Computer Estimating (ACE), should be considered for a desk review of all estimates where an appraiser is not assigned. American Computer Estimating (ACE) (http://www.ace-it.com/), is one firm that provides desk reviews of automobile, property (building and contents), and subrogation damage supporting documentation to determine if the estimates are fair and reasonable. If the claim involves an automobile accident, request an estimate from the auto body shop where the vehicle is going to be repaired.

It should be noted that some states, such as New York, prohibit an adjuster from requesting a body shop estimate from more than one body shop. The rationale is that the claimant should have a choice as to where the repairs are to be completed and not have to request multiple estimates so that the insurance company can select the lowest repair estimate. The process of securing multiple estimates is time-consuming, and body shops are not always cooperative if they sense that the vehicle owner is simply requesting a comparison estimate. It is always important to secure an agreed appraisal with the claimant's choice of body shop.

Property damage estimates involving other than automobile damages (i.e., building damage caused by automobile) should be requested from the contractor the claimant has identified as the party contracted to repair the damages. Claims adjusters should refrain from recommending a contractor to the claimant, or any other party to a loss, unless required to do so by the insurer. It is recommended that an agreed appraisal be obtained from the claimant's body shop or contractor. However, if the liability investigation is incomplete and still ongoing, the appraisal should be assigned without prejudice. This means that no rights of the party concerned are to be considered as waived or lost.

Depending on the state involved, the property damage settlement offer may take into consideration the percentage of liability assessed on the insured and claimant. Comparative negligence varies by state and is discussed further in Chapter 14, Claims Process—Evaluation and Resolution, beginning on page 155. Generally, if the claimant vehicle is declared a total loss, some claim facilities may not want to become involved in processing the vehicle salvage.[1] The estimated salvage value would be reduced from the total loss settlement offer. However, there may be circumstances, because of state regulations, where a settlement offer must be extended to the claimant with the full total loss amount and then the vehicle salvage is processed in the same fashion as first-party automobile physical damage claims. Auto salvage is discussed in more detail in Chapter 22 beginning on page 273.

Some states, such as New York, require an acknowledgement letter to the claimant explaining comparative negligence, providing an explanation of loss of use, and requesting completion of a driver statement form and estimate. Be sure to consult individual state regulations for individual requirements peculiar to that jurisdiction. Any indication of an injury during the property damage claims handling process should be referred to the claims manager for reserve entry and assignment to a bodily injury adjuster.

Loss of Use/Rental Reimbursement

Loss of use reimbursement should be offered in property damage liability claims in accordance with various state regulations, and to the extent of the insured's negligence. Generally, reimbursement is made for loss of use at a reasonable daily rate (plus tax), excluding costs associated with mileage, gasoline, and insurance. All loss of use arrangements should be confirmed in writing and include any state-mandated language as well as an explanation as to the loss of use details and parameters. Some claim facilities have direct payment arrangements with rental car companies.

Closing Documentation

At the conclusion of a liability claim, a release should be taken from the claimant as outlined in the closing documentation section of Chapter 11, page 115.

[1]When the vehicle owner retains the vehicle salvage, the adjuster calculates the total loss payment and reduces the payment by the vehicle salvage amount, leaving the handling of the salvage with the claimant vehicle owner. This eliminates the need for referral of the salvage to an auction facility and the payment of the storage costs. However, it may create other problems, therefore is not recommended as a regular course of handling. For example, the claimant may repair the vehicle and put it back on the road in an unsafe condition. Unprocessed salvage could create the potential for fraud by using the vehicle title information to register a vehicle that does not exist. An ISO ClaimSearch® should always be submitted when the claimant retains the salvage to avoid the potential for fraud. If the claimant vehicle owner retains the vehicle salvage, an Affidavit of Salvage Retention should always be requested. See sample Affidavit of Salvage Retention at http://www.claimspages.com/.

Chapter 24: PIP/No-Fault Claims Handling Guidelines

Statutory or written law is set down by a state or federal legislature or an administrative body in response to a perceived need. The purpose of enacting statutes may include clarifying the functioning of government, improving civil order, answering a public need, codifying existing law, or, for an individual or company, providing special treatment. For insurance matters, state statutory laws are paramount, and federal statutory laws play a more supporting role. There is a tremendous variety of state statutes, and personal injury protection (PIP)/ no-fault statutes are no exception.

PIP provides basic "no-fault" auto coverage that meets state-mandated coverages and limits. Some state laws call for protection that applies to drivers, passengers, and/or pedestrians and may extend to their family members and dependents. Coverages vary by state and can include payment of medical expenses, lost income, ongoing services to those injured (nursing home, therapy, medical transportation, etc.), funds to replace injured family member services, a death benefit, funeral expenses, and survivor benefits. Added personal injury benefits provide optional or higher no-fault limits in addition to the basic no-fault benefits mandated by the state.

The objective in handling PIP or no-fault claims is to effectively manage the claims process, control loss and expenses, and bring the claim to an equitable resolution, while strictly adhering to state regulations and statutes.

Coverage

In addition to the typical coverage verification requirements outlined in the general auto physical damage and liability claims handling guidelines, Chapters 22 (page 273) and 23 (page 279), respectively, a review of the applicable PIP coverage endorsement, if any, needs to be conducted. This endorsement outlines the specific state coverage provided, including an explanation of the benefits payable. The handling adjuster should evaluate coverage for each PIP claim, including the following, if applicable:

- ***Eligibility conditions***—For example, only certain individuals are eligible for PIP benefits, such as the vehicle operator, passengers, and pedestrians or bicyclists struck by the vehicle. Typically, PIP benefits are not available to any person who was driving while intoxicated, under the influence of drugs, intentionally caused their own injuries, or in the process of committing a felony.

- ***Limitations***—Certain aspects of PIP coverage have monetary limitations such as limits for monthly wage benefits (i.e., 80 percent of gross wages to a maximum of $1,000 per month for period not exceeding 3 years), limits for death benefits or funeral expenses, and policy limitations for overall benefits (i.e., $8,000, $50,000, $250,000). In some states, you can purchase additional PIP benefits to increase some of these limitations as well as the overall amount of coverage. There are also limitations in that the application for benefits must be filed within a prescribed time period (i.e., within 30 days of the accident).

- ***Deductibles***—Some states, such as Florida, allow insurance companies to offer a PIP deductible (i.e., $250, $500) in exchange for a reduced premium. However, the deductible does not typically apply to passengers who are not relatives of the insured or pedestrians.
- ***Offsets***—PIP coverage is usually offset by other primary coverage such as any applicable Social Security benefits for wage loss and workers compensation benefits if the claimant was in the course and scope of employment at the time of the accident.
- ***Priority of order***—PIP benefits usually follow the vehicle; however, in some states, the coverage may follow the individual—the injured person's own PIP coverage would apply first or be primary. In the absence of individual coverage, the vehicle being occupied would provide coverage.
- ***Medical fee schedule***—In some states, such as New York, PIP medical benefits are paid in accordance to a mandatory medical fee schedule, which may be comparable to the workers compensation fee schedule in that state. In states that do not have a mandatory medical fee schedule, medical and hospital bills are paid according to "usual and customary" fees.
- ***Coinsurance issues***—Some PIP benefits are paid on a coinsurance basis, meaning that the eligible injured person pays a portion or percentage of the medical bills. For example, in Florida, the medical benefits may be paid at a rate of 80 percent of the submitted medical expense and wages, paid at a rate of 60 percent.

Investigation

The following should be considered during the investigation of PIP claims:

- Review the applicable PIP regulations and statutes as well as any PIP caselaw and/or regulatory publications.
- Determine whether any medical fee schedules are required or if medical is paid on a usual and customary basis. This means the typical charges for certain medical treatment in a particular jurisdiction.
- Identify all applicable PIP coverage available to the claimant.
- Confirm that the PIP claim is eligible, and there are no exclusions or issues precluding benefits.
- Confirm the injury, causal relationship, prior medical history, treatment, and prognosis.
- Obtain the completed and signed Application for No-Fault (PIP) Benefits.

- Obtain signed wage and medical authorization forms.
- Secure statements of the claimant, passengers, witnesses, and the insured operator.
- Acquire attorney allegations, including specific information on injury and disability periods.
- Identify any bodily injury (BI) tort claims and uninsured/underinsured motorist claim exposures.
- Conduct a search using the ISO ClaimSearch® database on all PIP claimants.
- Hire or consult with local defense counsel who can provide specialized legal representation for PIP claims, if necessary.
- When warranted, consider an examination under oath (EUO) deposition of the claimant to confirm the eligibility of the PIP claims and testimony regarding medical treatment and disability. Used to enable the insurer to obtain information necessary to process a claim, an EUO may be required when a coverage question exists or any other issue arises that requires the insured's testimony. An EUO is a formal deposition held in the insurer's attorney's office with a court stenographer. The insured may or may not be represented by an attorney. An insured's failure to comply with the policy requirement for an EUO is, by definition, prejudicial, absent extraordinary circumstances. If the insured does not comply with the EUO request, coverage may be denied for failure to cooperate.
- Aggressively pursue PIP subrogation, loss transfer, and lien rights, when applicable. (See Chapter 17: Claims Process—Recovery, page 205.)
- Initiate effective fraud investigations regarding accident and treatment activities. If necessary, retain a Special Investigative Unit (SIU) to investigate questionable claims involving policyholders, claimants, and various providers. An SIU is typically a division or department within an insurance company involved in detecting and pursuing action against fraudulent activities on the part of insureds or claimants.
- Obtain copies of all official reports, including:
    - Police accident reports
    - Police statements
    - Police photos
    - Police accident reconstruction reports
    - Weather reports
    - Traffic light sequence reports
    - Death certificates
    - Medical examiner or autopsy report

Claim File Documentation and File Management

It is important that all activities pertaining to the PIP claim be properly documented by letter or telephone. Below are some recommendations:

- Use transmittal forms and letters to facilitate the distribution of PIP forms and benefit explanations to claimants.
- Itemize and document PIP claim reserve management in the claim file.
- Evaluate and confirm disability dates.
- Clearly document PIP wage calculations and medical payment details in the claim file notes and on the claim check and/or the explanation of benefits (EOB). An EOB is a document often included with a claim payment explaining the basis for the amount paid.
- Applicable wage or medical benefit offsets, and/or priority of coverage issues, must be clearly documented in the claim file notes (i.e., workers compensation, Social Security, disability).
- Determine if wages are placed on a repetitive payment schedule.
- Proper diary management is essential to comply with statutory requirements for issuance of forms and benefits.
- Organize claim file documentation by individual PIP claimant to facilitate the claim process.
- Utilize a PIP payment register to sort payments by claimant, service, date, provider, and amounts.
- Submit PIP claim denials in writing, in a timely manner, and in accordance with statutory requirements (including utilization of proper statutory forms).

PIP Claim Forms

Use the state specific claim forms[1] when handling PIP claims, including, but not limited to, the following:

- No-fault application for benefits (including any required cover letters and attachments, such as a Statutory Disability Benefit Form [NY])
- No-fault medical and hospital verification forms
- No-fault wage verification forms
- No-fault denial forms
- No-fault wage offset forms (i.e., workers compensation, Social Security, or state disability)
- No-fault subrogation and loss transfer forms (intercompany reimbursement forms)
- Other required no-fault forms

Medical Management and Disability Management

Medical management is the process by which the delivery of health care is structured and monitored, with the goal of providing medical services that are both appropriate and economically reasonable. An effective medical management or managed care program includes timely independent medical examinations (IMEs) to assist in the claims handling process, nurse

[1] PIP claim forms are usually available at the state insurance department or through a third-party vendor.

case management, medical and hospital bill repricing, utilization review, and physician peer reviews. Early intervention with an effective medical management program will assist in securing appropriate reports and the control of medical treatment, as well as lead to a reduction in lost time days and total loss costs.

Proper medical and disability management should include:

- ***PIP medical and hospital bill review or repricing***—Medical bill repricing or bill review means that the medical or hospital bill is reviewed either internally or by a third-party vendor to make sure the bill is either billed in accordance with the state mandated fee schedule or complies with the usual and customary charges for that procedure. If the bill is repriced or reduced, the payment is changed and an Explanation of Benefits (or EOB) is sent to the medical provider explaining the basis for payment.

- ***Nurse case management***—When applicable, a nurse may be assigned via telephone or in the field to assist with a claim, with the goal of returning the claimant to work. The nurse may also work in a triage capacity with the attending physician and injured worker.

- ***Timely payment of medical and hospital bills***—Bills and other medical-related benefits should be paid in a timely manner in accordance with statutes.

- ***Utilization reviews***—Referrals to either a physician or nurse case manager to ascertain the necessity and cost or type of treatment being recommended and medical peer reviews (of a physician's treatment by a fellow physician) should be made to determine the necessity and course of medical treatment.

- ***Proper review of medical documentation***—Look for causation, treatment, prior medical history, disability periods, and other issues.

- ***Narrative medical reports***—If necessary, clarify the medical diagnosis, prognosis, disability, permanency, and future treatment. These reports, requested from an attending physician, should include the diagnosis, prognosis, necessity and duration of further treatment, permanency, disability, and the causal relation to the accident. An adjuster should secure a narrative medical report in advance of an IME, if possible.

- ***Copies of diagnostic reports***—Request these to confirm injuries, treatment, disability, and permanency.

- ***Independent medical examinations (IME)***—These are medical exams of a claimant on behalf of the insurance company, and should be conducted in a timely manner, by specialty. When presented with a questionable soft tissue injury, consider scheduling an IME upon receipt of the completed no-fault application for benefits. IMEs are commonly conducted for soft tissue injuries—a major source of pain and disability. The four fundamental tissues that are affected are the epithelial, muscular, nervous, and connective tissues.

Regulatory Compliance

When handling PIP claims, it is important to note that the handling process is governed by various state statutes and regulations. There are specific time periods for submission of the no-fault application, payment of medical and hospital bills, and payment of wage benefits. If PIP benefits are paid late, interest may apply, and if audited by the state insurance department, fines could apply as well. Oftentimes, medical providers will file suit for late payment of medical bills, claiming interest and penalties. PIP adjusters who have excessive workloads will incur PIP fines and interest expense as backlogs occur and PIP benefits tend to get paid late.

Special Notes

After the initial investigation is completed, the primary handling of a PIP claim is to manage the claim process using effective medical management. PIP claims which are not medically managed properly incur higher loss and expense payments.

Diary management is very important in the PIP claims handling process. If a PIP adjuster is behind in diary management, claimants may end up receiving continued wage loss payments that should not have been paid and possibly overtreatment, resulting in a higher loss ratio. For example, assume a PIP claimant has been out of work for 8 weeks. The adjuster needs to secure an updated medical report, but is behind on diary, so when he finally gets the time to secure the updated medical report, he realizes the claimant can return to work. Since the adjuster needs to issue a partial PIP denial to the claimant to cease paying wage benefits, he ends up overpaying the lost wage claim. The adjuster also realizes that an IME report has been received in the interim indicating that the claimant no longer requires any further medical treatment, yet he continues to seek chiropractic adjustments. The adjuster ends up overpaying the medical benefits as well.

Managing PIP claims requires good organizational skills and proper diary management. These cannot be stressed enough.

FOR MORE INFORMATION ON:	GO TO:	PAGE(S):
Claims Handling Guidelines	Chapters 21–30	271–354
Auto Physical Damage	Chapter 22	273
Auto Liability	Chapter 23	279
First-Party Property and Inland Marine	Chapter 25	295
Cargo	Chapter 26	305
General Liability	Chapter 27	311
Professional and Management Liability	Chapter 28	323
Public Entity	Chapter 29	331
Workers Compensation	Chapter 30	337

Chapter 25: First-Party Property and Inland Marine Claims Handling Guidelines

We often think of property in categories of buildings, equipment (machinery), business personal property, and stock (finished goods); but other types of property are also subject to loss. Some examples are tenant improvements, piers and wharves, fences, landscaping, and dams, and any other structure that is not classified as a building. Property is either real or personal in nature. Real property is fixed and immobile, such as land and buildings; personal property is all other movable property. Personal property can be further classified as: (1) tangible, such office equipment, stock, furniture, etc.; or (2) intangible, such as patents, copyrights, stocks and personal annuities.

Insurable Interest

The concept of insurable interest is vital to understanding property insurance; no property may be insured by an entity without an insurable interest. So it goes that no claim should be paid to an insured or claimant who lacks an insurable interest. The nature and extent of insurable interest must be proven at the time of loss. Financial interests that fall within this broad definition of insurable interest include those of:

- The owner
- The lessor (one who leases a building or space to a lessee)
- A secured creditor (mortgagors, lenders, etc.)
- A holder of a mechanic's or contractor's lien
- A bailee or other agent of the owner
- A lessee or renter of property (to the extent of the lessee's legal obligation)
- A party who has made improvements upon real property owned by another (such as the tenant or lessee)
- A party with a contractual interest in property (such as the interest of a life tenant)
- A party with a legal right to use another's property (such as easements, permanent use of storage buildings, private roads)

The insurable interest may be direct, such as when physical destruction to property occurs, or indirect, such as loss of average daily attendance payments after destruction of a school building.

Claims Handling

Direct Damage versus Time Element Coverage

Another facet of a first-party[1] property claims is time element coverage. If an organization's facilities are damaged or destroyed by a fire or a tornado, the physical damage to the buildings and contents is said to be a direct damage loss. Direct damage property insurance provides funds to pay for the repair or replacement of the damaged property.

An organization that suffers a direct damage loss also may suffer a loss of income or an increase in operating expenses as a result of not being able to use the damaged property while it is being repaired or replaced. These losses are called time element losses because the amount of the income loss or expense increase generally depends on how long it takes to repair or replace the damaged property. Time element property insurance pays for the loss of income or the increase in operating expenses that result from suspended or makeshift operations while the damaged property is being repaired or replaced.

Types of Property Policies

Property exposures are generally covered by a single property insurance policy to cover all real and personal property with a reasonable deductible high enough to eliminate frequent claims. Policies also are available to cover highly protected risks (HPR).

The major divisions of types of property policies are:

- ***Property insurance***—Covers buildings and contents.
- ***Inland marine insurance***—Covers property in transit and unusual fixed property, such as bridges, communication towers, tunnels, contractor's equipment, and other risks associated with land transportation.
- ***Ocean marine insurance***—Covers cargo aboard ocean-going vessels or vessels using internal waterways, such as the Mississippi River (Claims handling guidelines for these exposures are addressed in Chapter 26, beginning on page 305.)

First-party property and inland marine losses should be assigned to adjusters who are experienced at handling first-party property losses.

Coverage

The claim file should be fully documented with copies of all the applicable policy forms and endorsements. The claim notes must address application of coverage including:

- Coverage forms and endorsements
- Policy deductibles
- Settlement valuation (actual cash value, replacement cost, or agreed value)
- Insurable interest

[1] Claims involving the policyholder are typically referred to as first-party claims, and claims involving a third-party claimant are referred to as a third-party claims.

- Insurance to value[2] and any applicable coinsurance[3]
- Coverage limits
- Coverage sublimits
- Coverage extensions
- The existence of any other available insurance coverage

A thorough review of the coverage forms and endorsements, including the application of any coinsurance penalties, deductibles, and any policy limitations need to be indicated in the claim file notes. If coverage does not exist or is excluded or limited by the policy language, the policyholder should be advised in writing as soon as possible.

If an adjuster is unsure of coverage applying to a particular loss, then the adjuster should seek assistance from the claims manager and the Underwriting Department. The claims manager may have experience with the policy coverage issue, and the underwriter or underwriting manager will be able to explain the intent of the policy language.

[2]Insurance to value refers to insurance written in an amount approximating the value of the subject of the insurance or which meets coinsurance requirements.

[3]Coinsurance is a property insurance provision that penalizes the insured's loss recovery if the limit of insurance purchased by the insured is not at least equal to a specified percentage (commonly 80 percent) of the value of the insured property. A business income coverage coinsurance provision penalizes the insured's loss recovery if the business income limit of insurance is not at least equal to a specified percentage of the business income that would have been earned during the 12-month policy period. The coinsurance provision specifies that the insured will recover no more than the following: the amount of the loss multiplied by the ratio of the amount of insurance purchased (the limit of insurance) to the amount of insurance required (the value of the property on the date of loss multiplied by the coinsurance percentage), less the deductible.

Property Inspection and Damage Appraisal

An estimate of damages should always be requested from the insured. All first-party property and inland marine claims with damages exceeding the agreed appraisal inspection limit (e.g., $500 or $1,000) need to have a staff field adjuster or independent adjuster assigned to inspect the damaged property, unless the claims handling instructions state otherwise. It is up to the handling adjuster's own judgment as to when to assign independent property adjusters on claims under $1,000. The adjuster/appraiser secures an agreement on the price of repairs with the insured's contractor of choice relative to the property damage. This is called an "agreed appraisal." Simply preparing a damage estimate without the amounts being agreed to by the insured will not provide the necessary basis to settle the claim.

A full adjustment may be necessary if the property loss is serious or complex. This involves completion of all elements of the property adjustment process (including the items that may be completed by the desk staff adjuster) along with a fully captioned report. Due to the increased expense, some companies require management approval for a full adjustment assignment by an independent property adjuster.

Scope of Damages

Property inspections should be completed immediately after the loss. The property adjuster develops a formal scope of damages to include:

- Preliminary indication of the cause of loss
- Comment on the necessity of a cause-and-origin expert
- Photographs and diagrams of the damaged property
- Measurements of the property
- Property replacement cost valuation
- Building and contents damage projections
- Business interruption/extra expense projections
- Debris removal expense projections
- Comment on any public adjuster involvement in the loss adjustment process (discussed later)
- Assessment of whether a building contractor[4] will be necessary to assist the field adjuster with the building damage estimate process

[4]A building contractor or "builder" is a contractor specializing in residential or commercial buildings. The contractor is retained to prepare a detailed estimate of damages. Contractors are often retained by insurance adjusters and public adjusters.

The scope of damage is used by the adjuster (both field and desk adjusters) to evaluate the total exposure of the claim as well as the application of coverage. The initial scope of damage may trigger a coverage position letter or nonwaiver agreement based on damaged property not being covered and is also used to establish initial claim reserves.

Business Interruption and Extra Expense Claims

Business interruption or business income insurance provides loss of income coverage to the insured as a result of a covered loss causing damage to the premises resulting in discontinued or suspended operations. Business interruption insurance may include rental value insurance, providing coverage for loss of rental income when a covered loss causes building damage. It basically provides coverage for loss of income due to the policyholder being unable to continue operations resulting from vacating the premises after a covered loss, such as a fire. The coverage provides for the loss of profit and continuing operating expenses (e.g., electricity, gas).

Extra expense coverage is time element property insurance that pays for expenses in excess of normal operating expenses that an insured incurs to continue operations while its property is being repaired or replaced after having been damaged by a covered cause of loss. Extra expense coverage can be purchased in addition to or instead of business income coverage, depending on the needs of the insured.

Business interruption and extra expense claims provide coverage for the indirect losses or time element claims as a result of the direct property damage claim. These types of claims may require the use of an accountant or an adjuster with knowledge of business operations and accounting to determine the amount of the loss. Business and financial records must be reviewed to evaluate claims under this coverage, usually on site at the insured's location, unless the documents are copied and forwarded to the adjuster.

Cause and Origin/ Use of Experts

The property adjuster should provide a comment as to the cause and origin of the loss. Telephone contact with the field staff adjuster or independent property adjuster after the initial inspection will determine whether a cause-and-origin expert will need to be assigned. This is an expert retained to determine the cause of loss. Experts may include building engineers, electrical engineers, mechanical engineers, architects, plumbing experts, accountants, fire investigators, and general cause-and-origin experts. The decision to engage a cause-and-origin expert is typically included in the initial scope of damages. Claims involving potential arson or potential subrogation require an immediate assignment of a cause-and-origin expert.

Use of Building Contractors

Depending on the size of a property loss, the field staff adjuster or independent property adjuster may retain a building contractor to determine the replacement cost and/or prepare a detailed repair estimate for the property. The use of building contractors is usually reserved for the more serious property losses that require an extensive amount of time to prepare a damage estimate.

Basic Investigation

The basic property claim investigation may include the following:

- Coverage verification and coverage analysis
- On-site inspection of loss
- Interviews with and statements by the insured and witnesses
- Identification of the insured's repair contractor of choice
- Photographs and diagrams of the property
- Preparation of building damage estimate/agreed appraisal
- Copies of all official reports, including all fire and police reports
- Copies of leases and other applicable contracts
- Copies of all applicable insured records
- Code violations issues
- Prior loss history
- Ownership confirmation
- Lien and mortgagee information

- Personal property/contents damage list
- ISO ClaimSearch® entries for all fire and theft losses (See Appendix B, page 363.)
- Proof of loss
- Loan receipts

Personal Property Theft Claims

All personal property theft losses should include the following investigation:

- Statement of the insured
- Stolen item or contents list
- Police report
- Photographs (if applicable)
- Copies of any verification documents (i.e., receipts, warranties, guaranties, product literature, photographs, videos)
- Theft affidavit
- Proof of loss
- Loan receipts

Public Adjuster (PA) Involvement

PAs are adjusters retained by policyholders to represent their interests in first-party claims against an insurance company. PAs are paid by the insured, typically a percentage of the settlement amount. PAs are the only types of adjusters who represent the insured and not the insurance company. A public adjuster represents the policyholder in personal lines and commercial lines first-party property claims.

In the past, in the event of a disagreement with the insurer over the claim amount involving a large fire loss, the insured may have hired a PA. Now, the use of public adjusters is very common in all types and sizes of property losses. The continued use of public adjusters highlights the public's attitude toward and trust of insurance companies and adjusters. Insureds are willing to give up a portion of the settlement in exchange for the certainty that they are being treated fairly and equitably by the insurer. If the adjuster treats the insured fairly, a PA can often be avoided.

The PA is retained to protect the interests of the insured and works closely with the staff or field property adjuster. PAs prepare detailed estimates and consult often with the insured to compile all the necessary information for the claim. If a PA is retained by the insured, request a written letter of confirmation or retainer and comply with the request for the PA to be listed as a payee on the settlement checks.

Special Investigative Unit (SIU) Assignment

All claims involving potentially fraudulent activity should be assigned to an SIU investigator. An SIU is a division or department within an insurance company involved in detecting fraud and pursuing actions against insureds or claimants involved in fraudulent activities. Some companies have their own SIU assigned to investigate all potentially fraudulent claims, while others may outsource this activity.

It is important that the SIU investigation be completed promptly and timely. If the claim is legitimate, and there is no evidence of fraudulent activity on the part of the insured, the claim should be evaluated and resolved. An SIU investigation should not be allowed to continue without any substantive evidence of fraud.

Examination under Oath (EUO)

An EUO should be requested when there are claims involving potentially fraudulent activity or when additional information or documentation is needed to evaluate coverage. Basically, an EUO enables the insurer to obtain information necessary to process a claim. An EUO may be required when a coverage question exists or any other issue that requires the insured's testimony. An EUO is a formal deposition, held in the insurer's attorney's office, with a court stenographer present. The insured may or may not be represented by an attorney. An insured's failure to comply with the policy requirement for an EUO is, by definition, prejudicial, absent extraordinary circumstances. This could result in a coverage denial if the insured does not cooperate.

Nonwaiver Agreements and Reservation of Rights

In the event that there is a question regarding whether the claim is covered, the field adjuster or independent property adjuster should be instructed to secure a signed nonwaiver agreement. Thereafter, the handling adjuster will prepare a coverage position letter to the insured, with client approval.

A nonwaiver agreement is a form of reservation of rights and is used in property and casualty claims, but is used more often in the handling of property and inland marine claims. Nonwaiver agreements allow the investigation to continue and the adjustment of a claim, with each party understanding that a potential coverage issue exists. It preserves the rights of both the insurance company and the insured.

The primary difference between the reservation of rights letter and the nonwaiver agreement is that the nonwaiver agreement is signed by both the insurance company representative and the insured and is, therefore, considered a bilateral agreement. Typically, nonwaiver agreements are brief and do not go into any detail with respect to the coverage issue and policy language. They may be used by the field claim staff and sometimes by the desk adjuster.

Nonwaiver agreements are not indefinite. At some point, the nonwaiver agreement needs to be converted into a detailed coverage position letter in the form of a reservation of rights, partial coverage disclaimer, or full coverage disclaimer.

Proof of Loss and Subrogation Loan Receipt

All property losses require a proof of loss and subrogation/loan receipt if there is a potential for subrogation. A proof of loss is a formal statement made by the insured to the insurer regarding a claim, especially in property insurance, so that the insurer may determine its liability under the policy. A subrogation loan receipt is a document attached or incorporated into a proof of loss that provides the insurance company with the right of subrogation.

Replacement Cost and Actual Cash Value

There are two methods for establishing the value of most of the insured property for purposes of determining the amount the insurer will pay in the event of loss. Replacement cost is the cost to replace the damaged property with materials of like kind and quality. Actual cash value is the cost to replace the damaged property, less depreciation.

If the policy is written on a replacement cost basis, and it applies to a property loss, the adjuster should consider settling the loss based on actual cash value and "holding back" the difference between the replacement cost value and the actual cash value until the repairs are actually completed. This will require a proof of loss and a replacement cost "hold back" form. This is a document signed by the policyholder indicating that payment will be made based on actual cash value until the repairs are completed or items are actually replaced, at which time the difference between actual cash value and replacement cost will be paid.

Some property insurance forms may specify that replacement cost will be paid without any deduction for depreciation or hold back if the building loss is under a certain monetary threshold, such as $2,500. Replacement cost provisions apply to both building and contents losses.

Mortgagees, Loss Payees, and Lien Holders

All mortgagees, loss payees, and lien holders need to be listed on all claim payment checks unless written authority for the removal of the name from the claim check by the designated mortgagee, loss payee, or lien holder has been provided.

Use of Payment Advances

Advance payments are sometimes used to assist the insured with the cost to initiate repairs and reduce business interruption or extra expense claims. It is generally not recommended to provide advance payments until the cause of a loss has been determined. Otherwise, if advance payments were issued on an arson or intentional claim, the payment could affect any chance of denying coverage.

Special Notes

The handling of property and inland marine claims requires special training in estimating damages and understanding coverage. Due to the specialized training, property adjusters usually only handle property losses and do not work on casualty losses.

Most property adjusters attend basic and advanced property training schools that train adjusters in estimating damages. Many years ago, the damage estimates were prepared by reviewing various regional contracting manuals for the price of materials and labor rates. Now, most companies use specialized estimating software that allows the adjuster to plug in the damaged property item description, measurements, and dimensions, as well as the zip code for labor rates, to generate a damage estimate.

Field adjusters may use computer laptops to prepare damage estimates, uploading the damage estimate and digital photos to their computers. As technology progresses, particularly with the use of video technology, the need to use field adjusters to actually write or prepare the damage estimates in the field may dwindle. Video technology will allow live wireless video to be streamed back to the desk adjuster who can use the video with computerized estimating software, along with the measurements provided by a field person (with minimal adjusting experience), to prepare the damage estimates, e-mailing them directly to the insured.

FOR MORE INFORMATION ON:	GO TO:	PAGE(S):
Claims Handling Guidelines	Chapters 21–30	271–354
Auto Physical Damage	Chapter 22	273
Auto Liability	Chapter 23	279
Auto PIP/No Fault	Chapter 24	289
Cargo	Chapter 26	305
General Liability	Chapter 27	311
Professional and Management Liability	Chapter 28	323
Public Entity	Chapter 29	331
Workers Compensation	Chapter 30	337
ISO ClaimSearch®	Appendix B	363
Ethics in Claims Handling	Appendix E	409
Legal Theory and Doctrines	Appendix G	427

Chapter 26: Cargo Claims Handling Guidelines

Inland marine cargo claims involve damage to property in transit on trucks, railroads, and in the air. Marine cargo refers to damage to property in transit on the ocean or other large bodies of water.

The carrier is the company that is transporting the merchandise from one point to another. The carrier can be a boat, airplane, truck, or train. A common carrier is a commercial individual or organization carrying persons or property from one place to another for payment, e.g., a trucker. As contrasted with contract carriers, a common carrier is one that transports or handles the goods of the general public. Since enactment of the Interstate Commerce Commission (ICC) Termination Act of 1995, a carrier can hold operating authority as both a common carrier and contract carrier, but a separate registration fee is required for each type of authority. An applicant for common carrier authority must file proof of cargo insurance, while a contract carrier is not required to do so.

A contract carrier is a commercial individual or organization carrying persons or property of certain customers only rather than the goods of or the public in general. Unlike a common carrier, a contract carrier has a right to choose or refuse to convey passengers or freight for payment.

History

All common carriers have extraordinary responsibility for the goods they carry. However, they are not liable for:

- Acts of God—accidents or events resulting from natural causes (e.g., floods, lightning, earthquake, storms)
- Acts of a public enemy, war, or hostile acts of a foreign nation (e.g., terrorism, civil war)
- Acts of a public authority (e.g., confiscation of property, delay due to closure of roads)
- Defects or inherent vice in the goods shipped
- The neglect or fault of the shipper or delay in transit at the shipper's request, unless the carrier is proven negligent

The air or sea cargo carrier is not usually responsible for loss to the cargo unless it is manifestly negligent, because all participants in an ocean voyage are traditionally joint ventures, each taking their own chances. The responsibilities of shipper and carrier are delineated by the U.S. Carriage of Goods by Sea Act (COGSA) based on the internationally accepted "Hague Rules" of 1921. These rules excuse ocean carriers from liability if they have exerted due diligence to provide a seaworthy ship before the voyage and exercise care for the goods during carriage on the ship. COGSA makes direct or subrogation claims against the carrier somewhat more difficult than those against inland carriers that generally are excused only for "Acts of God."

If the carrier can prove that there was no fault or privity on its part, it can limit its liability to a certain prescribed amount for each package or unit. In 1968, a protocol known as the Hague-Visby Rules was developed. This raised the amount of the limitations per package and dealt with the problems of containerization and other unitization of cargo.

Marine insurance is more flexible than property insurance and far less restrictive. Use of an aggregate deductible has become a legitimate method of controlling costs, using a commercial insurer as a provider of documentation (certificates of insurance, etc.) and catastrophe protection.

Timeliness of Handling and Adjuster Assignment

It is important that immediate notice be given in case of cargo loss or damage, particularly if salvage or abandonment has to be considered. Timely handling serves to protect a shipment or load from further damage ensures prompt delivery of any undamaged goods, and facilitates obtaining maximum salvage return for any damaged cargo.

Cargo claims should handled on a priority basis and assigned to a cargo adjuster specialist. That adjuster will review the loss, initiate the investigation, and may assign an independent cargo adjuster or appraiser for an on-site assessment of the loss, mitigation of damages, and preservation of salvage. Based on area of specialization and expertise, a national or regional independent salvor may need to be engaged for early evaluation and disposition of salvage.

If field staff cargo adjusters are not available, an independent adjuster/appraiser should be assigned. All assignments to independent adjusters need to provide specific instructions concerning the assignment. Include copies of shipment documents, any damage estimates, claim details, contact information for interested parties, and any special handling instructions in the file.

The independent adjuster should be instructed to telephone the handling adjuster with initial findings as soon as the initial assessment is completed, whether the inspection is conducted on-site or at a storage location. The independent adjuster should also be requested to complete the assignment within 5 days and forward the damage report with digital photographs to the claims handler's office via e-mail.

To maximize salvage recovery, the adjuster must work hand in hand with the insured, the owner, and the cargo adjuster or appraiser.

Coverage Determination

The applicable bill of lading and coverage forms need to be examined closely to determine whether coverage will be afforded for a particular loss. A bill of lading is a document issued by a shipping carrier, or by a company's shipping department, acknowledging that specified goods have been received onboard as cargo for conveyance to a named place for delivery to the consignee (the person to whom the shipment is to be delivered), who is usually specifically identified. The bill of lading must contain (1) the names of the shipper and consignee, (2) the origin and destination points, (3) the number of packages, (4) the description of the freight, and (5) the weight, volume, or measurement of the freight.

Review carefully the coverage forms, the insuring agreement, policy exclusions, exceptions and limitations, applicable deductibles or retentions, the settlement valuation provisions, and the insured's duties in the event of a loss. Cargo coverage forms will vary, and in some instances, specified perils coverage will afford relatively narrow coverage. For example, a tarping endorsement will only afford coverage where a load is properly tarped, i.e., protected by a tarp, at the time of loss. A refrigeration endorsement will only provide coverage for loss to a refrigerated load if the refrigeration unit is inspected at defined intervals by a certified heating, ventilating, and air-conditioning (HVAC) technician.

Motor Truck Cargo (MTC) Insurance

Motor truck cargo carriers have specific coverage forms available. The Motor Carrier Act of 1980 makes it a requirement that certain vehicles carry minimum limits of insurance coverage to satisfy public liability and environmental restoration claims that may arise from accidents. The minimum required limits range from $750,000 to $1 million to $5 million per accident, depending on the type of commodity transported (i.e., nonhazardous or hazardous and, in the case of hazardous substances, the specific category of such).

MTC insurance is liability insurance for truckers, for both common carriers and contract carriers who transport property of others. It is an inland marine coverage form covering loss of property in the course of transit, either by common carrier or on the insured's own vehicles, depending on the form used.

Basic Investigation

It is important to conduct a detailed investigation concerning the circumstances of the loss, including the following:

- Prompt contact with the insured for complete details
- Statements of the parties to the loss, such as the insured, drivers, adverse operators, and witnesses
- Copies of all shipping documentation and contracts (see Documentation of Loss section below)
- Information pertaining to shipment seals,[1] locks, alarms, and Global Positioning Satellite (GPS) systems

[1]A container seal is a metal or plastic device used as a locking mechanism on a container to prevent theft or tampering. Container seal numbers may be indicated in the shipping documents along with the container number.

- Official reports, such as police and fire reports
- Photographs and diagrams
- Federal and state agency reports, including inspection reports of perishable goods
- Drivers' logs and weigh station reports, as necessary
- Determination of parties responsible for loading and unloading a shipment
- In-depth subrogation investigation to identify responsible parties

Contact with the Insured

Upon receipt of a new cargo loss, the handling adjuster should contact the insured to determine the facts surrounding the loss, such as the following:

- The exact location of the loss
- The on-site contact for the insured and his/her contact information
- Nature of the cargo
- Type of damage (concealed loss or damage, shortages, etc.)
- Estimated amount of the damage
- Driver's notation of visible damage
- Insured's photographs of the damaged cargo
- Steps taken to preserve the damaged packaging and contents
- Steps taken to protect the cargo from further damage
- Condition of any salvage and potential disposition of same
- Any lease agreements or other contracts relating to the load or shipment
- Local authorities, if any, on-site

Following this initial contact with the insured, every effort should be made to contact the insured's on-site representative to supplement the above items and obtain a current status of the loss.

Documentation of Loss

There are various types of losses which can occur to cargo, such as collision, overturn, theft, water, wind (hurricane, tornado, etc.), fire, refrigeration malfunction, explosion, etc. All aspects of the claim must be documented with sufficient detail to determine the exact nature and scope of the loss, and make a determination of liability. This involves obtaining and analyzing the following items, where applicable:

- Copy of the written claim against the carrier
- Statement of claim showing an itemization of the loss
- Policy declaration page with schedules, certificate of insurance, or identification of the report of risk or "declaration" to the insurer
- Policy forms and endorsements, including any endorsements for specified perils, such as tarping or refrigeration

- Bill of lading (front and back) (*Note:* A "clean" bill of lading is when the carrier has not indicated any problems with the condition of the cargo at the time of its acceptance for shipment.)
- Freight bill (front and back)
- Commercial invoices, including invoices covering the entire shipment (in some cases, a certified copy)
- Lease arrangement in effect between the motor carriers and any other entity
- Any other written contracts
- Packing slips or lists
- Delivery receipts, with or without delivery exceptions (*Note:* A "clean" delivery receipt is when the party receiving the goods has not indicated any "exceptions"[2] or "shortages" at the time of receiving the shipment.)
- Photographs and diagrams
- Survey or inspection reports
- Repair estimates
- Replacement estimates
- Missing cargo report
- Salvage reports
- Reports by various local, state, or federal authorities investigating the loss (e.g., health department if food perishables are involved)
- Police report for lost or stolen cargo
- Fire report
- Weather reports
- For losses involving a sealed shipment, information concerning the seal and condition or inspection reports completed at the time the shipment was sealed
- Proof of loss

Put all requests for documentation in writing. Telephone conversations concerning required documentation should be confirmed in writing. The front and back of all documentation need to be secured as important information may be indicated on the reverse side of the documents.

Identification of Responsible Parties

Identify all parties involved in the chain of the shipping sequence and place them on notice of the claim as appropriate. Although the insured may be called on to pay a loss, there may be another responsible party from whom contribution or reimbursement may be obtained.

Damages

Generally, the shipper is only entitled to recover the "actual loss" to the property unless the shipping documentation specifi-

[2]An exception is a note on the delivery receipt indicating damage to or shortage of merchandise. Failing to note any exceptions may make a future claim difficult to present against the carrier.

cally provides for special or consequential damages arising out of a loss. Lost profits, for example, are generally not recoverable.

As a general rule, the "actual loss" is limited to the value of the merchandise at the point of shipment or the "fair market value" of the shipment, as determined by the difference between market value of the shipment in the condition in which it should have been delivered, and the market value of the shipment at the time of delivery or the time the shipment was damaged.

A thorough review of the policy language (including any applicable coinsurance) and endorsement provisions, the bill of lading, and damage report is necessary to determine the scope of damages for any given loss.

Salvage

As appropriate, a salvor should be engaged to minimize the scope of the loss by maximizing the salvage recovery for the damaged shipment. The handling adjuster must work closely with the insured, owner, and independent adjuster or appraiser to identify the appropriate salvor for a given loss based on the salvor's experience with the type of shipment, the salvor's location and availability to handle the salvage in a timely manner, and the salvor's ready accessibility to available markets.

Following notice to the owner and any other parties of interest, cargo should be disposed of in a manner that is fair and protects the best interests of the owner.

FOR MORE INFORMATION ON:	GO TO:	PAGE(S):
Claims Process	Chapters 10–17	105–220
Claims Handling Guidelines	Chapters 21–30	271–354
Auto Physical Damage	Chapter 22	273
Auto Liability	Chapter 23	279
Auto PIP/No Fault	Chapter 24	289
First-Party Property and Inland Marine	Chapter 25	295
General Liability	Chapter 27	311
Professional and Management Liability	Chapter 28	323
Public Entity	Chapter 29	331
Workers Compensation	Chapter 30	337
Ethics in Claims Handling	Appendix E	409

Chapter 27: General Liability Claims Handling Guidelines

General liability is commonly described as insurance that protects commercial insureds from most liability exposures, other than automobile and professional liability. General liability coverage is a commercial lines coverage form, either written within a package policy along with other coverages, such as property, or as a standalone policy. In this section, when we refer to general liability, we are including dwelling owner personal liability, homeowner liability, farm owner liability, as well as commercial liability coverage forms.

There are a wide variety of claims that fall within the general liability category, including the following:

- ***Premises liability***—These claims are made in conjunction with the ownership, maintenance, or control of the building and land. Examples of premises claims include visitor trip and falls on sidewalks due to snow and ice, in interior hallways from standing water, on stairs because of concrete defects or a lack of handrails, and any other claim resulting from liability due to maintenance and control of the premises. Premises liability exposures pertain to both the tenant and building owner or landlord. Typically, the lease agreement between the landlord and tenant will address maintenance responsibility and any relevant indemnification provisions.
- ***Operations liability***—This liability occurs as a result of the insured's business operations, often involving maintenance, repairs, and construction activities. Typically, there are two operations categories: operations in progress and completed operations.[1] An example would be where a contractor, who is replacing an existing tile floor, ruptures the water pipes underneath the tile, causing immediate water damage to occur. Another example is a drywall contractor who pierces an electrical conduit with a nail, leaves the job site, and the building sustains a fire loss 2 days later due to the electrical problem. The latter is a completed operations claim as the insured had finished the drywall job and left the premises.
- ***Tenant legal liability***—This includes claims for damage to the building by the landlord. Since the space leased to the tenant is in the care, custody, and control of the tenant, the damages to the building would be excluded under the standard general liability coverage form, but supplementary coverage may exist under the "Tenant Legal Liability" or "Damage to Premises Rented

[1]Under a general liability policy, completed operations is work of the insured that has been completed as called for in a contract; or work completed at a single job site under a contract involving multiple job sites; or work that has been put to its intended use.

Claims Handling

to You" provisions. An example of this type of claim is an insured tenant leaving a candle burning in his rental space, causing a fire that damages the building.

- ***Product liability***—These claims are for bodily injury or property damage incurred as a consequence of some defect in a product sold or manufactured. Examples of product liability claims abound in the news, including those against car manufacturers for design defects or those against restaurants by patrons who contract salmonella poisoning due to the improper handling or storage of food.

- ***Personal injury liability***—This category includes claims for insurable offenses that produce harm other than bodily injury. Liability policies may cover claims for libel, slander, defamation, malicious prosecution, wrongful eviction, invasion of privacy, and false arrest, detention, or imprisonment. For example, an insured may defame a business competitor by making statements about its financial condition. The competitor may make a claim for monetary loss sustained as a result of losing customers who believed the insured's statements. Another example would be an incident involving a department store security guard who detains a customer believed to be shoplifting. The customer could file a lawsuit based on false arrest, detention, and malicious prosecution.

- ***Advertising liability***—These claims arise from advertising injury—damage sustained in connection with the insured's advertising of its goods or services, e.g., libel, slander, invasion of privacy, copyright infringement, and misappropriation of advertising ideas. An example would be an insured inappropriately using a competitor's copyrighted business ideas, causing damage to the competitor, who files a claim.

- ***Contractual liability***—This liability is imposed on an entity by the terms of a contract. As used in insurance, the term refers not to all contractually imposed liability, but to the assumption of the other contracting party's liability under specified conditions. An example would be a slip and fall injury claim at the landlord's building. The claim is referred to the tenant for handling based on the indemnity provisions in the lease agreement, as the accident occurred in the space rented to the tenant and the tenant assumed responsibility for all interior maintenance.

- ***Employment practices liability (EPL)***—EPL claims occur as a result of wrongful acts arising out of the employment relationship. The most frequent types of claims alleged under such policies include: wrongful termination, discrimination, and sexual harassment. An example of an EPL claim is when an employee is sexually harassed by a supervisor or manager on a consistent basis and then files a claim against the employer (insured) for damages.

- ***Animal liability***—These claims arise from injuries or damages due to the control or ownership of a domestic animal. For example, a business may have a guard dog on the premises which gets loose and bites a person. The injured person files legal action against the business for injuries and damages.

- ***Garage liability***—Garages (automobile dealer garages, repair shops, service stations, etc.) require general liability insurance to cover claims involving bodily injury and property damage arising out of business operations. They also require coverage for "bailment" regarding damage to automobiles left in their custody for safekeeping or repair, called garagekeepers legal liability coverage. An example would be a claim made against a repair shop for damage to the vehicle caused by paint overspray while the car was at the shop for repair.

- ***Pollution liability***—The contamination of the environment by substances regarded as pollutants can give rise to a great many claims against the polluters. While liability from pollution is normally excluded by liability policies, separate environmental impairment liability policies may provide coverage. An example of a pollution liability claim is when an insured dumps toxic waste into an adjacent reservoir, poisoning the water supply, and residents sue for damages. Cleanup costs are typically very expensive, making pollution liability claims costly.

- ***Umbrella or excess liability***—As their names suggest, umbrella and excess policies provide insurance coverage over various primary liability policies, such as the business auto policy, commercial general liability (CGL) policy, and watercraft and aircraft liability policies. The umbrella policy provides excess limits when the limits of underlying liability policies are exhausted by the payment of claims, drops down and picks up where the underlying policy leaves off when the aggregate limit of the underlying policy is exhausted by the payment of claims, and provides protection against some claims not covered by the underlying policies. An excess policy is a policy issued to provide limits in excess of an underlying liability policy. The underlying liability policy can be, and often is, an umbrella liability policy. An excess liability policy is no broader than the underlying liability policy; its sole purpose is to provide additional limits of insurance.

  Claims that reach the umbrella and excess layers are handled by the senior claims staff and involve working closely with the primary insurer's claim facility. An example of this type of claim is when the insured has $1 million in primary liability coverage and the claimant is seeking $10 million in damages. The primary insurer's claim facility will handle the claim but report developments to the umbrella or excess insurer so it can monitor any exposure to its policy limits. The umbrella or excess insurer may assume the direct handling of the claim depending on its complexity and severity.

The investigation and documentation necessary in handling a liability claim will vary depending on the type of claim. Likewise, claim guidelines will also vary depending on individual company or client requirements. The following are general liability claims handling guidelines for claims staff or third-party administrator (TPA) adjusters and claim attorneys. It is the adjuster's job to effectively handle liability claims through proper coverage analysis, appropriate claim investigations, and effective litigation management.

Basic Investigation

As with all claims, proper investigation and evaluation of liability, as well as an evaluation of the full damage exposure, is critical. The investigation is crucial to determine whether a liability claim will be settled or prepared for defense. The results of the claim investigation are also the basis for evaluating and establishing the claim reserves.

Liability claim investigations are the foundation for the ultimate disposition of each claim; therefore, the investigation must be timely and complete. When a liability claim is assigned to the handling adjuster, the adjuster should prepare an action plan and document it in the claim file notes, outlining the elements of the claims investigation to be completed.

At times, the independent adjuster may assist in the investigative process and may report directly to defense counsel to protect the adjuster's work product as being attorney-client privileged. Attorney-client privileged information and documents are protected from discovery as they represent a confidential information exchange or communication between attorneys and their clients for preparation of a defense. The legal doctrine or concept fosters open and honest communication between attorneys and their clients.

Statements

For the portions of the liability investigation conducted by telephone, recorded statements should be secured from the interviewed parties involved in the loss as necessary and appropriate. When working in the field, the adjuster needs to secure either recorded or signed statements from the insureds, claimants, and any witnesses. Statement guides can help. These are generally a series of questions that adjusters should ask to achieve the full picture of the liability accident and claim. (See Appendix C beginning on page 369 for various statement guidelines.)

Many insurers have developed their own statement guides. Another source of online statement guides for use by adjusters can be found at www.claimspages.com. These statement guides include claims involving animal bites, product liability, slip and falls, vehicle accidents, swimming pool accidents, workers compensation, and many others. The website is an excellent resource, and many claims people bookmark the site for daily use and reference.

Independent adjusters take both recorded and signed statements. Signed statements are typically more costly and should be reserved for those claims where securing a signed statement is appropriate (i.e., serious injury, subrogation potential). Recorded statements taken by an independent adjuster may need to be transcribed. The independent adjuster should provide the statement in a computerized digital format for storage in the electronic claim file. The independent adjuster should provide a summary of the recorded statement or summarize it within the independent adjuster's report.

Exhibit 27.1: Attorney Allegations

Secure the following information from the claimant's attorney as soon as possible after a claim has been made:

- Attorney and law firm name, business address, telephone and fax numbers, and e-mail address
- Claimant(s) full name, permanent address, age, date of birth, and marital status
- Date and time of accident, description of accident scene, and weather conditions
- Attorney's theory of liability, i.e., who is to blame, degree of fault
- Claimant occupation, employer name and address, wage rate, and disability period
- Physician names, addresses, and specialties; injuries, diagnosis, treatment, and prognosis
- Hospital name and address with inpatient or service dates
- Itemized special damages (objectively assessed monies awarded to an injured party for tangible losses), including wage loss, loss of use, nursing care, hospital and medical expenses, property damage, etc.
- Third-party involvement/other parties on notice, including contact information, insurer, and attorney information
- Witness names, addresses, and telephone numbers
- Responding police agency and/or ambulance company
- Claimant vehicle make, model, and year; claimant vehicle damage and any available estimates.
- Photographs of accident scene and vehicles
- Workers compensation and no-fault insurer and claim reference numbers
- Litigation: yes/no (If yes, consider securing an extension of time to answer without waiving any defenses.)
- Names of any experts retained

Some claim facilities may also utilize a statement form and other accident reporting forms (for claimants, insureds, and witnesses) when handling liability property damage claims, which require statements from the parties to a loss. This type of an investigation technique can be appropriate in the handling a small claims or lower value claims.

Attorney Allegations

General liability claims are much more likely to involve an attorney than basic property damage claims. When contacting a claimant attorney, secure as much information as possible to properly evaluate the claim exposure. Always request that the claimant attorney allow statements to be taken from the claimants. Occasionally, claimant attorneys do allow statements that will assist the adjuster in evaluating the claim. The primary reason claimant attorneys will not allow statements from their client, or the claimant, is that they do not want their client disclosing information that may be detrimental to their claim. Most claimant attorneys prefer that their client provide a statement prepared by the attorney or wait for legal discovery and a formal deposition. The information in Exhibit 27.1 on page 315 provides basic information that should be garnered from the attorney during the initial contact.

Note that some states require a written disclosure of policy limits in a state specific format when contacting or requesting information from the claimant attorney (i.e., Florida). This emphasizes the importance of becoming familiar with the jurisdictions where claims are handled to avoid costly errors.

Authorizations

For every injury claim presented, be sure to request and receive signed medical and wage authorization forms. Most claim facilities have various template authorization forms for the release of medical and hospital records, wage and salary information, and release of the no-fault or workers compensation claim file information from the insurer. It is important that the authorizations contain any necessary required language to comply with state and federal laws, e.g., the Health Insurance Portability and Accountability Act (HIPAA). HIPAA provides protection to an individual's personal and confidential information from being used inappropriately or disclosed illegally to third parties.

According to the U.S. Department of Health and Human Resources:

> The HIPAA Privacy Rule provides federal protection for personal health information held by covered entities and gives patients an array of rights with respect to that information. At the same time, the Privacy Rule is balanced so that it permits the disclosure of personal health information needed for patient care and other important purposes.

Information on HIPAA can be found at http://www.hhs.gov/ocr/privacy/hipaa/understanding.

When an attorney represents the claimant, acknowledge the claim in writing and attach authorization forms to be signed and returned. Although some attorneys may not want to provide authorizations, they should always be requested by the adjuster since they will accelerate the claims handling process. Often, the claimant attorneys will provide their own signed authorizations or copies of the hospital and medical reports along with itemized bills.

Upon receipt of the signed authorizations, request the appropriate records from the medical providers and employers. Most claim facilities generally have various forms on file to be completed by attending physicians and employers. Hospital records should always be requested as well. When requesting hospital records, be sure to indicate whether the treatment was on an emergency room basis or as an inpatient. If the claimant was an inpatient, indicate the dates hospitalized and the discharge date, and specify whether the entire hospital record is requested or simply the hospital discharge summary.

Special Damages

Special damages are objectively assessed monies awarded to an injured party for tangible losses, such as wage loss and medical, hospital, diagnostic, and nursing care expenses. To properly evaluate bodily injury claims, the investigation needs to include copies of all itemized special damages, including all hospital, medical, and physician reports, diagnostic reports and records, and itemized bills. The records will provide a detailed analysis of the claimant's diagnosis, prognosis, treatment regime, disability periods, and other information necessary to evaluate the claim. It is important to include itemized medical and hospital bills in the analysis or evaluation of the claim. A list of such damage documentation is shown in Exhibit 27.2 below.

In addition, an independent medical examination by the insurer's own physician, expert, or consultant should be considered if the claim so merits. Physical examinations are usually assigned by specialty. For example, if a clamant is treating with an orthopedic surgeon, the physical exam, commonly referred to as an independent medical exam (IME), should be assigned to an orthopedic surgeon as well. If the claimant is treating with multiple specialties, multiple IMEs may be necessary.

Exhibit 27.2: Special Damage Documentation—Injury Claims

- Attending Physician Reports
- Medical Narrative Reports
- Diagnostic and Radiology reports
- Physical Therapy Reports
- Hospital Emergency Records
- Hospital Records (Full Record and Discharge Summary)
- All Medical and Hospital Bills
- Dates of Disability Confirmation
- Employer Wage Loss Records
- Claimant Tax Returns (If Self-Employed)

Bodily Injury Claim Evaluation

All bodily injury claims require an evaluation, and the evaluation must be documented in the claim notes. Items to include in the evaluations are:

- Claimant name, age, and occupation
- Brief summary of the claim facts
- Theory of liability alleged
- Defenses available
- Third-party involvement
- Summary of special damages (medical, hospital, wage loss/disability period, etc.)
- Gross damage exposure of claim
- Liability percentage on the insured
- Claim value calculation (i.e., $100,000 gross value X 50% liability = $50,000)

A bodily injury claim evaluation will assist the adjuster and manager in establishing an accurate claim reserve. Remember, bodily injury claims can vary widely in value depending on a variety of circumstances. Try to avoid the use of pattern injury claim values; that is, claim values established based on the handling of prior claims, which may or may not have similar circumstances or damages. While it may seem that general liability claims are similar enough to replicate the outcome, each must be evaluated on its own merits.

Photographs and Diagrams

Scene photographs and diagrams are very important to evaluate both liability and damage exposures and should always be considered as part of the adjustment process. Photographs and diagrams should be taken and made early on in a claim investigation so that the accident scene remains substantially unchanged from the accident date.

Diagrams are very helpful in understanding how an accident happened and in ascertaining responsibility. Adjusters should consider using diagrams when taking statements, particularly if the statement is being taken in person. The diagram also assists the witness in recollecting the accident details. It is not unusual for the adjuster to ask the witness to sign and date the diagram as further confirmation of the accident description.

Diagrams also help assist in viewing the photographs of the accident scene, providing measurements, compass direction, and an overall simulation of the accident. Most liability claims should have a diagram of the accident scene to assist the adjuster in evaluating the liability issues.

Official Reports

Copies of official reports should always be requested to evaluate both liability and damage issues. The following is a list of some available official report and where they can be secured:

- ***Police aided reports (non-auto)***—Police aided reports can be secured from the police precinct or trooper barracks, by making a formal request to the police agency records department, or by using a third-party company which requests police reports for claim facilities and insurance companies, such as ISO ClaimSearch.®

- ***Police statements***—Generally, in serious accidents, the police agency will take written statements from witnesses and other parties to a loss. The police report will indicate if statements were taken by the responding police officers. These statements should be specifically requested from police agency records department, providing the police accident report reference number(s).

- ***Police photos***—Generally, in serious accidents, the police agency will take photographs of the accident scene. The police report will indicate if photographs were taken by the responding police officers at the accident scene. The photographs should be specifically requested from police agency records department, providing the police accident report reference number(s).

- ***Police accident reconstruction reports***—In serious accidents, the police agency will complete an accident reconstruction and prepare a written report. The accident reconstruction is completed by specially trained law enforcement officers and includes measurements, video, photos, and compilation and analysis of other evidentiary documentation and information. The purpose of the report is to support the police agency's findings with regard to the persons or conditions deemed responsible for the accident and whether any criminal charges will be brought. The accident reconstruction report will typically include photographs taken by the responding police officers at the accident scene. The accident reconstruction report should be specifically requested from police agency records department, providing the police accident report reference number(s).

- ***Fire reports***—Fire reports can be secured from the local fire department responding to the fire (particularly immediately after a fire occurs) or by making a formal request to the fire department records department. A third-party company can sometimes be used, which requests fire reports for claim facilities and insurance companies.

- ***Weather reports***—Weather reports can be very helpful in documenting the weather on a specific date, such as whether it was raining or snowing, indicating the specific accumulation, etc. Weather reports can be secured from the National Climatic Data Center (NCDC) at http://www.ncdc.noaa.gov/oa/ncdc.html.

- ***Death certificates***—Death certificates can be requested from local municipality or county offices which retain these records, such as a county clerk's office.

- ***Medical examiner or autopsy reports***—These reports can be requested from the local municipality or county medical examiner's or coroner's office.

- ***Occupational Safety and Health Administration (OSHA) reports***—OSHA is a division of the U.S. Department of Labor (http://www.osha.gov). When a serious accident occurs at a business, the local authorities may call in OSHA investigators to determine whether the business owner has violated any statutes. The OSHA reports are important as they may contain important investigative information, including statements of witnesses. The OSHA information is available under the Freedom of Information Act and can be requested with a letter to Freedom of Information Act Officer, Occupational Safety and Health Review Commission. There are several regional locations for Freedom of Information requests listed on the OSHA website.

- ***Building code and violation reports***—These reports can be requested from the local municipality or county building department or building inspectors office.

Experts

Experts should always be considered during the adjustment process. The following is a list of some expert types that might prove useful in evaluating a general liability claim:

- Medical (e.g., doctors)
- Engineers
- Heating, ventilating, and air conditioning (HVAC) professionals
- Accident reconstructionists
- Accounting
- Legal professionals
- Economists

The assignment of experts should be reserved for serious claims or to support a subrogation claim, given the cost involved. Locating experts can be accomplished by consulting with defense counsel, other claim professionals, or through various outside firms that provide experts for a variety of claims, such as the Technical Advisory Service for Attorneys (TASA) at http://www.tasanet.com/.

When considering an expert, be sure to request a detailed curriculum vitae (or résumé), references, and fee schedule. Determine if the expert has testified in the past and whether their expert services have been provided primarily to plaintiffs or defendants, or both.

ISO Claim Search®

All bodily injury claims should be entered electronically in the ISO ClaimSearch system within 10 days from the claim report date and every 6 months thereafter, or in accordance with the claim facility's claims handling guidelines. The ISO ClaimSearch system (discussed in more detail in Appendix B, page 363) is an all claims database utilized for property, casualty, and automobile claims. It is the industry's most comprehensive resource for claims professionals. The ISO ClaimSearch database contains information from the former Property Insurance Loss Register (PILR), the former Index System (CIB) for bodily injury claims, and the vehicle information databases formerly administered by the National Insurance Crime Bureau (NICB).

Today, all of those claims are part of a single database that lets adjusters search all lines of business and all types of claims simultaneously.

Property Damage Liability Claims

When presented with a property damage liability claim, always request a damage estimate from the claimant or assign an appraiser or adjuster to reach an agreed price with the claimant's choice of repair contractor. An agreed price is when the appraiser meets with the contractor which provided the repair estimate and agrees on the repair costs so that a settlement offer can be extended to the claimant to cover those costs. An appraisal review service, such as American Computer Estimating (ACE) should be considered for a desk review of all estimates where an appraiser is not assigned. American Computer Estimating (ACE) (www.ace-it.com) is one firm that provides desk reviews of automobile, property (building and contents), and subrogation damage supporting documentation to determine if the estimates are fair and reasonable.

Property damage estimates should be requested from the contractor the claimant has identified as the party contracted to repair the damages. Claims adjusters should refrain from recommending a contractor to the claimant, or any other party to a loss, unless required to do so by the insurer. It is recommended that an agreed appraisal be obtained from the claimant's contractor. However, if the liability investigation is incomplete and still ongoing, the appraisal should be assigned without prejudice. This means that no rights of the party concerned are to be considered as waived or lost.

Depending on the state involved, the property damage settlement offer may take into consideration the percentage of liability assessed on the insured and claimant. Comparative negligence varies by state and is discussed further in Chapter 14, beginning on page 155. Any indication of an injury during the property damage claims handling process should be referred to the claims manager for reserve entry and assignment to a bodily injury adjuster.

Closing Documentation

At the conclusion of a liability claim, a release should be taken from the claimant as outlined in the closing documentation section of Chapter 10 (see page 113).

Chapter 28: Professional Liability and Management Liability Claims Handling Guidelines

Professional liability and management liability claims handling is a specialty in itself, and although basic fundamental claim investigative tools may be utilized (i.e., statements, interviews), claim investigations may differ widely depending on the type of professional or management liability claim being handled. While they sound synonymous, professional liability and management liability are two separate insurance coverages.

Professional liability coverage is designed to protect traditional professionals (e.g., physicians) and quasi-professionals (e.g., real estate brokers) against liability incurred as a result of errors and omissions in performing professional services. Although there are a few exceptions, most professional liability policies cover economic losses suffered by third parties, as opposed to bodily injury and property damage (which is typically covered under commercial general liability policies). The vast majority of professional liability policies are written with claims-made coverage triggers.

Thus, when we refer to professional liability, we are including errors and omissions (E&O) coverage as well. Ordinarily, the insurance policies have similar language, but may not involve a "profession" in the formal sense of what society may refer to as a profession. For example, professional liability coverage for an adjuster may be referred to as an E&O policy, while professional liability coverage for a physician will be referred to as a professional liability policy. The terms are frequently used interchangeably. For claims handling purposes, both terms are used as the fundamental coverage issues and claims handling are the same.

Management liability insurance covers exposures faced by directors, officers, managers, and business entities that arise from governance, finance, benefits, and management activities (also called "executive liability insurance"). This includes directors and officers (D&O) liability insurance, employment practices liability (EPL) insurance, fiduciary liability insurance, and "special crime" insurance (covering kidnap, ransom, and extortion exposures). These coverages may be written as stand-alone insurance policies or combined into a single "package" policy.

The claim investigation for both professional and management liability claims is basically the same. Most professional and management liability claims will involve some type of a coverage issue due to the complex nature of the coverage. Special attention must be paid to:

- ***The definition of "wrongful act," i.e., the event triggering coverage***—De-

Claims Handling

fined as an act, error, or omission that takes place within the course of performing professional services.

- ***The coverage trigger***—These policies are written on a claims-made basis, i.e., coverage will only apply if the claim is reported during the applicable policy period.

- ***The retroactive date***—Found in many claims-made policies, coverage does not apply for injuries or damage that occurred prior to a specified date even if the claim is first made during the policy period.

- ***The various policy exclusions, exceptions, and limitations.***

It would not be unusual for an adjuster to issue a reservation of rights letter on most professional and management liability claims as the first aspect of the claim investigation.

The claim investigation of a professional or management liability claim is rarely "template," meaning that each investigation will need to be tailored to the particular claim being investigated. During the investigative process, the adjuster may ask defense counsel to assist with the investigation to protect the investigative work product under attorney-client privilege. Experts may be retained to assist with the investigation and defense of the claim.

The adjuster handling a professional or management liability claim needs to understand the "profession" or "management responsibilities" to properly investigate a claim and anticipate the various types of claims that might arise under the policy. Understanding the profession or management responsibilities allows the adjuster to direct and complete the claim investigation properly.

Professional Liability

Anyone who gives advice that others have reason to rely on may be subject to legal action if the advice proves faulty. Others may be subject to liability if certain activities are not handled properly in accordance with statutes or common law, or provisions within a contract. For example, an adjuster may have mishandled a claim, triggering a "bad faith" claim, which would result in an E&O claim against the claim facility. Insurance protection for these activities is needed and is available in a variety of forms. These policies typically do not cover bodily injury or property damage; they involve supplemental protection for "wrongful acts" by various occupations or businesses, such as lawyers, insurance agents, architects and engineers, physicians, hospitals, opticians, druggists, blood banks, adjusters, real estate brokers, and a host of other professional and personal services.

Most professional liability policies use the errors and omissions approach. They agree to:

> ... pay on behalf of the insured all sums which the insured shall become obligated to pay by reason of the liability imposed upon him by law for damages resulting from any claim made against the insured, arising out of the performance of professional services for others in the insured's capacity as a professional, and caused by any act, error, or omission of the insured or any other

person for whose acts the insured is legally liable.

The insuring agreement thus covers affirmative negligence as well as failure to perform properly and failure to perform at all. The major exclusions in the professional liability policy are:

1. Any dishonest, fraudulent, criminal or malicious act or omission

2. Bodily injury from other than professional causes (usually covered under a general liability policy)

3. Property damage in some policies

Note that the insuring agreement above refers to liability imposed by law but not to liability assumed by contract. Some professional liability policies do not provide coverage for contractually assumed liability. Check the exclusions and the insuring agreement.

Ideally, professional and general liability policies are purchased from the same insurer as it is not always clear which of the two policies might apply, triggering a coverage issue and reservation of rights letter to the insured. Unfortunately, few general liability insurers write professional liability, and several different insurers' policies may apply. This is another reason why these types of claims are so complicated.

Sometimes, professionals (such as attorneys, accountants, and architects) work for a company as well as for themselves. If they work for the company, they should be covered by the company liability policy—but their personal acts outside the company would be excluded. Thus, both the professional's own policy and the company's policy need to be examined closely.

Professional Liability Settlements

Most professional liability policies state that the insurer may not settle a claim without the written consent of the insured. This is to protect the reputation of professionals and to prevent them from being impaired by compromise, even though it might be less expensive to settle a claim than to fight it. It works like this: The insurer recommends a certain settlement, but the insured elects to contest the claim. If the cost of the claim rises above that of the proposed settlement, in excess of the insured's deductible or retention, the insurer will not be liable for the excess amount, nor the costs and expenses incurred since the date of the insured's refusal to settle.

The consent-to-settle provision is usually found under the defense and settlement provisions of the professional liability policy. While the insurer agrees not to settle any claim without the consent of the insured, consent must not be unreasonably withheld. The consent-to-settle provision is commonly referred to as the hammer clause. Sometimes an insurer will soften the hammer clause by providing defense and indemnification after the insured refuses consent to settle; however, the insurance company will only pay a percentage (i.e., 75 percent) of the defense and settlement.

These provisions need to be carefully reviewed, and there should be open communication with the insured concerning the recommended disposition of claims.

Management Liability

Under the broad category of "management liability" falls directors and officers liability, both inside and outside the company, including employment practices and fiduciary liability. Directors and officers are fiduciaries entrusted with the management of corporations. Should a failure on their part result in loss to the corporation or its shareholders, they can be held personally liable. Corporations can also be sued for the acts of their directors or officers. Under state law, directors and officers owe their corporations three duties:

- ***Duty of care***—Directors and officers owe a fiduciary duty of care to the corporation and its shareholders, and must serve in good faith.
- ***Duty of loyalty***—Directors owe a fiduciary duty of loyalty to the corporation they serve, which requires them to place the corporation's interests above their own.
- ***Duty of obedience***—Directors and officers must act within the authority granted them by the corporation or its bylaws.

Failure in the performance of these duties can result in claims against the organization itself and against the directors and officers personally. Six types of suits can be brought against directors and officers:

1. Direct action suits may be brought by shareholders on their own behalf.
2. Derivative action suits can be brought by shareholders on behalf of the corporation.
3. Class action suits may be brought by a representative shareholder on behalf of all shareholders.
4. The corporation can file suits against former directors or officers who breached a fiduciary duty owed to the corporation and/or its shareholders.
5. Employees of the corporation can bring suits against the corporation and its directors and officers.
6. Third-party actions can be brought by individuals outside the corporation, such as government officials, previous owners, creditors, or even competitors.

If directors are sued for bodily injury, property damage, libel, slander, or false arrest, they are usually protected by the corporation's general liability policy. If they are sued for other kinds of "wrongful acts," neither the company's general liability policy nor their own personal liability policy will cover because the former does not cover "wrongful acts," and the latter excludes business pursuits.

In addition, the directors may be insured under the organization's D&O liability insurance, which may provide some employment practices liability (EPL)[1] cov-

[1]Employment practices liability insurance covers liability arising from employment activities. It is a form of liability insurance covering wrongful acts arising from the employment process. The most frequent types of claims alleged under such policies include: wrongful termination, discrimination, and sexual harassment. The policy forms are written on a claims-made basis and generally exclude coverage for large-scale, companywide layoffs. In addition to being written as a stand-alone coverage, EPLI is frequently available as an endorsement to directors and officers liability policies.

erage. A stand-alone EPL policy might also be involved; it provides broader coverage, such as that for personal injury claims, claims from non-officer employees, and insured-versus-insured claims. General partnership liability (GPL) policies and fiduciary liability policies are two other forms of insurance that could come into play. It is especially important in management claims to find all the policies that might apply and read them very carefully.

Coverage Verification and Analysis

Many claim facilities utilize their own professional liability claim adjusters and claim attorneys to handle professional liability and management liability claims. The objective should be to effectively handle professional liability claims through proper coverage analysis, appropriate claim investigations, and effective litigation management. General guidelines, such as those outlined below, are used to handle professional and management liability claims, but specific client and special claims handling guidelines would modify these guidelines.

As mentioned above, many different insurance policies may be involved in professional and management liability claims. Coverage verification is the responsibility of the handling adjuster or claims attorney and the claims manager. A review of the policy declarations page, as well as copies of all pertinent policy forms and endorsements, must be carefully conducted. The policy declarations page should clearly indicate the forms and endorsements attached to the policy, including any manuscript endorsements.

Analyzing and evaluating coverage also rests with the claims handler and the claims manager. Consideration should be given to retaining coverage counsel to assist with the coverage analysis depending on the complexity and severity of the coverage issues.

The claim file notes should clearly outline the coverage analysis, including reference to the applicable policy forms and endorsements. Particular attention should be paid to the following:

- Insuring agreement
- Definition of "professional services"
- Definition of "wrongful act"
- Definition of "claim" and "potential claim"
- Definition of "damages"
- Exclusions and exceptions
- Actual date of notice and loss date on claims-made policies
- Prior loss history
- Prior and pending issues, i.e., an exclusion found in professional liability and management liability policies that precludes coverage for claims that were pending prior to the inception of the policy
- Retroactive dates
- Any supplemental or extended reporting period (ERP), i.e., a designated period of time after a claims-made policy has expired during which a claim may be made and coverage triggered as if

the claim had been made during the policy period

- Consent-to-settle provisions
- Self-insured retention (SIR) and deductible amounts, and the collection process for these
- Limits of liability, especially whether the limits include or exclude expenses
- Any applicable sublimits
- Any applicable ancillary coverage (loss or defense costs)

Reservation of Rights and Coverage Disclaimers

Coverage position letters (reservation of rights and coverage disclaimers) should be issued as soon as the adjuster is in a position to formulate a coverage opinion, but no later than 30 days from the report date. The adjuster or claim attorney should consider having coverage counsel assist with the preparation of coverage position letters, especially when tricky coverage issues are involved.

Most professional liability and management liability claims require some type of reservation of rights letter, due to the complexity of the coverage forms and claims. Of necessity, these letters tend to be very detailed, citing specific policy language.

Basic Investigation

The objective in handling professional and management liability claims is to properly investigate each claim to evaluate liability on the insured as well as to assess the full damage exposure. It is important to determine whether a liability claim will be settled or prepared for defense. The results of the claim investigation are the basis for evaluating claim reserves.

The professional liability and management liability claim investigation is the foundation for the ultimate disposition of each claim; therefore, the investigation must be timely and complete. When a professional liability or management liability claim is assigned to the handling adjuster or claim attorney, an action plan should be prepared, outlining the elements of the claims investigation to be completed.

Depending on the type of claim involved, defense counsel may be used to assist in the investigation process and pre-suit avoidance activities. For instance, defense counsel may need to conduct investigation as a prerequisite to an administrative hearing, court motion, petition, or other pre-suit legal hearing or motion. Defense counsel may especially be needed to assist in conducting an investigation involving an employment practices liability claim, due to the sensitive nature of the claim and damages, as well as to protect the work product under attorney-client privilege. At times, an independent adjuster may report directly to defense counsel to protect the adjuster's work product from discovery.

When investigating professional and management liability claims, focus on the allegations set forth in the claim letter, notice of claim, or lawsuit. The investigation includes claimant or plaintiff attorney contact information to help with details, claim interviews, and securing relevant documents during the process. The documents are obtained from the claimant or their legal representative, the insured, insurers, and various other sources. The following represents a sample list of basic investigation items to be considered during the investigation of professional and management liability claims. Of course, the claim investigation should be specifically tailored to the type of claim involved. The investigation outline is not a template; the adjuster needs to develop a specific investigation strategy for each claim based on the facts presented.

- Statements of the insured, claimant and witnesses
- Copies of all relevant records and reports
- Contracted scope of services
- History of prior incidents
- *Curriculum vitae,* professional licensing, and education
- Retention of experts
- Any industry legal requirements or violations
- Research on industry custom and practice
- Copies of any relevant professional or licensing administrative hearing transcripts or minutes
- Corporate structure
- Copies of all corporate records and documents
- Copies of all discovery documents, including pleadings, depositions, discovery, and other relevant court documents
- Annual meeting minutes and other documents
- All internal communication related to the subject of the claim, including notes, letters, memorandums, and e-mail
- Copies of computer system documents
- Any available videotapes
- Identification of relevant experts and copies of all expert reports
- Copies of industry best practice protocols
- All official records and reports
- The insured's published procedures, processes, and protocols pertinent to the incident
- Newspaper articles and other published accounts of the incident(s)
- Copies of all contracts and agreements pertaining to the incident
- Copies of any relevant insurance certificates and additional insured endorsements
- Employee personnel records, employee manuals, employment procedures and policies, and other human resource/personnel records (EPL claims)
- List of board members and board meeting or other departmental meeting minutes

- Corporate bylaws or limited liability company operating agreements
- History of prior relevant incidents

Special Notes

Although a comprehensive investigation checklist would be helpful as we may use in an automobile or general liability claims, the complexity of these types of professional and management claims requires a custom investigation tailored to each individual claim. After any relevant coverage issues are addressed, the adjuster needs to identify the primary allegations against the insured and then tailor the claim investigation accordingly.

Chapter 29: Public Entity Claims Handling Guidelines

Public entities include cities, counties, school districts, special districts, and state governments. They differ from private sector risks in the following respects:

1. Public entities are accountable to the public, not stockholders.

2. They must provide a large range of public services, such as police and fire protection, roads, stadiums, airports, and hospitals.

3. They may have different liabilities than private firms, depending on the laws of the state. The distinction between *governmental* functions (those inherent in the nature of the entity, such as police, fire protection, public health, and education) and *proprietary* functions (those taken on by choice, such as recreation, utilities, and public halls) is diminishing, as is governmental immunity (discussed below).

4. They have available to them specially designed insurance forms. The coverages offered to public entities are often broader and consolidated into fewer policies than those offered to corporations.

Governmental Immunity

There are various statutes at the local, state, and federal level that provide public entities immunity from prosecution. Governmental immunities stem from English common law, or sovereign immunity, wherein the sovereign entity or state cannot commit a legal wrong and is immune from civil lawsuits. For example, the U.S. federal government has sovereign immunity under certain circumstances. The cases that are brought against it are usually brought under the jurisdiction of the Federal Tort Claims Act.

States may do the same; Massachusetts, for example, may limit the monetary amount of damages claimed against a municipality under certain circumstances. Other states, such as New York, may require prior written notice of a defect before a claim can be brought against the municipality. Certain officials of a municipality may be insulated from liability unless their actions were considered to be grossly negligent.

However, governmental immunity against legal action, long enjoyed by public bodies, is diminishing, though some important immunities or limitations of liability exist in many states. Limitations are of two types:

- Caps on the amount of damages, often from $100,000 to $1 million per person

- Immunities (i.e., complete exemption) from some types of claims

Liability caps apply to claims brought in the home state, not to accidents that occur out of state or to claims in federal court (e.g., discrimination claims). Thus, while caps reduce the exposure to large judgments, they do not eliminate it.

Public Officials

Those who govern a public entity, whether elected, appointed, or hired, have a varying degree of personal liability. Certain positions have absolute immunity: federal and state legislators, judges, prosecuting attorneys, and jurors. Others have some immunity, but for the most part, there is a need for individual protection. Since commercial general liability policies do not protect against "wrongful acts," special public officials liability policies are needed to fill this gap.

Coverage Verification and Analysis

Typically, a claim facility will utilize professional liability adjusters or claim attorneys to handle the public entity claim exposures. The objective should be to effectively handle public entity claims through proper coverage analysis, appropriate claim investigations, and effective litigation management. The guidelines below were developed as an outline to handle public entity professional liability and general liability claims.

As mentioned above, many different insurance policies may be involved in public entity claims. Coverage verification is the responsibility of the handling adjuster or claims attorney and the claims manager. It is a good idea to look for applicable coverage in the following policies:

- Public officials liability
- Law enforcement legal or police professional liability
- School board legal or educators liability
- Directors and officers (D&O) liability
- Employment practices liability (EPL)
- General liability

A review of the policy declarations page and all pertinent policy forms and endorsements must be carefully conducted. The policy declarations page should clearly indicate the forms and endorsements attached to the policy, including any manuscript endorsements.

Analyzing and evaluating coverage also rests with the claims handler and the claims manager. Consideration should be given to retaining coverage counsel to assist with the coverage analysis depending on the complexity and severity of the coverage issues.

The claim file notes should clearly outline the coverage analysis, including reference to the applicable policy forms and endorsements. Particular attention should be paid to the following:

- Insuring agreement
- Definition of "professional services"
- Definition of "wrongful act"
- Definition of "claim" and "potential claim"

- Definition of "damages"
- Exclusions and exceptions
- Actual date of notice and loss date on claims-made policies
- Prior loss history
- Prior and pending issues, i.e., an exclusion found in some liability policies that precludes coverage for claims that were pending prior to the inception of the policy
- Retroactive dates, i.e., a provision found in many claims-made policies that eliminates coverage for injuries or damage that occurred prior to a specified date, even if the claim is first made during the policy period
- Any supplemental or extended reporting periods (ERP), i.e., a designated period of time after a claims-made policy has expired during which a claim may be made and coverage triggered as if the claim had been made during the policy period
- Consent-to-settle provisions
- Self-insured retention (SIR) and deductible amounts, and the collection process for these
- Limits of liability, especially whether the limits include or exclude expenses
- Any applicable sublimits
- Any applicable ancillary coverage (loss or defense costs)

Reservation of Rights and Coverage Disclaimers

Coverage position letters (reservation of rights and coverage disclaimers) should be issued as soon as the adjuster is in a position to formulate a coverage opinion, but no later than 30 days from the report date. The adjuster or claims attorney should consider having coverage counsel assist with the preparation of coverage position letters, depending on the complexity and severity of the coverage issues.

Most public entity liability claims require some type of reservation of rights letter, due to the complexity of the coverage forms and claims. Of necessity, these letters tend to be very detailed, citing specific policy language. When handling public entity claims, there may be a town administrator or town attorney involved who may need to be a copy recipient of the coverage position letter.

Governmental Immunities and Legal Remedies

As mentioned above, there are various governmental immunities available at the local, state, and federal level that are available to public entities which limit liability and damages. Every public entity claim should address any available public entity governmental immunities during the initial claims investigation process. Copies of any available statutes or caselaw need to be posted to the claim file. Governmental immunities may be researched through in-house reference material and through discussions with local defense counsel and the municipal attorneys.

Public entities may also have formal "notice of claim" requirements, which require formal pleadings prior to litigation, as well as the potential opportunity to depose the claimant prior to litigation being filed. Ordinarily, a notice of claim is filed against the public entity within 90 days from the loss date; however, this time period may range from 30 days to 365 days, depending on the state. Generally, the notice of claim does not require a response pleading, but it may require notice of an appearance from the assigned defense attorney. After the notice of claim is filed, the public entity usually deposes the claimant and may be able to conduct pre-suit discovery, such as requests for medical and other documentation. The deposition is taken under oath with a court stenographer present. Many states require that suit be filed no later than 1 year and 90 days from the accident or loss date, if there is a 90-day notice of claim requirement. The deposition transcript is usually admissible at trial.

Public entities may also have prior written notice statutes concerning incidents or accidents. A prior written notice statute is a written law pertaining to a public entity, such as a local village, town, or county, indicating that the municipality is insulated from any liability unless there was prior written notice of the defect or dangerous condition causing or contributing to the accident. Typically, the municipality will not be insulated from liability if it created the dangerous condition. Prior written notice is a form of "actual notice"; however, the prior notice must be in writing. These statutes protect the public entity and should be vigorously pursued. Governmental immunities and notice statutes may be available at the local, town, state, and federal level.

Consent-To-Settle Provisions

Public entity professional liability coverage forms may contain consent-to-settle provisions. This provision is typically found under the defense and settlement sections of the public entity liability policy. While the insurer agrees not to settle any claim without the consent of the insured, consent must not be unreasonably withheld. The provision further states that if the insured refuses to consent to any settlement recommended by the insurance company, and that settlement is acceptable to the claimant, the insurance company's liability will not exceed the amount that the claim could have been settled in excess of the insured's deductible or retention.

The consent-to-settle provision is commonly referred to as the hammer clause. Sometimes an insurer will soften the hammer clause by providing defense and indemnification after the insured refuses to consent to settle; however, the insurance company will only pay a percentage (i.e., 75 percent) of the defense and settlement.

These provisions need to be carefully reviewed, and there should be open communication with the insured concerning the recommended disposition of claims.

Basic Investigation

The objective in handling public entity liability claims is to properly investigate each claim to evaluate liability on the insured as well as to assess the full damage exposure. The investigation is specifically utilized to evaluate whether a liability claim will be settled or prepared for defense. The results of the claims investigation are the basis for setting claim reserves.

The public entity liability claims investigation is the foundation for the ultimate disposition of each claim; therefore, the investigation must be timely and complete. When a public entity liability claim is assigned to the handling adjuster or claim attorney, an action plan should be prepared, outlining the elements of the claims investigation to be completed.

Depending on the type of claim involved, defense counsel may be used to assist in the investigation process and pre-suit avoidance activities. For instance, defense counsel may need to conduct investigation as a prerequisite to an administrative hearing, court motion, petition, or other pre-suit legal hearing or motion. Defense counsel may especially be needed to assist in conducting an investigation involving an employment practice liability claim, due to the sensitive nature of the claim and damages, as well as to protect the work product under attorney-client privilege. At times, an independent adjuster may report directly to defense counsel to protect the adjuster's work product from discovery.

When investigating public entity liability claims, focus on the allegations set forth in the claim letter, notice of claim, or lawsuit. The investigation includes claimant or plaintiff attorney contact information to help with details, claim interviews, and securing relevant documents during the process. The documents are obtained from the claimants or their legal representatives, the insureds, insurers, and various other sources. The following represents a sample list of basic investigation items to be considered during the investigation of public entity liability claims. Of course, the claim investigation should be specifically tailored to the type of claim involved. The investigation outline is not a template; the adjuster should develop a specific investigation strategy for each claim based on the facts presented.

- Statements of the insured, claimant, and witnesses
- Scene photographs and diagrams
- Any available video
- Pertinent governmental immunities, caselaw, and statutes favoring the insured's defense
- All other pertinent laws, ordinances, and statutes
- Any applicable prior written notice statutes
- Insured's records regarding prior notice
- The insured's internal records and reports concerning the incident
- All official reports
- Police reports, police statements, arrest warrants, and police officer notes
- The insured's published procedures and protocols pertinent to the incident
- Police officer personnel files and training files (i.e., weapon training)
- Newspaper articles and other published accounts of the incident(s)

- All contracts and agreements pertaining to the incident
- Employee personnel records, employee manuals, employment procedures and policies, and other human resource/personnel records (EPL claims)
- Correctional facility inmate records
- List of board members and board meeting or other departmental meeting minutes
- History of prior relevant incidents
- Copies of any relevant professional administrative hearing minutes

Special Notes

Public entities require all types of insurance coverage, including property, inland marine, automobile, general liability, workers compensation, public officials liability, police professional liability, school board legal liability, and other various coverages. This chapter focused primarily on liability claims handling because of its nuances specifically related to public entities, and not on private industry such as governmental immunities, notice of claim requirements, and prior written notice statutes.

Handling pubic entity claims requires a special expertise that involves understanding the jurisdictions involved and the special reporting requirements and immunities available to the public entity. If an adjuster is not familiar with a specific jurisdiction, particularly the various immunities and defenses available, a claim could be paid mistakenly when governmental immunity was available, or the claim could be barred by the notice of claim not being filed timely, or lack of prior written notice.

Adjusters handling public entity claims also need to understand the many different coverage forms that could apply to a professional liability claim.

FOR MORE INFORMATION ON:	GO TO:	PAGE(S):
Claims Process	Chapters 10–17	105–220
Claims Handling Guidelines	Chapters 21–30	271–354
Auto Physical Damage	Chapter 22	273
Auto Liability	Chapter 23	279
Auto PIP/No Fault	Chapter 24	289
First-Party Property and Inland Marine	Chapter 25	295
Cargo	Chapter 26	305
General Liability	Chapter 27	311
Professional and Management Liability	Chapter 28	323
Workers Compensation	Chapter 30	337

Chapter 30: Workers Compensation Claims Handling Guidelines

Workers compensation was the first "no-fault" form of insurance where employees, if injured on the job, would be guaranteed payment from the employer for medical costs and lost wages, in return for which they would not sue. Each state has its own workers compensation law. Some allow insurance only through a state fund (North Dakota, Ohio, Washington, and West Virginia). Other states have a state fund competing with private insurers (Arizona, California, Colorado, Hawaii, Idaho, Kentucky, Louisiana, Maine, Maryland, Michigan, Minnesota, Missouri, Montana, New Mexico, New York, Oklahoma, Oregon, Pennsylvania, Rhode Island, Texas, and Utah). Wyoming requires insurance only for "extrahazardous" industries and occupations. The state fund competes with private insurers and self-insurers for other industries and occupations.

Workers compensation benefits may be paid through a state-approved self-insurance program or by insurance. The self-insurance option varies by state, and will typically involve an insurance company providing excess workers compensation coverage above the self-insured retention program.

Today, the system is under immense pressure due to the following factors:

- Rising healthcare costs
- Claims never anticipated when the system was designed: long-term health care, workplace stress, AIDS, long latency occupational diseases, mental injuries
- Degradation of the "exclusive remedy"[1]
- High medical provider expenses that are less subject to systematized cost containment programs than other medical programs
- Politicized charges resulting in depressed rates for workers compensation insurers
- Increased use of assigned risk pools
- Fraud

Industry analysts are deeply concerned about the future of our free-enterprise system of workers compensation, and various states have amended their statutes. Additional changes are expected.

Controlling Claims Costs

The way a workers compensation claim is handled can greatly influence how soon the injured employee returns to work. The

[1]Attorneys have found ways to bypass the exclusive remedy of workers compensation with lawsuits filed directly against employers.

adjuster should work with the medical providers and the employer to facilitate the return-to-work process and also control the medical and rehabilitation costs. Remember, controlling medical costs does not mean that all claimants are "over treated"; therefore, medical care should not be limited or denied as a matter of course. Each claim should be handled and evaluated on its own merits, which may not necessarily result in the same medical care and disability period as a prior claim with a similar injury.

If the workers compensation adjuster handles the claim timely, and in accordance with statutory guidelines and unfair claim practices regulations, the claimant does not need to be represented by an attorney during the claims handling process. The workers compensation claimant should not be an adversary! It is the adjuster's job to assist claimants by making sure they receive the benefits entitled under the workers compensation law and provide the necessary means to facilitate any medical care, rehabilitation, and return to work.

Components of effective workers compensation claims handling include:

- Timely reporting
- Coverage verification
- Investigation and three-point contact, i.e., contact with the claimant, employer and treating physician
- Workers compensation form filings
- Medical management/managed care
- Return-to-work coordination
- Nurse case management
- Independent medical exams (IMEs)
- Fraud recognition
- Utilization of private investigators
- Litigation management
- Utilization and peer review
- Third-party recovery (subrogation/liens)
- Second injury funds

Each of these is discussed in detail below. Keep in mind that these claim guidelines are for the handling of workers compensation claims and may vary by individual company or client.

Timely Reporting

It is very important that employers (the policyholder) report all new losses in a timely fashion. The sooner the first notice of injury is received and assigned to an adjuster, the quicker the adjuster can make the necessary contacts, conduct a thorough claim investigation, and evaluate compensability. Timely reporting also allows for the coordination of medical care and the timely payment of medical and wage benefits, as well as maintaining claimant control, in lieu of the claimant retaining an attorney.

The timely reporting of claims is also important in that many states impose penalties or fines on the employer if a workers compensation claim is not reported within a given time period. Even a few days or a week can impact the result of the claim. For example, the claimant may undergo unnecessary treatment or even surgery during the period that the claim remains unreported or may be out of work longer than necessary. Some employers may attempt to circumvent the workers compensation laws (to avoid any increased premiums) by paying the medical bills directly or paying the claimant continued wage benefits, not realizing that certain injuries may also result in a sizeable workers compensation award[2] after treatment has been completed. After the employer receives a notice of hearing (i.e., permanency rating hearing) from the workers compensation commission or board, the claim ends up being reported to the insurance company, which results in a late report.

Coverage Verification

It is the responsibility of the adjuster, as well as the claims manager, to properly confirm coverage through the established verification process for a particular company or client. When verifying coverage, it is important to focus on the name of the insured (employer), policy effective dates, states covered (Section 3(A)[3]), class codes and descriptions, payroll, any exclusions for officers or principals, and policy exclusions.

There are certain types of coverage issues that need to be addressed at the time of coverage verification. For example, most workers compensation statutes exclude sole proprietors as being covered unless they specifically request to be covered and file an appropriate form with the state. Also, some states allow members of a limited liability company (members are usually owners) to exclude themselves by filing an appropriate form with the state. Both of these situations are premium driven, in that the sole proprietor pays less insurance premium for not being covered and the multi-member limited liability company may pay less premium if the members are excluded from coverage. The workers compensation records and statutes should be able to clarify these issues.

It is important to note that the industry differentiates two categories of workers compensation claims: indemnity and medical-only claims.

Indemnity claims may include an indemnity reserve and medical reserve, as well as reserves for allocated loss adjustment expense (ALAE). Typically, indemnity claims involve lost time from work and/or a potential permanency award. Indemnity claims require a claims investigation and are more labor intensive for the following reasons:

- Investigation requirements (by insurer)
- Wage payment processing
- Use of medical management and return-to-work programs

[2]Workers compensation awards can be based on a scheduled loss award (i.e., specified monetary compensation for body parts, such as an arm, hand, finger, leg) or based on a percentage of permanency provided by the primary treating physician (i.e., 10 percent overall permanency rating).

[3]Within the workers compensation policy, Section 3 provides an indication of what states the insurance company will provide benefits in. Section 3(A) will typically list the primary states within which the policyholder will have locations or operations. For example, if the business only operates in Connecticut, then Connecticut will only be listed under Section 3(A). Section 3(C) provides workers compensation coverage for the other states that an employee may be injured in where the policyholder does not have locations or operations. Often, bordering states or states where employees may occasionally travel are included in Section 3(C).

- Utilization of various workers compensation forms during the claims process
- Various required filings with the workers compensation board or commission
- Arrangements for IMEs
- Scheduled awards and permanency awards
- Workers compensation hearings
- Reserve management

Medical-only claims are less labor intensive and typically only involve paying one or several medical bills without the need to pay any indemnity benefits or make any necessary filings with the workers compensation commission or board. These claims do not have any lost time or any potential for a permanency award. Some insurers do not reserve medical-only claims on a case-reserve basis and simply use a bulk reserve based on the historical paid amounts.

It is important to note that medical-only claims could turn into indemnity claims with either lost time benefits being paid or the potential for permanency awards. The claim will then be converted to an indemnity claim with an indemnity and medical reserve (and an expense reserve, if necessary).

The workers compensation policy provides coverage for statutory workers compensation benefits subject to the state act or statutes. The workers compensation policy also provides coverage for employers liability under Section B of the policy. Employers liability provides coverage for situations not covered under workers compensation laws where an employee could sue for injuries sustained under common-law liability. These types of claims involve similar handling as liability claims, including litigation management.

Investigation and Three-Point Contacts

After the claim is reported, and coverage is verified by the assigned adjuster or claims service representative,[4] the assigned adjuster initiates the claim investigation by making contact with the parties to the claim. The parties to the claim are the claimant (employee), employer (policyholder), and the treating physician. In the industry, this referred to as the "three-point contact."

Required contacts should be made within 24 hours of the loss being reported to the insurance company or self-insured. On serious injury claims, it is recommended that contacts be made the same day the claim is reported. Throughout the claim, the adjuster will continue with the three-point contact process when lost time is involved (i.e., the claimant has not returned to work) on a regular basis to facilitate the return to work. Regular ongoing contact with the claimant is absolutely necessary in the handling of workers compensation claims to effectively manage the claims process.

[4]Often, an adjuster will work with a claims service representative, claims assistant, or processor who will assist with various claim functions such as coverage verification, claim payment processing, arrangements for independent medical examinations, etc. Depending on the state involved, these positions may require adjuster licensing.

Within the insurance industry, some companies use acronyms to describe the claims process or summarize the initial claim investigation. For example, some companies use the acronym ANCR as a method to summarize the compensability of a workers compensation claim. ANCR stands for accident, notice, and causal relationship. Below is a further description of these terms:

> ***Accident***—An accident occurred within the meaning of the coverage and workers compensation statute.
>
> ***Notice***—The employer has received proper notice in accordance with the workers compensation statute.
>
> ***Causal relationship***—The claimant's physician has confirmed that the injuries are causally related to the accident.

Ordinarily, if ANCR has been established, the claim is compensable.

Contact with the claimant or injured worker is crucial within the first 24 hours as it enables the adjuster to verify the circumstances of the accident and determine the causal relationship. It can also create trust between the adjuster and the injured worker. Open communications facilitate the claims handling process.

Contact with the employer is also important. It allows the adjuster to confirm the accident and injury information, and secure other relevant information, such as wage rate and return-to-work records, evidence, witness information, and other records.

Lastly, contact is made with the treating physician. The treating physician can provide information regarding the diagnosis, prognosis, causal relation, disability confirmation, the recommended treatment plan, and return-to-work prognosis. This allows the adjuster to determine what benefits may be due or perhaps request nurse case management to aid in the return-to-work process.

If voice-to-voice contact cannot be completed with these parties, a contact letter should be mailed and the appropriate documentation recorded in the electronic claim notes the same day. Medical information should be gathered by telephone within 24 hours of the claim assignment. The telephone calls should be documented in claim notes, and the details confirmed through written communication with the medical providers. Medical reports should always be requested from each attending physician as soon as possible and received no later than 30 days from the request date.

Most states have mandated workers compensation medical report forms, or utilize a Health Care Financing Administration (HCFA)[5] form, a standardized medical report and billing form used by physicians and medical facilities. When requesting medical reports, including narrative reports to supplement a medical report form, it is important to highlight specific requests such as diagnosis, prognosis, necessity and duration of further treatment, disability period, and causal relationship of the injury to the accident. When permitted by law, medical bills should not

[5]The HCFA is now known as the Centers for Medicare and Medicaid Services (CMS), a federal agency that governs the Medicare program, Medicaid, and health insurance standards.

be paid until written documentation is received to confirm the necessity of treatment and causal relationship of the injury to the accident.

All claims must contain investigative reports or file notes that clearly state the basis for accepting or rejecting the claim, using the facts and applying the statute and any applicable caselaw. Simplistic statements such as: "The claim is deemed to be uncompensable" or "The case has been denied" are not acceptable explanations. Exhibit 30.1 provides an example of an appropriate explanation of compensability issues within a claim report or file note.

All workers compensation claims should be entered in the ISO ClaimSearch® system at the time the claim is set up and every 6 months thereafter.

Prompt initial payments or declinations must be done within the time frame required by the workers compensation law

Exhibit 30.1: Sample Compensability Comments

The claimant, represented by an attorney, alleged that she injured her lower back at work when bending down from her desk to pick up a pencil. An investigation was conducted and determined that the claimant actually injured her lower back at home the day before.

A statement was secured from a coworker witness who indicated the claimant told him she sustained the injury to her back at home while lifting boxes during her move the previous day. When contacting the attending physician's office, it was confirmed that the claimant had treated for the lower back injury the day before the alleged workers compensation accident.

After establishing contact with the employer (including taking a statement from the coworker), as well as contacting the attending physician, it appears that ANCR has not been established. Although an accident did occur, and notice was established timely with the employer, the employer, witness, and claimant's attending physician have confirmed that the injuries sustained by the claimant were not causally related to the alleged accident. The injuries sustained by the claimant were preexisting and resulted from an accident at the claimant's home the day before, and are not considered during the course and scope of employment. Therefore, the injury is not compensable, and the claimant is not entitled to workers compensation benefits.

The claim has been controverted (denied) and the appropriate filing with the workers compensation commission has been made. We have received written communication from the claimant attorney that they have withdrawn their representation of the claimant. If the claimant continues to pursue the claim, we will consider contacting the state fraud bureau.

in the applicable jurisdiction. Note the following:

- For third-party administrators (TPAs), penalties for late payments caused by failure of the adjuster to act in a timely manner and in compliance with the applicable statutes or regulations are the TPA's responsibility.
- Overpayments caused by the adjuster's failure to properly obtain a wage statement, calculate the indemnity rate, or verify ongoing disability are the responsibility of the TPA and should be reimbursed to the claim file.
- Wage statements must be used to calculate all indemnity benefit rates unless otherwise provided by law. Corrections and adjustments must be explained in the claim notes.
- State form filings must be timely, accurate, and in accordance with applicable statutes and regulations.

Depending on the severity of the claim and the possibility of subrogation or lien potential, an on-site field claim investigation may be necessary. The field investigation may include witness statements, photographs and diagrams, as well as other field activities. As part of the investigation process, the insured (employer) should be asked if the validity of the claim is in question. If there is a question of compensability, thoroughly investigate the situation before the claim is accepted as being compensable. Discuss the issue of compensability with the insured (employer) to foster open communication between the claims adjuster and the insured, and to gain a consensus on whether the claim should be accepted or denied.

A thorough claim investigation will have a positive impact on the adequacy of claim reserves and the ultimate disposition of the claim. It will also serve as the foundation for any third-party involvement (i.e., lien or subrogation). Recorded or written statements should be taken on most lost-time indemnity claims and on unwitnessed and/or questionable claims. Generally, statements are secured from the claimant's supervisor or manager and any available witnesses. Statements of claimants should be secured on most indemnity claims and should adequately:

- Clarify and confirm the facts and description of loss, including the date, time, and place.
- Determine the full extent of the injuries sustained.
- Limit the injury being claimed.
- Discover prior or existing medical conditions.
- Develop and maintain witness information.
- Develop the basis for acceptance or declination of the claim.
- Help determine the need for an independent medical examination (IME) or special medical or diagnostic testing.
- Aid in determining whether there is a need to retain a private investigator for further background investigation or surveillance.
- Establish where there is potential for subrogation or other third-party re-

covery, and capture the critical details needed to accomplish such recoveries.

Workers Compensation Form Filings

There are many statutory guidelines to follow throughout the claims process, including the timely payment of wage and medical benefits, and utilization of state-prescribed claim forms during various stages. These state-mandated forms are an integral part of the workers compensation claims process. Failure to file these forms timely or properly could result in fines or penalties.

The following are examples of state-mandated forms or industry standard workers compensation forms that may be necessary:

- ***First notice of injury report***—By employer
- ***First notice injury report***—By employee
- ***Initial filing with notice of accepting claim***
- ***Initial filing with notice of denying claim***—Also called "controvert" in some states
- ***Initial filing with wage payment***—Detailing wage rate and wage payment period
- ***Subsequent filing with modified wage payment***—Detailing wage rate and wage payment period and reason for any wage payment modification or termination
- ***Claimant medical authorization forms***
- ***Request for medical and hospital reports/records***
- ***Physician medical report forms***—Required to be filed by attending physicians
- ***Request for employers wage verification report***—Required to be filed by the employer
- ***Request for hearing***—By claimant or insurer
- ***Settlement agreements and stipulations***—By claimant or insurer
- ***Death claim form***
- ***Rehabilitation report***—By insurer
- ***Applications and reimbursement requests involving the second injury fund***[6]
- ***Fraud complaint form***—By insurer

Copies of these forms may be required to be sent to the workers compensation board or commission, which may maintain a file on each claim, depending on the type of claim involved.

Medical Management/ Managed Care

The claim facility should have an effective medical management or managed care program in place. This is a process by which the

[6]Certain states have implemented second injury funds to encourage employers to hired disabled employees. See section on second injury funds later in this chapter.

delivery of health care is structured and monitored, with the goal of providing medical services that are both appropriate and economically reasonable. An effective medical management program includes requests for narrative medical reports from the attending physicians; timely IMEs to assist in evaluating the injuries, diagnosis, prognosis, and treatment regime; nurse case management; medical and hospital bill repricing; utilization reviews; and physician peer reviews.

The objective of medical management is to return the employee to gainful employment through appropriate medical treatment to yield prompt recovery and, when possible, to facilitate return to work so as to minimize lost time and temporary total disability. Rehabilitation services can reduce loss of earnings benefits for injured workers who are unable to return to the pre-injury occupation. These services can be useful to enhance the injured worker's transferable skills to meet qualifications for alternative work.

A nurse case manager is assigned to achieve quality and cost-effective medical care by working closely with the claimant and the claimant's attending physician(s) to coordinate appropriate medical treatment and return to work (part time or full time). The nurse case manager also assists the claimant through any emotional periods resulting from the accident and injury, coordinating medical visits and arrangements for therapy surgery and prescriptions. The nurse case manager also assists in securing the appropriate medical reports and records for the adjuster to facilitate the adjuster's payment of medical and wage benefits.

Early intervention with an effective medical management program will assist in controlling medical treatment and its costs, and lead to a reduction in indemnity costs by reducing disability periods. Managed care vendors provide a variety of services, including medical bill review or repricing, utilization review, nurse case management, and pharmacy benefit programs.

Return-to-Work Programs

Return-to-work programs are post-injury programs that return injured employees to some type of work as soon as medically possible. Even if the injured workers are partially impaired, temporary or modified duties can be assigned that take into consideration the physical impairments. The end result of an effective return-to-work program is a reduction in indemnity and medical costs.

It has been proven that only half of the employees receiving workers compensation benefits who remain out of work for more than 6 months actually return to work. If employees receiving benefits are out of work for a year, the chances for a return to work drop even more. After 2 years of being out of work and collecting workers compensation benefits, the chances of returning the employee back to work are very low. Therefore, early intervention and an effective return-to-work program are often necessary and should be incorporated into any workers compensation claims handling guidelines.

Nurse Case Management

As indicated above, the assignment of nurse case managers is an effective way to control medical costs and assist in having the employee return to work as soon as medically possible. There are two categories of nurse case management: telephonic case management (TCM) and field case management (FCM). The primary difference between the two is that the activities involving telephonic case management are done by telephone, as opposed to field case management, which is done in person in the field. For example, when using telephonic case management, the nurse case manager will contact the claimant, employer, and physician by telephone to facilitate the coordination of medical treatment and control the disability period. A field nurse case manager may use the telephone for some activities but will visit the claimant in person and physically go to the physician's office.

Many claim facilities have criteria for nurse case management. Listed below are sample criteria for the assignment of both telephonic case and field case management:

- Most lost-time claims
- Back injuries
- Burns (second and third degree, and electrical)
- Cardiac conditions
- Chemical inhalation exposures
- Concussion/head injuries
- Crush injuries of any body part
- Cumulative trauma, e.g., carpal tunnel syndrome and tendonitis
- Dislocations
- Electric shock
- Foreign body in eye requiring follow-up visit
- Fractures
- Hearing loss
- Hernia
- Hospitalization postaccident
- Injuries needing immediate inpatient hospitalization
- Knee injuries
- Lacerations involving tendons/muscles and/or requiring stitches
- Psychological and stress claims
- Recidivism claims
- Rotator cuff injuries
- Sprains and strains

Referrals by an adjuster to the TCM at a later time are appropriate if any of the following occurs:

- Hospitalizations
- Injured worker in noncompliance with treating provider's recommendations
- Provider quality concerns
- Reinjury of the same body part
- Specialty provider referrals

Indicators for referral to an on-site nurse case manager or FCM by the adjuster and/or recommended to the adjuster by telephonic case manager include the following:

- Catastrophic injury (e.g., severe burn, spinal cord, amputation)
- Attorney prevents telephonic intervention
- Chemical dependency/substance abuse related to the injury
- Communication difficulties
- Employer refuses to accept employee back to work
- Jurisdictional requirement for on-site intervention
- Limited intelligence or education of injured worker
- Mental health/psychiatric issues
- Suspected fraud
- Uncooperative behavior
- Unexplained lack of progress
- Vocational rehabilitation services

Limited assignments appropriate for referral by the adjuster to either TCM or FCM include the following:

- Attendance at an independent medical evaluation
- Attendance at a physician appointment
- Completion of job modification planning
- Evaluation of home setting
- Job analysis

Utilization and Peer Review

An uncontrolled workers compensation claim can result in unnecessary medical treatment, surgery, and/or diagnostic testing or medical costs that may be excessive. In an effort to control medical costs and reduce unnecessary medical treatment, an adjuster will assign a nurse case manager or physician to conduct a utilization review or peer review.

A utilization review involves a referral to either a physician or nurse case manager to ascertain the necessity and cost or type of treatment being recommended. Not every claim will require a utilization review. A medical peer review is when one physician's recommended course of treatment is reviewed by a fellow physician to assess the necessity and course of that medical treatment.

There are certain types of issues which may prompt utilization or peer review. Some of these issues are indicated below:

- Direct medical expenses over $500
- Experimental procedures
- Extended services, e.g., chiropractic and/or physical therapy
- Facet, trigger point, or steroid injections

- High costs of diagnostic services
- Inpatient or outpatient surgeries
- Inpatient or outpatient chemical dependency or psychological services
- Inpatient rehabilitation

Independent Medical Exam (IME)

Typically, the workers compensation law or statute allows for IMEs of the claimant during the claims process. These are medical exams of a claimant on behalf of the insurance company or self-insured. Adjusters will want to consider an IME if the claimant is out of work beyond 30 days (or sooner, depending on the injury and treatment), for claims involving soft tissue injuries, apparent cases of overtreatment, or the indication of surgery that may not be warranted. IMEs are also used to determine the residual or permanency disability rating as a basis for any award, if the permanency rating provided by the attending physician appears to be inappropriate, or a need to confirm the permanency rating.

IMEs should be arranged by specialty in a timely manner, providing the examining physician with copies of all relevant medical and hospital records.

Fraud Recognition

As with other types of claims, the adjuster should always be cognizant of potential fraud. Red flags are indicators that a workers compensation claim may be potentially fraudulent which may be uncovered or recognized during the investigation and claims handling process.

It is important to note that fraud may be as simple as the claimant embellishing the injury and pain or persuading their attending physician to provide another 2 weeks of unwarranted disability, to fabricating or staging the entire accident and injuries. Fraud may involve not only a claimant but may also involve medical providers, attorneys, adjusters, and other parties involved in the claims process.

Some examples of red flags include:

- Injury occurs on a Monday.
- Cross-outs or white-outs appear on claim documents.
- Inconsistent home addresses are listed.
- Injured worker who claims to be disabled cannot be reached at home.
- Injured worker moves out of state shortly after the accident.
- Injury is not consistent with the nature of the job.
- Injured worker lacks recall of the accident details.
- The alleged accident occurred without any witnesses.
- The employee does not report the accident timely.
- The claim is made by a disgruntled or terminated employee.

- The injured worker is due to retire in the near future.
- The injured worker is having financial difficulty.
- There is no physical injury.
- Tips are received from coworkers.

Although these claims may be legitimate, each claim should be investigated thoroughly to confirm that the claim is not fraudulent, with no question that the injury is work related and compensable.

Claims identified as having potential for fraud, should be discussed immediately with the claims manager. It is important to involve a special investigative unit (SIU) investigator and possibly defense counsel in reviewing all facts of the claim so that if a referral to the attorney general's office and/or the appropriate state fraud unit is warranted, they can help to facilitate the referral and investigation process. Communication with all parties involved should continue as long as the issue of fraud is present.

Utilization of Private Investigators

Private investigators are often utilized during the handling of workers compensation claims for surveillance, activity checks, neighborhood interviews, and other measures to determine whether injuries and disability are legitimate. Oftentimes, the injuries and disability are legitimate, and the investigation by the private investigator simply confirms the medical documentation. However, there are claims that involve fraudulent activity, and the use of a private investigator can assist in these types of claims.

In cases of suspected fraud, when a private investigator is being considered, the following guidelines should be utilized:

- Use of private investigators should be limited to cases that require fieldwork, surveillance, neighborhood activity checks, obtaining Department of Motor Vehicle (DMV) records, credit records, court records, police interviews, past employer investigations, or SIU investigations.
- A budget should be established at the time of the assignment with the agreement that any charges beyond that budget must be approved in advance.
- Prior to doing any field activity, the private investigator should be able to identify the employee and provide the background information available from public records or local business records.
- Surveillance needs to be scheduled when there is a strong likelihood that the subject will actually be on the move. This should include nights and weekends. Days of doctor visits, receipt of benefit checks, and after bad weather are other examples of times when a subject might be active.
- Copies of the billing rates should be available for reserving and auditing purposes.
- Bills must be audited to be sure the fees are consistent with the rates and the services obtained.

- If a service provider seems to consistently come back with meaningless information or video, change service providers.

Litigation Management

The most important aspect of litigation management is control of the litigation process with attentive claims management. Litigation management involving *statutory* workers compensation claims may be different than liability claim litigation management as outlined in Appendix F, Litigation Management, beginning on page 421.

The primary reason that the litigation process is different with statutory workers compensation claims is that the initial filing and information exchange process is not the same. Typically, there is no initial formal lawsuit filed by the plaintiff, such as a writ or summons and complaint,[7] nor is there a formal discovery process with interrogatories (a bill of particulars in New York).

In a statutory workers compensation claim, the primary forum, unless there is an appeal, is at an administrative hearing, which takes place at the workers compensation commission or board, with depositions taken in front of a court stenographer. Sworn testimony is taken, and various medical and employment records are admitted into evidence, with information and documentation exchanged. Testimony will be taken from the claimant, employer, witnesses, and sometimes medical experts. An administrative law judge presides over the hearing and may assign a medical expert to examine the claimant. The employer/insured is represented by an attorney retained by the insurance company. The claimant may or may not be represented by an attorney. As the claim progresses, multiple hearings may be held throughout the claims process. Ultimately, a final hearing is conducted to determine the compensability or the extent of any permanency award to the claimant.

Ordinarily, workers compensation claims will not involve a hearing until the claim reaches the permanency award stage, disability rates or weekly wage benefits are being modified and challenged by the claimant, or the claim has been denied, in which case a hearing will be scheduled shortly after the claim has been denied by the insurance company.

An effective litigation management program is important during the workers compensation claims handling process. Workers compensation claims involve various administrative hearings and litigation. Law firms specializing in workers compensation should be retained to represent the interests of the insured or employer. When referring a workers compensation claim to defense counsel, the following guidelines are recommended:

- A litigation referral letter or litigation referral form should be utilized providing the factual details of the incident and accident, injury and treatment details, lost-time information, benefits paid to date, the scheduled hearing details, the adjuster's analysis of the claim, specific instructions to defense counsel regarding attendance at the hearing

[7] A lawsuit brought against an employer under the employers liability section of the workers compensation policy will have a similar format as a lawsuit involving a claim under a liability policy.

and the type of report required, and a request for a legal budget.

- The claim investigation needs to be completed by the adjuster and not by defense counsel.
- Require litigation budgets on all litigation claims. The litigation budget can be used as one element of the expense reserve evaluation.
- Keep all legal billing on a minimum 3-month cycle. Each legal bill should reflect a complete itemization of charges down to the tenth of an hour, by date, by legal activity, and by the handling attorney or paralegal. The bill must also reflect the hourly rate by legal handler with a summary of hours billed. Deem unacceptable charges for unnecessary activities, or any activities not approved, unless the activity was a necessary responsive pleading or correspondence in response to other parties in the litigation.
- Expect prompt communication by defense counsel and compliance with reporting requests.
- Actual deposition transcripts are usually not needed; summary reports of each deposition, which are normally prepared by the handling attorney for the legal file, will usually suffice.
- All appeals, at any level, should require management approval. Defense counsel should project the total cost of the appeal process as well as the percentage chance of success.
- All motions must be approved by the adjuster or manager. Defense counsel should request written approval to pursue any motion practice and include the reason for the motion, the projected cost, and the percentage chances of success, if applicable.
- All legal research requires the adjuster's prior approval. Defense counsel should provide the projected cost of the research and comment on the impact of the research relative to the claim result. Place a copy of the legal research brief in the claim file.
- The use of all experts requires prior approval by the claims operation.
- During the litigation process, the assigned defense attorney represents the employer or the policyholder. Although the litigation may be assigned by the insurance company, the defense attorney represents the insured as his or her client. Therefore, if a coverage dispute is involved, do not request a coverage opinion from the same defense firm defending the insured. Coverage opinions or disputes need to be referred to the defense firm that will represent the insurer in the event coverage litigation develops.
- Refer all allocated loss adjustment expenses (ALAE) to the claims operation for payment processing. These are not paid by defense counsel or included within the legal bill.

It's not defense counsel's job to direct the overall litigation activities of a workers compensation claim without involvement from the claims staff. The adjuster controls the litigation process and provides direction to the handling attorney, in accordance with the litigation management program.

Consider the defense attorney's advice to be one element of the claim evaluation, but do not exclusively rely on defense counsel's opinion. An effective litigation management program (including control of the legal billing) will help control defense activities and contribute to the reduction of loss and expense costs.

Third-Party Recovery/Liens

The right of subrogation or recovery in a workers compensation claim exists due to the rights specified in the insurance policy language and under the workers compensation law or statute. Recovery through subrogation or liens is an offset that must be identified during the initial investigation of the claim. If a viable subrogation claim exists, the adjuster needs to conduct a comprehensive investigation, including statements, photographs and diagrams, official reports as well as securing records, contracts, and other information or documentation which will support the subrogation or recovery claim. Contact with any available witnesses or coworkers that were in the area at the time of the injury can provide important information that could lead to a subrogation/lien recovery.

The party pursued for subrogation is referred to as the "third party." Subrogation may involve the workers compensation insurer placing a lien on any third-party claim brought by the claimant/employee against the responsible third-party equivalent in the amount of workers compensation benefits paid, or an action may be brought directly against the responsible third party by the workers compensation insurer on behalf of the claimant/employee. This is called an assignment.

It is recommended that all workers compensation claims with recovery potential—such as claims involving motor vehicle accidents, slips and falls, products, construction accidents, injuries sustained due to loose or flying objects, and injuries involving machinery—be completely investigated *prior* to subrogation/lien potential being ruled out as an offset. Send out lien letters in a timely manner, early in the claims process, so the various statutes of limitations are protected, when applicable. A lien letter is simply a letter placing the claimant on notice of the right of subrogation, indicating that the amounts paid by the workers compensation insurer must be satisfied from any third-party settlement or judgment. Frequently, the claimant attorney will take a third of the lien recovery as a fee, leaving two-thirds as the net recovery to the insurance company.

An example of workers compensation recovery is outlined in Exhibit 30.2 for illustrative purposes.

The claimant retained an attorney to pursue the property owner at the client's location for negligent maintenance of the property. The workers compensation insurance company filed a lien against any recovery the claimant may receive in the third-party claim. The claimant settles the claim for $100,000, which would mean that the workers compensation lien would need to be satisfied in the amount of $35,000. The claimant attorney is entitled to a one-third collection fee, which means the workers compensation insurer would receive a net recovery of approximately $23,100. It should be noted that workers compensation liens are often compromised, particularly if there are questionable liability issues.

Exhibit 30.2: Workers Compensation Lien Example

The employee claimant tripped and fell during a sales call at a client's location. The fall was the result of a defective walkway and had existed for over a year. The claimant had never been to the location previously. As a result of the accident, the claimant fractures her right arm, requiring surgery. The workers compensation insurer or insurance company pays the claimant $5,000 in indemnity wage benefits and $15,000 in medical and rehabilitation benefits. At a final hearing, the claimant received a scheduled loss award of $15,000. The total benefits paid to the claimant were $35,000. After completing its investigation, the insurer would have filed a lien notice if it was determined that a potential third-party claim existed. The workers compensation lien would need to be satisfied from the proceeds of any tort claim recovery received by the claimant.

Second Injury Funds

Yet another source of recovery is a second injury fund. In workers compensation insurance, claim apportionment between insurance companies may apply in situations where there are preexisting injuries or illnesses to an employee who has now presented a claim under the current policy. This may trigger more than one policy applying to the claim under certain situations in some states. Usually this means dividing the claim exposure among a group of employers the claimant worked for, during which time the employee was exposed to the conditions that contributed to the illness. It can also mean division of liability between an employer and a fund, such as a second injury fund, that pays for the portion of a claim attributable to preexisting conditions.

Certain states have implemented second injury funds to encourage employers to hire disabled employees. An example of a second injury fund would be the insurance company only being responsible for the first 104 weeks of workers compensation benefits. Thereafter, all future payments are reimbursed by the second injury fund. The second injury funds are typically subsidized from the premium on every workers compensation insurance policy issued in a particular state. Many states have eliminated or are phasing out second injury funds due to a lack of funding.

Ordinarily, the second injury fund potential is part of the initial claim investigation. If it is determined that the claimant had a preexisting injury or illness, then a written knowledge statement would be secured from the employer, as well as an authorization to secure the medical records. A formal submission, with the knowledge statement and second injury fund application, are submitted to a separate department at the state workers compensation commission or department.

Special Notes

The handling of workers compensation claims differs from the handling of other property and casualty claims. There are many statutory guidelines to follow throughout the claims process, including the timely payment of wage and medical benefits, and the utilization of state-prescribed claim forms. The claim investigations may involve similar tools, such as statements and medical report documentation, but liability is not an issue, only whether the claim is deemed to be compensable.

The adjuster's objective is to confirm that the accident occurred during the course and scope of employment and process the claim in accordance with the workers compensation act or statute. It is not to look for ways to deny the claim or intentionally limit benefits without supporting evidence or medical documentation. Workers compensation insurance is an employee benefit, mandated by the state, and provided by the employer. It does not matter how the accident happened, or whether the employer is responsible for the accident, the only requirement is that the accident occur during the course and scope of employment, and comply with the workers compensation act or statute.

The handling of workers compensation claims is a specialty that will usually involve adjusters who handle these types of claim exclusively. The handling and management of the claims is different than other property and casualty claims, and most claim facilities segment the workers compensation claim unit from other claim units involving other lines of business.

FOR MORE INFORMATION ON:	GO TO	PAGE(S):
Claims Handling Guidelines	Chapters 21–30	271–354
Auto Physical Damage	Chapter 22	273
Auto Liability	Chapter 23	279
Auto PIP/No Fault	Chapter 24	289
First-Party Property and Inland Marine	Chapter 25	295
Cargo	Chapter 26	305
General Liability	Chapter 27	311
Professional and Management Liability	Chapter 28	323
Public Entity	Chapter 29	331
Ethics in Claims Handling	Appendix E	409
Litigation Management	Appendix F	421
Legal Theory and Doctrines	Appendix G	427

Appendix A: Alternative Market

The "alternative market" is a term commonly used in risk financing to refer to one of a number of risk funding techniques (e.g., self-insurance, captive) or facilities (e.g., ACE, XL) that provide insurance coverages or services outside the realm of that provided by most traditional property and casualty insurers. The alternative market may be utilized by large corporations, for example, to provide high limits of coverage over a large self-insured retention (SIR), or by smaller entities participating in a risk retention group (RRG) or group captive program. Note that the distinction between traditional and alternative markets tends to blur over time as many traditional insurers expand their offering of products to encompass alternative-type funding techniques, and vice versa. Also, retrospective rating plans, especially paid loss plans, are sometimes identified with the alternative market.

The following are considered part of the alternative market, often referred to as the alternative risk transfer (ART) market:

- Captives
- Risk retention groups
- Risk purchasing groups
- Self-insurance pools

This Appendix discusses these ART options.

Captives

A captive is an insurance company that has as its primary purpose the financing of the risks of its owners or participants. Captives are licensed under special purpose insurer laws and operate under a different regulatory system than commercial insurers. This is because captives provide insurance to sophisticated insureds who require less policyholder protection than does the general public.[1]

Because a captive is wholly owned and controlled by its insureds, its primary purpose is to insure the risks of its owner-members—the primary beneficiaries of its underwriting profits. The captive has a contractual obligation for payment of future losses, and not just the administrative responsibility for processing payments. This is why captives require a contribution of risk capital and are regulated under insurance laws.

A captive may be a direct writer of insurance or be formed as a reinsurance company. Captives facilitate the financing of

[1]Much of this discussion is derived from Kathryn A. Westover, *Captives and the Management of Risk*, 2nd ed., Dallas: International Risk Management Institute, Inc., (2006), with permission.

risk and also provide the following benefits:

- Underwriting and investment income
- Improved cash flow from premium and loss reserves
- Reward for favorable loss experience
- Incentives for loss control
- Direct access to the reinsurance market
- Rate stabilization and independence from the commercial market fluctuations
- Reduced or stabilized insurance costs
- Opportunity for improved claims handling
- Control of risk management
- Potential tax advantages
- Tailored or manuscript coverage

There are many types of captive insurance companies, differentiated by their ownership and purpose. These include the following:

- ***Single-owner captive***—This is a captive with a single shareholder, and may be referred to as a "single-parent" captive. When it insures only the risks of the parent organization or its subsidiaries, it is called a "pure" captive.
- ***Group captive***—This is a captive that has as its owner a group of nonrelated organizations or parents. The captive finances risks for each of these entities. This type of captive offers some transfer opportunities that are outside the economic family of a particular parent. Thus, it provides a combination of retention and risk transfer to its various parents. A group captive is also referred to as a multiple-parent captive. This could be a stock captive, a mutual captive, or a reciprocal. In the case of a stock captive, shares can be owned by some or all of the insureds, or by non-insureds, subject to the captive domicile's license classification. For example, there are captives set up for contractors, for truckers, and for taxicab companies.
- ***Rental captive***—This is a captive insurance company that allows unrelated parties ("participants") to use the captive for a fee, thereby eliminating the need for formation and operation of a new company. The participant may or may not be required to contribute capital, and may or may not be a preferred shareholder in the rental captive. Provided such use is permitted in a domicile, rental captive participants may be insureds or non-insureds, such as insurance agents. These arrangements are also called "rent-a-captives."
- ***Cell captive***—This is a sponsored captive or rental captive that maintains underwriting accounts separately for each participant. It may also be called a protected cell captive (PCC) or segregated cell insurer. If the cells are legally segregated, this type of captive may be used to securitize risk.
- ***Segregated cell captive (SCC)***—This special purpose insurer (typically oper-

ating as a rental captive) establishes legally segregated cells or underwriting accounts. The objective is to ensure that assets in one underwriting account may not be used to satisfy liabilities in another underwriting account, nor the general (noncellular) liabilities of the SCC. Noncellular assets may or may not be available to satisfy cellular liabilities. This form of captive may also be called a segregated portfolio company (SPC), a protected cell company (PCC), or a separate account company (SAC).

- ***Profit center captives***—This is a captive that has the primary function of earning underwriting income by writing unrelated risk.

- ***Producer-owned reinsurance company (PORC)***—This is a captive or a rent-a-captive cell owned or used by a broker or managing general agent (MGA) for reinsurance of selected risks that it produces for the purposes of retaining the underwriting income. It may be set up by insurance companies to circumvent state laws regarding the amount of commissions that can be paid to their producing agents.

- ***Agency captive***—Unlike other forms of captives, agency captives are not designed to provide insurance for their owners. Instead, they benefit the insurer, agent, or broker that owns the company. Agents and brokers are often

Exhibit A.1: Group Captive Illustration

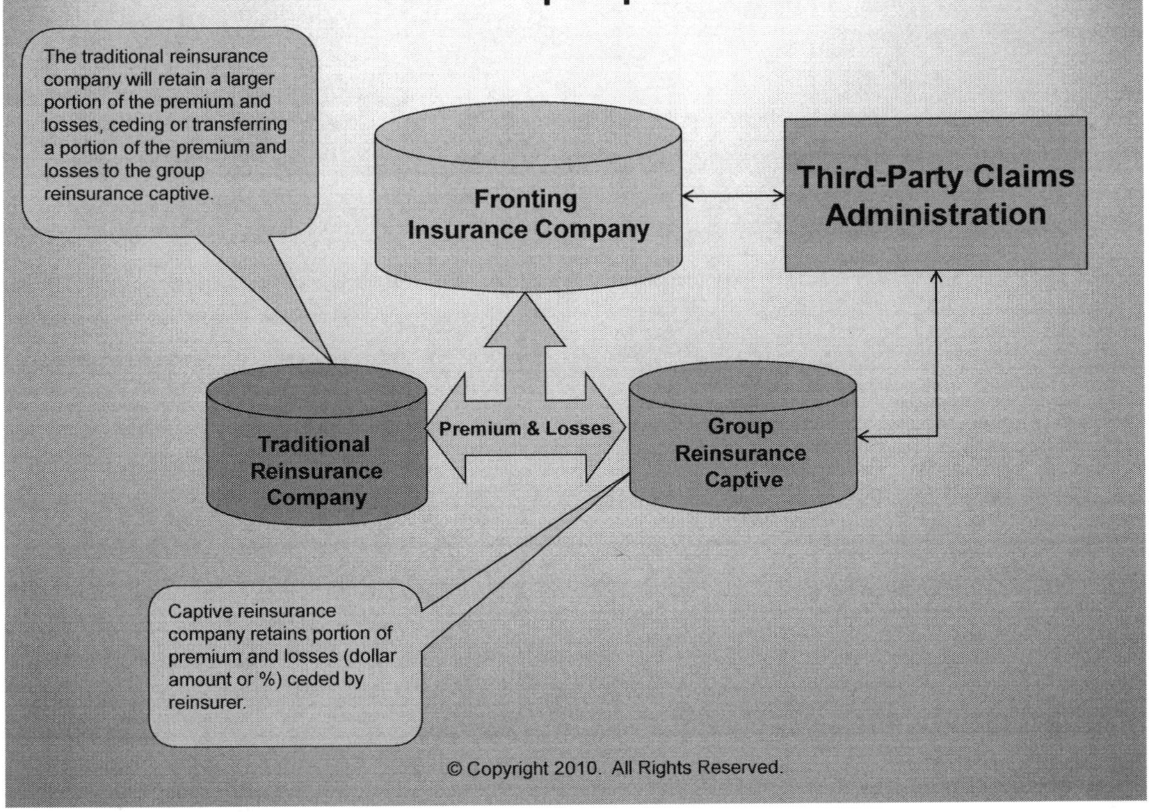

compelled to form captives to provide markets for their clients when the insurance market is in a "hard cycle," and commercial insurance is unavailable.

- ***Insurer-sponsored agency captive***—The most popular and innocuous form of agency captives, this captive is typically created and sponsored by large multiline insurance companies. They are enhanced profit-sharing schemes structured as offshore captive facilities. Participating agents and the sponsoring insurer each purchase one share of the captive's stock, which funds the captive's capital and surplus. The sponsoring insurer provides reinsurance, fronting, and ancillary services. Agents take a share of the captive's retention; the sponsoring insurer takes the rest. Participating agents commit to placing a minimum amount of business with the sponsoring insurer who cedes the captive's percentage.

- ***Reinsurance captive***—This special purpose insurer operates only on a fronted basis, assuming risk from a ceding company. The reinsurance captive does not issue policies directly to insureds and typically operates on a non-admitted basis. This is also referred to as a fronted captive.

Exhibit A.1 provides an illustration of a group captive. The captive, structured as a reinsurance company, retains a portion of the premium and losses along with the traditional reinsurance company. The fronting insurance company may or may not retain a portion of the risk, ceding or transferring the premium and losses to the reinsurers (or to the traditional reinsurance company, which will then transfer to the reinsurance captive).

Risk Retention Groups

In 1981, Congress passed the federal Liability Risk Retention Act (LRRA) in response to the hard market, i.e., a shortage of underwriting capacity that left many U.S. insureds unable to obtain or afford product liability insurance. The purpose of the LRRA was to allow groups of insureds to join together to form RRGs and risk purchasing groups (RPGs). The LRRA was amended in 1986 to allow entities authorized under its powers to write or purchase not only product liability insurance, but all types of liability insurance.

The Liability Risk Retention Act is a valuable piece of legislation, allowing smaller insureds (those without the financial strength to retain risk or assert economic strength in the marketplace) to attain bulk buying power in the purchase of liability insurance. It also allows them to avoid the "fictitious group" laws passed in some states to prevent groups forming solely for the purpose of buying insurance. It was also the intention of the LRRA to make it easier for insurers to handle multistate filings for rates and policy forms, thereby encouraging risk capital to enter the market. This creates underwriting capacity for insurance of difficult-to-place risks. Since it is more efficient for an insurer to underwrite a group of similar risks, rather than separately underwriting each insured entity, it was hoped that the federal legislation would reduce insurance costs.

An RRG must be owned by its insureds. Most RRGs are formed as captives and must be domiciled onshore, except for those grandfathered under the 1981 Act. RRGs cover all the liability exposures, other than workers compensation exposures, of their owners. They are not subject to the individual state laws that would otherwise prohibit the formation of group captives or make it difficult to form or operate them.

RRGs are often formed from trade and professional associations, which serve as the sponsor for the RRG liability insurance program. Owned by their members, a key advantage is control over the liability program. This control can mean lower insurance rates, broader coverage, effective loss control and risk management programs, participation by RRG members in favorable loss experience, access to reinsurance markets, and stability of coverage, depending on insurance market cycles. Most RRGs are regulated as captives, with lower initial capitalization and surplus requirements.

Exhibit A.2 provides an illustration of an RRG. In an RRG, favorable results will yield underwriting income, and unfavorable results will yield an underwriting loss. Favorable results will provide distributions to members in the form of increased surplus, premium reduction, and dividends, depending on the RRG structure.

Risk Purchasing Groups (RRGs)

As mentioned above, an RPG is another group formed in compliance with the Risk

Exhibit A.2: Risk Retention Group Illustration

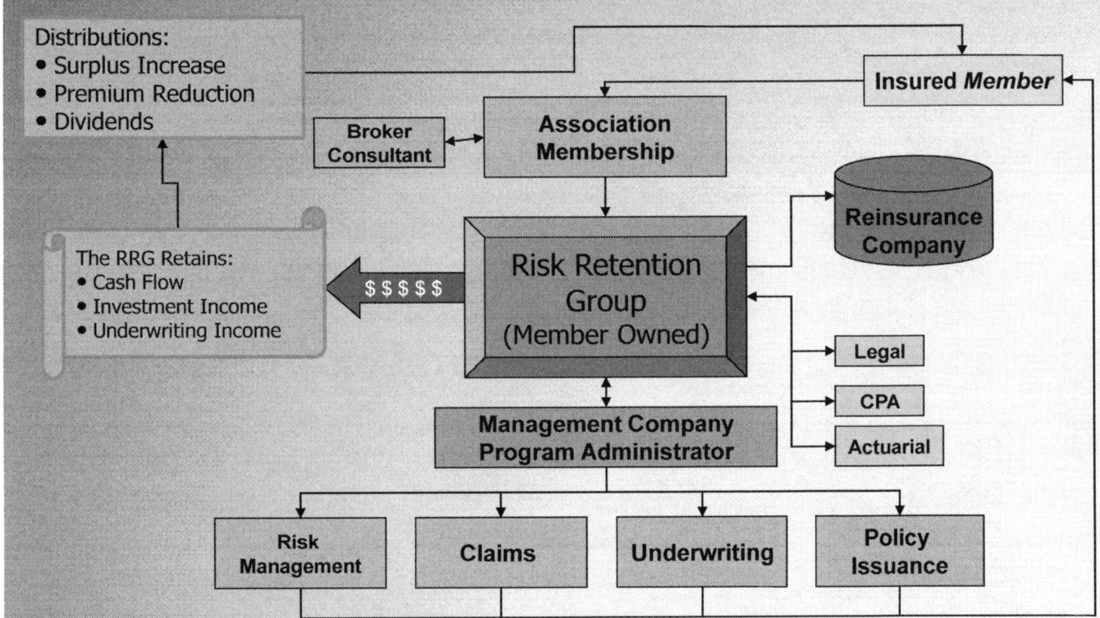

In the member owned risk retention group (RRG) model, the RRG bears risk, cedes (or transfers) a portion of the risk to a reinsurance company, and provides services to the insured though a management company and other service providers. The RRG retains investment income and cash flow from the operations.

Exhibit A.3: Risk Purchasing Group Flowchart

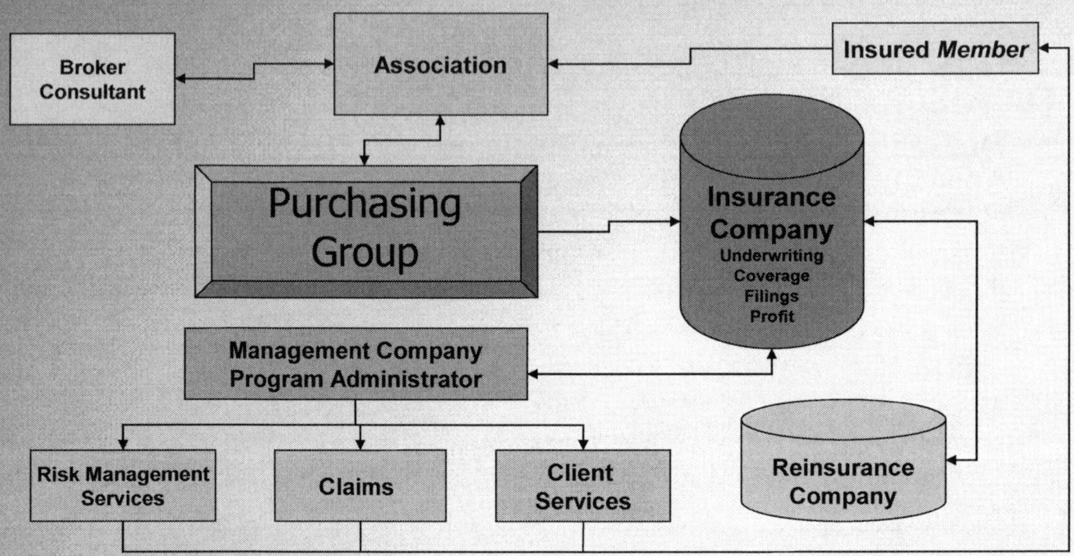

In a risk purchasing group, the RPG bears no risk. The insurance company bears all the risk, cedes (or transfers) a portion of the risk to a reinsurance company, and provides services to the insured either directly or through a management company.

Retention Act of 1986 authorizing a group of insureds engaged in similar businesses or activities to purchase insurance coverage from a commercial insurer. This is in contrast to an RRG, which actually bears the group's risks rather than obtaining coverage on behalf of group members.

Even though purchasing groups are not captives, insureds in a purchasing group have many of the same objectives as captive insureds. They want access to coverage in hard markets, lower costs for both insurance and insurance-related services, such as claims handling, and customized policy forms.

What the purchasing group insured does not do is transfer risk to an alternative risk financing mechanism. Because the RPG does not assume risk, there is no contribution of risk capital from the insureds to the group, and generally no commitment—contractual or implied—to remain a member of the group beyond the insurance policy anniversary. These are the defining characteristics that help to differentiate risk purchasing groups from a captive. It is possible for a risk purchasing group to reorganize as a risk retention group.

Exhibit A.3 provides an illustration of an RPG. As with RRGs, favorable results yield underwriting income. Insurance rates and availability fluctuate with the market cycles.

Self-Insurance Pools

Self-insurance pools have many objectives in common with purchasing groups: to provide a mechanism for joint access to coverage and claims services and to allow the pool members to stabilize loss costs and improve control over purchasing coverage from commercial insurers. They differ in that the function of administering claims payments for losses within each member's retention is assumed by the pool.

Pools can be funded or unfunded. If they operate as a mutual benefit association, the pool can assess members to pay losses as they occur. If funded by its members, a pool may do many things that an insurer does, such as setting up loss reserves and paying losses. As a result, pool members have a longer-term commitment and are required to post collateral to ensure future payment of the pool losses. Pool members also have joint and several liability, meaning that, although there may be pool participation agreements stating that each member will pay its own losses, if one pool member defaults, the other members may jointly become responsible for the unfunded losses. When joint and several liability exists, a claimant may sue the members of a group separately as well as the group as a whole.

Workers compensation pools are an example of a frequently used type of funded risk financing mechanism. The WC self-insurance pool is regulated under special purpose laws and provides reports to state insurance regulators. Pool participants must be qualified self-insurers, meaning that they have passed minimum net worth or other tests established by the state where the workers compensation coverage is provided. Public entity pools, which finance liability risk for states, cities, or other governmental organizations, are another frequently used type of self-insurance pool. As legal entities, the pools have the ability to enter into contracts on behalf of their members and will have a board of directors and elected officers.

The key difference between a self-insurance pool and an insurance company is that the risk of loss remains with the pool members.

Appendix B: ISO ClaimSearch®

ISO Services, Inc., the company that owns ISO ClaimSearch,® was kind enough to provide detailed information about the history of the ISO ClaimSearch® system and an explanation of the services associated with the product. This data is incorporated into this Appendix. Much of the information is directly quoted from ISO Services, Inc., with its permission.

Introduction

The ISO ClaimSearch® system is used by most insurance companies and third-party claim administrators (TPAs). It is an excellent industry tool for the review and exchange of claims history information between subscribers or claim facilities. Adjusters use this service in the handling of most property and casualty claims by reporting new claims, updating existing claim history, and exchanging detailed information on claims already reported.

In the author's opinion, the ISO ClaimSearch® database is the most comprehensive in the industry, providing historical claim information that helps identify fraudulent claim activity and assists in complying with reporting requirements mandated by various state insurance regulations (i.e., New York).

TPAs and self-insureds are charged an annual subscription fee by ISO Services for the ISO ClaimSearch services per database, plus a fee for each individual report. Insurance companies are charged as a percentage of their direct written premium for the lines of business pertaining to the individual databases.

The various databases include *casualty* (general liability, auto liability, workers compensation, medical payments, errors and omissions, etc.); *property* (fire, allied lines, inland marine, homeowners, burglary and theft, etc.); and *auto* (vehicle theft, physical damage, and salvage). Insurance companies pay a percentage of their annual written premium as a subscriber fee and do not pay for any individual reporting entries.

Appendix B examines the history of the ISO ClaimSearch® system and the host of services available to its subscribers.

History

For several decades, claims personnel did not have a single source of historical insurance claim information for claims evaluation and special investigations support. Claims information was maintained in three separate systems:

- Index system for bodily injury claims, also called the Central Index Bureau (CIB)
- *Property Insurance Loss Register (PILR)* for property claims

Appendix B

REMEMBER PROFITABILITY

With data on property, casualty, and vehicle claims, ISO ClaimSearch® is the insurance industry's most comprehensive resource for claims professionals. The ISO ClaimSearch database contains information from the former *Property Insurance Loss Register (PILR),* the former *Index System* for bodily injury claims, and the vehicle information databases formerly administered by the *National Insurance Crime Bureau* (NICB).

Today, all of those claims are part of a single database that allows searches of all lines of business and all types of claims simultaneously.

The ISO ClaimSearch database has three major segments: casualty, property, and auto. Each segment contains comprehensive information on claims submitted by hundreds of insurers and other users. Subscribers can participate in one or more segments of the database.

Source: ISO Claims Solutions brochure. ISO ClaimSearch.® Jersey City, NJ: Insurance Services Office, Inc., 2005, 2006, page 2.

- National Insurance Crime Bureau (NICB) database of vehicle claims (formerly the National Auto Theft Bureau)

Over 30 years ago, the reporting and exchanging of claim information was done by submitting handwritten forms to these various organizations. The submission of information was a manual process for the claim facility and was not consolidated among various reporting agencies.

At the urging of claims and investigations personnel across the industry, Insurance Services Office, Inc., the parent of ISO Services, Inc. (both herein referred to as "ISO"), developed a plan to create an all-claims system that could provide information on a claimant's history of claims across all lines of business. It would also support special investigations and offer proactive fraud detection capabilities. In 1997, ISO acquired the American Insurance Services Group, a subsidiary of the American Insurance Association, which operated two of the claims systems: the Index System and the *Property Insurance Loss Register.* In 1998, ISO came to an agreement with the National Insurance Crime Bureau to acquire its data processing assets and function as the processor of its vehicle information system.

In 2000, ISO launched the integrated ISO ClaimSearch® system. The system has grown over the past few years and, as of 2010, the database contains nearly 700 million claims. It processes over 50 million new claims and 20 million investigations queries each year. Participants in the system include hundreds of insurers, public and private self-insured organizations, TPAs, and state workers compensation insurance funds. It also services the National Insurance Crime Bureau, thousands of law enforcement agencies, state insurance fraud bureaus, and state fire marshals. The system is the information and technology foundation of the property and casualty insurance industry's anti-fraud efforts.

Universal Format

The ISO ClaimSearch® system touts a "universal format," which offers many benefits, including:

- A single input format for all claim types (property, casualty, and auto)
- Cross-line search results in match reports
- A variety of reporting options, including Internet, system-to-system, and Extensible Markup Language (XML)
- The flexibility to deliver new products, such as public records and scoring tools.

Before universal format, participants transmitted claim reports and received results in monoline formats designed for the three independent systems—casualty, property, and auto. Those formats were inflexible and couldn't accommodate cross-line search results, changes in data requirements, or other enhancements. Also, the monoline formats could not accommodate the addition of information from other sources, such as public records or from new fraud-detection products.

When the ISO ClaimSearch® system first implemented universal format, limited communication methods were available. Users would enter claims manually through the ISO ClaimSearch® website and then receive match reports from the system. If participants were interested in automated interfaces, they could choose from only two communication options:

- ***File Transfer Protocol (FTP)***—Input and return, which processed data in batches and returned an electronic file the following day.
- ***IBM's MQ-Series***—Input and return, which processed the data in real time and returned an electronic output match report.

Both of those output options required participants to program their own systems to create match reports from the information they received from the ISO ClaimSearch® database.

To meet customer needs, ISO implemented additional system-to-system communication options. If participants wished to send the input files automatically but did not have adequate internal resources to program their own systems, they could also choose one of these options:

- ***Web output***—Allows adjusters to log onto the ISO ClaimSearch® website to view and print match reports.
- ***PDF files***—Send back an electronic file of all matches to the company's system in portable document format (PDF) files. Participants can then store the PDF files on their system or distribute them to users.

In addition, ISO developed an Extensible Markup Language (XML) interface to transmit and receive data.

Claims Reporting and Processing

The primary service of the ISO ClaimSearch® system is claims reporting, also known as the claim-processing service. To use the service, subscribers submit a claim through their own claims system or the ISO ClaimSearch® website. The system then provides a match report with information on other claims filed by the same individual or business.

The system provides a phonetic search for names and addresses that recognizes alternative spellings, such as Green and Greene or Smith and Smyth. The system also checks possible nicknames and alternative forms of a name, such as Elisabeth, Liz, Lizzie, and Beth.

The system also uses its advanced "address hygiene" function to standardize address information. It checks the validity of all information submitted to the database. For example, the system will make sure that the zip code and state are compatible and that the reported vehicle identification number is a valid number. The system then searches the database for other claims with matching information in key data fields, such as:

- Name
- Address
- Vehicle Identification Number (VIN)
- Tax Identification Number (TIN)
- Social Security Number (SSN)
- License plate number
- Driver's license number
- Telephone number

The ISO ClaimSearch® database can be accessed through several electronic transmission methods, including:

- ISOnet℠—ISO's Internet information service for insurance professionals.
- Batch and interactive system-to-system transmissions in a number of formats.

Statutory and Regulatory Reporting

An added service of the ISO ClaimSearch® system provides required claims data to state fraud bureaus, fire marshals, or other entities on behalf of insurers. Some states have direct access to the ISO ClaimSearch® system for follow-up on individual cases.

Workers Compensation—wcPrism®

wcPrism® is a comprehensive suite of data management, compliance, and analytic solutions for workers compensation. For insurers, wcPrism can handle reporting of all workers compensation data on their behalf from a single transactional feed and offers sophisticated analytics. For states, the wcPrism suite offers an efficient, cost-effective way to collect insurers' first report of injury (FROI), subsequent report of injury (SROI), and medical data claims to perform their own in-depth analysis.

Claims Inquiry

Special investigations units (SIUs) and claims personnel use the ISO ClaimSearch® Claims Inquiry for follow-up fraud investigations. Users may customize queries to search on any field of information to support a specific claims investigation. Queries can be submitted online, in real time, to receive instant search results for property, casualty, and vehicle claims. System reports provide information to help identify a claimant's or insured's full loss profile, individuals with suspicious patterns of claims, and fraud-ring activity. Claims Inquiry is an extension of the ISO ClaimSearch® claim reporting service. A claim must be entered in the ISO ClaimSearch system prior to using Claims Inquiry to expand the search for those claims that require additional investigation. The company claim number, entered in the ISO ClaimSearch database when reporting the claim is required on the claim number field in Claims Inquiry. Red flags and other exception criteria are used to assure compliance with ISO privacy and security procedures.

Office of Foreign Assets Control Compliance Service

The ISO ClaimSearch® system offers an Office of Foreign Assets Control (OFAC) Compliance Service that provides an automated method of checking claimants and other contacts against the government's watch list of potential terrorists and drug traffickers. The OFAC of the U.S. Department of the Treasury administers and enforces economic and trade sanctions against certain foreign governments, organizations, and individuals. OFAC has compiled a master list of more than 5,000 "specially designated nationals and blocked persons." U.S. insurance companies and their employees are responsible for screening claims against that master list. Subscribers to the OFAC service automatically have their claims data compared to the OFAC watch list on a daily basis. If the system finds a match, ISO notifies the designated company representative by e-mail.

ISO offers the service in four tiers:

1. **Standard Service:** ISO compares all involved parties against the OFAC watch list. The comparison includes businesses and individuals based on name (plus aliases) and date of birth.

2. **Premium Service:** In addition to the standard service, ISO will automatically perform public record searches to help verify the identity of individuals or businesses.

3. **Historical Sweep:** There is an option to searching all claims previously submitted to the system or searching claims submissions over a specific segment of time, such as the last 2 or 5 years.

4. **Enterprisewide Service:** ISO conducts searches on individuals and businesses for all departments within the subscriber's organization. Claims, Human Resources, Accounts Payable, and other departments can perform searches against the OFAC watch list.

OFAC LookUp

The ISO ClaimSearch® system also offers OFAC LookUp service, which lets subscribers initiate a query to check if a name is on the OFAC master list. Decision Net® users can enhance their OFAC queries with public records searches. OFAC LookUp is not a replacement for the OFAC Compliance Service, which automatically checks all incoming claim reports against the OFAC lists without additional effort on the subscriber's part.

Summary and Conclusion

The ISO ClaimSearch® system is an investigative tool that should be used during the claims handling process. All claims that meet the reporting protocol should be reported to the ISO ClaimSearch® database. When the handling adjuster receives information through the ISO ClaimSearch® system indicating a history of prior claims (or new claim activity after the date of loss), the handling adjuster should follow up to request the claim details and document the claim file accordingly. The prior claim history should be carefully analyzed and be a component of any claim evaluation.

For more information concerning the ISO ClaimSearch® system, contact:

ISO ClaimSearch®
545 Washington Boulevard, 22-11
Jersey City, NJ 07310-1686
(800) 888-4476
Email: info.claimsearch@iso.com
http://www.iso.com

APPENDIX C: STATEMENT GUIDES

As discussed in Chapter 27, statement guides are used as a claim tool to help the adjuster during the investigation process. They are particularly useful for new adjusters at the scene of the accident or incident. The following guides are contained in this appendix:

Appendix C

Automobile Accidents Statement Guide

- ❑ Vehicle involved: year, make, model, and color
- ❑ Vehicle owner: name and contact information
- ❑ Any trailer attached?
- ❑ Vehicle operator: name, address, age, and contact information
- ❑ Drivers' license information: type, license number, state issued, and restrictions
- ❑ Driving experience
- ❑ Permissive use issues
- ❑ Prior accidents or violations
- ❑ Date, time, and place of accident
- ❑ Description of road and markings
- ❑ Any road defects or obstructions?
- ❑ Weather conditions
- ❑ Lighting
- ❑ Visibility
- ❑ Posted speed limit
- ❑ Traffic conditions
- ❑ Passengers: names, addresses, and contact information.
- ❑ Passenger positions in car
- ❑ Any mechanical condition issue with vehicles prior to and after the accident.
- ❑ Purpose of trip—business or pleasure
- ❑ Departure point and time
- ❑ Any stops during trip?
- ❑ Alcohol or drugs (including prescription drugs)? Quantity? Where?
- ❑ Any physical impairment?
- ❑ Seatbelts used by all occupants? Airbags deployed?
- ❑ Any distractions in vehicle (e.g., stereo, I-Pod, cell phone, GPS system, smoking, eating, children, texting, etc.)?
- ❑ Any passenger objections to driving?
- ❑ Traffic controls—working?
- ❑ Describe the accident in your own words.
- ❑ Position of all vehicles
- ❑ Direction of your travel

Page 1 of 5

Automobile Accidents Statement Guide (cont.)

- ❑ Direction of the other vehicle(s)
- ❑ Speed just prior to the accident
- ❑ Speed of other vehicle(s)
- ❑ When did you first see the other vehicles?
- ❑ Distance—view—obstructions
- ❑ Signals given; signals seen
- ❑ Warning by anyone?
- ❑ Attempts to avoid accident?
- ❑ Points of impact
- ❑ If pedestrian involved, address the following with any party to the claim:
    - o Location when first seen
    - o View and obstructions
    - o Distance away
    - o Direction person facing
    - o In crosswalk or distance from intersection
    - o Color of clothes
    - o Carrying anything: umbrella, I-Pod, package, books, cell phone, food, smoking, children, etc.
    - o Walking or running—distraction
    - o Position when danger realized
    - o Evasive action taken by driver
    - o Evasive action taken by pedestrian
    - o What part of vehicle struck the pedestrian (scratches or indentations on car)
    - o Stopping distance
    - o Where was pedestrian after accident?
    - o Conversation after accident
    - o Evidence of intoxication
    - o Evidence of physical impairment
- ❑ Position of vehicles after accident
- ❑ Stopping distances
- ❑ Skid marks—both vehicles
- ❑ Skids measured? By whom and how?
- ❑ Location of dirt or debris

Automobile Accidents Statement Guide (cont.)

- ❑ Persons thrown from vehicle—positions
- ❑ First person on scene—witnesses
- ❑ Conversations—with whom?
- ❑ Cars moved prior to police arrival?
- ❑ Police investigation: report number, officer name and shield number, any tickets or arrests, any accident reconstruction or police photos
- ❑ Any official hearings scheduled
- ❑ Any intoxication tests performed by police
- ❑ Witnesses to accident: name and contact information
- ❑ Do you personally know other parties to the claim?
- ❑ Any photos taken at accident scene?
- ❑ Ambulances: name of ambulance company
- ❑ Other vehicle(s)
  - o Other vehicle(s) involved: year, make, model, and color
  - o Other vehicle owners: name and contact information
  - o Other driver information: name, age, and contact information
  - o Passengers: names, contact information, and positioning vehicles
  - o Description of vehicles
  - o Apparent injuries—complaints
- ❑ Trucking supplement:
  - o Commercial driver's license (CDL)
  - o Driver training?
  - o Trip records
  - o Driving how long?
  - o Federal filings
  - o State filings
- ❑ Damages to all vehicles:
  - o Specific parts damaged
  - o Extent of damage
  - o Estimates obtained
  - o Disposition of vehicles
  - o Present location

Automobile Accidents Statement Guide (cont.)

- o Tow trucks on scene
- o Previous damage to vehicles (prior accident, rust, general condition)

❑ Injuries—Special Damages

- o How were injuries caused?
- o Treatment at scene of accident
- o Were you rendered unconscious?
- o Nature of treatment after the accident
- o Ambulance and police involved?
- o Name of hospital
- o Emergency room treatment
- o Hospitalization (duration and dates)
- o Name and address of hospital
- o Name and address of all physicians (with specialties)
- o X-rays? Name of radiologist
- o Previous accidents, injuries, or illnesses (details)
- o Disability dates
- o Paid by employer?
- o Wage rate
- o Lost wages to date
- o Expected return-to-work date
- o Expected future disability
- o All medical and hospital bill related expenses to date
- o If fatality claim:
  - — Funeral and other expenses
  - — Length of time between accident and death—conscious pain and suffering?

❑ Witness Supplement

- o Identification of person
- o Accident location
- o Witness location
- o What attracted attention?
- o View of accident

Page 4 of 5

Automobile Accidents Statement Guide (cont.)

- Actually saw accident?
- Coming from/going to where
- Accident details
- Post-accident details
- Vehicle(s) involved—describe
- Driver(s) involved
- Number of people in vehicle
- Damages
- Injuries noted
- Know parties involved?

General Liability Accidents Statement Guides

Premises Accidents

Statement of an owner, tenant, resident witness:

- ❑ Describe the premises involved (address, structure, and age)
- ❑ Ownership of premises
- ❑ Maintenance of premises
- ❑ Control of premises
- ❑ Tenants of premises
- ❑ Type of premises—when purchased?
- ❑ Use of premises
- ❑ Condition of premises
- ❑ Any lease agreement involved (responsibilities and hold harmless and indemnity)
- ❑ Exact location of accident
- ❑ Any recent repairs or alterations—by whom?
- ❑ Prior knowledge of defective condition (actual or constructive notice)
- ❑ How long has defect been in existence
- ❑ Any post-accident or prior photographs
- ❑ Inspection of premises—by whom and how often (any records kept)
- ❑ Condition visible/hidden
- ❑ Previous complaints or accidents
- ❑ Description of any alleged defect:
    - o Structural
    - o Wear and tear
    - o Weather elements
    - o Faulty construction or repairs
    - o Foreign object or foreign substance
- ❑ Lighting
- ❑ Weather conditions
- ❑ When last cleaned, scrubbed, waxed, swept, or inspected
- ❑ Post-accident details
- ❑ First knowledge of accident
- ❑ Witness to accident—details, visible injuries, inspection of accident area, etc.

Page 1 of 8

General Liability Accidents Statement Guides (cont.)

- ❑ Why injured on premises?
- ❑ Person on premises before?
- ❑ How well known?
- ❑ Other witnesses to accident
- ❑ First aid given—by whom?
- ❑ Police or ambulance
- ❑ Photos taken by anyone?
- ❑ Repairs—removal of defect—by whom?
- ❑ Claimant under influence of alcohol or drugs?

Statement of Claimant:

- ❑ Pre-accident details
- ❑ Pinpoint location of accident
- ❑ Date and time of accident
- ❑ Purpose of trip
- ❑ Route taken
- ❑ Accompanied by anyone
- ❑ Familiarity with premises
- ❑ Weather conditions
- ❑ Lighting
- ❑ Distractions
- ❑ Claimant under influence of alcohol or drugs?
- ❑ Type of footwear
- ❑ Running—walking
- ❑ Accident details—how did accident happen
- ❑ Cause of accident—describe
- ❑ Description of any alleged defect:
    - o Structural
    - o Wear and tear
    - o Weather elements
    - o Faulty construction or repairs
    - o Foreign object or foreign substance

General Liability Accidents Statement Guides (cont.)

- ❑ Knowledge of any defect
- ❑ Other parties involved
- ❑ Exact position after accident
- ❑ Did you report accident? To whom?
- ❑ Assistance provided by anyone?
- ❑ Immediate medical care details
- ❑ Witnesses to accident—name and contact information
- ❑ What did witnesses say?
- ❑ Police investigation: report number, officer name and shield number, any accident reconstruction or police photos?

Construction Accidents

- ❑ Specific accident location
- ❑ Name and contact information of building or property owner
- ❑ Architect, general contractor, subcontractors
- ❑ Ownership, maintenance, and control
- ❑ Supervision and inspection
- ❑ Contracts and responsibility
- ❑ Description of accident
- ❑ Witnesses
- ❑ Workers on job site and experience
- ❑ Safety measures/safety meetings
- ❑ Occupational Safety and Health Act (OSHA) compliance
- ❑ Safety equipment
- ❑ Permits and code compliance
- ❑ Police or ambulance
- ❑ Road construction:
    - o Control of area
    - o Description of construction area
    - o Time period under construction
    - o Flares, barriers, or signs used
    - o Prior accidents
    - o Notice (actual or constructive)

General Liability Accidents Statement Guides (cont.)

Floor Accidents

- ❑ Composition of floor (carpet, wood, concrete, tile)
- ❑ Condition of floor:
    - o Damaged, defective, worn, or torn
    - o Wet
    - o Slippery
    - o Recently waxed or polished
    - o Debris
    - o Foreign substance
    - o Foreign object
    - o Slope/level
    - o Color
    - o Illusions created with multilevel floors and any warnings
- ❑ Claimant carrying anything or distracted
- ❑ Claimant footwear and clothing
- ❑ How long did hazard exist?
- ❑ Notice (actual or constructive)
- ❑ Prior accidents
- ❑ Lighting
- ❑ Weather conditions
- ❑ Police or ambulance
- ❑ Use of interior/exterior mats
- ❑ If fall due to wax application:
    - o Maintenance company
    - o Last wax application
    - o Type of wax (name and manufacturer)
    - o Carpets or mats involved—is this process done by another company?

General Liability Accidents Statement Guides (cont.)

Sidewalk or Walkway Accidents

- ❑ Construction of sidewalk: concrete, stone, brick, etc.
- ❑ Company that constructed sidewalk
- ❑ Abutting landowner
- ❑ Age and condition
- ❑ Lighting
- ❑ Weather conditions
- ❑ Claimant carrying anything or distracted?
- ❑ Claimant footwear and clothing
- ❑ Level or sloped
- ❑ Public or private
- ❑ Notice (actual or constructive)
- ❑ Exact location of accident
- ❑ Describe defect in detail (if sidewalk flag elevated, measure defect)
- ❑ Cause of defect
- ❑ Length of time defect has existed
- ❑ Attempts to repair defect or damage
- ❑ If snow or ice:
    - o Natural accumulation or man-made
    - o Last snowfall: duration and accumulation
    - o Snow removal done?
    - o Salt applied?
    - o Third-party snow-removal company
- ❑ Police or ambulance

Stairway Accidents

- ❑ Ownership, maintenance, and control
- ❑ Composition of stairs and landing (carpet, wood, concrete, tile)
- ❑ Description of stairway
- ❑ Who uses stairway and where does it lead to?
- ❑ Measurements of steps (height and width)

Page 5 of 8

Appendix C—GL

General Liability Accidents Statement Guides (cont.)

- ❑ Number of steps and uniformity
- ❑ Covering of steps: mats, carpet, etc.
- ❑ Condition of covering and steps
- ❑ Mats at top or bottom of stairway
- ❑ Condition of step nosing, rise, and facing
- ❑ Building code compliance
- ❑ Handrail (left, right, or both sides)
- ❑ Any obstructions?
- ❑ Cause of fall
- ❑ Lighting and switch location
- ❑ Prior falls on stairs
- ❑ Weather conditions
- ❑ Claimant carrying anything or distracted?
- ❑ Claimant footwear and clothing
- ❑ Police or ambulance

Product Liability Claims

- ❑ Product name and manufacturer codes
- ❑ Purchaser of product—contact information and date delivered
- ❑ Purchase contract, invoice or shipping documentation
- ❑ Manufacturer, distributor, and retailer in the product chain
- ❑ Who uses the product?
- ❑ Where is the product now?
- ❑ Description of product (batch or lot number and serial number)
- ❑ Any printed material and labels related to product
- ❑ Is product a component part manufactured by another company (name)?
- ❑ When was product defect discovered?
- ❑ Date product delivered and its condition
- ❑ Describe the quality control process
- ❑ Is the product unreasonably dangerous?
- ❑ Has the product undergone any inspection, testing, or analysis?
- ❑ Was product used as directed?

General Liability Accidents Statement Guides (cont.)

- ❑ Describe the injury and when it manifested
- ❑ Names of all parties who used the product
- ❑ If food-borne illness, what else was eaten at same time and what common foods were eaten by all who became ill?
- ❑ When was a complaint first made and to whom?
- ❑ Complete details of manufacturing, canning, and packaging
- ❑ Describe the method of storing and handling from the point of manufacture to distributor, retailer, and then to the end user
- ❑ Did defect exist at time product left manufacturer?
- ❑ Was the product "state of the art" at time of manufacture?
- ❑ Date, location of accident (exact)
- ❑ Police or ambulance

Animal Bite Claims

- ❑ Ownership and control of animal
- ❑ Did accident occur on public or private property?
- ❑ Animal type, breed, name, weight, disposition, and age
- ❑ Licensing
- ❑ Collar worn
- ❑ Medical history and shots
- ❑ Prior bite history
- ❑ Leashed
- ❑ Fenced
- ❑ Electric fence utilized—signs posted?
- ❑ Police or ambulance
- ❑ Did claimant attempt to pet animal?
- ❑ Did claimant torment, tease, or attempt to feed animal?
- ❑ Bite location
- ❑ Public authority notified
- ❑ Police or ambulance

General Liability Accidents Statement Guides (cont.)

Swimming Pool Claims

- ❑ Ownership, maintenance, and control
- ❑ Type of pool, age, and installation date
- ❑ Pool surface and surrounding surface
- ❑ Pool manufacturer, distributor, retailer, and installer
- ❑ Pool warranties and guarantees
- ❑ Pool warning signs
- ❑ Pool alarms/roping
- ❑ Pool fence
- ❑ Pool depth and markings
- ❑ Rope separating low and deep end of pool
- ❑ Slide or diving board
- ❑ Diving allowed
- ❑ Any life guard on duty
- ❑ Life preservers available
- ❑ Lighting
- ❑ Maintenance
- ❑ Any pool usage guidelines or instructions
- ❑ Supervision (including children)
- ❑ Number of toys in pool at time of accident
- ❑ Warnings by owner to people using the pool
- ❑ Pool defects
- ❑ Record of pool maintenance and repairs
- ❑ Police or ambulance
- ❑ Prior pool accidents
- ❑ Any alcohol or drug involvement
- ❑ Description of accident details (including date and time)

Page 8 of 8

Workers Compensation Statement Guides

WC Claimant Statement:

- ❑ Name and contact information of employer
- ❑ Excluded employment? Independent contractor? Loaned employee?
- ❑ Wage rate. How paid? Hours per week? Salary? Hourly?
- ❑ Any other employment? Wage rate?
- ❑ Prior work history?
- ❑ Dependents: name and ages
- ❑ Any physical impairments or prior injuries?
- ❑ Are pre-employment physicals or medical examinations given to employees?
- ❑ Date, time, and location of accident or incident
- ❑ Description of accident/incident
- ❑ Weather conditions
- ❑ Were you drinking any alcohol prior to or at the time of the accident/incident?
- ❑ Were you taking any medication at the time of the accident/incident?
- ❑ Were you with anyone at the time of the accident/incident?
- ❑ Any witnesses? Names and contact information
- ❑ Who did you give notice of the accident and injuries? Name and position at employer
- ❑ Any violation of safety regulations?
- ❑ Any third-party involved? Name and details of the third-party involvement
- ❑ Any police? Name of department? Report taken? Any arrests? Citations?
- ❑ Any ambulance? Name of department?
- ❑ Nature and extent of the injuries? Describe in detail. Unconscious?
- ❑ Treatment details:
    - o Treated at the accident scene?
    - o Any immediate medical care? By whom?
    - o Hospital emergency care? Name and address of hospital
    - o Hospital impatient care? Name and address of hospital, admission/discharge dates
    - o Treating physician(s) names and contact information
    - o Any other treating physician(s)?
    - o X-rays taken? Where and by whom? Results of x-rays?
    - o Was any follow-up treatment authorized by your employer?

Page 1 of 3

Workers Compensation Statement Guides (cont.)

- ❑ Any previous accidents, injuries, or illnesses or other pertinent medical history? Provide full details including physician names, hospitals, and treatment dates. Full recovery?
- ❑ Any Second Injury Fund or apportionment issues?
- ❑ Disability to date? Date last worked?
- ❑ Lost time? Actual out-of-pocket wage loss?
- ❑ Return to work? At full wages?
- ❑ Expected date of return to work? Full-time or part-time work?
- ❑ Expected future disability? Any date certain?
- ❑ Any bills or expenses to date? Paid or unpaid? Provide details.
- ❑ If eye claim: prior visual acuity?
- ❑ If heart claim: any unusual stress or strain? Temperature?
- ❑ If fatality claim:
  - o Prior marriages?
  - o Verify prior divorces
  - o Separated for justifiable causes?
  - o Any other dependents?
  - o Obtain death, birth, and marriage certificates
  - o Funeral and other expenses
  - o Length of time between accident and death?

WC Employer Statement:

- ❑ Name and contact information of employer
- ❑ Title, position, and job description with employer
- ❑ Employee personal information
- ❑ Employee position, wage rate, and days worked per week
- ❑ Any physical impairments or prior injuries?
- ❑ Are pre-employment physicals or medical examinations given to employees?
- ❑ Date, time, and location of accident or incident
- ❑ Description of accident/incident
- ❑ Weather conditions
- ❑ Any alcohol or medication involvement?

Page 2 of 3

Workers Compensation Statement Guides (cont.)

- ❑ Any witnesses? Names and contact information
- ❑ To whom did the employee report the accident and injuries? Name and position at employer
- ❑ Any violation of safety regulations?
- ❑ Any third-party involvement? Provide name, contact information, and details of the third-party involvement.
- ❑ Any police? Name of department? Report taken? Any arrests? Citations?
- ❑ Any ambulance? Name of department
- ❑ Nature and extent of the injuries and treatment
- ❑ Any previous accidents, injuries, or illnesses or other pertinent medical history?
- ❑ Any Second Injury Fund or apportionment issues?
- ❑ Lost time? Disability to date? Date last worked?
- ❑ Expected date of return to work? Full-time or part-time work?
- ❑ If heart claim: any unusual stress or strain on the employee? Temperature?

APPENDIX D: ACORD LOSS NOTICE FORMS

The four primary ACORD loss notice forms are shown on the following pages:

These forms are reproduced with permission of ACORD. They are provided solely for educational and reference purposes. Insurance companies must be licensed directly by ACORD to use these forms. ACORD forms are changed periodically to reflect changing legal, industry, and other requirements. Use of unauthorized, outdated forms violates ACORD's proprietary rights. In addition, use of outdated ACORD forms may also violate the law and increases the risk to you of lawsuits arising from the use of the outdated ACORD form.

ACORD®

PROPERTY LOSS NOTICE

DATE (MM/DD/YYYY)

AGENCY	INSURED LOCATION CODE	DATE OF LOSS AND TIME	AM / PM
	PROPERTY / HOME POLICY		
	CARRIER	NAIC CODE	
CONTACT NAME:	POLICY NUMBER		
PHONE (A/C, No, Ext):			
FAX (A/C, No):	FLOOD POLICY		
E-MAIL ADDRESS:	CARRIER	NAIC CODE	
CODE: / SUBCODE:			
AGENCY CUSTOMER ID:	POLICY NUMBER		
	WIND POLICY		
	CARRIER	NAIC CODE	
	POLICY NUMBER		

INSURED

NAME OF INSURED (First, Middle, Last)			INSURED'S MAILING ADDRESS
DATE OF BIRTH	FEIN (if applicable)	MARITAL STATUS	
PRIMARY PHONE # ☐ HOME ☐ BUS ☐ CELL	SECONDARY PHONE # ☐ HOME ☐ BUS ☐ CELL		PRIMARY E-MAIL ADDRESS:
			SECONDARY E-MAIL ADDRESS:
NAME OF SPOUSE (First, Middle, Last) (if applicable)			SPOUSE'S MAILING ADDRESS (if applicable)
DATE OF BIRTH	FEIN (if applicable)	MARITAL STATUS	
PRIMARY PHONE # ☐ HOME ☐ BUS ☐ CELL	SECONDARY PHONE # ☐ HOME ☐ BUS ☐ CELL		PRIMARY E-MAIL ADDRESS:
			SECONDARY E-MAIL ADDRESS:

CONTACT ☐ CONTACT INSURED

NAME OF CONTACT (First, Middle, Last)		CONTACT'S MAILING ADDRESS
PRIMARY PHONE # ☐ HOME ☐ BUS ☐ CELL	SECONDARY PHONE # ☐ HOME ☐ BUS ☐ CELL	
WHEN TO CONTACT		PRIMARY E-MAIL ADDRESS:
		SECONDARY E-MAIL ADDRESS:

LOSS

LOCATION OF LOSS	POLICE OR FIRE DEPARTMENT CONTACTED
STREET:	
CITY, STATE, ZIP:	REPORT NUMBER
COUNTRY:	
DESCRIBE LOCATION OF LOSS IF NOT AT SPECIFIC STREET ADDRESS:	
KIND OF LOSS ☐ FIRE ☐ THEFT ☐ LIGHTNING ☐ HAIL ☐ FLOOD ☐ WIND ☐ ________	PROBABLE AMOUNT ENTIRE LOSS
DESCRIPTION OF LOSS & DAMAGE (Attach ACORD 101, Additional Remarks Schedule, if more space is required)	
REPORTED BY	REPORTED TO

ACORD 1 (2010/02) Page 1 of 3

Appendix D

AGENCY CUSTOMER ID: ______________________

REMARKS (Attach ACORD 101, Additional Remarks Schedule, if more space is required)

APPLICABLE IN ALASKA

A person who knowingly and with intent to injure, defraud, or deceive an insurance company files a claim containing false, incomplete, or misleading information may be prosecuted under state law.

APPLICABLE IN ARIZONA

For your protection, Arizona law requires the following statement to appear on this form. Any person who knowingly presents a false or fraudulent claim for payment of a loss is subject to criminal and civil penalties.

APPLICABLE IN ARKANSAS, DELAWARE, KENTUCKY, LOUISIANA, MAINE, MICHIGAN, NEW JERSEY, NEW MEXICO, NEW YORK, NORTH DAKOTA, PENNSYLVANIA, RHODE ISLAND, SOUTH DAKOTA, TENNESSEE, TEXAS, VIRGINIA, AND WEST VIRGINIA

Any person who knowingly and with intent to defraud any insurance company or another person, files a statement of claim containing any materially false information, or conceals for the purpose of misleading, information concerning any fact, material thereto, commits a fraudulent insurance act, which is a crime, subject to criminal prosecution and [NY: substantial] civil penalties. In LA, ME, TN, and VA, insurance benefits may also be denied.

APPLICABLE IN CALIFORNIA

For your protection, California law requires the following to appear on this form: Any person who knowingly presents a false or fraudulent claim for payment of a loss is guilty of a crime and may be subject to fines and confinement in state prison.

ACORD 1 (2010/02) **Page 2 of 3**

AGENCY CUSTOMER ID: ____________________

APPLICABLE IN COLORADO

It is unlawful to knowingly provide false, incomplete, or misleading facts or information to an insurance company for the purpose of defrauding or attempting to defraud the company. Penalties may include imprisonment, fines, denial of insurance, and civil damages. Any insurance company or agent of an insurance company who knowingly provides false, incomplete, or misleading facts or information to a policy holder or claimant for the purpose of defrauding or attempting to defraud the policy holder or claimant with regard to a settlement or award payable from insurance proceeds shall be reported to the Colorado Division of Insurance within the Department of Regulatory Agencies.

APPLICABLE IN THE DISTRICT OF COLUMBIA

Warning: It is a crime to provide false or misleading information to an insurer for the purpose of defrauding the insurer or any other person. Penalties include imprisonment and/or fines.

APPLICABLE IN FLORIDA

Pursuant to S. 817.234, Florida Statutes, any person who, with the intent to injure, defraud, or deceive any insurer or insured, prepares, presents, or causes to be presented a proof of loss or estimate of cost or repair of damaged property in support of a claim under an insurance policy knowing that the proof of loss or estimate of claim or repairs contains any false, incomplete, or misleading information concerning any fact or thing material to the claim commits a felony of the third degree, punishable as provided in S. 775.082, S. 775.083, or S. 775.084, Florida Statutes.

APPLICABLE IN HAWAII

For your protection, Hawaii law requires you to be informed that presenting a fraudulent claim for payment of a loss or benefit is a crime punishable by fines or imprisonment, or both.

APPLICABLE IN IDAHO

Any person who knowingly and with the intent to injure, defraud, or deceive any insurance company files a statement of claim containing any false, incomplete or misleading information is guilty of a felony.

APPLICABLE IN INDIANA

A person who knowingly and with intent to defraud an insurer files a statement of claim containing any false, incomplete, or misleading information commits a felony.

APPLICABLE IN MARYLAND

Any person who knowingly and willfully presents a false or fraudulent claim for payment of a loss or benefit or who knowingly and willfully presents false information in an application for insurance is guilty of a crime and may be subject to fines and confinement in prison.

APPLICABLE IN MINNESOTA

A person who files a claim with intent to defraud or helps commit a fraud against an insurer is guilty of a crime.

APPLICABLE IN NEVADA

Pursuant to NRS 686A.291, any person who knowingly and willfully files a statement of claim that contains any false, incomplete or misleading information concerning a material fact is guilty of a felony.

APPLICABLE IN NEW HAMPSHIRE

Any person who, with purpose to injure, defraud or deceive any insurance company, files a statement of claim containing any false, incomplete or misleading information is subject to prosecution and punishment for insurance fraud, as provided in RSA 638:20.

APPLICABLE IN OHIO

Any person who, with intent to defraud or knowing that he/she is facilitating a fraud against an insurer, submits an application or files a claim containing a false or deceptive statement is guilty of insurance fraud.

APPLICABLE IN OKLAHOMA

WARNING: Any person who knowingly and with intent to injure, defraud or deceive any insurer, makes any claim for the proceeds of an insurance policy containing any false, incomplete or misleading information is guilty of a felony.

APPLICABLE IN WASHINGTON

It is a crime to knowingly provide false, incomplete, or misleading information to an insurance company for the purpose of defrauding the company. Penalties include imprisonment, fines and denial of insurance benefits.

ACORD 1 (2010/02) Page 3 of 3

ACORD®

AUTOMOBILE LOSS NOTICE

DATE (MM/DD/YYYY)

AGENCY	INSURED LOCATION CODE	DATE OF LOSS AND TIME AM / PM
	CARRIER	NAIC CODE
	POLICY NUMBER	
CONTACT NAME:	POLICY TYPE	
PHONE (A/C, No, Ext):		
FAX (A/C, No):		
E-MAIL ADDRESS:		
CODE: SUBCODE:		
AGENCY CUSTOMER ID:		

INSURED

NAME OF INSURED (First, Middle, Last)			INSURED'S MAILING ADDRESS
DATE OF BIRTH	FEIN (if applicable)	MARITAL STATUS	
PRIMARY PHONE # ☐ HOME ☐ BUS ☐ CELL	SECONDARY PHONE # ☐ HOME ☐ BUS ☐ CELL		PRIMARY E-MAIL ADDRESS:
			SECONDARY E-MAIL ADDRESS:

CONTACT ☐ CONTACT INSURED

NAME OF CONTACT (First, Middle, Last)		CONTACT'S MAILING ADDRESS
PRIMARY PHONE # ☐ HOME ☐ BUS ☐ CELL	SECONDARY PHONE # ☐ HOME ☐ BUS ☐ CELL	
WHEN TO CONTACT		PRIMARY E-MAIL ADDRESS:
		SECONDARY E-MAIL ADDRESS:

LOSS

LOCATION OF LOSS	POLICE OR FIRE DEPARTMENT CONTACTED
STREET:	
CITY, STATE, ZIP:	REPORT NUMBER
COUNTRY:	
DESCRIBE LOCATION OF LOSS IF NOT AT SPECIFIC STREET ADDRESS:	
DESCRIPTION OF ACCIDENT (Attach ACORD 101, Additional Remarks Schedule, if more space is required)	

INSURED VEHICLE

VEH #	YEAR	MAKE:	BODY TYPE:	PLATE NUMBER	STATE
		MODEL:	V.I.N.:		

OWNER'S NAME AND ADDRESS ☐ (Check if same as insured)	PRIMARY PHONE # ☐ HOME ☐ BUS ☐ CELL	SECONDARY PHONE # ☐ HOME ☐ BUS ☐ CELL
	PRIMARY E-MAIL ADDRESS:	
	SECONDARY E-MAIL ADDRESS:	
DRIVER'S NAME AND ADDRESS ☐ (Check if same as owner)	PRIMARY PHONE # ☐ HOME ☐ BUS ☐ CELL	SECONDARY PHONE # ☐ HOME ☐ BUS ☐ CELL
	PRIMARY E-MAIL ADDRESS:	
	SECONDARY E-MAIL ADDRESS:	

RELATION TO INSURED (Employee, family, etc.)	DATE OF BIRTH	DRIVER'S LICENSE NUMBER	STATE	PURPOSE OF USE	USED WITH PERMISSION? (Y/N)

DESCRIBE DAMAGE

1. WAS A STANDARD CHILD PASSENGER RESTRAINT SYSTEM (CHILD SEAT) INSTALLED IN THE VEHICLE AT THE TIME OF THE ACCIDENT?	Y / N
2. WAS THE CHILD PASSENGER RESTRAINT SYSTEM (CHILD SEAT) IN USE BY A CHILD DURING THE TIME OF THE ACCIDENT?	Y / N
3. DID THE CHILD PASSENGER RESTRAINT SYSTEM (CHILD SEAT) SUSTAIN A LOSS AT THE TIME OF THE ACCIDENT?	Y / N

ESTIMATE AMOUNT:	WHERE CAN VEHICLE BE SEEN?:	WHEN CAN VEHICLE BE SEEN?:
OTHER INSURANCE ON VEHICLE - CARRIER:		POLICY NUMBER:

ACORD 2 (2010/01) Page 1 of 4

Appendix D

AGENCY CUSTOMER ID: ______

OTHER VEHICLE / PROPERTY DAMAGED — NON - VEHICLE? ☐

VEH #	YEAR	MAKE: / MODEL:	BODY TYPE: / V.I.N.:	PLATE NUMBER	STATE

DESCRIBE PROPERTY (Other Than Vehicle)	OTHER VEH/PROP INS? (Y/N) ☐

CARRIER OR AGENCY NAME	NAIC CODE	POLICY NUMBER

OWNER'S NAME AND ADDRESS

PRIMARY PHONE # ☐ HOME ☐ BUS ☐ CELL — SECONDARY PHONE # ☐ HOME ☐ BUS ☐ CELL

PRIMARY E-MAIL ADDRESS:

SECONDARY E-MAIL ADDRESS:

DRIVER'S NAME AND ADDRESS ☐ (Check if same as owner)

PRIMARY PHONE # ☐ HOME ☐ BUS ☐ CELL — SECONDARY PHONE # ☐ HOME ☐ BUS ☐ CELL

PRIMARY E-MAIL ADDRESS:

SECONDARY E-MAIL ADDRESS:

DESCRIBE DAMAGE

ESTIMATE AMOUNT	WHERE CAN DAMAGE BE SEEN?	

INJURED

NAME & ADDRESS	PHONE (A/C, No)	PED	INS VEH	OTH VEH	AGE	EXTENT OF INJURY
		☐	☐	☐		
		☐	☐	☐		
		☐	☐	☐		
		☐	☐	☐		

WITNESSES OR PASSENGERS

NAME & ADDRESS	PHONE (A/C, No)	INS VEH	OTH VEH	OTHER (Specify)
		☐	☐	
		☐	☐	
		☐	☐	

REPORTED BY	REPORTED TO

REMARKS (Attach ACORD 101, Additional Remarks Schedule, if more space is required)

ACORD 2 (2010/01) Page 2 of 4

AGENCY CUSTOMER ID: ______________

APPLICABLE IN ALASKA

A person who knowingly and with intent to injure, defraud, or deceive an insurance company files a claim containing false, incomplete, or misleading information may be prosecuted under state law.

APPLICABLE IN ARIZONA

For your protection, Arizona law requires the following statement to appear on this form. Any person who knowingly presents a false or fraudulent claim for payment of a loss is subject to criminal and civil penalties.

APPLICABLE IN ARKANSAS, DELAWARE, KENTUCKY, LOUISIANA, MAINE, MICHIGAN, NEW JERSEY, NEW MEXICO, NORTH DAKOTA, PENNSYLVANIA, RHODE ISLAND, SOUTH DAKOTA, TENNESSEE, TEXAS, VIRGINIA, AND WEST VIRGINIA

Any person who knowingly and with intent to defraud any insurance company or another person, files a statement of claim containing any materially false information, or conceals for the purpose of misleading, information concerning any fact, material thereto, commits a fraudulent insurance act, which is a crime, subject to criminal prosecution and civil penalties. In LA, ME, TN, and VA, insurance benefits may also be denied.

APPLICABLE IN CALIFORNIA

For your protection, California law requires the following to appear on this form: Any person who knowingly presents a false or fraudulent claim for payment of a loss is guilty of a crime and may be subject to fines and confinement in state prison.

APPLICABLE IN COLORADO

It is unlawful to knowingly provide false, incomplete, or misleading facts or information to an insurance company for the purpose of defrauding or attempting to defraud the company. Penalties may include imprisonment, fines, denial of insurance, and civil damages. Any insurance company or agent of an insurance company who knowingly provides false, incomplete, or misleading facts or information to a policy holder or claimant for the purpose of defrauding or attempting to defraud the policy holder or claimant with regard to a settlement or award payable from insurance proceeds shall be reported to the Colorado Division of Insurance within the Department of Regulatory Agencies.

APPLICABLE IN THE DISTRICT OF COLUMBIA

Warning: It is a crime to provide false or misleading information to an insurer for the purpose of defrauding the insurer or any other person. Penalties include imprisonment and/or fines.

APPLICABLE IN FLORIDA

Pursuant to S. 817.234, Florida Statutes, any person who, with the intent to injure, defraud, or deceive any insurer or insured, prepares, presents, or causes to be presented a proof of loss or estimate of cost or repair of damaged property in support of a claim under an insurance policy knowing that the proof of loss or estimate of claim or repairs contains any false, incomplete, or misleading information concerning any fact or thing material to the claim commits a felony of the third degree, punishable as provided in S. 775.082, S. 775.083, or S. 775.084, Florida Statutes.

APPLICABLE IN HAWAII

For your protection, Hawaii law requires you to be informed that presenting a fraudulent claim for payment of a loss or benefit is a crime punishable by fines or imprisonment, or both.

APPLICABLE IN IDAHO

Any person who knowingly and with the intent to injure, defraud, or deceive any insurance company files a statement of claim containing any false, incomplete or misleading information is guilty of a felony.

APPLICABLE IN INDIANA

A person who knowingly and with intent to defraud an insurer files a statement of claim containing any false, incomplete, or misleading information commits a felony.

APPLICABLE IN MARYLAND

Any person who knowingly and willfully presents a false or fraudulent claim for payment of a loss or benefit or who knowingly and willfully presents false information in an application for insurance is guilty of a crime and may be subject to fines and confinement in prison.

APPLICABLE IN MINNESOTA

A person who files a claim with intent to defraud or helps commit a fraud against an insurer is guilty of a crime.

ACORD 2 (2010/01) Page 3 of 4

AGENCY CUSTOMER ID: ______________

APPLICABLE IN NEVADA

Pursuant to NRS 686A.291, any person who knowingly and willfully files a statement of claim that contains any false, incomplete or misleading information concerning a material fact is guilty of a felony.

APPLICABLE IN NEW HAMPSHIRE

Any person who, with purpose to injure, defraud or deceive any insurance company, files a statement of claim containing any false, incomplete or misleading information is subject to prosecution and punishment for insurance fraud, as provided in RSA 638:20.

APPLICABLE IN NEW YORK

Any person who knowingly and with intent to defraud any insurance company or other person files an application for commercial insurance or a statement of claim for any commercial or personal insurance benefits containing any materially false information, or conceals for the purpose of misleading, information concerning any fact material thereto, and any person who in connection with such application or claim knowingly makes or knowingly assists, abets, solicits or conspires with another to make a false report of the theft, destruction, damage or conversion of any motor vehicle to a law enforcement agency, the Department of Motor Vehicles or an insurance company, commits a fraudulent insurance act, which is a crime, and shall also be subject to a civil penalty not to exceed five thousand dollars and the value of the subject motor vehicle or stated claim for each violation.

APPLICABLE IN OHIO

Any person who, with intent to defraud or knowing that he/she is facilitating a fraud against an insurer, submits an application or files a claim containing a false or deceptive statement is guilty of insurance fraud.

APPLICABLE IN OKLAHOMA

WARNING: Any person who knowingly and with intent to injure, defraud or deceive any insurer, makes any claim for the proceeds of an insurance policy containing any false, incomplete or misleading information is guilty of a felony.

APPLICABLE IN WASHINGTON

It is a crime to knowingly provide false, incomplete, or misleading information to an insurance company for the purpose of defrauding the company. Penalties include imprisonment, fines and denial of insurance benefits.

ACORD 2 (2010/01) Page 4 of 4

ACORD®

GENERAL LIABILITY NOTICE OF OCCURRENCE / CLAIM

DATE (MM/DD/YYYY)

AGENCY	INSURED LOCATION CODE	DATE OF LOSS AND TIME	AM / PM
	CARRIER	NAIC CODE	
	POLICY NUMBER		
CONTACT NAME:			
PHONE (A/C, No, Ext):			
FAX (A/C, No):			
E-MAIL ADDRESS:			
CODE: SUBCODE:			
AGENCY CUSTOMER ID:			

INSURED

NAME OF INSURED (First, Middle, Last)			INSURED'S MAILING ADDRESS
DATE OF BIRTH	FEIN (if applicable)		
PRIMARY PHONE # ☐ HOME ☐ BUS ☐ CELL	SECONDARY PHONE # ☐ HOME ☐ BUS ☐ CELL		PRIMARY E-MAIL ADDRESS:
			SECONDARY E-MAIL ADDRESS:

CONTACT ☐ CONTACT INSURED

NAME OF CONTACT (First, Middle, Last)		CONTACT'S MAILING ADDRESS
PRIMARY PHONE # ☐ HOME ☐ BUS ☐ CELL	SECONDARY PHONE # ☐ HOME ☐ BUS ☐ CELL	
WHEN TO CONTACT		PRIMARY E-MAIL ADDRESS:
		SECONDARY E-MAIL ADDRESS:

OCCURRENCE

LOCATION OF OCCURRENCE	POLICE OR FIRE DEPARTMENT CONTACTED
STREET:	
CITY, STATE, ZIP:	REPORT NUMBER
COUNTRY:	
DESCRIBE LOCATION OF OCCURRENCE IF NOT AT SPECIFIC STREET ADDRESS:	
DESCRIPTION OF OCCURRENCE (Attach ACORD 101, Additional Remarks Schedule, if more space is required)	

TYPE OF LIABILITY

PREMISES: INSURED IS ☐ OWNER ☐ TENANT ☐	TYPE OF PREMISES	
OWNER'S NAME & ADDRESS (If not insured)	PRIMARY PHONE # ☐ HOME ☐ BUS ☐ CELL	SECONDARY PHONE # ☐ HOME ☐ BUS ☐ CELL
	PRIMARY E-MAIL ADDRESS:	
	SECONDARY E-MAIL ADDRESS:	
PRODUCTS: INSURED IS ☐ MANUFACTURER ☐ VENDOR ☐	TYPE OF PRODUCT	
MANUFACTURER'S NAME & ADDRESS (If not insured)	PRIMARY PHONE # ☐ HOME ☐ BUS ☐ CELL	SECONDARY PHONE # ☐ HOME ☐ BUS ☐ CELL
	PRIMARY E-MAIL ADDRESS:	
	SECONDARY E-MAIL ADDRESS:	
WHERE CAN PRODUCT BE SEEN?		

ACORD 3 (2010/02) Page 1 of 4

Appendix D

AGENCY CUSTOMER ID: ______________________

INJURED / PROPERTY DAMAGED

NAME & ADDRESS (Injured/Owner)		EMPLOYER'S NAME & ADDRESS	
PRIMARY PHONE # ☐ HOME ☐ BUS ☐ CELL	SECONDARY PHONE # ☐ HOME ☐ BUS ☐ CELL	PRIMARY PHONE # ☐ HOME ☐ BUS ☐ CELL	SECONDARY PHONE # ☐ HOME ☐ BUS ☐ CELL
PRIMARY E-MAIL ADDRESS:		PRIMARY E-MAIL ADDRESS:	
SECONDARY E-MAIL ADDRESS:		SECONDARY E-MAIL ADDRESS:	
AGE / SEX / OCCUPATION		DESCRIBE INJURY	
WHERE TAKEN		WHAT WAS INJURED DOING?	

DESCRIBE PROPERTY (Type, model, etc.)	ESTIMATE AMOUNT	WHERE CAN PROPERTY BE SEEN?

WITNESSES

NAME AND ADDRESS	PRIMARY PHONE # ☐ HOME ☐ BUS ☐ CELL	SECONDARY PHONE # ☐ HOME ☐ BUS ☐ CELL
	PRIMARY E-MAIL ADDRESS:	
	SECONDARY E-MAIL ADDRESS:	
NAME AND ADDRESS	PRIMARY PHONE # ☐ HOME ☐ BUS ☐ CELL	SECONDARY PHONE # ☐ HOME ☐ BUS ☐ CELL
	PRIMARY E-MAIL ADDRESS:	
	SECONDARY E-MAIL ADDRESS:	
NAME AND ADDRESS	PRIMARY PHONE # ☐ HOME ☐ BUS ☐ CELL	SECONDARY PHONE # ☐ HOME ☐ BUS ☐ CELL
	PRIMARY E-MAIL ADDRESS:	
	SECONDARY E-MAIL ADDRESS:	

REMARKS (Attach ACORD 101, Additional Remarks Schedule, if more space is required)

REPORTED BY	REPORTED TO

ACORD 3 (2010/02) Page 2 of 4

AGENCY CUSTOMER ID: ______________________

APPLICABLE IN ALASKA

A person who knowingly and with intent to injure, defraud, or deceive an insurance company files a claim containing false, incomplete, or misleading information may be prosecuted under state law.

APPLICABLE IN ARIZONA

For your protection, Arizona law requires the following statement to appear on this form. Any person who knowingly presents a false or fraudulent claim for payment of a loss is subject to criminal and civil penalties.

APPLICABLE IN ARKANSAS, DELAWARE, KENTUCKY, LOUISIANA, MAINE, MICHIGAN, NEW JERSEY, NEW MEXICO, NEW YORK, NORTH DAKOTA, PENNSYLVANIA, RHODE ISLAND, SOUTH DAKOTA, TENNESSEE, TEXAS, VIRGINIA, AND WEST VIRGINIA

Any person who knowingly and with intent to defraud any insurance company or another person, files a statement of claim containing any materially false information, or conceals for the purpose of misleading, information concerning any fact, material thereto, commits a fraudulent insurance act, which is a crime, subject to criminal prosecution and [NY: substantial] civil penalties. In LA, ME, TN, and VA, insurance benefits may also be denied.

APPLICABLE IN CALIFORNIA

For your protection, California law requires the following to appear on this form: Any person who knowingly presents a false or fraudulent claim for payment of a loss is guilty of a crime and may be subject to fines and confinement in state prison.

APPLICABLE IN COLORADO

It is unlawful to knowingly provide false, incomplete, or misleading facts or information to an insurance company for the purpose of defrauding or attempting to defraud the company. Penalties may include imprisonment, fines, denial of insurance, and civil damages. Any insurance company or agent of an insurance company who knowingly provides false, incomplete, or misleading facts or information to a policy holder or claimant for the purpose of defrauding or attempting to defraud the policy holder or claimant with regard to a settlement or award payable from insurance proceeds shall be reported to the Colorado Division of Insurance within the Department of Regulatory Agencies.

APPLICABLE IN THE DISTRICT OF COLUMBIA

Warning: It is a crime to provide false or misleading information to an insurer for the purpose of defrauding the insurer or any other person. Penalties include imprisonment and/or fines.

APPLICABLE IN FLORIDA

Pursuant to S. 817.234, Florida Statutes, any person who, with the intent to injure, defraud, or deceive any insurer or insured, prepares, presents, or causes to be presented a proof of loss or estimate of cost or repair of damaged property in support of a claim under an insurance policy knowing that the proof of loss or estimate of claim or repairs contains any false, incomplete, or misleading information concerning any fact or thing material to the claim commits a felony of the third degree, punishable as provided in S. 775.082, S. 775.083, or S. 775.084, Florida Statutes.

APPLICABLE IN HAWAII

For your protection, Hawaii law requires you to be informed that presenting a fraudulent claim for payment of a loss or benefit is a crime punishable by fines or imprisonment, or both.

APPLICABLE IN IDAHO

Any person who knowingly and with the intent to injure, defraud, or deceive any insurance company files a statement of claim containing any false, incomplete or misleading information is guilty of a felony.

APPLICABLE IN INDIANA

A person who knowingly and with intent to defraud an insurer files a statement of claim containing any false, incomplete, or misleading information commits a felony.

APPLICABLE IN MARYLAND

Any person who knowingly and willfully presents a false or fraudulent claim for payment of a loss or benefit or who knowingly and willfully presents false information in an application for insurance is guilty of a crime and may be subject to fines and confinement in prison.

APPLICABLE IN MINNESOTA

A person who files a claim with intent to defraud or helps commit a fraud against an insurer is guilty of a crime.

ACORD 3 (2010/02) Page 3 of 4

AGENCY CUSTOMER ID: ______________________

APPLICABLE IN NEVADA

Pursuant to NRS 686A.291, any person who knowingly and willfully files a statement of claim that contains any false, incomplete or misleading information concerning a material fact is guilty of a felony.

APPLICABLE IN NEW HAMPSHIRE

Any person who, with purpose to injure, defraud or deceive any insurance company, files a statement of claim containing any false, incomplete or misleading information is subject to prosecution and punishment for insurance fraud, as provided in RSA 638:20.

APPLICABLE IN OHIO

Any person who, with intent to defraud or knowing that he/she is facilitating a fraud against an insurer, submits an application or files a claim containing a false or deceptive statement is guilty of insurance fraud.

APPLICABLE IN OKLAHOMA

WARNING: Any person who knowingly and with intent to injure, defraud or deceive any insurer, makes any claim for the proceeds of an insurance policy containing any false, incomplete or misleading information is guilty of a felony.

APPLICABLE IN WASHINGTON

It is a crime to knowingly provide false, incomplete, or misleading information to an insurance company for the purpose of defrauding the company. Penalties include imprisonment, fines and denial of insurance benefits.

ACORD® WORKERS COMPENSATION - FIRST REPORT OF INJURY OR ILLNESS

EMPLOYER (NAME & ADDRESS INCL ZIP)	CARRIER / ADMINISTRATOR CLAIM NUMBER *	REPORT PURPOSE CODE *
	JURISDICTION *	JURISDICTION LOG NUMBER *
	INSURED REPORT NUMBER	OSHA CASE NUMBER
INDUSTRY CODE / EMPLOYER FEIN	EMPLOYER'S LOCATION ADDRESS (IF DIFFERENT)	LOCATION #: / PHONE #

CARRIER / CLAIMS ADMINISTRATOR

CARRIER (NAME AND ADDRESS)	POLICY PERIOD ___ TO ___	CLAIMS ADMINISTRATOR (NAME AND ADDRESS)
PHONE (A/C, No, Ext):	CHECK IF APPROPRIATE: ☐ SELF INSURANCE	PHONE (A/C, No, Ext):
CARRIER FEIN *	POLICY / SELF-INSURED NUMBER	ADMINISTRATOR FEIN *
AGENT NAME:	AGENT CODE NUMBER:	

EMPLOYEE / WAGE

NAME (LAST, FIRST, MIDDLE)	DATE OF BIRTH	SOCIAL SECURITY NUMBER	DATE HIRED	STATE OF HIRE
ADDRESS (INCL ZIP)	SEX: ☐ MALE ☐ FEMALE ☐ UNKNOWN	MARITAL STATUS: ☐ UNMARRIED/SINGLE/DIVORCED ☐ MARRIED ☐ SEPAR ATED ☐ UNKNOWN	OCCUPATION / JOB TITLE	
E-MAIL ADDRESS:			EMPLOYMENT STATUS	
PHONE	# OF DEPENDENTS		NCCI CLASS CODE *	
RATE PER: ☐ DAY ☐ WEEK ☐ MONTH OTHER:	AVERAGE WEEKLY WAGES	# DAYS WORKED / WEEK	FULL PAY FOR DAY OF INJURY? (Y / N) ☐ DID SALARY CONTINUE? (Y / N) ☐	

OCCURRENCE / TREATMENT

TIME EMPLOYEE BEGAN WORK ☐ AM ☐ PM	DATE OF INJURY / ILLNESS	TIME OF OCCURRENCE ☐ AM ☐ PM ☐ CANNOT BE DETERMINED	LAST WORK DATE	DATE EMPLOYER NOTIFIED	DATE DISABILITY BEGAN
CONTACT NAME		TYPE OF INJURY / ILLNESS		PART OF BODY AFFECTED	
PHONE (A/C, No, Ext):					
DID INJURY / ILLNESS EXPOSURE OCCUR ON EMPLOYER'S PREMISES? (Y / N) ☐		TYPE OF INJURY / ILLNESS CODE *		PART OF BODY AFFECTED CODE *	

DEPARTMENT OR LOCATION WHERE ACCIDENT OR ILLNESS EXPOSURE OCCURRED	ALL EQUIPMENT, MATERIALS, OR CHEMICALS EMPLOYEE WAS USING WHEN ACCIDENT OR ILLNESS EXPOSURE OCCURRED
SPECIFIC ACTIVITY THE EMPLOYEE WAS ENGAGED IN WHEN THE ACCIDENT OR ILLNESS EXPOSURE OCCURRED	WORK PROCESS THE EMPLOYEE WAS ENGAGED IN WHEN ACCIDENT OR ILLNESS EXPOSURE OCCURRED
HOW INJURY OR ILLNESS / ABNORMAL HEALTH CONDITION OCCURRED. DESCRIBE THE SEQUENCE OF EVENTS AND INCLUDE ANY OBJECTS OR SUBSTANCES THAT DIRECTLY INJURED THE EMPLOYEE OR MADE THE EMPLOYEE ILL	CAUSE OF INJURY CODE *

DATE RETURN(ED) TO WORK	IF FATAL, GIVE DATE OF DEATH	WERE SAFEGUARDS OR SAFETY EQUIPMENT PROVIDED? (Y / N) ☐ WERE THEY USED? (Y / N) ☐	
PHYSICIAN / HEALTH CARE PROVIDER (NAME & ADDRESS)		HOSPITAL OR OFFSITE TREATMENT (NAME & ADDRESS)	INITIAL TREATMENT: ☐ NO MEDICAL TREATMENT ☐ MINOR: BY EMPLOYER ☐ MINOR CLINIC / HOSP ☐ EMERGENCY CARE ☐ OVERNIGHT HOSPITALIZATION ☐ FUTURE MAJOR MEDICAL/ LOST TIME ANTICIPATED
WITNESS NAME: PHONE (A/C, No, Ext):		WITNESS NAME: PHONE (A/C, No, Ext):	
DATE ADMINISTRATOR NOTIFIED	DATE PREPARED	PREPARER'S NAME / TITLE	PHONE NUMBER

ACORD 4 (2010/02) Page 1 of 5

IAIABC 1A-1 (1/1/02)

APPLICABLE IN ALASKA

A person who knowingly and with intent to injure, defraud, or deceive an insurance company files a claim containing false, incomplete, or misleading information may be prosecuted under state law.

APPLICABLE IN ARIZONA

For your protection, Arizona law requires the following statement to appear on this form. Any person who knowingly presents a false or fraudulent claim for payment of a loss is subject to criminal and civil penalties.

APPLICABLE IN ARKANSAS

Any person or entity who willfully and knowingly makes any material false statement or representation or who willfully and knowingly omits or conceals any material information, or who willfully and knowingly employs any device, scheme or artifice for the purpose of obtaining any benefit or payment, or for the purpose of defeating or wrongfully decreasing any claim for benefit or payment or obtaining or avoiding workers' compensation coverage or avoiding payment of the proper insurance premium (or who aids and abets for either said purpose), under this chapter shall be guilty of a Class D. felony.

APPLICABLE IN CALIFORNIA

Any person who makes or causes to be made any knowingly false or fraudulent material statement or material representation for the purpose of obtaining or denying workers compensation benefits or payments is guilty of a felony.

APPLICABLE IN COLORADO

It is unlawful to knowingly provide false, incomplete, or misleading facts or information to an insurance company for the purpose of defrauding or attempting to defraud the company. Penalties may include imprisonment, fines, denial of insurance, and civil damages. Any insurance company or agent of an insurance company who knowingly provides false, incomplete, or misleading facts or information to a policy holder or claimant for the purpose of defrauding or attempting to defraud the policy holder or claimant with regard to a settlement or award payable from insurance proceeds shall be reported to the Colorado Division of Insurance within the Department of Regulatory Agencies.

APPLICABLE IN CONNECTICUT

This form must be completed in its entirety. Any person who intentionally misrepresents or intentionally fails to disclose any material fact related to a claimed injury may be guilty of a felony.

APPLICABLE IN DELAWARE AND OKLAHOMA

Any person who knowingly and with intent to injure, defraud, or deceive any Insurer, files a statement of claim containing any false, incomplete or misleading information is guilty of a felony. The lack of such a statement shall not constitute a defense against prosecution under this section. *Delaware Statutes Regulations: Del #C Section 913(B)

APPLICABLE IN THE DISTRICT OF COLUMBIA

Warning: It is a crime to provide false or misleading information to an insurer for the purpose of defrauding the insurer or any other person. Penalties include imprisonment and/or fines.

APPLICABLE IN FLORIDA

Pursuant to S. 817.234, Florida Statutes, any person who, with the intent to injure, defraud, or deceive any insurer or insured, prepares, presents, or causes to be presented a proof of loss or estimate of cost or repair of damaged property in support of a claim under an insurance policy knowing that the proof of loss or estimate of claim or repairs contains any false, incomplete, or misleading information concerning any fact or thing material to the claim commits a felony of the third degree, punishable as provided in S. 775.082, S. 775.083, or S. 775.084, Florida Statutes.

APPLICABLE IN HAWAII

For your protection, Hawaii law requires you to be informed that presenting a fraudulent claim for payment of a loss or benefit is a crime punishable by fines or imprisonment, or both.

APPLICABLE IN IDAHO

Any person who knowingly and with the intent to injure, Defraud, or Deceive any Insurance Company Files a Statement of Claim Containing any False, Incomplete or Misleading information is Guilty of a Felony.

EMPLOYEE SIGNATURE: ______________________________

ACORD 4 (2010/02) **Page 2 of 5**

APPLICABLE IN INDIANA

A person who knowingly and with intent to defraud an insurer files a statement of claim containing any false, incomplete, or misleading information commits a felony.

APPLICABLE IN KENTUCKY, LOUISIANA, MAINE, MICHIGAN, NEW JERSEY, NEW MEXICO, NEW YORK, NORTH DAKOTA, PENNSYLVANIA, RHODE ISLAND, SOUTH DAKOTA, VIRGINIA AND WEST VIRGINIA

Any person who knowingly and with intent to defraud any insurance company or another person files a statement of claim containing any materially false information, or conceals for the purpose of misleading, information concerning any fact material thereto, commits a fraudulent insurance act, which is a crime, and subjects the person to criminal and [NY: substantial] civil penalties. In LA, ME and VA, insurance benefits may also be denied.

APPLICABLE IN MARYLAND

Any person who knowingly and willfully presents a false or fraudulent claim for payment of a loss or benefit or who knowingly and willfully presents false information in an application for insurance is guilty of a crime and may be subject to fines and confinement in prison.

APPLICABLE IN MINNESOTA

A person who files a claim with intent to defraud or helps commit a fraud against an insurer is guilty of a crime.

APPLICABLE IN NEVADA

Pursuant to NRS 686A.291, any person who knowingly and willfully files a statement of claim that contains any false, incomplete or misleading information concerning a material fact is guilty of a felony.

APPLICABLE IN NEW HAMPSHIRE

Any person who, with purpose to injure, defraud or deceive any insurance company, files a statement of claim containing any false, incomplete or misleading information is subject to prosecution and punishment for insurance fraud, as provided in RSA 638:20.

APPLICABLE IN OHIO

Any person who, with intent to defraud or knowing that he/she is facilitating a fraud against an insurer, submits an application or files a claim containing a false or deceptive statement is guilty of insurance fraud.

APPLICABLE IN TENNESSEE

It is a crime to knowingly provide false, incomplete or misleading information to any party to a workers compensation transaction for the purpose of committing fraud. Penalties include imprisonment, fines and denial of insurance benefits.

APPLICABLE IN TEXAS

Any person who knowingly presents a false or fraudulent claim for the payment of a loss is guilty of a crime and may be subject to fines and confinement in state prison.

APPLICABLE IN UTAH

Any person who knowingly presents false or fraudulent underwriting information, files or causes to be filed a false or fraudulent claim for disability compensation or medical benefits, or submits a false or fraudulent report or billing for health care fees or other professional services is guilty of a crime and may be subject to fines and confinement in state prison.

APPLICABLE IN WASHINGTON

It is a crime to knowingly provide false, incomplete, or misleading information to an insurance company for the purpose of defrauding the company. Penalties include imprisonment, fines and denial of insurance benefits.

EMPLOYEE SIGNATURE: ________________________________

ACORD 4 (2010/02) **Page 3 of 5**

EMPLOYER'S INSTRUCTIONS

DO NOT ENTER DATA IN FIELDS MARKED *

DATES:
Enter all dates in MM/DD/YY format.

INDUSTRY CODE:
This is the code which represents the nature of the employer's business which is contained in the Standard Industrial Classification Manual or the North American Industry Classification System published by the Federal Office of Management and Budget.

OSHA CASE NUMBER:
Transfer the case number from the OSHA 300 log after you record the case there.

CARRIER:
The licensed business entity issuing a contract of insurance and assuming financial responsibility on behalf of the employer of the claimant.

CLAIMS ADMINISTRATOR:
Enter the name of the carrier, third party administrator, state fund, or self-insured responsible for administering the claim.

AGENT NAME & CODE NUMBER:
Enter the name of your insurance agent and his/her code number if known. This information can be found on your insurance policy.

OCCUPATION / JOB TITLE:
This is the primary occupation of the claimant at the time of the accident or exposure.

EMPLOYMENT STATUS:
Indicate the employee's work status. The valid choices are:

Full-Time	On Strike	Unknown	Volunteer
Part-Time	Disabled	Apprenticeship Full-Time	Seasonal
Not Employed	Retired	Apprenticeship Part-Time	Piece Worker

DATE DISABILITY BEGAN:
The first day on which the claimant originally lost time from work due to the occupation injury or disease or as otherwise deigned by statute.

CONTACT NAME / PHONE NUMBER:
Enter the name of the individual at the employer's premises to be contacted for additional information.

TYPE OF INJURY / ILLNESS:
Briefly describe the nature of the injury or illness, (eg. Lacerations to the forearm).

PART OF BODY AFFECTED:
Indicate the part of body affected by the injury/illness, (eg. Right forearm, lower back).

DEPARTMENT OR LOCATION WHERE ACCIDENT OR ILLNESS EXPOSURE OCCURRED:
(eg. Maintenance Department or Client's office at 452 Monroe St., Washington, DC 26210)

If the accident or illness exposure did not occur on the employer's premises, enter address or location. Be specific.

ACORD 4 (2010/02) **Page 4 of 5**

ALL EQUIPMENT, MATERIAL OR CHEMICALS EMPLOYEE WAS USING WHEN ACCIDENT OR ILLNESS EXPOSURE OCCURRED:

(eg. Acetylene cutting torch, metal plate)

List all of the equipment, materials, and/or chemicals the employee was using, applying, handling or operating when the injury or illness occurred. Be specific, for example: decorator's scaffolding, electric sander, paintbrush, and paint.

Enter "NA" for not applicable if no equipment, materials, or chemicals were being used. NOTE: The items listed do not have to be directly involved in the employee's injury or illness.

SPECIFIC ACTIVITY THE EMPLOYEE WAS ENGAGED IN WHEN THE ACCIDENT OR ILLNESS EXPOSURE OCCURRED:

(eg. Cutting metal plate for flooring)

Describe the specific activity the employee was engaged in when the accident or illness exposure occurred, such as sanding ceiling woodwork in preparation for painting.

WORK PROCESS THE EMPLOYEE WAS ENGAGED IN WHEN ACCIDENT OR ILLNESS EXPOSURE OCCURRED:

Describe the work process the employee was engaged in when the accident or illness exposure occurred, such as building maintenance. Enter "NA" for not applicable if employee was not engaged in a work process (eg. walking along a hallway).

HOW INJURY OR ILLNESS / ABNORMAL HEALTH CONDITION OCCURRED. DESCRIBE THE SEQUENCE OF EVENTS AND INCLUDE ANY OBJECTS OR SUBSTANCES THAT DIRECTLY INJURED THE EMPLOYEE OR MADE THE EMPLOYEE ILL:

(Worker stepped back to inspect work and slipped on some scrap metal. As worker fell, worker brushed against the hot metal.)

Describe how the injury or illness / abnormal health condition occurred. Include the sequence of events and name any objects or substance that directly injured the employee or made the employee ill. For example: Worker stepped to the edge of the scaffolding to inspect work, lost balance and fell six feet to the floor. The worker's right wrist was broken in the fall.

DATE RETURN(ED) TO WORK:

Enter the date following the most recent disability period on which the employee returned to work.

ACORD 4 (2010/02) **Page 5 of 5**

Appendix E: Ethics in Claims Handling

What drives a person to be unethical? Is it money? Greed? Stupidity? There are different ways of being unethical, and being unethical doesn't necessarily mean there is a financial gain. People may be unethical because they are angry and use their control within their job responsibilities to express their anger. This situation creates a poor reputation for the insurance industry.

There have been many books and articles written about ethics in the insurance industry. It is such an important topic, yet oftentimes does not get the attention it should, particularly in a real-world work environment. Attention to ethics needs to be companywide. The hiring process for adjuster positions should always include questions concerning ethical issues, and a copy of the firm's ethical guidelines distributed to every employee.

It's very easy to develop a companywide ethics code of conduct, but implementation is something else. If senior management treats the ethics code as simply a procedural document, employees will never embrace it as an integral part of their daily work activities. Most large companies have a code of conduct, which includes ethics-related topics; however, many employees, including officers, may not even know the content of the code, and more importantly, do not promote it within the organization.

Adherence to an ethical standard always starts at the top of the hierarchy of an organization. When senior management embraces a comprehensive code of conduct, which includes a strict emphasis on strong ethical behavior, line management will embrace it as well. If line management embraces the code of conduct, subordinate employees will do likewise.

Appendix E examines some industry codes of conduct, provides examples of unethical behavior, discusses the lack of trust of the public toward the insurance industry, and suggests ways to improve this image.

Industry Ethical Codes of Conduct

The most prestigious insurance designation in the insurance industry is the Chartered Property Casualty Underwriter (CPCU) designation, which requires passing rigorous undergraduate and graduate level examinations, meeting experience requirements, and agreeing to be bound by a strict code of professional ethics. The CPCU Society has adopted a very comprehensive code of professional ethics for its professional membership that can be found at http://www.cpcusociety.org. These rules can be specifically applied to the claim profession.

Many insurance and non-insurance organizations have codes of ethics and conflict of interest policies outlined within human resource or personnel manuals. An example of a code of ethics and conflict of interest policy is listed below:

> A corporation's reputation for integrity is its most valuable asset and is directly related to the conduct of its officers and employees. Therefore, employees must never use their positions with the corporation, or any of its clients, for private gain, to advance personal interests, or to obtain favors or benefits for themselves, members of their families, or any other individuals, corporations, or business entities.
>
> The corporation adheres to the highest legal and ethical standards applicable in our business. The corporation's business is conducted in strict observance of both the letter and spirit of all applicable laws, and the integrity of each employee is of utmost importance.
>
> Employees of the corporation shall conduct their personal affairs such that their duties and responsibilities to the corporation are not jeopardized and/or legal questions do not arise with respect to their association or work with the corporation.

A code of ethics that includes some of the above sections is a standard which most claim organizations should adopt.

Ethics in Claims Organizations

There are various claim organizations and associations that embrace their own code of ethics or code of conduct. The Society of Registered Professional Adjusters' ethics guidelines are outlined in Exhibit E.1. Its welcome message on http://www.rpa-adjuster.com states:

> The Society of Registered Professional Adjusters is the organization implemented to oversee the qualifications and designations of Registered Professional Adjusters (RPA). The Society was formed by industry professionals that felt continuing education was critical and that there needed to be a designation that recognized the professionalism of an adjuster. The Board of Directors is made up of insurance company top management and support organizations, independent claims adjusters, and attorneys that work directly with the industry. It is the first and only designation formed by and for the insurance claims professional. The Society is a nonprofit organization and supported by volunteers and member donations. RPA designees have demonstrated excellence and proficiency in the insurance claims field, have met Continuing Education Requirements, comply with ethics standards imposed by the RPA, and have sustained a level of competence ... something all current member designees must demonstrate and something that all insurers should demand....

Codes of ethics and conflict of interest policies serve a purpose and should be carefully communicated to all employees and officers so that there is a clear understanding of the intent, content, and compliance. Issues with regard to ethics, codes of conduct, and conflict of interest should be topics of discussion at various stages throughout the year. Reinforcement of company policy, including the impact of noncompliance, should be conducted on a regular basis.

Exhibit E.1: Society of Registered Professional Adjusters' Ethics Guidelines

The work of adjusting insurance claims is a profession of public trust. Accordingly, RPAs must maintain a standard of integrity that will promote the goal of building public confidence and trust in the insurance industry.

RPAs will only discharge claims responsibilities for which they possess sufficient technical competence or can acquire adequate training.

RPAs will seek only information they believe to be relevant, timely, and accurate, and use only legal and ethical means of obtaining that information. They will handle claims with no intent to mislead or misinform.

RPAs will be sensitive to individuals' rights of privacy, and will take reasonable measures to protect sensitive information from illegal or unauthorized examination.

RPAs will avoid illegal discrimination, and will strive to keep personal feelings and prejudices from influencing their judgment.

RPAs will maintain a courteous and sensitive attitude in their interactions with insureds and claimants, seeking to understand their concerns during times of distress. They will assist insureds in presenting and documenting their losses, and will not place the interests of their employer above those of the insured.

RPAs will maintain their business relationships with others in a manner that will promote the goal of bringing credit and honor to the profession. They will have no undisclosed financial interest in any direct or indirect aspect of an adjusting transaction.

RPAs will obey the laws and regulations related to handling claims.

They will resist fraudulent, unmeritorious, or exaggerated claims, and support public and industry organizations involved in the detection and prevention of insurance fraud.

Recognizing that litigation is costly and time-consuming, when appropriate, RPAs will seek out all available alternatives to litigation to resolve issues in an expeditious and conciliatory manner.

RPA. "Society of Registered Professional Adjusters Ethics Guidelines." Downers Grove, IL: Society of Registered Professional Adjusters, 2007. http://www.rpa-adjuster.com/ethics.html.

Regulating Ethics

Unfortunately, even in recent times, the insurance industry has become tarnished because of behavior by a few insurance professionals that was viewed as both unethical and illegal. Some of these issues have been reported extensively in the trade press and in worldwide news. These unethical issues involved bid rigging, financial statement impropriety, and deceiving the public in a number of ways, including unethical behavior by adjusters during catastrophes. As a result, some offenders have been held to be criminally responsible, even industry professionals with over 20 years' experience. Why turn to criminal behavior? They may have thought they were above the law or perhaps out of pure greed. There will always be arrogant behavior with the attitude that success is necessary at all costs, even if it means conducting business practices which are illegal or unethical.

The insurance industry is heavily regulated by various state and federal agencies. As an industry, our core insurance services involve the public, whether in personal or commercial lines. Thus, the industry is always under intense scrutiny by regulators, the public, and the press. Many of the insurance regulations and statutes, including unfair claim practice regulations, have developed as a result of the public being poorly treated by the insurance industry. Market conduct reviews of insurance companies and claim facilities, i.e., investigation by insurance regulators to determine if an insurer has followed laws relating to the distribution of products to consumers and settlement of claims, have also led to increased regulation.

Improper claims handling leads to even greater regulation. For example, most states have adopted unfair claim practice regulations which dictate that a fair settlement offer must be extended within a certain period after the loss. This regulation did not develop as a result of a regulator's whim, but in response to poor behavior by industry claim professionals. To this day, there are claim facilities that intentionally delay an offer of settlement to a third-party claimant, attempting to force them to pursue their own first-party coverage as it is an easier process for the adjuster.

Also, consider adjuster workloads—a topic which has been a focal point throughout this book. If adjuster workloads are too high, the adjuster may be unable to handle the new incoming claim volume as well as the pending claim volume on a timely basis. This may indirectly precipitate unethical behavior in the sense that the adjuster may not be able to keep up with the work and comply with unfair claim practice regulations. The adjuster may take shortcuts and use unethical tactics to reduce the volume of work.

Unethical Examples

Some claim facilities may promote unethical activities either intentionally or unintentionally. It is perfectly ethical for an adjuster to work with a claimant toward a resolution of a bodily injury claim and advise the claimant that retaining an attorney is unnecessary. This approach, termed claimant control, allows the adjuster to reach an equitable settlement resolution of the claim with the claimant directly. If this is handled properly and ethically, the claimant will receive more money since the attorney's fee (one-third of the gross settlement proceeds) has been eliminated, and the insurance company or claim facility will pay less, presumably because the gross settlement payout will be less.

However, some adjusters may settle a claim at a substantially lower value than it is worth because they were able to convince the claimant not to retain an attorney. In this situation, the payment to the claimant would be less than the two-thirds of the gross settlement proceeds the claimant would have received if an attorney was involved. This approach is unethical, as the adjuster is taking advantage of the claimant who may not be sophisticated enough to understand the claim process or claim values. Here's a more detailed example:

> Peter Johnson, the claimant, age 22, tripped and fell on a walkway at the insured's premises. As a result of the accident, he sustained a fractured calcaneus or heel bone that required surgical intervention. The claimant was hospitalized for 1 week and lost 12 weeks of wages. The adjuster's investigation indicates the walkway was defective. The insured had received complaints, both written and oral, on several prior occasions about the walkway. Therefore, the adjuster evaluates liability as "probable."
>
> During the course of the investigation, the adjuster establishes a rapport with the claimant and indicates that when treatment and disability have been concluded, he'll make sure Peter receives a fair settlement. Peter indicates that his uncle advised him to retain an attorney so that his interests would be protected. The adjuster advises Peter that doing so would only result in Peter receiving one-third less of the settlement proceeds, the portion that would go to the attorney. The claimant heeds the adjuster's advice, completes medical treatment, and returns to work after 12 weeks. However, the attending physician indicates the heel fracture could develop into more severe problems at a later date.
>
> The adjuster discusses the claim with his supervisor who extends claim settlement authority up to $25,000. The adjuster approaches the claimant with a settlement at $15,000, which Peter accepts, and a general release is secured. Six months later, the claimant undergoes surgery that results in extensive disability, including the claimant having a residual limp for the rest of his life.

Was the adjuster ethical in settling this claim at $15,000? If the adjuster was trained properly, he would've known that a claim involving a fractured heel has the propensity to be very severe and could result in a residual problem. Yes, the adjuster may have been correct advising the claimant that by retaining an attorney, he might give up a third of the settlement for the attorney's fee; however, if the total valuation of the claim is far less than an attorney's evaluation (the claim should be evaluated at a fair value either way), the statement by the adjuster is unethical. If the claimant had retained an attorney, the attorney would not have allowed the claimant to prematurely settle the claim at that particular stage, and the gross value of the claim would have been more.

This example of unethical behavior by an adjuster is sometimes condoned (or even encouraged) by claim management in some organizations. Adjusters are trained to investigate claims and direct them toward settlement. If claims are not settled, work volume increases, resulting in the need to hire additional staff, which in turn negatively impacts profitability. In an effort to conclude claims and be looked upon favorably by their supervisor, adjusters may settle claims at less than the claim value, feeling that they have saved the company money. If a supervisor or manager congratulates the adjuster in the above example for controlling the claimant effectively and achieving a low settlement, the supervisor or manager is not behaving ethically. The adjuster who feels they have been successful in settling the claim for an amount less than the actual value, because the claimant was not sophisticated enough to understand claim values or the potential for problems to develop with injuries at a later date, is behaving unethically.

When an adjuster engages in this type of behavior, it only adds to the negative attitude of the public toward adjusters and insurance companies. It is unethical for an insurers or any other claim facility to train adjusters how to persuade unrepresented claimants not to retain an attorney when the resulting settlements are not fair and equitable. (More examples of unethical behavior are shown in Exhibit E.2.) In a nutshell, it is unethical if the claimant is not treated fairly and equitably.

First-Party versus Third-Party Claims

Some claims people may differentiate the level of service or handling depending on whether the claim involves a third-party claimant or a first-party policyholder. This is based on the premise that the first-party policyholder pays a premium to the insurer—the adjuster's employer—as opposed to a third-party claimant trying to collect money under the policy written for the insured. Although unfair, this type of process may be condoned by management, and some companies may even mandate that first-party claims be handled more expediently since policyholders paid the premium to the company; therefore, they are entitled to better service.

Let's look at this issue from an ethical viewpoint. As an adjuster, you have received two new claims at the same time. The first claim involves a policyholder who has presented a collision claim for $2,500. The second claim, involving a third-party claimant, has a basement filled with water as a result of a liability claim caused by the plumber who is your policyholder. Which claim do you handle first?

Some may choose to handle the collision claim first because it involves a policyholder. Other adjusters may more appropriately handle the third-party claim, knowing that it requires immediate handling. Although this may not be an obvious ethical issue, it does highlight a situation where an adjuster may choose to not treat a third-party claimant as fairly as a first-party insured, or delay the claims handling because of either a company mandate or an individual decision that all first-party claims involving policyholders require priority handling.

Litigation Gone Awry

Insurance company executives complain about society becoming increasingly or continually litigious with an abundance of claimant attorneys involved in the claim

Exhibit E.2: Examples of Unethical Adjuster Behavior

This list is not meant to be all-inclusive, and there are many other areas of adjusting that may result in unethical behavior. This list provides clear examples unacceptable claim practices.

- Intentionally not making contact with parties to a loss, hoping a claim will not be presented.
- Extending a low settlement offer knowing the claimant is unrepresented by an attorney.
- Convincing a claimant to settle a claim prematurely to save loss dollars.
- Not returning telephone calls, hoping the party will abandon the claim.
- Failing to explain coverage under a policy that may have a material effect on the party's settlement.
- Not offering coverage under a policy when coverage applies.
- When evaluating coverage, looking for a way to deny the claim versus looking for coverage availability.
- Making an insured or claimant provide an unreasonable amount of documentation to support a claim, even though enough information has been submitted to resolve the claim properly.
- Recording telephone conversations without the other party's permission.
- Delaying the inspection and handling of third-party claims, forcing the parties to collect from their own first-party coverage.
- Providing a low settlement offer, forcing the parties to collect from their own first-party coverage.
- Taking a statement from a party and not honoring the request for a copy or transcription.
- Intentionally underreserving or delaying the reserve entry of a claim to positively affect the loss ratio and amount of the adjuster's projected bonus.

continued

Exhibit E.2: Examples of Unethical Adjuster Behavior (cont.)

- When interviewing job candidates, being dishonest about the job environment, culture, workloads, or expectations.
- Overloading an adjuster with work, with unrealistic expectations, resulting in a performance action plan or termination.
- Reporting dishonest information to the claim file.
- Visiting a claimant in the hospital immediately after an accident occurs to obtain a statement, when the claimant may be under medication or traumatized and unable think clearly. In some states it is illegal to visit a third-party injured claimant in the hospital unless a certain time period has passed (i.e., 15 days).
- Falsely reporting that a claimant or an insured is involved in fraudulent activity.
- Intentionally misleading a supervisor or manager into providing claim authority when the information recorded was inaccurate.
- Being dishonest to a claimant, insured, or witness for personal gain.
- Inflating or deflating damage estimates or claim valuations for personal gain.
- Sharing personal claim information with anyone not authorized to see it.
- Discussing claim details with any person not a party to the claim.
- Being employed as both a claims adjuster and a public adjuster at the same time.
- Working as a claims adjuster and for a claimant law firm simultaneously.
- Contacting or interviewing the claimant without including their attorney, knowing the claimant is represented.
- Interviewing a witness who was employed by the codefendant in a lawsuit, knowing the witness is represented by the codefendant attorney.

process. Litigation adds to both unallocated and allocated loss adjustment expenses, and also requires a more experienced adjuster handling claims. As more examples of adjuster unethical or unfair behavior are publicized, it just adds to a poor reputation and increases litigation due to lack of trust. If an insurance company or claims facility handled the claim example above properly and ethically, including a proper evaluation of Peter Johnson and advising him to hold off on settlement to determine whether any residual problems might arise, Peter would have received a proper settlement and probably would not have needed to retain an attorney.

It sounds like a simplistic approach toward a longstanding problem; however, it starts with individual claims handling at the adjuster level. If the company trains its adjusters to be ethical, honest, and helpful during the claims process, the company will achieve better results in loss costs, expenses, and overall reputation. It will probably also gain market share at the same time. In the claim example above, the adjuster saved the company money by paying less loss dollars but, by doing so, added to the tarnished reputation of the insurance industry.

If claims adjusters make reasonable settlement offers to both unrepresented and represented claimants, eventually the public may regain its trust of the insurance industry. The plaintiff attorneys also contribute to the problem when they use scare tactics to persuade a third-party claimant to retain legal services. Unfortunately, when adjusters handle claims improperly, as outlined above, plaintiff attorneys are correct.

It's important to clarify that the entire industry does not handle claims as illustrated in the example above. However, even just a few claims handled this way may be widely publicized in the media, adding to the problem. The value of a claim should be no higher because a claimant is represented by an attorney. Each claim should be evaluated based on its own individual merits in terms of liability and damages. If claimants who retain attorneys receive larger settlements than those who do not, even after the attorney's fees are deducted, all claimants will consider retaining attorneys.

Why does the insurance industry not want claimant attorneys involved in the claims process? It's because claims involving represented claimants have the propensity to reach the litigation stages. In litigation, expenses and human resource costs skyrocket as claims tend to be pending longer with increased values over time.

The issues of ethical claims handling go beyond the individual handling of claims by adjusters. Unethical claims handling tends to evolve from a corporate culture or environment condoned or supported by line management and even executive management. Complimenting adjusters for saving the company money when the claim was clearly underpaid is unethical on the part of management. Instead, the adjuster should be either reprimanded or retrained regarding how to handle claims properly.

Ethics in Business Relationships

The insurance business, particularly in the claims area, involves financial transactions. The financial transactions include reserve management and the payment of claims.

The basis for the financial transactions and payment of claims are commonly performed by the claims staff. For example, adjusters prepare estimates and appraisals, evaluate bodily injury claims, negotiate settlements, process total loss vehicles, including salvage, and manage litigation claims. All of these processes could result in some type of unethical behavior on the part of the adjuster, manager, and other business professionals.

In the business environment, vendors take clients to lunch or dinner, provide them with various gifts, and provide entertainment and other forms of gratuity. In some businesses, this is acceptable. In the insurance business, however, this has historically been a problem. The reason it represents a problem is because these actions may end up establishing the foundation for unethical behavior.

For example, an attorney providing defense work to your company takes you and your spouse to dinner. As time progresses, you develop a friendship which includes providing the defense firm with all of your claim legal work. If the defense attorney makes a mistake or error, it will place you in a very difficult situation to handle the situation objectively. If you looked the other way, it would be unethical on your part.

Another example would be a property adjuster who establishes a very friendly relationship with a public adjuster with whom she works with extensively. As the public adjuster submits estimates and appraisals, her objectivity may be adversely affected by the friendship. Although, it may be subtle, it also has the appearance of impropriety. The mere appearance of impropriety could lead others to believe that an unethical situation exists.

A litigation adjuster may have an extensive volume of litigation claims with a particular plaintiff's law firm. As the adjuster develops a friendship with the law firm, it allows for an environment to settle claims effectively prior to litigation. The law firm and the litigation adjuster continue be friendly, and the law firm offers to let the adjuster stay at the company beach house for a week, all expenses paid. The adjuster accepts the invitation, thinking it will continue to improve both the relationship and the ability to settle claims in the future.

Unfortunately, most will view this arrangement as being very unethical. The litigation adjuster evaluates claims for a law firm that provides gratuities and entertainment. The adjuster's objectivity in both liability and damages valuations may be adversely affected. In this situation, the adjuster may lose all credibility with regard to claim of evaluations—and probably lose his job.

Here's another example. A policyholder has an extensive fire loss in excess of $100,000. During the adjustment process, the property adjuster provides great service throughout the claim process, and the insured is very happy with the claim resolution. A letter was sent to the president of the adjuster's company indicating what a great job she had done. Thereafter, the adjuster receives a telephone call from the insured indicating that he was very happy with the claim result and wanted to give her a token of his appreciation. He asks for her home address and, a week later, she receives a case of very expensive wine, which she keeps. The situation went from a very positive one, including a letter of commendation from the president of the company, to a situation where her acceptance of the wine may give the impression, rightly or wrongly, that the loss was overpaid, with the possibility of fraud on the adjuster's part.

When gifts, entertainment, or other items of gratuity are extended to the adjuster or manager, there is the opportunity for objectivity to be compromised and an unethical issue—real or perceived—can develop. Sometimes people become involved in situations because they use poor judgment. Poor judgment is not necessarily an indication of being unethical; however, poor judgment can lead to an unethical situation if the adjuster is not strong enough to recognize and withdraw from the situation. The best approach is to avoid the situation in the first place. The next time an independent adjuster or defense attorney wants to take you to an expensive restaurant for lunch, either politely refuse, or if the meeting is necessary, go to a less expensive restaurant and either pay for your own lunch or offer to pay for the other party's.

There is another area of unethical behavior which is worth mentioning. In the third-party administrator (TPA) environment, the client may request that the adjuster handle investigation and adjusting activities in a manner that is not compliant with unfair claim practice regulations. This places the adjuster in a very difficult situation. In all cases, the adjuster should refuse to engage in any behavior that is unethical, illegal, or not compliant with insurance regulations.

Appendix F: Litigation Management

Successful claims operations develop and implement litigation management guidelines for their claims staff. The litigation management program primarily involves liability claims handling. This Appendix provides a detailed litigation management program along with a litigation procedural outline for defense counsel that can be provided to the handling attorney with each new suit referral to defense counsel.

Generally, a litigation management program is a collaborative effort between the claims staff and defense firms to manage the entire litigation process, with a specific focus on control of the litigation process and its costs. Litigation management guidelines serve the purpose of providing a consistent and uniform approach toward handling claims pending in litigation. Even an experienced adjuster will want to refer to the litigation management program to understand the company's requirements and methodology being utilized.

Below is a sample comprehensive litigation management program for XYZ Claim Facility.

Litigation Management Program

XYZ Claim Facility has implemented a claim litigation management program that meets these obligations and effectively manages the litigation process. We retain only qualified and experienced attorneys on our approved panel to represent policyholders and handle litigation on behalf of our clients in a professional manner. All litigation handling is conducted in a manner that fully meets our obligation to provide competent and qualified defense counsel on behalf of our clients and their policyholders.

Initial Review of New Litigation

All new lawsuits and other legal process are immediately referred to the claims manager for review via e-mail with attachments. Copies of all documents are also scanned to the claim file. The claims manager will enter the new lawsuit into the suit log (a report recording incoming and outgoing lawsuit activity) and enter a management diary date. Litigation screens will be completed within the claims system.

Upon receipt of a new lawsuit, the handling adjuster will contact the insured (and/or other defendants insured under our policy) to determine the details of how service was effected on the parties being represented.

All new suits will be immediately referred to defense counsel. The handling adjuster will contact defense counsel by telephone, well in advance of the answer due date, to alert defense counsel of any time restrictions.

Extension of Time To Answer

We will instruct defense counsel to request all extensions of time to answer, i.e., the time extended by a plaintiff attorney to respond to a summons and complaint. These extensions must be confirmed in writing by defense counsel, with a copy of the letter or stipulation sent to our office. Extensions will only be utilized if there are time restrictions in defense counsel preparing a timely answer and appearance.

Litigation Screen and Suit Log

The claims manager will complete the litigation status screen in the claims system indicating the date the petition or suit was filed, the answer due date, and the answered date. In the event an extension of time to answer is secured, the status screen will indicate the specific extension of time to answer date. The answered date will only be completed when the litigation is actually referred to defense counsel and we have received confirmation by defense counsel indicating an answer has been filed.

The claim management system generates a suit log for monitoring purposes.

Selection of Defense Counsel

Subject to any specific instructions from the client, all defense firms being utilized must be on the XYZ Claim Facility's list of approved attorneys or "Panel Counsel List."

Our policy is to select defense firms of the highest quality to defend and represent the insured and the Client Company. The selection process is based on the attorney's ability, expertise, and past results. We expect all assigned defense attorneys to adhere to our litigation procedures, guidelines, and instructions. We insist on timely reporting and being responsive to our requests. Law firms that do not comply with our litigation management requirements will be removed from the approved list.

Control of the Litigation Process

XYZ Claim Facility is responsible for controling the litigation process through effective communication with defense counsel and retains the responsibility to investigate, analyze, evaluate, and negotiate claims. However, settlement authority may be delegated to defense counsel as an exception.

The handling adjuster provides specific instruction for litigation handling at the time of the initial suit referral and throughout the litigation process until the claim is concluded. The handling adjuster will provide written instructions to defense counsel outlining specific activities to be completed (i.e., answer and/or appearance, basic discovery, interrogatories, depositions, cross-claims, admissions).

Effective control of the litigation process will provide more focused direction and control of legal costs. All new suit referrals to defense counsel will include a complete copy of all relevant claim file documentation. The initial suit referral to defense counsel must include the following:

- Copies of pertinent claim file documentation
- Details concerning the service of legal process on the defendants we plan to represent
- Details concerning any extension of time to answer/appear

- The style of the case (names of the plaintiff and defendant)
- Court and venue
- Named insured and contact person at insured (include any additional named insureds)
- Name of the parties we intend to defend and/or indemnify
- Policy numbers, effective dates, and policy limits (include any excess or umbrella policy)
- Plaintiff law firm information
- Plaintiff name and available personal data
- Incident and accident facts and details
- Injury and special damage information
- The handling adjuster's liability analysis and damage evaluation
- Specific follow-up adjuster action plan[1]
- Specific litigation management plan.
- Request for copies of all response pleadings
- Confirmation of the agreed hourly billing rate
- Request for projected legal budget up to the point of trial
- Request for interim legal billing at least every 3 months
- Enclose a copy of the Defense Counsel Litigation Procedures[2]

The suit referral will request an acknowledgement within 30 days from the referral date. The handling attorney's acknowledgement letter must include any additional comments not addressed in the referral letter, defense counsel's analysis, and evaluation (liability and damages) as well as any further handling recommendations. The acknowledgement should include copies of the response pleadings and a projected litigation budget up to the point of trial so that legal costs can be reserved. Defense counsel must send a representation letter to the defendants being represented in the pending litigation, with a copy to XYZ Claim Facility.

We expect defense counsel to handle the legal activities, and XYZ Claim Facility to handle the claim activities. However, we do understand the necessity to make exceptions to this procedure based on the merits of each individual claim. Litigation management is an ongoing process of controlling all legal-related activities throughout the duration of the claim.

Administrative Hearings

When referring a matter to defense counsel involving a hearing at an administrative board or commission, such as a municipal hearing, defense counsel needs to be advised of our litigation management pro-

[1]Typically consists of the activities to be handled by the adjuster, such as continued investigation, securing documents, etc.

[2]Comprehensive litigation procedures and protocol for defense counsel to follow during the handling of litigation claims.

gram, with specific legal activities outlined. A legal budget must also be requested.

Should the insured's records be needed in preparation of the administrative hearing, the records will be requested from the insured by the XYZ Claim Facility claims staff, unless there are attorney client privilege issues, in which case defense counsel will request the records directly. Attorney-client privilege is a legal concept that protects communications between a client and his or her attorney and keeps those communications confidential.

Legal Billing

We recognize the hourly rate billed may differ by jurisdiction. We want to be billed at a rate based on the industry average in a particular jurisdiction and commensurate with the volume of work referred to the law firm.

All legal billing should be on a minimum of a 3-month cycle. Each legal bill must reflect a complete itemization of charges down to the tenth of an hour, by date, by legal activity, and by the handling attorney or paralegal initials. The bill must also reflect the hourly rate by legal handler with a summary of hours billed. We should not be charged for unnecessary activities, or any activities not approved, unless the activity was a necessary responsive pleading or correspondence in response to other parties in the litigation. We do not want to pay for redundant or duplicate activities conducted by both the partner and legal associate.

Defense counsel must provide a legal budget with their initial acknowledgement of the new lawsuit. The legal budget must project the total costs up to the point of trial.

Use of Excess Letters

When the amount of the suit exceeds the policy limits, a letter must be sent to each defendant in a lawsuit who is covered under the liability policy advising them of this fact. These are called excess ad damnum letters, and must be sent by the XYZ Claim Facility claims staff, by certified mail, to each named defendant we represent in the pending action. In certain jurisdictions, the amount sued for is open or provisional; therefore, a letter will need to be sent to each defendant on all claims pending in litigation. If the amount sued for is open or provisional, a proper excess letter must be issued at the appropriate time. If there are pending coverage issues, including claims for punitive or exemplary damages, the excess letter must incorporate these issues as well. Should any of these issues require reporting to the Client Company, the excess letter must be referred to the Client Company for preapproval.

Handling Trial Activity

XYZ Claim Facility must be notified of all trials and arbitration proceedings at least 30 days in advance of the scheduled trial or hearing date, if possible. At least 30 days prior to the scheduled trial or arbitration hearing date, we require defense counsel's opinion (written pretrial report) concerning jury verdict or arbitration award exposure potential, settlement value, negligence percentages on all parties involved in the litigation, and the handling attorney's written recommendations. We also ask that defense counsel project the total trial or arbitration costs to properly evaluate any potential settlement options.

While the trial or hearing is ongoing, the handling attorney must contact XYZ Claim Facility on a daily basis, providing updates. Reporting by defense counsel should begin with the initial jury selection, providing information on the jury panel selected.

XYZ Claim Facility should be kept advised on a daily basis and will, in turn, provide updates to the Client Company in accordance with its instructions.

Unfortunately, we are unable to ever predict the outcome of a jury verdict or arbitration award. Therefore, we do not want any claim tried to a verdict, or allow a claim to be decided by an arbitration panel, without prior approval by XYZ Claim Facility and the Client Company. Therefore, it is absolutely essential that the Client Company be kept advised concerning the continued handling of any litigation claim at the trial or arbitration stages.

Miscellaneous Litigation Procedures

Following are some procedures not addressed by the above discussion.

- We expect prompt communication by defense counsel and compliance with our reporting requests.
- All litigation claims resulting in a default judgment, either on liability or damage issues, must be immediately reported to the XYZ Claim Facility Vice President of Claims.
- We do not require actual deposition transcripts. We require summary reports of each deposition, which are normally prepared by the handling attorney for the legal file.
- All appeals, at any court level, must be approved by XYZ Claim Facility before defense counsel files them. Appeals require prior approval by the Client Company. We want defense counsel to project the total cost of the appeal process as well as our percentage chance of success.
- All motions must be approved by XYZ Claim Facility before defense counsel files them. Defense counsel must request written approval to pursue motion practice and include the reason for the motion, the projected cost, as well as our percentage chances of success, if applicable.
- All legal research requires prior approval by the claim operation. Defense counsel must provide the projected cost of the research and comment on the impact of the research relative to the claim result. A copy of the legal research brief must be contained in the claim file.
- The use of all experts requires prior approval by the claim operation.
- When retaining defense counsel for coverage opinions (or coverage litigation), representation should never be requested from the same defense firm that is handling the underlying action. The reason for this is that defense counsel represents the insured in the underlying action, and in a coverage action (or in providing a coverage opinion), defense counsel represents the insurance company. By represent-

ing both, there would be a conflict of interest.

- All allocated loss adjustment expenses (ALAE) must be referred to XYZ Claim Facility for payment processing and not be paid by defense counsel or included within the legal bill. Examples of ALAE are court reporter fees, expert fees, etc.

- Litigation budgets are required on all litigation claims, and XYZ Claim Facility should request updates to the litigation budget during the litigation process. The litigation budget will also be used as one element of our expense reserve evaluation.

- Defense counsel will receive specific instructions when assigned cases involving nonlitigation matters, such as municipality hearings, administrative hearings, pre-suit discovery, examinations under oath, and coverage opinions.

Thank you.

XYZ Claim Facility

Litigation Procedures for Defense Counsel

A litigation procedural outline should be provided to the handling attorney with each new suit referral. The outline should include the salient points of the litigation management program as a reminder of the requirements and to ensure compliance.

Appendix G: Legal Theory and Doctrines

This Appendix includes a discussion of various legal theories and doctrines encountered during the property and casualty claim process. Legal theories and doctrines will be explained, in alphabetical order, complete with practical applications to allow for a better understanding of each term. This section ends with a basic discussion of the judicial process. Definitions contained in the list of legal terms are shown in bold italics.

This Appendix is not meant to provide an in-depth analysis of legal issues from a lawyer's perspective. The purpose of this Appendix is to discuss these theories and doctrines and their application by an adjuster during the claims process. An important point to understand is that law varies from one state to the next. Therefore, this analysis is more of a general overview to help claims personnel understand the impact of legal issues during the claims process. These fundamental principles, along with the investigation results, establish the foundation for claim reserves and settlement values. If there is a lack of understanding of legal theories and the legal process, it may adversely affect the insurer's or third-party administrator's bottom line.

Legal Terms

absolute liability—Also known as strict liability, the legal doctrine under which liability is imposed with respect to injury or damage arising from certain types of hazardous activities. For example, under strict liability standards, the manufacturer or distributor of a dangerous product is liable to a person who is injured by the product, regardless of the degree of care exercised by the manufacturer or distributor in the production or sale of the product. In a claims situation, it usually means there is no fault placed on the claimant or injured party. Absolute liability can be placed on a defendant if their actions were egregious, e.g., damages caused by intentional pollution.

actual cash value (ACV)—In property and auto physical damage insurance, one of several possible methods of establishing the value of insured property to calculate the premium and determine the amount the insurer will pay in the event of loss. ACV is typically calculated as the ***replacement cost value (RCV)*** less depreciation. It is important to note that, in many jurisdictions, a plaintiff may only recover actual cash value and not replacement cost in a property damage liability claim. Also see ***broad evidence rule.***

administrative law—The body of law created by federal or state administrative agencies, with the consent of the respective legislatures. This law normally takes the form of rules and regulations, such as those promulgated by state insurance departments.

affiant—The person making an affidavit; the complainant.

affidavit—A ***sworn statement,*** voluntarily given by a declarant, and witnessed by a ***notary public.*** An affidavit may also be a legal sworn statement prepared by an attorney that provides details of a claim. The affidavit provides no mechanism to ask questions or a rebuttal to the content of the statement. It is basically a notarized prepared sworn statement. Sometimes an attorney will provide an affidavit in lieu of the adjuster taking a statement from the claimant or insured.

affirmative defense—A fact or issue that is a valid defense to a claim even assuming the alleged facts asserting liability are true. For example, despite a defendant's negligence in causing an automobile accident, the plaintiff's ***contributory negligence*** may establish an affirmative defense to a bodily injury claim if it is proven that the plaintiff would have suffered no injuries had he or she been wearing a seatbelt. Other affirmative defenses include ***assumption of risk*** and ***statute of limitations.***

answer—The formal written statement made by a defendant setting forth the grounds of his defense under the Codes and Rules of Civil Procedure.

appeal—The submission of a decision to a higher court for its review and possible reversal. An example is a plea to an appellate court for review of an order issued by a trial court.

appearance—Showing up in court, either as a party to litigation, an attorney, or an interested person.

assault and battery—Criminal in nature, assault is the threat of violence, and battery is the actual physical violent act. Assault and battery are typically not covered under a liability policy unless a manuscript endorsement has been specifically written to provide coverage for the risks. The reason that coverage is not provided for an assault and battery is that the acts are intentional and do not meet the definition of an occurrence or accident, which is usually defined as "a continuous or repeated exposure which results in bodily injury or property damage neither expected nor intended by the insured." However, there may be situations where the insurance company may be required to either defend or indemnify a policyholder involving an assault and battery claim, if it is determined that the injuries occurred as a result of an "unintentional consequence of an intentional act." Typically, these types of claims may require handling under a ***reservation of rights.***

assumption of risk—This is a common-law defense that has been used to pass the responsibility for loss or injury onto the injured party by asserting that the individual had knowledge and understanding of the hazards involved in the undertaking and is therefore not entitled to recovery for the loss. Legal decisions have eroded and narrowed the applicability of this defense.

attorney allegations—Detailed information secured by the adjuster during the investigation of a liability claim. Attorney allegations include securing the claimant attorney's theory of liability, the claimant's personal information, accident details, medical and hospital information, special damages, witness information, and other pertinent data related to the claim.

attorney-client privilege—A legal concept that protects communications between a client and his or her attorney and keeps those communications confidential.

attorney-in-fact—A trustee who has custody of the subscriber funds and uses those funds to pay insurance claims.

attractive nuisance doctrine—A legal doctrine that is a notable exception in the law relating to trespassers that imposes a special duty of care on a person maintaining an artificial condition on land which attracts children (e.g., a swimming pool). Under the attractive nuisance doctrine, children enjoy the status and protection of invitees. In some cases, the landowner has been held absolutely liable for injuries to children in connection with an attractive nuisance even though the children were trespassers.

bill of particulars—During the ***discovery*** stage, information and documentation is exchanged through various discovery demands. In some jurisdictions, these demands and responses may be called ***interrogatories,*** and in other jurisdictions, such as New York, the information exchange is referred to as a bill of particulars.

breach of contract—This is a material failure to fulfill one's contractual obligations. Insurance policies typically do not cover liabilities arising out of a breach of contract because it is viewed as a business risk that is within the control of the insured. In some cases, most notably construction defect claims, this has led to extensive litigation over what constitutes a breach of contract versus ordinary negligence. Liability claims handling will involve contractual issues. For example, during the claims handling process, particularly claims involving habitational risks, e.g., building owners, there will be lease agreements between the tenant and landlord outlining the specific responsibilities of each party with regard to structural repairs and maintenance. If the tenant is responsible for general maintenance of the premises, and an accident occurs as a result of the tenant's failure to maintain the premises, the tenant would have breached the contractual provision relating to maintenance of the premises. It is important to note that breach of contract is not covered under most liability policies because it does not meet the definition of bodily injury or property damage.

Some adjusters make the mistake of thinking if a policy provides contractual liability coverage it would cover all claims involving breach of contract. The actual breach of contract is not covered; however, the tort liability assumed in the contract resulting from the breach of contract would be covered, as long as it met the policy definition of bodily injury or property damage. Most general liability policies have contractual liability exclusions but provide coverage by exception for claims resulting from an insured contract, which includes lease agreements. The general liability policy can also be endorsed with blanket contractual liability coverage, which expands the coverage for any contract involving the named insured's business.

broad evidence rule—A method of valuation that has evolved in some states and does not adhere to the principle that the traditional measure of ***actual cash value*** (replacement cost value less depreciation) is the sole measure of value at the time of loss. This rule provides for the examination of every standard of value having a bearing on the property under consideration, such as the age of the property, the profit likely to accrue on the property, and the property's tax value. Ultimately, it calls for the selection of that "value" which, in the event of a total loss, will provide complete indemnification and no more.

caselaw—The body of judicial decisions within a particular jurisdiction.

class action lawsuits—Litigation involving many plaintiffs with the same cause of action. An example would be ill or dying plaintiffs joining together to sue cigarette companies claiming that ingredients in the cigarettes caused their cancers.

closing argument—At the end of a trial, this is the summation of the testimony and evidence presented during the trial made by both the plaintiff's and defendant's counsel urging the judge or jury to rule in their respective client's favor.

codefendant—In a legal action against multiple defendants, each defendant refers to the other defendant as a codefendant. When a complaint is served, each codefendant will be served separately.

collateral source rule—A procedural rule followed by the courts in many states that prohibits informing the jury that the plaintiff has received money for his or her injuries from other sources, such as from his or her employer's workers compensation policy or an insurance policy covering another defendant.

common law—Unwritten law derived from court case decisions based on custom and precedent. It is contrasted to ***statutory law.*** Common law develops as a result of various court decisions, called ***caselaw*** (laws based on judicial precedent). Common law is created through the judicial system and is used as the basis for subsequent decisions by the courts.

comparative negligence—The rule used in negligence cases in some states that provides for computing both the plaintiff's and the defendant's negligence, with the plaintiff's damages being reduced by a percentage representing the degree of his or her contributing fault. If the plaintiff's negligence is found to be greater than the defendant's, the plaintiff will receive nothing.

compensatory damages—A sum of money to which a plaintiff is entitled that, so far as is possible, makes amends for the actual loss sustained.

complaint—The original or initial pleading by which an action is commenced under the Codes and Rules of Civil Procedure. The pleading sets forth a claim for relief which includes (a) a short and plain statement of the grounds on which the court has jurisdiction, (b) a short and plain statement of the claim stating the pleader is entitled to relief, and (c) a demand for judgment for the relief sought.

constructive notice—By law, presumed knowledge of facts and circumstances by the party responsible to know, or take notice of, such facts and circumstances. For example, a defendant should have had knowledge of the defective or dangerous condition given the obvious nature of the condition and the defendant's involvement with the property.

continuance—A term used when a hearing or trial is put off until a later date.

contributory negligence—Negligence of a plaintiff constituting a partial cause or aggravation of his or her injury. This doctrine bars relief to the plaintiff in a lawsuit if the plaintiff's own negligence contributed to the damage. Contributory negligence has been superseded in many states by other methods of apportioning liability.

counterclaim—After a claim has been made, this is an action brought in response by the opposing party, typically a defendant against the plaintiff.

cross-claim—A suit by one defendant against a ***codefendant*** (or, more rarely, by one plaintiff against a coplaintiff) in a legal action related to the subject of the original claim or counterclaim.

***Cumis* counsel**—The 1984 California Court of Appeals decision in *San Diego Federal Credit Union v. Cumis Insurance Society, Inc.*, held that where an insurer is defending under a reservation of rights, a conflict of interest exists between the economic and litigation interest of the insurer and the insured. Under these circumstances, the traditional right of the insurer to select counsel and control the defense effort is lost. As a result, the insured selects counsel and controls the defense, but the insurer must pay the defense costs. Such counsel, selected and controlled by the insured at the expense of the insurer, is known as *Cumis* counsel.

damages relate to injuries or property destruction resulting from the breach of duty. Damages can be classified into several categories. ***Compensatory damages*** consist of general damages and special damages. ***General damages*** are subjective damages based on pain and suffering, loss of companionship, ***loss of consortium,*** disfigurement, loss of enjoyment of life, permanency, and mental or physical impairment. ***Special damages*** include expenses incurred by the plaintiff as a result of the accident, such as medical and hospital-related expenses, wage loss, property damage, and other out-of-pocket expenses. ***Punitive damages,*** sometimes called ***exemplary damages,*** refer to damages which serve to punish a defendant for its conduct. Typically, punitive damages are awarded when the defendant committed acts which are grossly negligent, intentional, or egregious. Punitive damage awards can far exceed general damage awards. In some jurisdictions, a plaintiff may receive treble or triple the general damages.

declaratory judgment (DJ) action—A special kind of judgment where a court declares the rights and obligations of parties to a written agreement. Where the parties to an insurance policy disagree as to the meaning of a policy term, either of them may file an action to obtain a declaratory judgment from a court as to what the policy term means. Sometimes a declaratory judgment action is referred to as a DEC action.

default judgment—This is the result of an answer or appearance not being filed timely in accordance with the jurisdiction's requirements. Default judgments can occur as a result of an insured not referring the pleadings to the claim facility timely, or as a result of an error on the part of the claim facility. Proper management control of incoming and outgoing lawsuit activity is critical for a claims operation, including date stamping pleadings as received. If a default judgment is received, some states are not lenient in vacating the judgment, which could result in a substantial judgment with no ability to challenge it.

defendant—The party against whom the plaintiff has filed a legal action.

discontinuance—A formal pleading submitted by the plaintiff in a legal action that stops the lawsuit. In a civil lawsuit, a discontinuance will be necessary if a claim is settled prior to or during trial.

discovery—Investigation of the facts of a claim or the alleged proximate cause of an injury. Discovery may include such activities as interrogatories, depositions, expert examination of a product, and review of a plaintiff's medical history.

dismissal—An order or judgment finally disposing of an action, suit, motion, etc., without a trial.

dramshop liability—Refers to the liability of bars, taverns, liquor stores, and other businesses that serve alcoholic beverages for loss arising out of the intoxication of patrons. Generally, dramshop laws establish liability arising out of the sale of alcoholic beverages to visibly intoxicated persons or minors who are subsequently involved in an accident causing injuries or even death to a third party. During the investigation process, an adjuster should always question the vehicle operators as to whether any drinking occurred prior to the accident. This may also be evident if an operator is cited or arrested at the scene of the accident for driving while intoxicated or driving while impaired.

Sometimes, a dramshop liability claim may result because the offending vehicle in an automobile accident has a low policy limit. If the injuries or damages are serious, the plaintiff may pursue a dramshop liability claim against the tavern that served the insured operator prior to the accident. If the tavern has liability limits of $1 million and the automobile carried limits of $100,000, ***joint and several liability*** may require a contribution by the tavern owner's insurance company even if the tavern owner was minimally negligent.

duty to defend and indemnify—Legal duties included in a liability insurance policy. Basically, the insuring agreement within the insurance policy states "We will pay all damages [indemnify] for bodily injury and property damage for which any insured may become legally responsible...we will settle or defend [indemnify and defend], as appropriate, any claim or suit asking for these damages. Our duty to settle or defend [indemnify and defend] ends when our limit of liability for coverage has been exhausted." The duty to defend involves an insurance company providing a defense to an insured under the policy, by assigning defense counsel to protect the interests of the insured. The duty to indemnify involves the insurance company paying any settlement or court judgment up to the policy limits.

It should be noted that the duty to defend is much broader than the duty to indemnify. Adjusters may encounter a lawsuit against a policyholder that has both covered and not covered causes of action under the insurance policy. These types of lawsuits may involve a defense under a ***reservation of rights.*** When evaluating the duty to defend, an adjuster should analyze each individual cause of action to determine whether coverage has been triggered. If there is an ambiguity or question as to whether coverage is provided, then any ambiguity should be ruled in favor of the policyholder, with coverage being provided, even if it is under a reservation of rights.

estoppel—See ***waiver and estoppel.***

evidence—Anything that can be used to prove or disprove an alleged fact.

examination before trial (EBT)—In the state of New York, a deposition taken prior to trial.

examination under oath (EUO)—Used to enable the insurer to obtain information necessary to process a claim. An EUO may be required when a coverage question exists or any other issue which requires the insured's testimony. An EUO is usually a formal deposition held in the insurer's attorney's office with a court stenographer present. The insured may or may not be represented by an attorney. EUOs are prevalent in first-party claims where fraud or misrepresentation is alleged on the part of the insured. An insured's failure to comply with the policy requirement for an EUO is, by definition, prejudicial absent extraordinary circumstances.

excess ad damnum letter—A letter sent to each defendant in a lawsuit who is covered under the liability policy, advising that the amount sued for exceeds the policy limits. In certain jurisdictions, the amount sued for is open or provisional; therefore, a letter will need to be sent to each defendant on all claims pending in litigation.

exclusive remedy—A component of workers compensation statutes that bars employees injured on the job from making a tort liability claim against their employers. The benefits provided under workers compensation are the sole remedy available to injured employees. There are exceptions to this rule, varying from state to state, that do provide the employee with a legal venue. The failure to obtain and maintain insurance as well as willful negligence on the part of the employer are two types of such deviations.

exculpatory language—A provision in a contract that relieves one party of all liability to the other in connection with the performance of the contract. The enforceability of an exculpatory clause may be restricted by ***common law*** or ***statutory law,*** or by legal precedent in a given jurisdiction. In some states, exculpatory language may not be enforceable as it is against public policy to transfer one's own negligence to avoid liability.

executor—The fiduciary specified by a will to settle a deceased's given estate.

exemplary damages—Damages in excess of that amount needed to compensate for the plaintiff's injury, awarded to punish the defendant for malicious or wanton conduct. Also called ***punitive damages.***

expert witness—An individual who has special training, skill, experiences, or knowledge so as to be qualified to render an authoritative opinion in a particular area of scientific, technical, or professional expertise.

fraud—Deception or artifice used to cheat or intentionally mislead. This is closely related to misrepresentation and concealment. Proof of fraudulent acts by an insured in procuring insurance may lead to a denial of coverage and voiding of the policy by the insurer. As a loss exposure, certain types of fraud can be insured by a commercial crime insurance policy.

general counsel—Often the highest-ranking lawyer within a corporation. General counsel is involved in all corporate activities including entity formation and filings, legal actions, employee related legal issues, corporate resolutions and other corporate documents, shareholder and board of director meetings, and contract preparation and review. General counsel is also typically involved in the development or review and maintenance of various corporate policies, such as a privacy policy. The general counsel position usually reports to executive management.

general damages—A subjective monetary award that is designed to compensate an injured person for his pain and suffering.

governmental immunity—Protection from prosecution based on statute at the local, town, state, and federal level.

hold harmless provision—This contractual provision requires one contracting party to respond to certain legal liabilities of the other party. For example, construction contracts typically require the contractor to indemnify the owner with respect to the owner's liability to members of the public who are injured or whose property is damaged during the course of the contractor's operations. There are a number of types of hold harmless clauses, differentiated by the extent of the liabilities they transfer. The most commonly used types of clauses are the limited, intermediate, and broad form hold harmless clauses:

- ***Limited form***—Where Party A holds Party B harmless for suits arising out of Party A's sole negligence. Party B is thus protected when it is held vicariously responsible for the actions of Party A.
- ***Intermediate form***—Where Party A holds Party B harmless for suits alleging sole negligence of Party A or negligence of both parties.
- ***Broad form***—Where Party A holds Party B harmless for suits against Party B based on the sole negligence of A, joint negligence of A and B, or the sole negligence of B. Broad form hold harmless agreements are unenforceable in a number of states.

hotel and innkeeper liability—Refers to liability claims by guests at a motel, hotel, or inn. Ordinarily, the hotel proprietor will not be liable for loss or damage to valuables in excess of a certain dollar amount, e.g., $500 per loss. This liability limitation will only apply if the proprietor has posted an appropriate notice in the room indicating the limitation and that a safe for valuables is available at the hotel upon request.

house counsel attorney—An attorney employed by a law firm that is actually part of an insurance company operation. The law firm will have a separate law firm name, and may even be a separate entity, but only provides legal services to the insurance company Claims Department.

indemnification—The promise to reimburse another party for damages.

infant compromise order—A formal pleading submitted to the court requesting the court to approve the infant claimant's settlement. The judge will generally request an updated medical report from the claimant's attending physician to evaluate the injuries, diagnosis, and prognosis. The infant claimant is a ward of the court until age 18, and the claimant's parents cannot sign a release on behalf of the infant claimant. After the judge approves the settlement, a formal order will be prepared, which is a legal pleading filed with the court. The court order will outline how the settlement payments are to be made. An attorney is necessary to assist in filing an infant compromise order or petition, and if the claimant is unrepresented, the claim facility may retain an attorney to represent the infant claimant.

insurable interest—An interest by the insured person in the value of the subject of insurance, including any legal or financial relationship. Insurable interest usually results from property rights, contract rights, and potential legal liability. For example, if a fire loss caused damages to a home, the owners of the home would sustain a loss and have an insurable interest in the property. During the investigation of a property claim, it is important to determine who has an insurable interest in the property. Insurable interests will include not only the homeowner, but also the mortgagee. When handling automobile claims, the owner of the vehicle has an insurable interest in the vehicle, as does the lienholder or loss payee.

interrogatories—A written list of questions put to a party—plaintiff or defendant—to a lawsuit. Answers provided are used to prepare questions for depositions or for trial.

joint and several liability—This legal doctrine, applicable in some states, allows an injured person to sue and recover from any one or more of several wrongdoers at his option, regardless of that wrongdoer's degree of negligence. The injured party cannot receive double compensation but can choose to recover 100 percent of a damages award from any defendant who is found liable to any extent. Many states have joint and several statutes.

The significance of joint and several liability is that the plaintiff has the option of pursuing any one of several defendants named in a lawsuit. If one defendant has a higher policy limit than the other defendant, the plaintiff will surely pursue the defendant with a higher policy limit, which may preclude that defendant from recovering from the responsible defendant with low policy limits.

When investigating claims involving serious injuries, it is always important to determine the policy limits of all potential defendants in any future lawsuit. This will allow the adjuster and manager to evaluate any impact regarding joint and several liability. If the responsible codefendant has low policy limits, and the insured has high policy limits, even a minimal amount of liability percentage on the part of the insured, could mean being responsible for the entire jury verdict. Opponents of joint and several liability commonly refer to it as choosing the defendant with the deepest pockets. Some states have undergone tort reform which has modified joint and several liability to require a minimum percentage of liability on the defendant targeted to pay the verdict.

loss of consortium claims—A legal action often brought by the spouse of the injured party that alleges the loss of spousal services, including (but not limited to) companionship, help with household duties, and sexual relations. Suits of this type can also be brought by parents or children of the injured party claiming the loss of services, typically companionship. Many jurisdictions have allowed these type of actions to be heard even when the injured party is a worker already receiving workers compensation benefits. Coverage for a lawsuit of this type is provided by the employers liability section of the workers compensation policy. In a claims situation, it's important that a general release be taken from both the husband and wife when settling a bodily injury liability claim.

motion—An application made to a court or judge for the purpose of obtaining a rule or order directing some act to be done in favor of the applicant.

negligence—The concept of negligence is a crucial part of every liability claim investigation because liability policies are designed to cover claims of negligence. Negligence is a tort, or civil wrong, and generally means a person's conduct does not meet the standard of a reasonable or prudent person. Acts of either omission or commission, or both, may constitute negligence. The four elements of negligence are: a duty owed to a plaintiff, a breach of that duty by the defendant, proximate cause, and an injury or damage suffered by the plaintiff. A duty owed means a duty of care has been established to prevent injury or damage, such as the duty to prevent someone invited to your home from being injured. Breach of duty is basically one party's failure to protect another party from injury or damages.

Understanding the concept of negligence is important for all adjusters. At one time, to determine negligence, there was an emphasis on the various levels of a claimant's status. For example, the term business invitee describes a person on the premises who was invited, e.g., a customer or patron to whom the insured owes the highest degree of care. A licensee is a person who is on the premises with permission for a specific reason. Here, the insured's obligation is to warn of a dangerous situation. For a trespasser, who should not be on the property for any reason, the insured's obligation is to not willfully harm or injure the person.

negligence per se—The legal doctrine which states that certain conduct violates standards of care as established by statute or law. Depending on state law, violating a statutory standard of care can be interpreted as (1) conclusive proof of negligence, making the defendant automatically liable without giving the defendant a chance to explain his or her actions, (2) presumptive proof of negligence, making the defendant liable unless the defendant can rebut the presumption of negligence by explaining the reasons for his or her actions, or (3) evidence of negligence, which can be considered when deciding if the defendant should be liable at all.

negligent entrustment—This refers to the failure to exercise the appropriate degree of care in allowing someone else to operate or use one's auto, aircraft, or watercraft. Under an insurance policy that excludes liability arising out of the use of an auto, aircraft, or watercraft owned by an insured, negligent entrustment may still constitute a separate—and therefore not excluded—category of negligence, unless a contrary provision is made specific in the policy.

negligent supervision—This refers to one party not properly or adequately watching or directing another party for whom they have accepted responsibility. Negligent supervision can sometimes take place in an employer and employee environment, where the employer is held to be liable for the negligent supervision of its employee. In some states, parents may be held liable for the negligent supervision of their children.

nonparty witness—Someone who has seen or has knowledge of the claim event, but who is not directly involved in the litigation, who is subpoenaed to testify at trial or at a deposition.

notary public—An authorized public official who administers and takes oaths and affirmations, confirms the validity of signatures, certifies documents, and performs other tasks.

notice—In civil actions, particularly actions against property owners, notice may need to be established to prove that the property owner was aware of a defective or dangerous condition. Actual notice means that the defendant has had prior notice in either written form or verbally. ***Constructive notice*** means that the defendant should have had knowledge of the defective or dangerous condition given the obvious nature of the condition.

Issues of notice will typically come up in the handling of general liability premises claims. The insured, as the property owner, may have received written or verbal notice of a defect or dangerous condition on the property. For example, the main stairway to the premises may have had stairs that were in disrepair or broken. The investigation indicates several tenants had written a letter to the landlord or property owner advising of the potential for an accident. In this situation, the insured had actual notice of the defective condition. If you take the same situation, with no actual notice by a tenant, the insured may still be liable if the insured should have had knowledge of the defective condition given its obvious nature and the fact that the insured visits the premises on a daily basis, resulting in constructive notice.

oath—A solemn, formal affirmation of the truth of one's words or actions, usually by swearing before God. In law, oaths are made by a witness to a court of law before giving testimony. Breaking this oath is called ***perjury*** and is a crime.

paralegal—Someone who is trained and certified to perform any function of assistance to a lawyer. Paralegals perform summaries, research, investigation, and the retrieval of records.

parol evidence—Facts outside a contractual agreement that may be used to interpret the agreement. Contract law prescribes a complicated set of tests—termed the parol evidence rule—by which the admissibility of parol evidence in discerning the contracting parties' intent may be decided. The admissibility of parol evidence is extremely limited in cases of an integrated agreement—a contract whose provisions make it clear that it contains within itself all the terms of the agreement between the parties. The "entire contract" clause found in many insurance policies are intended to make those policies integrated agreements and prevent the use of parol evidence in interpreting them.

pecuniary loss—A monetary/financial loss, such as a loss of earnings and future earning capacity.

peremptory challenge—In a jury trial, this refers to a right to reject a certain number of potential jurors who appear to have an unfavorable bias without having to give any reason for the rejection.

perjury—Deliberately breaking an ***oath,*** which could be a punishable offense.

personal injury claims—Under general liability coverage, this is a category of insurable offenses that produce harm other than bodily injury. Personal injury claims include libel, slander, defamation of character, false arrest, false imprisonment, malicious prosecution, wrongful eviction, or invasion of privacy. It should be noted that coverage for personal injury claims is not included in every liability policy. Some policies require a specific endorsement to provide coverage.

Adjusters handling claims involving department stores will often face personal injury claims. In an effort to deter shoplifters, department stores' internal security may detain and potentially arrest suspected shoplifters. If the charges are dismissed, there may be a personal injury claim filed against the department store for false arrest, false imprisonment, and malicious prosecution.

It is very difficult to evaluate a personal injury claim, particularly claims involving libel and slander. An adjuster evaluating this type of personal injury claim may not fully understand the damages resulting from the libel and slander activity. If the reputation of a professional person is tarnished, resulting in loss of income for that person and their company, these types of claims can result in large awards.

petition—Similar to a writ or summons and complaint, this is a formal pleading submitted to the court requesting certain legal action.

plaintiff—In a civil action, the party bringing suit and seeking damages from the defendant.

pleadings—The formal allegations of the respective claims and defenses by the parties to a lawsuit, consisting of a complaint, an answer, a reply to a counterclaim, an answer to a cross-claim, a third-party complaint, and answer to a third-party complaint.

prejudgment and postjudgment interest—Prejudgment interest is interest accruing on the amount of a legal award from the time of the injury or damage to the time the judgment is entered by the court. Prejudgment interest, when awarded as part of a judgment against the insured, is covered by the supplementary payments provision of standard general liability policies. Typically, prejudgment interest applies to liability claims involving property damage. Postjudgment interest refers to interest accruing after a verdict has been rendered. If an insurance company does not pay a judgment timely, postjudgment interest will accrue from the date judgment was entered by the court.

prima facie case—This means that enough factual information has been legally established to proceed with an action.

punitive damages—Damages in excess of those required to compensate the plaintiff for the wrong done, which are imposed to punish the defendant because of the particularly wanton or willful nature of his wrongdoing. Also called ***exemplary damages.*** Although the standard commercial general liability (CGL) and business auto policies (BAP) contain no punitive damage exclusion, many umbrella and excess liability policies do.

reasonable care—A legal duty to act as an ordinary and prudent person and not cause injury or damage to another person. In a negligence claim, this is the test for liability.

release—The document relinquishing a claim. A plaintiff or claimant signs a release in exchange for monetary payment, thereby giving up the right to pursue further indemnity in connection with the claim. The release sets forth the date and place of the loss, the settlement amount, the defendants being released, and the date signed. The general release is signed by the claimant or plaintiff, releasing the defendant, or insured from any and all claims resulting from the accident or incident. The general release is typically signed by both husband and wife and should be notarized. A signed and notarized general release should be taken on all bodily injury and property damage liability claims. Some claim facilities only use a general release if the settlement exceeds a dollar threshold amount, or when in the judgment of the handling adjuster a general release is required to protect the interest of the insured and/or the client company. If the claim is pending in litigation, a ***discontinuance*** and/or withdrawal should be filed with the court.

replacement cost value (RCV)—A property insurance term that refers to one of the two valuation methods for establishing the value of most insured property for purposes of determining the amount the insurer will pay in the event of loss. (***Actual cash value*** is the other.) It is usually defined in the policy as the cost to replace the damaged property with materials of like kind and quality, without any deduction for depreciation. Also see ***broad evidence rule.***

reservation of rights—This is an insurer's notification to an insured that coverage for a claim may not apply. Such notification allows an insurer to investigate (or even defend) a claim to determine whether coverage applies (in whole or in part) without waiving its right to later deny coverage based on information revealed by the investigation. Although a reservation of rights protects an insurer's interests, it also alerts the insured to the fact that some elements of a claim may not be covered, thereby allowing the insured to take necessary steps to protect its potentially uninsured interests.

res ipsa loquitur—A Latin term which means "the thing speaks for itself." This is a legal doctrine used to assess liability (often against professionals) when there is no evidence as to how an injury took place. For instance, if a sponge is inadvertently left in a patient's stomach, the doctrine is typically invoked to establish liability because such an event is presumed not to occur in the absence of negligence.

res judicata—A Latin legal term which basically states that the same parties are precluded from relitigating the same legal action in another court. This rule prevents a plaintiff from filing legal action against a defendant, receiving a judgment, and then prosecuting another action against the same defendant in a different court based on the same claim.

respondeat superior—This is a Latin term meaning "let the superior make answer." It is a legal doctrine under which an employer can be held liable for the actions of employees.

special damages—Objectively assessed monies awarded to an injured party for tangible losses, such as wage loss, loss of use, nursing care, and medical expenses.

stare decis—A Latin phrase meaning "to stand by the decision." As a principle of law, it refers to courts adhering to judicial precedents and not changing established rulings.

statute—Written law developed through legislative action.

statute of limitations—The time limitations that a plaintiff has to file legal action against a defendant. Statutes of limitations vary by state or jurisdiction and can be from 1 year to 6 years depending on whether the action is based on common law or contract law. When handling liability claims, it is important to document the statute of limitations. The statute of limitations is also important when handling subrogation claims. If a claim is made beyond the time limitation, the subrogation claim may be barred.

There may be situations where a statute of limitations may be waived. For example, an adjuster has been working directly with an unrepresented claimant throughout the claim process. The claim is not yet ready to be settled, as the claimant continues to be treated medically. In an effort to avoid litigation being filed, the statute of limitations may be waived. In this situation, the adjuster should seek approval from the insured to waive the statute limitations.

The statute of limitations also applies to claims presented by one insurance company against another insurance company. For example, an insurance company files a subrogation claim against the other insurer. In order for the statute of limitations to be protected, the insurance company pursuing the subrogation claim, must either a file for intercompany arbitration or litigation, or it may be barred from recovery. Occasionally, if negotiations are underway, an insurance company may waive the statute of limitations in a subrogation matter.

statute of repose—A law that cuts off a right of action after a specified period of time has elapsed, regardless of when the cause of action accrues. Most states have statutes of repose specific to construction projects that prohibit claims for construction defect beyond a specified number of years after the construction is completed. These statutes vary widely with regard to the limitation periods, what is covered, and who is protected. A statute of repose differs from a statute of limitation in that the time periods specified in statutes of limitations usually do not begin to run until the injury or damage actually occurs, irrespective of when the work was performed or the product was sold.

statutory law—That body of law enacted by legislative bodies. It is separate and distinct from ***common law.***

stipulation—An informal "agreement" reached between the parties. In civil litigation, a stipulation may be an agreement placed in the court record, such as a stipulation of ***discontinuance.*** In a workers compensation claim, a stipulation may be utilized to reflect a settlement.

***Stowers* Doctrine**—Named for a seminal Texas case, *Stowers Furniture Co. v. Am. Indem. Co.,* 15 S.W.2d 544 (Tex. Comm'n App. 1929), the *Stowers* Doctrine holds that a liability insurer that undertakes the defense of an insured has a duty to act in good faith in settling a liability claim. Courts have interpreted the "duty to defend" language in standard insurance policies as giving liability insurers absolute control over the conduct of the defense. Whether to settle a liability claim is therefore completely within the discretion of the liability insurer under the terms of the policy contract. If the injured party makes a pretrial offer to settle a liability claim for an amount within the liability policy limit, the insurer is not obligated to accept the offer and has the contractual right to take the claim to trial.

To protect insureds from abusive practices, courts impose an extracontractual duty on insurers to act in good faith when deciding whether to reject a pretrial settlement offer that is within policy limits. If the insurer acts unreasonably and rejects a good pretrial settlement offer within policy limits, unwisely takes the claim to trial, loses, and the jury returns a verdict against the insured for an amount above policy limits, the defaulting insured may be liable to pay the entire judgment under the *Stowers* Doctrine, even the excess portion above policy limits.

strict liability—This is a legal doctrine under which liability is imposed with respect to injury or damage arising from certain types of hazardous activities. For example, under strict liability standards, the manufacturer or distributor of a dangerous product is liable to a person who is injured by the product, regardless of the degree of care exercised by the manufacturer or distributor in the production or sale of the product. Also referred to as ***absolute liability,*** in a claims situation, it usually means there is no fault placed on the claimant or injured party. Absolute liability can be placed on a defendant if their actions were egregious, e.g., damages caused by intentional pollution.

subpoena—A command to appear at a certain time and place to give testimony.

subpoena *duces tecum*—A Latin term for "bring it with you," this form of subpoena requires not only the appearance of the subpoenaed party but also the production of books, papers, and other items.

summary judgment—A court judgment based on the judge's conclusion that the litigation involves only a question of law, with no associated questions of fact. Disputes as to the meaning of insurance policy provisions, when they involve only the interpretation of the policy itself and not the determination of the circumstances of the loss, are often the subject of a summary judgment.

summons—Instrument used to commence a civil action or special proceeding and as a means of acquiring jurisdiction over a party. Process directed to a sheriff or other officer requiring that they notify a person named that an action has been commenced against him or her. A general liability insured is required by the standard commercial general liability policy to provide the insurer immediately with copies of any summons received in connection with a claim or suit.

sworn statement—This is an ***oath*** given by an affiant in front of an officer of the court or a written ***affidavit*** attested to by a ***notary public*** outlining facts as understood by the claimant, witness, or other party to the litigation.

third-party claims—Liability claims brought by persons allegedly injured or harmed by the insured. The insured is the first party, the insurer is the second party, and the claimant is the third party.

third-party-over action—A type of action in which an injured employee, after collecting workers compensation benefits from the employer, sues a third party for contributing to the employee's injury. Then, because of some type of contractual relationship between the third party and the employer, the liability is passed back to the employer by prior agreement. Additionally, there are instances in which the third party can circumvent the exclusive remedy doctrine of workers compensation and enjoin the employer in the action. Depending on the nature and allegations of the action, coverage may be afforded under the contractual liability section of the employer's commercial liability policy or the employers liability section of the employer's workers compensation policy.

tort—A civil or private wrong giving rise to legal liability.

tortfeasor—A party accused of committing a tort; customarily, the defendant in a liability lawsuit.

unilateral contract—A contract in which only one party makes an enforceable promise. Most insurance policies are unilateral contracts in that only the insurer makes a legally enforceable promise to pay covered claims. By contrast, the insured makes few, if any, enforceable promises to the insurer. Instead, the insured must only fulfill certain conditions—such as paying premiums and reporting accidents—to keep the policy in force.

venue—The location in which an action is brought for trial.

verdict form—A vote is taken at the conclusion of the jury deliberation, which is presented to the judge on a signed verdict form. The verdict will include issues of liability and damages.

vicarious liability—This involves the liability of a principal for the acts of its agents. Vicarious liability can result from the acts of independent agents, partners, independent contractors, employees, and children.

voir dire—This refers to the jury examination process, wherein the defense, plaintiff, or judge may question jurors and potentially object to a particular juror.

waiver and estoppel—A waiver is generally the voluntary surrender of a right or privilege. Waivers can be written or oral. An estoppel occurs as a result of the waiver, which precludes the person who voluntarily surrendered the right or privilege from asserting its right later on.

writ—A written order by a court. For example, a party may appeal a nonfinal order issued by a trial court by use of a writ.

wrongful act—The event triggering coverage under many professional liability policies. Typically, a "wrongful act" is defined as an act, error, or omission that takes place within the course of performing professional services.

wrongful death claim—A claim made on behalf of survivors or beneficiaries when a person has died as a result of wrongful conduct (either negligent or intentional). Such claims are generally made by those who were financially dependent on the deceased. Damages recoverable as a part of wrongful death claims are measured as the loss incurred by virtue of the deceased's having been deprived of a natural lifespan. Such damages include medical expenses prior to death, loss of earnings during the expected natural life of the deceased, and ***loss of consortium.***

States have wrongful death statutes that dictate how actions are to be brought and the damages which can be claimed. Wrongful death actions can include ***general damages*** and ***special damages,*** as well as an action for conscious pain and suffering and expenses resulting from the death. A large aspect of any claim or award in a wrongful death action will include ***pecuniary loss.***

Wrongful death actions require comprehensive investigations to evaluate both liability and damages. A claim involving a decedent (deceased claimant) who is 75 years' old may have less value than a decedent or claimant who is 30 years' old with 3 children and a spouse. The evaluation of a wrongful death claim includes both conscious pain and suffering and pecuniary loss. The pecuniary loss can vary depending on the claimant's occupation, current wage earning capacity, future wage earning capacity, and age.

What would be the value of a claim which represents 100 percent liability on the insured, involving a 40-year-old stockbroker who is married with 3 children and earns $300,000 per year? Simple math would indicate the potential loss of earnings, if the claimant worked until age 65, would be $7.5 million. If the claimant underwent conscious pain and suffering prior to the death, an additional amount of exposure would be involved. Also, the claimant's spouse may have a claim for loss of companionship and consortium which will add to the value of the claim. Wrongful death claim evaluations are based on many factors. These factors include the potential for jury sympathy. Typically, when evaluating loss of earnings, mortality tables will be utilized (used to measure life expectancy) and the projected earnings will be discounted to net present value.

The Judicial Process

When a plaintiff files legal action against a defendant, the pleading may be called a ***writ, petition, summons*** and complaint, or just a ***complaint.*** This pleading details the plaintiff's claim with individual causes of actions detailed within the complaint. Each cause of action will have allegations detailing the reasons for the cause of action.

The complaint is typically personally served on each ***defendant*** or the defendant's legal representative. Sometimes, a defendant, its legal representative, or even an adjuster may secure an extension of time to answer, to provide more time to respond to the complaint, and to avoid the potential for a ***default judgment.*** Most legal complaints require a formal answer within 20 to 30 days from the date the complaint is served. If an extension of time to answer is required, the adjuster should make sure that the extension will not waive any ***affirmative defenses*** in the action.

After the defendant is served with the petition, writ, summons and complaint, or complaint, an ***answer*** is required, along with an ***appearance.*** The answer will provide detailed responses to the complaint in the form of admissions or denials. The appearance will indicate the defense firm representing the defendant.

If multiple defendants are involved, one defendant may file a ***cross-claim*** against another defendant in an effort to shift liability. The cross-claim is a separate cross-complaint served on the offending defendant. If a ***plaintiff*** is also negligent, the defendants may file a ***counterclaim*** against the plaintiff for damages, or based on liability. The counterclaim is a separate pleading served on the plaintiff.

After the answer and appearance are filed, the litigation progresses through a stage called ***discovery.*** During discovery, information and documentation are exchanged through various discovery demands. In some jurisdictions, these demands and responses may be called ***interrogatories,*** and in other jurisdictions such as New York, they are referred to as a ***bill of particulars.*** The discovery process will also include ***depositions*** of the plaintiffs and defendants, and may also include a deposition from a ***nonparty witness,*** who is basically a witness who is not a party to the litigation. The nonparty witness may have been forced to appear through a ***subpoena,*** which is a legal document served on a witness to appear at court. Subpoenas may be signed by the judge requiring or ordering the witness to appear. Subpoenas may also be utilized to request records as part of the discovery process or at the time of trial. These subpoenas are called record subpoenas or a ***subpoenas duces tecum.***

After discovery has been completed, if a defendant is not liable based on the results of discovery, a defendant may file a ***summary judgment*** motion with the court. A summary judgment is a detailed legal pleading with a summary of the litigation, with exhibits, requesting that the court rule in favor of the defendant, based on the discovery indicating that defendant is not liable. Factual questions or issues are reserved for a jury decision.

Upon review of the summary judgment motion, if a judge feels there are factual issues outstanding, the judge may rule against the summary judgment motion, meaning that the litigation will be directed toward trial. A summary judgment motion should not be confused with a ***declaratory judgment action,*** which may involve a defendant or plaintiff litigating a coverage issue. A declaratory judgment action is a legal action to decide the duties, rights, and obligations of the parties. These actions do not necessarily result in an award for damages.

After discovery is complete the litigation will move into the trial stage with the filing of a ***notice*** of trial. A jury is selected from a jury pool composed of laypeople who are required to participate in jury duty as part of their civic responsibility. The prospective jurors are questioned by both the judge and the participating attorneys. Depending on the jurisdiction, a participating attorney may challenge or reject a prospective juror who may be biased toward their particular case. This is commonly referred to as a ***peremptory challenge. Voir dire*** refers to the jury examination process, when the defense attorney, plaintiff attorney, or judge may question jurors and potentially object to a particular juror.

After jury selection, the trial begins with opening statements by both the plaintiff and defense attorneys. If there are multiple defendants, each defense attorney may provide its own opening statement. Thereafter, the plaintiff will have an opportunity to submit its case, commonly referred to as the plaintiff's case, which will include testimony from various witnesses as well as the admission of documentary evidence. The defendant will then have the opportunity to submit its case, commonly referred to as the defendant's case, including testimony from witnesses and admission of evidence.

After the plaintiff's case and defendant's case are concluded, each party will have an opportunity for a ***closing argument,*** which is basically a summary of the testimony and events of the trial. After closing arguments, the case is presented to the jury for ***jury deliberation,*** a secret meeting of the jurors behind closed doors. Prior to the deliberation, the judge will provide specific instructions to the jury, including an explanation of the law as it pertains to the case. A vote is taken at the conclusion of the jury deliberation, which is presented to the judge on a signed ***verdict form.*** The jury verdict or decision may be read by the court clerk, judge, or some other court official. The verdict will include issues of liability and damages. In some jurisdictions, the trial may be bifurcated, meaning that the liability issue is tried separately from the damage issue. If the defendant(s) are not found to be liable, the damage trial will not take place.

After the verdict is rendered, the judgment is entered by the court. The judgment is a formal pleading filed with the court. A copy of the judgment is provided to each party to the litigation. Depending on the type of damages involved, the judgment may include ***prejudgment interest.*** If the verdict involves monetary damages, the defendant has a certain amount of time to pay the damages to the plaintiff. If an insurance company is involved, it will pay the judgment up to its policy limit. If damages are not paid timely, ***postjudgment interest*** may apply.

Sometimes, the defense may make a motion to ***appeal*** the judgment to a higher court, such as a court of appeals or the appellate division of a superior court.

Bibliography

AAA. "Commercial Rules—Claims Programs." New York: American Arbitration Association, 2010. http://www.adr.org/sp.asp?id=32533

ACE. "About Us." West Chester, PA: American Computer Estimating, Inc., 2010. http://www.ace-it.com/ace/ace-it/about.html.

AF. "About Arbitration Forums." Tampa, FL: Arbitration Forums, Inc., 2010. https://www.arbfile.org/webapp/pgStatic/content/pgAboutAF.jsp.

Cutts, Karen, ed. *A Practical Guide to Purchasing Groups: A Comprehensive Reference Source on the Formation, Operation, and Regulation of Purchasing Groups Formed under the Liability Risk Retention Act.* 2nd ed. Pasadena, CA: Insurance Communications, 2004.

———. *Risk Retention Group Directory and Guide 2008.* Pasadena, CA: Insurance Communications, 2008.

Early, James M. *What Is a Structured Settlement?* Merrimack, NH: Ringler Associates, 2009.

Elliott, Michael W., Bernard L. Webb, Howard N. Anderson, and Peter R. Kensicki, *Principles of Reinsurance.* 2nd ed. Vols. I–II. Malvern, PA: Insurance Institute of America, Inc., 1995.

———, Michael W., George L. Head, and James D. Blinn. *Risk Financing.* 2nd ed. Malvern, PA: Insurance Institute of America, 2004.

FreeAdvice.® "Personal Injury Statute of Limitations" Sausalito, CA: Advice Company, 2009. http://www.freeadvice.com/resources/personal_injury_statute_of_limitations.htm.

Head, George L. *Risk Management—Why and How.* Dallas: International Risk Management Institute, Inc., 2009. http://www.irmi.com/online/riskmgmt/risk-management-why-and-how.pdf.

I.I.I. "Do I Need Business Interruption Insurance?" New York: Insurance Information Institute, Inc., 2010 http://www.iii.org/individuals/business/basics/interruption/.

IRMI. *Commercial Lines 101.* Dallas: International Risk Management Institute, Inc., 2006. http://www.irmi.webce.com/.

———. *Glossary of Insurance and Risk Management Terms.* Dallas: International Risk Management Institute, Inc., 1978–2010. http://www.irmi.com/online/insurance-glossary/.

———. IRMI.com Expert Commentary. Dallas: International Risk Management Institute, Inc., 2000–2010. http://www.irmi.com/expert/default.aspx.

ISO ClaimSearch®. Jersey City, NJ: Insurance Services Office, Inc. 1996, 2010. http://www.iso.com/Products/ISO-ClaimSearch/ISO-ClaimSearch-improve-claims-processing-and-prevent-fraud.html.

Launie, J.J., J. Finley Lee, and Norman A. Baglini. *Principles of Property and Liability Underwriting*, 3d ed. Malvern, PA: Insurance Institute of America, 1986.

Lorimer, James L., Harry F. Perlet Jr., Frederick G. Kempin Jr., and Frederick R. Hodosh. *The Legal Environment of Insurance.* 3rd ed. Vol. I. Malvern, PA: American Institute for Property and Liability Underwriters, 1987.

Mind Tools Ltd. "Leadership Styles—Using the Right One for Your Situation." London: MindTools Ltd., 1995–2010. http://www.mindtools.com/pages/article/newLDR_84.htm.

"OFAC Compliance Service." Jersey City, NJ: ISO ClaimSearch.® http://www.iso.com/Products/ISO-ClaimSearch/ISO-ClaimSearch-OFAC-Compliance-Service.html.

Olson, Robin K. *Personal Risk Management and Insurance.* Dallas: International Risk Management Institute, Inc., 2001–2010. http://www.irmi.com/products/.

The Professional Association for Chartered Property Casualty Underwriters. "About the CPCU Society." Malvern, PA: CPCU Society, 2010. http://www.cpcusociety.org/page/46169/.

———. "CPCU Society Ethics Code." Malvern, PA: CPCU Society, 2010. http://www.cpcusociety.org/page/65790/.

RPA. "Society of Registered Professional Adjusters Ethic Guidelines." Downers Grove, IL: Society of Registered Professional Adjusters. 2007. http://www.rpa-adjuster.com/ethics.html.

Scammell, Stephen, ed. *Captive Insurance Company Reports.* Dallas: International Risk Management Institute, Inc., 1998–2010. http://www.irmi.com/products/.

Society of Lloyd's. "What Is Lloyd's?" London: Lloyd's, 2010. http://www.lloyds.com/Lloyds/About-Lloyds/What-is-Lloyds.

United States Department of Labor. "Occupational Outlook Handbook," 2010–2011 ed. N.E. Washington, DC: U.S. Bureau of Labor Statistics, 2010. http://www.bls.gov/oco/ocos125.htm.

Urgent Business Forms. "Indemnity Agreement—Hold Harmless." Minneapolis: Orion Systems, 1997–2010. http://www.urgentbusinessforms.com/indemnity.asp.

Webb, Bernard L., Norman A. Baglini, Willis P. Rokes, and J. J. Launie. *Insurance Company Operations,* 3rd ed. Vol. II. Malvern, PA: 3rd ed. Vol. II. Malvern, PA: American Institute for Property and Liability Underwriters, 1984.

Westover, Kathryn A. *Captives and the Management of Risk,* 2nd ed. Dallas: International Risk Management Institute, Inc., 2006. http://www.irmi.com/products/.

———. *Captive Practices and Procedures.* Dallas: International Risk Management Institute, Inc., 2006. http://www.irmi.com/products/.

Williams Jr., Arthur, George L. Head, and G. William Glendenning. *Principles of Risk Management and Insurance.* Vol. II. Malvern, PA: American Institute for Property and Liability Underwriters, 1978.

Workman, Millicent W. *Practical Risk Management.* Dallas: International Risk Management Institute, Inc., 1974–2010. http://www.irmi.com/products/.

Topical Index

Q

R